Nonviolence before King

Justice, Power, and Politics

COEDITORS
Heather Ann Thompson
Rhonda Y. Williams

EDITORIAL ADVISORY BOARD
Peniel E. Joseph
Daryl Maeda
Barbara Ransby
Vicki L. Ruiz
Marc Stein

The Justice, Power, and Politics series publishes new works in history that explore the myriad struggles for justice, battles for power, and shifts in politics that have shaped the United States over time. Through the lenses of justice, power, and politics, the series seeks to broaden scholarly debates about America's past as well as to inform public discussions about its future.

More information on the series, including a complete list of books published, is available at http://justicepowerandpolitics.com/.

Nonviolence before King

The Politics of Being and the
Black Freedom Struggle

....

ANTHONY C. SIRACUSA

The University of North Carolina Press Chapel Hill

© 2021 Anthony C. Siracusa
All rights reserved
Set in Charis by Westchester Publishing Services
Manufactured in the United States of America

The University of North Carolina Press has been a member of the
Green Press Initiative since 2003.

Library of Congress Cataloging-in-Publication Data
Names: Siracusa, Anthony C., author.
Title: Nonviolence before King : the politics of being and the Black
 freedom struggle / Anthony C. Siracusa.
Other titles: Justice, power, and politics.
Description: Chapel Hill : University of North Carolina Press, [2021] |
 Series: Justice, power, and politics | Includes bibliographical
 references and index.
Identifiers: LCCN 2021012061 | ISBN 9781469662992 (cloth) |
 ISBN 9781469663005 (paperback) | ISBN 9781469663012 (ebook)
Subjects: LCSH: Civil rights movements—United States—History—20th
 century. | Nonviolence—United States—History—20th century. | Direct
 action—United States—History—20th century. | African Americans—Civil
 rights—History—20th century.
Classification: LCC E185.61 .S593 2021 | DDC 323.1196/0730904—dc23
LC record available at https://lccn.loc.gov/2021012061

Cover illustration: Nashville police arrest Rev. James M. Lawson Jr., center,
in front of the First Baptist Church on 4 March 1960. © USA Today Network.

To Natasha, for showing me how to love

Contents

Acknowledgments, xi

Introduction, 1

Part I
Imagining Nonviolence

1 Race and the Problem of Pacifism in the United States, 17

2 From Mere Quietus to Prophetic Religion, 48
   Howard Thurman Imagining Nonviolence in America

Part II
Practicing Nonviolent Direct Action

3 Jane Crow Must Also Go, 81
   Pauli Murray and Politics of Sex and Nonviolence in the Midcentury Freedom Movement

4 From Pacifism to Resistance, 111
   Bayard Rustin and the Roots of National Nonviolent Direct Action in Wartime America

Part III
Building a Movement
The Politics of Being

5 Disrupting the Calculation of Violence, 141
   James M. Lawson Jr. and the Religious Politics of Nonviolent Direct Action

Epilogue, 171
Of Agnostic Nonviolent Technicians and the Conscience of the Congress

Notes, 185

Bibliography, 249

Index, 263

Illustrations and Map

Illustrations

A young Howard Kester in the 1920s, 36

Howard Thurman circa 1930, 60

Pauli Murray in 1946, 95

A flier for a race relations institute organized by Bayard Rustin, 124

Rev. James M. Lawson Jr. being arrested in Nashville in March 1960, 162

Pauli Murray in her clerical robes in the late 1970s, 183

Map

Locations where Rev. James M. Lawson Jr. taught workshops or spoke between 1958 and 1960, 159

Acknowledgments

The origins of this book lie in my experiences growing up in Memphis, Tennessee. As a young person, I often wondered why the ghost of Dr. Martin Luther King Jr. and his dream seemed to linger in the city decades after his assassination. As I grew older, I realized that King came to Memphis against the advice of many of his closest advisors to ally with 1,300 striking sanitation workers, seeing in them the very people he hoped to organize in his burgeoning "Poor Peoples Campaign." But I wondered: Why did King come to Memphis against the advice of many of his closest counselors? I found that the answer was a relatively simple one. His most trusted associate in the area of nonviolent campaigns, Rev. James M. Lawson Jr., invited him to Memphis. In the Sanitation Strike of 1968, King saw an energy around nonviolent organizing he had not witnessed since the early 1960s. But who was this person, the Methodist minister Lawson? And how did he come to be such a well-respected intellectual and tactician that he could persuade King to come to Memphis over the advice of his other counselors? I pursued this question in the summer of 2007 in a Rhodes College Institute for Regional Studies paper under the guidance of Dr. Stephen Haynes. My initial focus was Lawson's activism in Memphis between his arrival in the city in 1962 as pastor of Centenary Methodist Church and his much more public role in the Sanitation Strike of 1968. Dr. Haynes assisted me greatly at the outset of this project and told me to pay attention to the fact that I enjoyed spending hours upon hours in front of the microfiche machine in the Benjamin L. Hooks Central Library in Memphis.

That summer left me wanting to learn more about Lawson and in particular the history of nonviolence in the United States he seemed to carry with him. I explored Lawson's role during the Sanitation Strike in the fall of 2007 under the guidance of Dr. Gail Murray and then completed a directed inquiry course in religion and nonviolence with Dr. Charles W. McKinney Jr. in the spring of 2008. All of this work led to an honors thesis on Lawson in the fall of 2008 under the guidance of Dr. Luther E. Ivory. Affectionately known as "the I-Man," Dr. Ivory helped me grapple with Howard Thurman and the 1949 volume edited by William Stuart Nelson, *The Christian Way in Race Relations*. I completed the honors thesis with support from Dr. Ivory, Dr. Murray, and Dr. McKinney in the spring of 2009. I am forever grateful to the members of the Rhodes College Department of History for their help and support throughout these early stages of this project. I am especially indebted to Dr. McKinney, who led a tour of the National Civil Rights Museum on my first day at Rhodes. He not only introduced me to the field of African American history but has been a steadfast supporter and an invaluable interlocutor for the past fifteen years. The early years of this project also benefited immensely from other Rhodes historians, including Dr. Timothy Huebner, Dr. Michael J. LaRosa, Dr. Michael Drommp, and Dr. Jeffery Jackson. Additionally, Dr. Steven McKenzie, Dr. John Kaltner, Dr. Ellen Armour, and Dr. Milton Moreland in the Department of Religious Studies were gracious with their time and insights. Dr. Zandria Robinson and Dr. Robert Strandburg also deserve special thanks, as do Dr. Natalie Person and Dr. Zach Casey.

As I prepared to continue my work on nonviolence in the Black freedom movement in graduate school, Dr. Charles Hughes, director of the Turley Memphis Center at Rhodes College, was an ardent supporter and helpful reader. Dr. Russell T. Wigginton was an essential advisor as I prepared for graduate school, and he introduced me to Dr. Dennis C. Dickerson at Vanderbilt University. Dr. Dickerson was not simply my dissertation advisor; he was also a source of counsel, strength, and guidance for me throughout the process of reading, research, and writing. I learned valuable lessons from Dr. Dickerson about life in the academy and about the critical vocation of researching and writing about the Black past. Words cannot express sufficiently my depth of gratitude to Dr. Dickerson.

Dr. Sarah Igo was the director of graduate studies in history at Vanderbilt when I arrived, and she has proven to be a valuable reader and constant source of feedback. She introduced me to the depth and breadth of the field of intellectual history, and the study of ideas has ever since captured my imagination. This project was influenced deeply by my study of social movements and social movement theory under the direction of Dr. Larry W. Isaac at Vanderbilt. Dr. Isaac shaped my understanding of what social movements are, how they form and are maintained, who joins them and why—often these conversations took place at the Twelfth Avenue Taproom in midtown Nashville. Dr. Paul A. Kramer read many iterations of this project at a number of different stages and provided invaluable insights about how to effectively frame the work. Dr. Thomas A. Schwartz at Vanderbilt proved to be a critical influence in thinking about politics in modern America, and the book would not have been possible without support from Dr. Samira Sheikh and Dr. Michael Bess. Thanks also to fellow graduate students at Vanderbilt: Mary Bridges, Justin Hubbard, Juliet Larkin Gilmore, Kyle Romero, Kayliegh Whitman, Jessica Lowe, Katie McKenna, Patrick Raisco, and Henry Gorman.

Multiple colleagues in the Department of History at Colorado College (CC) read the book proposal with enthusiasm and a careful eye. Dr. Carol Neel was an ever-present light throughout the process as I sought to maintain methodical progress despite my many other duties at the college. Dr. Amy Kohout read through my work and provided timely and important feedback. Dr. Jamal Ratchford was a constant presence of support through the process, and Dr. Tip Ragan and Dr. Dennis McEnnerney welcomed me with open arms from the moment I arrived at CC. Dr. Paul Harvey at the University of Colorado at Colorado Springs (UCCS) was an early supporter of this book project and provided important insights as it came to fruition. Thanks also go to other colleagues at CC, including Dr. Michael Sawyer, Dr. Steven Hayward, Dr. Aaron Stoller, Dr. Manya Whitaker, Dr. Tina Valtierra, Dr. Eric Popkin, Dr. Jordan Travis Radke, and Ms. Niki Sosa, and to my students Sophia Pray, Nan Elpers, and Talia Worth.

Additional thanks go to Dr. Gary Gerstle; Dr. Mona Frederick; Dr. Cade Smith; Dr. Bill Cafferro; and to my father, Anthony C. Siracusa Jr.; my sister, Natalie Siracusa; friends Anthony Carlson, John and Jessica Gladney, Matthew Farr, Kyle Wagenschutz, Ceylon Mooney, Christian Walker, Marvin Stockwell, and Shawn Apple; and Cheryl Cornish and Julia Hicks at First Congregational United Church of Christ. Most of all, I am grateful to my wife, Natasha S. Main, for her steadfast faith, for giving me way too many Sundays to write, and for being an ardent cheerleader who remained deeply interested in this work. She listened intently as I tried to make sense of Howard Thurman many, many more times than would otherwise be permissible.

Last, but certainly not least, I am deeply grateful to Dr. Rhonda Y. Williams for taking a real interest in this project, engaging it in such a rich and meaningful way, and pushing me to do my best work. Her mentorship and rigorous engagement with the ideas in this book will be something that I will cherish for the rest of my life.

I am in the debt of each of these people for the love and support and faith they showed in me over the course of the last twelve years. If I have done something worthwhile with this book, the credit is shared with each of them. The mistakes are mine alone.

Nonviolence before King

Introduction

The master's tools will never dismantle the master's house.
—Audre Lorde

In October 1928, the Black scholar of religion Howard Thurman delivered five "chapel talks" in Sister's Chapel at Spelman College, each dealing with a song whose origins were in Black enslavement.[1] Preaching on "Jacob's Ladder," Thurman suggested that as the enslaved sang "We are climbin' Jacob's ladder," they recalled that Jacob's situation was much like their own. The enslaved found themselves in a life space that was "crushing and depressing." They were treated like chattel, "driven and herded together like cattle, felled in their own blood if they resisted . . . these panic stricken souls found their present cruel and demoralizing. A future uncertain, an immediate past unspeakably bad, a present crowded with bitterness and misfortune—where is there hope?" It was the ladder, Thurman told the students, in the ladder there is hope. "The ladder!" he exclaimed, preaching that "there are no situations which are so depressing, so devoid of hope, that the human spirit cannot throw itself into a realm in which these conditions do not exist, and live in that realm despite all the hell about them. . . . I am enslaved,'" Thurman told the students, "I am beaten and brutalized by power-maddened men, but I shall see to it that my experiences and my environment do not crush me."[2]

With elegance and grace, Thurman connected the experience of a Jewish people persecuted 2,000 years before to that of the Black students seated before him. The enslaved people who created those songs of sorrow and hope felt an acute "kinship" with the "Hebrew children," Thurman said, as they maintained shared experiences of bondage and exile.[3] "Their records . . . have become ours," accounts of "sorrow and suffering" that remained relevant for Black Americans well beyond the end of slavery. In Jim Crow America, Thurman reminded the students, "intimate and primary interactions" between white and Black people remained elusive, often forbidden by law, and almost always under the threat of violence. "People who live under social pressure as in a master-slave society and its posterity find it almost impossible to be honest with each other," Thurman said from the pulpit, citing this lack of authentic interaction as among "the most vicious results of human slavery." "It robs people of the ability to be straight forward, honest, courageous," making "masters and the sons of masters, slaves and the sons of slaves monumental hypocrites." This "master-slave ethic" has brought "a moral famine to the land," he concluded, challenging his students to consider how they might transform the ethic of Black dehumanization central to American life since the nation's founding.[4]

If Thurman's sermon at Spelman in 1928 dealt squarely with an abiding source of rot in the fabric of the United States' social politics, Black dehumanization, it also pointed toward a revolution. The three-fifths clause in the U.S. Constitution codified in U.S. law the idea that Black people were less than 100 percent human, making it possible for the enslaved to be bought and sold like pigs and traded like sacks of grain. In the decades following the Civil War, a sinister new system of Black repression emerged—what Douglas A. Blackmon has described as "slavery by another name," a social arrangement whose ethic of Black dehumanization differed little from enslavement.[5] The public mutilation of Black bodies so common in the era of lynching made clear that the racial ethics of the United States had changed little since the founding of the republic: more than 4,400 Black people were killed by white vigilante forces between 1865 and 1945.[6] But in connecting the experience of Black people in the United States to the historic struggles of the Hebrew children, Howard Thurman located a powerful source of religious experience—a well-protected internal center for courageous, revolutionary, and ethical action that ran like a river from the ancient Jewish past to the seat of his Black students' spirits in the present. Thurman focused on how Black Americans might act from this core of courage to undertake risky activism in the decades following his Spelman sermon, and he established himself as the primary intellectual architect for a political philosophy of religious nonviolence—a source of real political power for Black people in the United States.

Historians and sociologists, political scientists and scholars of religion and law have acknowledged for decades the centrality of nonviolent direct action to the Black freedom movement. But we know much less about the evolution of the political philosophy of religious nonviolence, a set of ethics that led to the rise and appeal of nonviolent direct action for many Black Americans. This book unearths that lineage of activists and thinkers who acknowledged this reality—that nonviolence was not a legible political philosophy in the fight against Jim Crow, although it might become one—and narrates the contested effort to demonstrate how and why being nonviolent for Black Americans became a revolutionary vision for liberation. Inspired by the preaching and writing of Howard Thurman, three figures—Pauli Murray, Bayard Rustin, and James M. Lawson Jr.—organized around the idea that Black people could generate significant political power by collectively expressing their right to be, fully and freely, refusing to contort themselves to the pervasive intrusions of a racist, sexist, and homophobic society. They argued that adhering to Jim Crow's caustic demands ran contrary to their understanding of the purpose of human life, which was the full and creative expression of human freedom. They demonstrated this collective freedom through carefully staged nonviolent direct actions, and over the course of four decades each made vital contributions to the language, practice, and institutions that established nonviolence as a revolutionary force in the modern United States.

A radically democratic tactic, direct action has long been a hallmark of the struggle for Black freedom in the United States, one that had a profound impact both on individuals and on the nation.[7] The historian Paula Giddings writes of "the personal effect" that nonviolent direct action had on individual practitioners in the early student movement, citing the "Jail, No Bail!" strategy deployed by Fisk student Diane Nash and Spelman student Ruby Doris Smith in their 1960 Rock Hill campaign. Giddings argues that the practice of nonviolent direct action "forged a strong bond" among movement participants "and made them more determined than ever to devote their lives to the movement."[8] Nonviolent direct action was a widespread tactic in the student movement by the time of the 1960 Rock Hill campaign, a "developmental style of politics" that contributed directly to the growth of individual and collective power for Black youth activists.[9] Sometimes described as a "weapon of the weak," nonviolent direct action is perhaps better understood as a powerful tool for resilient local people—one that demanded courage and discipline but that also drew on, cultivated, and sustained power for rank-and-file demonstrators.[10]

But if nonviolent direct action proved to be an effective method for *how* local people might challenge Jim Crow, the philosophy of nonviolence became an answer to *why* people struggled in this way. Angeline Butler recalled the power of learning about nonviolence in a 1959 workshop taught by James M. Lawson Jr. "In these workshops what we were talking about was our future," Butler remembered. "A new phase of my life began as we addressed the truth about our place in the society and how society looked at us as a people. We studied Mahatma Gandhi, the life of Jesus Christ, and

Thoreau. Pretty soon we applied their teachings of nonviolence and civil disobedience to the fundamental inequality of people in Nashville's segregated society." The Nashville workshops led to the end of legal segregation in Nashville in 1960, but the impact on individual students was one that often lasted a lifetime. "The movement made each of us into a 'one person army,' strong enough to take the lead wherever we could visualize that change was needed," Butler remembered.[11] Butler and her fellow students learned the philosophy of nonviolence in preparation for dangerous direct action, becoming the "shock troops" of the early 1960s freedom movement. They risked their lives in public demonstrations challenging Jim Crow, but it was not at all clear that their efforts would change laws, policies, or customs.

So why did they choose nonviolence? Diane Nash, among those who participated in Lawson's workshops on nonviolence in the late 1950s, recalled being five months pregnant in the sweltering heat of Mississippi's Parchman Penitentiary following her arrest during the Freedom Rides of 1961. "I was scared the whole time. . . . But here's the thing—you had to do what was required or you had to tolerate segregation. And whenever I obeyed a segregation law I felt like I was agreeing that I was too inferior to do what the general population did."[12] Butler and Nash point to the power of nonviolence as a way of being in the world. Rather than "converting" an opponent to a different way of thinking or acting, the immediate act of claiming the freedom to be had a galvanizing impact on the students themselves, often Black students, fortifying a deep sense of internal security that could steel them for a lifetime of movement work.[13]

For a critical cohort of activists and intellectuals, this decision to take nonviolent direct action was just that: a choice about *how to be* in the world. It was a choice that flowed from the belief that the full flourishing of one's personality, allowing one's "inner light" to shine forth, was the great promise and guaranteed birthright of all human beings. The choice to be, fully and freely, was rooted in the conviction that all people deserved the opportunity to grow into the fullness of their being—that no one should shrink away from this raison d'être in the face of Jim Crow racism or Jane Crow sexism. Refusing cooperation with the disfiguring demands of a racist and sexist society, choosing to be fully and freely rather than to act from "behind the veil," these choices were made strategically and collectively to force whites in a Jim Crow society to see and confront the basic humanity—the distinct and complex individual personalities—of Black Americans.

These ways of being often provoked violence from white bystanders. But in responding to this violence with mercy, kindness, and forgiveness, nonviolent demonstrators patented a method designed carefully to contrast with and transform the cruel structure of domestic American politics. In responding to such violence with acts of mercy and compassion, these Black students demonstrated to the nation the world as it should be, a violent white society engaged and transformed by Black students embodying nonviolent acts of love and forgiveness. I describe this phenomenon as a politics of being and suggest that these collective acts of nonviolent being proved more powerful than Jim Crow because they did not replicate the institutional forms of power long used to subjugate and exploit Black people: law and violence. Instead, the politics of being drew on an ethic much older than the United States and its particular brand of white supremacy, one deployed strategically to force Black humanity to the center of a nation founded on white superiority.

The politics of being emerged in the transition from slavery to Jim Crow as possibilities for Black life in the United States both expanded and contracted. As the fetters of legal bondage loosened, de jure strictures of racial segregation tightened and white violence against Black communities became rampant. On this shifting terrain of racial politics, Black Americans made freedom through a host of pursuits: the development of organizations, associations, and mutual aid societies that supported Black life—including the National Association for the Advancement of Colored People (NAACP); the development of a robust Black press in cities and towns across the nation; internationally significant cultural expression through literature, art, and music; and the development of Black educational institutions. Within this distinct moment of possibility in the *longue durée* of African American history, the first generations born after enslavement redefined what it meant to be Black and free in the United States.[14] Black institutional spaces emerged as critical sites for this process of imagining and making freedom, Howard University foremost among them, and making freedom was just that—a process: one that began in 1619 and continues through to today. This idea is embodied well in the statue in the foyer of the National Civil Rights Museum in Memphis. Hundreds of people are scaling a mountain, all moving together, but no one has reached the top.[15]

The politics of being emerged in this moment against a backdrop of significant political constraint for Black Americans. Locked out of legislative processes and with practically no protection under the law, revolutionary violence was an increasingly unlikely option for African Americans. While many migrated out of the rural South, white violence and discrimination did not stop at the Mason-Dixon Line. The search for methods to end lynching and Jim Crow laws grew urgent in these opening decades of the twentieth century. Acts of "resistance" were common, whether refusing to sit in a Jim Crow rail car or participating in a boycott or work stoppage. But the relationship between such acts of resistance, the agency of the individual, and the impact on the social structure they engage is complex. The historian Walter Johnson offers some insight on this phenomenon in his work on Black enslavement, suggesting that we understand the lives of enslaved people "as powerfully conditioned by, though not reducible to, their slavery."[16] For Black Africans torn from their indigenous cultural conditions and brought to the United States against their will, apprehending life forces, culture, religion, and political action—in both origin and impact—requires understanding those elements that both preceded *and* were deeply conditioned by the United States' unique system of racial control.[17]

To be clear, white supremacy pervaded nearly every element of American life well after slavery. It remains an ongoing feature of national life, one contested powerfully by the Black Lives Matter movement contemporaneously. But there is a cost to centering white supremacy in our understanding of Black politics, culture, and religiosity. We run the risk of suggesting that Black culture was conditioned primarily by the demands of white supremacy and reactions to this system of social control, papering over a deeper, more complex, and older story of Black cultural life and experience.[18] The tendency to center white supremacy and Jim Crow and, subsequently, reactions of Black people to Jim Crow and white supremacy has led to the term "protest" becoming ubiquitous in characterizations of nonviolence and nonviolent direct action. And, indeed, much ink has been spilled chronicling the streetcar sit-ins, pickets, and boycotts that were in fact direct-action Black protests of white supremacy in the decades following the Civil War.[19]

But I suggest that the vision behind the politics of being was not simply a protest. That is, they were not *only* an effort to highlight and condemn white supremacy—protest as defined in its most elemental form. The politics of being were a vision for what social change is and how it might happen in the United States, a vision that went beyond contesting the particularities of nativist white supremacy in America. The politics of being were a vision for how personal and political liberation were bound together, how individual means were bound to collective, structural ends. They were a demonstration of the world as it should be through practices of mercy, kindness, and forgiveness in the face of white violence, acts deployed strategically to force the rehumanization of Black people in the

United States after more than 200 years of buying and selling Black human beings as objects. The politics of being were about Black people claiming the fundamental human freedom to be after eighty years in which they were lynched simply for being. The politics of being were a revolution in the most fundamental sense of the word, a transformation of the structure of American politics through a form of power that was neither violence nor law. The philosophy of nonviolence was at the heart of these politics of being, and this philosophy was a direct challenge to both the ethics and political culture of the United States.

As the intellectuals and activists in this book show, the origins of the political philosophy of nonviolence lay not in the particular social context of white supremacy in the United States, although it was strategically attenuated within this context precisely to transform this structure.[20] Black Americans claimed ways of being, created culture, and forged politics by drawing on ideas and traditions with origins much older than the particular brand of white supremacy common to the modern United States. As Howard Thurman preached to students at Spelman in 1928, the records and experiences of the "Hebrew children" had become those of Black Americans. Seeking not simply to gain advantage or even equality within U.S. structures using existing levers of power, the ethic of nonviolence began with the premise that state power flowed from a coercive ideological framework. The state disfigured people's proclivities toward building community, held people back from what Howard Thurman described as the desire for "true fellowship."

The antecedent cited routinely for how state power had been used unjustly in the past—state power buttressed by law and violence—lay in the life of Jesus of Nazareth, a community leader killed by the Roman state for practicing his religion of Judaism. As in the ancient context of the Jewish teacher, Thurman argued that law and custom in the United States forced African Americans under the threat of violence to shrink away from the full expression of the human freedom to be. Black dehumanization was the ethic that fueled this political system of racial oppression, a demeaning and diminishing of individual Black people intended to break the spirit of Black communities for the purpose of long-term economic and political subjugation.

For the people covered in this book, defying segregation was a rejection of these external attempts to impose internal inferiority. It was a challenge to the ethic of Black dehumanization, a claim on the right to live up to one's human potential, and for this reason a challenge to segregation was rooted in the same philosophy as a challenge to conscription. Because both segregation and conscription forced people to act according to state mandates under the threat of violence or jail, resisting Jim Crow and refusing to fight in war were rooted in the same ethical sensibility. Understanding this relationship between conscription and segregation is key to apprehending the revolutionary elements of nonviolence, an admittedly odd pairing given that wars often led to Black advancement in the United States. For the Black people in this book, segregation and conscription fundamentally distorted the human personality, prevented people from living their most deeply held beliefs about how to be in the world, and forced engagement with other humans that was toxic, deleterious, and damaging. As importantly, using violence to resolve problems—whether conflicts between nations or Jim Crow in America—made little sense because violence itself was a core part of the problem. Violence deepened mistrust, hardened prejudice, and made the opportunity for reconciliation more elusive. Violence had also been key to controlling Black behavior in America for centuries and was thus an unlikely candidate to shift the ethic animating Jim Crow. Violence might narrow Black unfreedom, but would it lead to a "greater freedom"?[21] The choice to be nonviolent flowed from a vision for this greater freedom, an effort to live by the highest ideals of Judeo-Christian practice—religious ideals also common to the Jain and Hindu traditions that inspired Gandhi and millions of others. The politics of being were about Black people making an immediate claim to be free to live their highest ethical ideals, and the effect was to expose as morally bankrupt the violence and law long used to hold together a Jim Crow society.

As countless historians and movement people have made clear, many participated in nonviolent direct-action campaigns while also practicing armed self-defense when necessary.[22] This is true, of course, but I argue the politics of being deepened and sharpened the contours of freedom for many Black Americans—an intrepid combination of ethics and political tactics that made lasting impacts on both adherents and the nation. Violence and law were political methods used by white colonial powers to subdue nonwhite peoples for generations, the same methods used by whites to "keep Blacks in their place" throughout enslavement and Jim Crow. There was nothing revolutionary about either as an approach to social change. Calling the Soviet, Chinese, and Cuban revolutions "false revolutions," James Lawson asked, "What really changed except the names of those using violence and law to maintain a hold on their power?" For the religious people in this book, the politics of being were a method that was, itself, the end they sought—a way of being centered in practices of mercy, kindness, and forgiveness that were a reflection of the world they envisioned. They believed that social change must come through one's own self, through one's way of being in the world, just as they saw in the life of Jesus of Nazareth—a way of being so revolutionary that it split time in two. A method of transforming—of revolutionizing—the structure of racial politics in the United States could not be mere means alone, an instrument discarded once the goal was achieved. That is exactly how violence worked: people were treated as objects, as things to be used as a means to an end—as in slavery and segregation. The politics of being, on the other hand, were the world as it should be.

A coterie of white pacifists was deeply interested in this project of making nonviolent direct action a common practice in the struggle against Jim Crow in the twentieth century, and over time the pacifist Fellowship of Reconciliation (FOR) emerged as a major source of organizational infrastructure in the nonviolent struggle for Black freedom in the United States.[23] The FOR was committed to ending the use of violence in all conflicts, and in the United States these white pacifists viewed white mob terror and lynching as domestic sites of work for their global crusade. Chapter 1 shows how, in the 1920s and 1930s, the FOR attempted to build interracial chapters in cities across the South and Midwest, with limited success, believing that authentic interactions between Black and white people unconditioned by the mandates of Jim Crow might cure the prejudice that produced ignorance and gave rise to barbaric white violence. But if their work to build interracial cells of committed pacifists did not succeed, the FOR's work in the early twentieth century did create the institutional infrastructure that proved valuable in supporting decentralized experimentation with nonviolent direct action in cities across the United States in the 1940s, 1950s, and 1960s. Perhaps the FOR's most significant contribution was cementing interracialism as both a strategy and an outcome for the nonviolent freedom movement.

Many Black people in the early twentieth century looked askance at the mostly white FOR counseling "pacifism" in the face of lynching. Howard Thurman was a foremost proponent of this line of criticism, calling pacifism an inept strategy for Black liberation in the United States. But Thurman noted a kernel of ethical truth in pacifism surrounded by an otherwise anemic politics. He joined the pacifist FOR as a second-year student at Morehouse College in 1920, but critiqued pacifist philosophy as "mere quietus to be put into the hands of the minority to keep them peaceful and controllable."[24] Thurman began to envision a different kind of religious philosophy, one that was nonviolent but forceful, and one that might cultivate the hope, courage, and resilience required to transform a cruel and violent Jim Crow society. Chapter 2 shows how Thurman worked through this puzzle with students at the Howard University School of Religion in the 1930s, an institution that afforded the time and space needed to imagine a political philosophy of religious nonviolence. The work of Thurman and his students proved essential to the burgeoning interwar freedom movement, ethical cornerstones for an "indigenous" method to struggle effectively against American white supremacy.

This religious vision for nonviolence is especially important in the continuing project of excavating the African American intellectual tradition. Clarence Taylor has rightly described African American intellectual history as primarily "a secularized endeavor," and the focus in many church histories—though not all—tends to be on Black church structures and denominational nuance, leadership succession, and the broader import of Black institutions to African Americans in a segregated society.[25] Explaining the revolutionary vision of religious nonviolence in the Black freedom struggle is especially important amid expanding work on what Nicholas Johnson has called "the black tradition of arms." Historians have rightly suggested that it was quite common for Black activists to own guns and use them for self-defense even if they were also involved in nonviolent direct actions. And like popular writers, these scholars routinely note that nonviolent direct action was simply a tactic for the majority of Black activists, although a small group saw nonviolence as "a way of life." But this continuing juxtaposition sharpens the need to answer the core question posed in this book: What do we mean when we say nonviolence was "a way of life," and how was this way of life combined powerfully with direct-action tactics to become a revolutionary political force in modern America? How did this politics of being, practiced by such a small group, come to have such an outsized impact on the movement and U.S. society?[26]

For decades, historical literature has relied on Gandhi to explain how and why nonviolence arose as "a way of life" in the years before 1960.[27] Writers have proven that the Mahatma was well known to Black audiences across the United States, citing especially the particular influence of Black religious intellectuals who met the Mahatma abroad.[28] And indeed, Gandhi coined the term "nonviolence"—a distinctly twentieth-century concept—but as most Black Americans encountered Gandhi in newspapers, study groups, or sermons, Gandhian influence is but a partial explanation of how and why nonviolence emerged as a revolutionary political philosophy in the United States. This book shows that for a cohort of Black religious people, ethical sensibilities and humanistic impulses derived from an effort to apprehend the Black experience in America in light of the biblical tradition and domestic labor movements—explorations that took place in study groups, churches, and workshops—and this work informed directly their understanding of nonviolence and their use of nonviolent direct action.[29] Religious ideas, interracial community formation, and personal spiritual disciplines combined with direct-action tactics to become the center of a new kind of politics in the United States, one premised on a vision for Black American liberation grounded in a form of power uncommon to U.S. politics.

But figuring out how to apply these ideas in the United States required dedicated experimentation and collective reflection. A student at the Howard University School of Law in the early 1940s, Pauli Murray co-led a successful and influential nonviolent direct-action campaign in wartime America. Murray earned top honors at Howard for her legal work, and her contributions underwrote Thurgood Marshall's approach to challenging de jure segregation in the 1954 *Brown v. Board of Education* case. But Murray grew increasingly frustrated with the law as a method for change, and chapter 3 outlines her pivotal role in making legible the "new technique" imagined by Thurman and his students of religion. Murray did not wait for permission from the largely male civil rights establishment in the 1940s to pilot these new methods, opting instead to organize and wage a nonviolent direct-action campaign with a cohort of women at Howard in the spring of 1943. Their nonviolent movement commanded national attention and forced a well-publicized conflict between Howard students and President Mordecai Wyatt Johnson. The conflict forced Murray to articulate an ethical justification for nonviolent direct action, and her writings provide an insight into the vision of greater freedom possible through this method—a vision grounded in her understanding of Gandhi, the philosophy of the FOR, and the religious ethics of Howard Thurman.

Murray's work in the wartime years proved critical in illustrating how the religious principle of nonviolence could be linked to direct-action labor tactics in public battles against Jim Crow. Murray was a crucial figure in the shift from imagining nonviolence to practicing nonviolent direct action, as she and her fellow students operationalized ethical ideas through collective political work at the local level. But it was Bayard Rustin who emerged as the most important wartime organizer in the national effort to build local nonviolent movements against racial violence and discrimination. Rustin was employed by the FOR and A. Philip Randolph's all-Black March on Washington Movement (MOWM) to build cells of local people dedicated to the study of nonviolence and the practice of nonviolent direct action. These "nonviolent institutes" became spaces where the ethics of nonviolence were joined with direct-action tactics in communities across the United States, establishing a template that might be used by local communities across the nation in the fight against Jim Crow. Together, the work of Rustin and Murray led to the crystallization of nonviolent direct action as clearly distinct from its pacifist roots. That neither Rustin nor Murray fit neatly into the prescribed gender and sex roles of their time was not merely incidental to their pioneering work. Their identities were, in fact, central to their quest for a greater freedom.

Chapter 5 centers on James M. Lawson Jr., a Methodist minister routinely called upon to teach nonviolent direct action in local communities during the "heroic era" of the early 1960s Black freedom movement. As the FOR's southern field secretary, Lawson continued the tradition of interracial nonviolent institutes launched by the FOR in the 1920s, teaching the "indigenous" method of resistance Howard Thurman envisioned in the 1930s, and methodically utilizing a template for nonviolent demonstrations by establishing what he called "the anatomy of a demonstration." In doing so, he recalled the intellectual and organizing work of Pauli Murray during the 1940s. Lawson organized nearly fifty nonviolence workshops across the South and Midwest in 1958 and 1959, teaching students that nonviolence was a personal practice that always afforded them a choice about how to be: abide by Jim Crow's disfiguring demands, or refuse cooperation and express your freedom to be—fully and freely—in spaces reserved for whites by violence. Lawson taught his students that in being together, fully and freely, and by responding to white violence with mercy, kindness, and forgiveness, they were actively transforming the social order of segregation by demonstrating a more just world. He taught that this way of being in the world was, as a collective practice, at once an act of powerful political insurgency against Black dehumanization and a demonstration of the world as it should be. He trained his students in the personal discipline required to publicly practice mercy and kindness in the face of violent white hostility, to steel themselves internally from the violence of the outside world, and their example became an innovative form of political power that toppled de jure Jim Crow and revolutionized racial politics in the United States.

In the conclusion, I challenge declension narratives so common to the rise and fall of nonviolence in the Black freedom movement by suggesting that the freedom practice of nonviolence did not end in the gazebo in Greenwood, Mississippi, when Stokely Carmichael called for Black Power in 1966, nor did it die with Martin Luther King Jr. on the balcony of the Lorraine Motel in Memphis in 1968. Nonviolence belonged to the longer search for a "greater freedom" stretching back to the arrival of the first Africans in America in 1619 in Virginia. It emerged from the joining of imagination and action, thinking and theorizing, demonstrating and doing. In the conclusion, I return to Pauli Murray to highlight the implications of the politics of being for people facing marginalization today. Murray worked throughout her life to live a complex gender identity in a binary society, finding some peace and liberation near the end of her life in a long-term partnership with a woman and through her ordination as the first Black woman priest in the Episcopal Church in 1978. In her clerical robes, her slight frame and slender build often led her to be mistaken as an altar boy—a mistake she relished as she fancied herself an "E-pixie-palion."[30]

Like so many freedom movement activists, Murray rarely shied away from confronting the dehumanizing structures of racism and sexism during her lifetime. Today, she serves as an inspiration for people seeking to organize in the face of forces that might diminish our humanity—sexism and racism, homophobia and violence—on the long walk to freedom and a more perfect union. Remembering the life and work of Murray, and this broader history of the politics of being, reminds us that who we are, who we are becoming, and the stories we bear with us—the identities we carry—can be a source of profound political power in the United States.

Part I **Imagining Nonviolence**

1 Race and the Problem of Pacifism in the United States

The Fellowship of Reconciliation (FOR), a pacifist organization dedicated to ending violence, was central to the nonviolent fight against Jim Crow. Founded in 1916 as the Great War wracked Western Europe and Jim Crow hardened into a violent way of life in the United States, the FOR believed that the segregation of Black and white people, like the isolating distance between the capital and laboring classes, was the root of widespread lynching in the United States. These American pacifists saw social isolation from one other, and the ignorance and enmity that resulted from such segregation, as the primary driver of racial violence in the United States. American racism and class conflict were analogs to the caustic nationalism fueling the bloodletting in Western Europe, and FOR leaders believed that meaningful engagement across lines of difference among people from different backgrounds could cure the U.S. of its scourge of lynching.

Over the course of its first three decades, the FOR intentionally entered violent conflicts to test a political "method" steeped in the religious "principles" of Quaker pacifism with the goal of building interracial and cross-class alliances that proved violence was not the only way to solve seemingly intractable conflicts. Its work contributed directly to the process of imagining nonviolence in the United States, and later proved indispensable to local experiments with nonviolent direct action.[1]

But by themselves, the pacifist politics of noncooperation—the refusal to fight—proved to be a threadbare response to the violence of lynching in the United States. As hundreds of thousands of Black Americans migrated from the southern countryside to cities across the United States during the First World War, they were routinely met with brutal mob violence. Self-defense was a common choice for Black families facing armed vigilantes, both in the South and along the trail of the Great Migration, and the birth of the National Association for the Advancement of Colored People (NAACP) in 1909 made litigation a premier strategy in the fight against Jim Crow. For most Black people, religious or otherwise, pacifism was irrelevant at best and foolish at worst, and the philosophy of nonviolence that became so central to the Black freedom movement was neither a staple of Black thought in the early twentieth century nor a legible philosophy in the fight against Jim Crow.

The FOR launched a process of imagining nonviolence—including experimentation with nonviolent direct action—that stretched over decades and contributed to the development of religious nonviolence as a political philosophy in the Black freedom struggle. The white southerner Howard Kester was at the leading edge of the FOR's effort to conceptualize and advance a constructive nonviolent force in the fight against Jim Crow in the 1920s and 1930s. He organized interracial southern groups around an "aggressive pacifism" in the interwar era, but was fired by the FOR late in 1933 for organizing interracial groups of striking workers who kept and used guns for self-defense. To his white bosses in New York, the purity of a pacifist commitment to do no violence outweighed the importance of Kester's interracial organizing in the South.

The lily-white FOR ultimately failed to demonstrate the "positive" nonviolent force it wrote about so often in the 1920s. But in the wake of Kester's firing, a cohort of Black intellectuals and organizers joined the FOR to serve in staff and leadership positions—Howard Thurman, Bayard Rustin, and James Farmer—and the work of these men moved the FOR from idea to action in developing the nonviolent "social force" envisioned by the pacifists. Each was a pacifist upon joining the FOR, and each was committed to the project of joining personal ethical practice with effective nonviolent politics. As Black pacifists, they brought unique sensibilities and new networks to the FOR. And Thurman's ideas, in particular, contributed directly to imagining nonviolence as a practical and powerful force for Black Americans. The organizing acumen of Rustin and Farmer bolstered the FOR's fledgling effort to develop a political technique—nonviolent direct action—that expressed the ethics of nonviolence.[2]

By the early 1940s, the FOR's effort to develop "techniques which are themselves immediate ends" began to bear fruit as the organization became the first in the United States to formally support and actively experiment with nonviolent political methods in what they called the "field of race relations." The FOR's work was foundational to imagining nonviolence as a politics of being, and the FOR's local organizing led to nonviolent direct-action campaigns in communities across the country—a cornerstone in the foundation of the midcentury nonviolent revolt against Jim Crow.

Origins of the U.S. Fellowship

The Fellowship of Reconciliation was founded in Cambridge, England, one week after Germany and Russia declared war on each other in August 1914.[3] The group came together after the publication of English Quaker Henry Hodgkin's "Message to Men and Women of Goodwill," where Hodgkin declared, "War spells the bankruptcy of much that we too lightly call Christian."[4] He implored his fellow Christians to find better methods than war to solve the world's major conflicts, and nearly seventy U.S. activists heeded his call at Garden City, Long Island, in early November 1916. These U.S. pacifists, previously "unknown to one another" and emerging from "different social groups and various faiths," found themselves "drawn together by a common feeling that the time was ripe for a deeper expression of the Christian message." These founders belonged primarily to existing Christian peace organizations—the Student Christian Movement, the World Alliance of Churches for Promoting International Friendship, and the Women's International League for Peace and Freedom, among others—but they were joined in their belief that the newly organized Fellowship of Reconciliation offered the best chance to meet the "profound need of uniting men and women of all nations."[5]

Establishing an office in New York City in 1916, the FOR named Quaker Edward W. Evans as its first secretary and appointed Young Men's Christian Association (YMCA) youth leader Gilbert A. Beaver to the General Affairs Committee. Helen S. Daley was appointed head of the Study Group Committee, and Haverford philosophy professor Rufus Jones was appointed to head the Conference Committee.[6] While its charter commitment was a refusal to "take part in war," the FOR believed its charge "clearly involves . . . very much more than the question of War." Such conflicts are not an "isolated phenomenon," the founders wrote, but are rather "one out of many unhappy consequences of the spiritual poverty of society." Acknowledging "the gulf between the present state of society and the ideal conceived," FOR members stated in 1916 their belief that the "immediate realization of that ideal" was possible by acting in a "spirit of love" in all aspects of one's "personal and social life."[7] This idea, that a social ideal might be realized through personal acts of love, became a hallmark of the FOR's approach and a core element of the politics of being, the animating impulse in the FOR's search for a method to transform the violence plaguing American life.

The FOR's primary orientation to social change was Christian. The organization called "the life and teaching and death of Jesus" a "revolutionary principle" and implored its small but growing membership to live like Jesus "here and now, in every relationship," across the spectrum of "personal, social, commercial, national, and international life."[8] FOR leaders believed it unnecessary to wait for social change, suggesting instead that such change would emerge from living in new ways here and now. FOR leaders believed their unique charge was to discover the "full implications" of applying this way of life "to all the great problems of industrial and social life," and they sought the "development of local groups" to apply FOR principles to domestic conflicts in the United States. The FOR cited its tactics as "conversation," "correspondence," and "the use of literature," and said its goal was to "enlist and develop spiritual and intellectual leaders who can make special contributions to Christian thought and practice."[9]

This almost exclusively white group of pacifists belonged to a much wider movement in the early twentieth century that sought to square Christian ideas with the scientific revolution and an emerging positivism. This shift in epistemology gave rise to a religious modernist movement that included intellectuals who placed the Bible in a historical context to explain its meaning. The FOR's claim that "the life, death, and teachings of Jesus" provide a "revolutionary principle" was part of a broader intellectual movement to understand the historical figure Jesus of Nazareth within the political and social context of first-century Palestine. A focus on what Albert Schweitzer called the "historical Jesus" challenged the biblical literalism of fundamentalist Christians, who argued that the Bible was the direct and infallible word of God. This modern religious movement was buoyed by positivist notions of social perfectibility, a vision that informed the work of Social Gospel advocates like Walter Rauschenbusch and Washington Gladden, among many others. These religious people and the thousands of others who preached the Social Gospel coordinated outreach programs that provided clothes, food, and health services for increasingly urban populations concentrated in subpar living conditions. Some of these religious leaders, seeking to bolster their ethical argument in favor of charity and outreach, suggested that socialist practices were clearly evident in the life of Jesus. In this Progressive Era moment, an epoch of "superabundant organizations" as associational life grew dramatically in the United States. The FOR staked out its claim as the "central organization" to facilitate the "growth of the Movement" designed to bring together people of all classes and races in a "common quest" to apply the revolutionary and nonviolent principles of Jesus of Nazareth "to the problems of social and national and international life."[10]

But the FOR struggled to move beyond its primary charge of opposing war, which it named as among the most acute problems in "social and international life." "As Christians we are forbidden to wage war," the FOR's founders wrote in 1916, seeking instead to apply "the broad and fundamental principles of Christianity to International Affairs."[11] For the vast majority of Black Americans, however, opposing war was neither a spiritual imperative nor an activist endeavor. American wars tended to produce significant advancement for African Americans. Crispus Attucks, a New England man of African descent, was a hero to many for being among the first patriots to die in the years leading up to the Revolutionary War.[12] More than 200,000 Black troops fought for freedom on the side of the Union in the American Civil War, what Frederick Douglass called "an abolition war" whose "comprehensive and logical object" was ending slavery.[13] At the turn of the twentieth century, more than 3,000 African Americans fought in the Spanish-American War in both Cuba and the Philippines, demonstrating bravery and commitment to nation alongside whites despite fighting in segregated units. In the First World War, more than one million African Americans responded to draft calls from the U.S. government, and more than 370,000 served in the U.S. Army.[14] And while he later regretted the decision, W. E. B. Du Bois called for Blacks to "close ranks" and support President Woodrow Wilson in "the Great War."[15] As the United States fought wars both overseas and at home under the banner of democratic ideals, Black Americans urged the nation, through sacrifice and loyalty, to vouchsafe the promise of life and liberty for every American.

A. Philip Randolph, a son of the African Methodist Episcopal (AME) Church and an emerging Black labor organizer, notably broke from Du Bois in condemning the First World War as a "sham" and a "mockery" of American ideals. Writing with his co-editor Chandler Owen in their Harlem newspaper *The Messenger* in 1919, the two argued that "the sham democracy about which Americans prate" would be revealed as "a rape on decency and a travesty on common sense." Owen and Randolph questioned the wisdom of Black Americans fighting in a segregated army for a Jim Crow society that lynched them with impunity.[16] The two were well aware that Black Americans were expected to "accommodate white expectations" under the threat of death, and African Americans were often killed as a matter of common practice with no consequences for their killers.[17] As Richard Wright has written, Black Americans in this period "were shot, hanged, maimed, lynched, and generally hounded until they were either dead or their spirits broken," a grim reality that led a generation of historians to characterize this early twentieth-century moment as the "nadir" of Black life in America.[18]

The Black response to this routine violence was manifold. The Great Migration led to an exodus of nearly two million Black Americans out of the former Confederacy between 1915 and 1940.[19] Many of those who stayed in the South moved from rural to urban areas, but whether in rural areas or urban, North or South, Black Americans committed themselves to developing their own institutions as segregation and violence hardened in the early twentieth century. Black banks, businesses, schools, and churches expanded dramatically before 1940 and provided critically important space for day-to-day life for Black people in America.[20] These efforts at building Black institutions emerged as among the most important efforts at making freedom in the age of Jim Crow.

Efforts to formalize collective resistance to white supremacy and Jim Crow took a number of forms in the early twentieth century, as African Americans launched the Niagara Movement in 1905 to wage a legal war against the violence and discrimination meted out against Black Americans daily—work that led to the incorporation of the NAACP in 1909. Jamaican leader Marcus Garvey cultivated pan-African sensibilities and organized a massive grassroots network of local groups to encourage mutual aid for those in the United States, and a journey "back to Africa" for others.[21] These processes of emigration and immigration, institutional development and litigation, all proved vitally important for Black Americans seeking to make freedom amid the violent and hostile environment of early twentieth-century America.

Armed self-defense was also a staple of Black life, North and South, amid the nadir. "The Winchester rifle deserves a place of honor in every Black home," wrote the courageous anti-lynching journalist Ida B. Wells. Run out of Memphis in 1898 after exposing what she called that "old threadbare lie" that Black men rape white women, Wells's newspaper *The Free Speech* was burned to the ground by a lynch mob intent on taking her life. By then, Wells had escaped to Chicago, but her perspective on guns reflected the common commitment to self-defense among Black Americans in this epoch.[22] A young professor at Atlanta University in 1906, W. E. B. Du Bois "bought a Winchester double-barreled shotgun and two dozen rounds of shells filled with buckshot." After the lynching of Sam Hose, Du Bois wrote that "if a white mob had stepped on the campus where I lived, I would without hesitation have sprayed their guts over the grass."[23] Mordecai Wyatt

Johnson, the famed Black minister who later became the first Black president of Howard University, wrote in 1921 that "the swift succession and frank brutality" of Reconstruction's end and Jim Crow's beginning was "more than Negro people could bear.... Multitudes took weapons in their hands and fought back violence with bloody resistance. If we must die, they said, it is well that we die fighting."[24] The Black socialists Randolph and Owen declared in the August 1919 issue of *The Messenger* that if a choice "has to be made" between one's life and the life of a lyncher, "destroy that of the lynching mob." They encouraged Black Americans to "act on the manly and lawful principle of self-defense," writing that "violence must be met with violence."[25]

Armed self-defense was a common choice for Black Americans because it was a survival technique amid the routine and vicious violence common to the opening decades of the twentieth century. This was true also for those Black Americans migrating out of the South.[26] In East St. Louis, where thousands of Black Americans moved during the First World War, hordes of white men marched through Black neighborhoods in May 1917 and attacked Black men, women, and children with impunity. Many whites were angered that Black Americans were filling jobs historically held by whites at the Aluminum Ore Company and American Steel Company, and they responded with violence that lasted throughout the summer and culminated in the firebombing of dozens of buildings in the Black district in early July 1917. At least thirty-nine Black Americans were killed.[27]

A clash between Black soldiers in the Twenty-Fourth U.S. infantry and white authorities in Houston in 1917 led ultimately to the deaths of thirteen Black men by hanging and life in prison for sixty others.[28] These violent incidents, among many others, presaged the so-called Red Summer of 1919, a period wherein more than twenty-five "anti-black riots" in cities across the country were ultimately punctuated by the unprecedented killing of Black women, men, and children in Elaine, Arkansas.[29] More than 200 African Americans, most of them sharecroppers, were killed at the hands of white mobs and federal troops in Elaine.[30] In this context of violence, the Black socialists Owen and Randolph argued that African Americans must be "thoroughly permeated, saturated, and shot through with treason to the institutions of Jim Crowism, lynching, race discrimination, segregation, disfranchisement, and to every instrument which maintains, perpetuates, and fosters these pernicious institutions."[31]

For the white activists in the Fellowship of Reconciliation concentrated primarily in northeastern cities, the brutality of white violence in the

Midwest and the South was quite literally a distant concern. But some FOR leaders identified Jim Crow segregation as the animating impulse behind the brutal violence they read about in newspapers, arguing that lynching was the cancerous outgrowth of a society that dehumanized and segregated Black people. These leaders saw in lynching a horrific example of how racial prejudice, underwritten by a lack of interaction between people from different backgrounds, led to barbaric acts of violence. In 1918, a small band of white pacifists partnered with the Federal Council of Churches to launch a literature program on what it called the "Negro Question," establishing a subcommittee on lynching charged with considering "whether there is any action as is desirable for the Fellowship to take."[32] The NAACP tasked Black field secretary James Weldon Johnson to spearhead the effort along with the white New York attorney L. Hollingsworth Wood. The two men eventually contributed to what they called a "Statement on Christianity and the Negro Problem," which FOR secretary and Quaker leader Edward W. Evans delivered to FOR members via mail.[33]

Evans became a prominent voice among pacifists in challenging U.S. racial mores. "We are not dealing with a subject race," he wrote in 1919, echoing the language of self-governance for colonized populations central to the Versailles peace talks, "but a body of our own citizens with a record of real achievement and with a promise of great contributions to our common treasure of democracy."[34] Black Americans are seeking "all the rights of American citizenship guaranteed to [them] by the constitution," Evans wrote to FOR members, "the fulfillment of the rights already guaranteed and the impartial interpretation and application of existing laws." Treating Black Americans as citizens is not, Evans stated, to "grant a privilege or bestow a favor. It is to cease withholding from him that which is rightfully his, that of which he is being illegally deprived. The withholding of the rights of citizenship from the American Negro is both a moral and a legal wrong."[35] Evans told FOR members that Black Americans were "denied the opportunity to earn their bread in many of the lines of labor and industry," and he argued that they faced "humiliating discriminations" across the pantheon of public life. "All of these practices are not only undemocratic and unchristian," he said, but "unjust and cruel." Calling the U.S. effort "to spread democracy abroad" as "hypocrisy," Evans characterized these international efforts as meaningless "until we have faced and are attempting to remedy these conditions at home."[36]

Evans described the lynching of thousands of Black Americans in the thirty-five years since the end of Reconstruction the most "severe indictment" of the nation, one of "positive barbarity and inhumanity." Describing lynching as "a great national disgrace and danger," Evans told FOR members:

> It must strike every American who has regard for the good name of his country with unutterable shame that the United States is the only civilized country in the world, more than that, the only governed land on the face of the globe where human beings are burned alive, and with impunity. It is the business of men and women, north and south, to crush out this vile thing, the growth of the mob spirit, the outgrowth of intolerance and prejudice, which otherwise will in time undermine all law and order in our land.[37]

Using the gendered Christian language common to the period, Evans called "upon the ministry and membership of the churches throughout the country to strive earnestly to create and arouse a public sentiment, which will include our Negro fellow citizens within the meaning of the 'Fatherhood of God and Brotherhood of Man.'" He concluded his letter by suggesting that the "negro question" was not merely "a problem" for Christians in the United States, but the "supreme test both of our democracy and our Christianity."[38]

While more than 1,600 people subscribed to the FOR's newsletter *New World* by the middle of 1918, growth among Black Americans remained sparse despite Evans's appeals.[39] The FOR struggled mightily to build interracial chapters focused on racial violence in the years after the First World War. The FOR's Morningside Heights chairman in New York wrote of a "vast longing for international brotherhood, freedom for the oppressed peoples under every flag, elimination of the forces that repress the free expansion of the spiritual life of men and women and children," but did not speak to the plight of Black New Yorkers.[40] Philadelphia members argued for a "progressive interpretation of this spirit and way of life as applied in the complexity of personal, social, industrial and international relationships in the modern world," and named as their goal "the constructive application of this spirit and way of life in service of creative personality and of personal relationships which satisfy Christian ideals." Yet no emphasis was given to African Americans by FOR members in the City of Brotherly Love.[41]

In the heart of New York City, where most members were concentrated in 1920, the FOR did make some modest progress with interracial organizing through their "Religious Forums," events designed to unite political "radicals" and "religious people." Citing the separation between political radicals and Christians as being as "clear cut as with a knife," the Methodist Episcopal minister Clarence V. Howell designed the forums to "reconcile" the two groups, with a goal of increasing the "spiritual dynamic" among radical movements while injecting a "new social vision" into churches.[42] Launched in Harlem as an interracial initiative, the Religious Forums brought together Harlem's sixty-two churches and seventeen synagogues with what Howell estimated to be 100,000 labor activists. Initially organized as open-air forums featuring a socialist speaker who was also religious, the Religious Forums grew to include a midweek devotional meeting and the organization of a speakers bureau. The initiative "worked so well" in the first year that the Methodist Episcopal Church offered to pay Howell's salary in 1922. A "group of praying radicals . . . is the heart of this service," Howell reported, asking the FOR to supply "speakers with a spiritual message for labor groups and speakers with a social message for church groups."[43]

The Religious Forums, which Howell later continued as interracial "Reconciliation Tours" in the 1920 and 1930s, were among the first programmatic efforts by FOR members and friends to cultivate interracial political work. But as lynching continued at alarming rates, the FOR struggled to make "the race question" more than a subject for papers, studies, or discussion groups. The organization did not have a clear approach to addressing what Edward Evans called the "supreme test of both our democracy and our Christianity." Instead, the 1920s were spent searching for "practical ways in which members of the fellowship might express their principles in action."[44] National leadership began to encourage more "practical experiments" for "constructive service," and the FOR's limited staff began to "aid individuals and groups who wish to undertake such service or make such experiments." After a decade spent envisioning a "method" that might bring about the new society they envisioned, the FOR was primed for experimental nonviolent action.[45]

The Primacy of Personality and the Search for Methods

By March 1922, the FOR's membership had grown to 2,000 people and the executive council began to write about the notion of personality—an idea that referred to those qualities wholly unique to each individual. This idea that each individual had a distinct personality was, paradoxically, a universal characteristic that united all humanity across lines of race, nation, and ethnicity. The FOR believed that any social or political system that interfered with the growth and evolution of individual personality should be resisted and transformed, noting that war in particular "inevitably involves violation . . . and disregard of the supreme value of personality." But for pacifists active in the years following the Great War's armistice, grappling with the broader social implications of this teaching beyond noncooperation with war was a profound challenge. In the 1920s, FOR members in the United States searched earnestly for a new method, a political technique more powerful than a refusal to fight, that might express a supreme reverence for personality and transform both individuals and the structures of law and politics that dehumanized people.[46]

This link between individual and social transformation was important to the FOR's burgeoning political philosophy. Calling for "fundamental changes in the spirit of man and in the structure of the social order," the FOR's executive council sent a letter to President Woodrow Wilson in February 1923 articulating the imperative to move from resisting war toward the proactive work of constructing a new and different social order. While the goal had been "to prevent war," it was now to "secure peace . . . by methods which shall not increase hate but which shall help to create a spirit of forgiveness and goodwill." This language echoed ideas that later became common among nonviolent activists in the Black freedom struggle, but in the early 1920s FOR leadership were in a phase of "investigations and experiments," seeking to devise that concrete "technique" that might "grip people and transform them into individuals fired with an enthusiasm for that way of life which eliminates all bitterness and conflict."[47]

FOR members debated fiercely whether "the distinctly Christian emphasis of the fellowship" was useful, noting that this religious orientation often jeopardized relationships with those in radical movements beyond the church. FOR cofounder A. J. Muste called for a "new creed," one that made clear the religious principles of the FOR while also avoiding dogmatism. "We must have some statement of our aims and purposes," Muste told the New York committee, urging leadership to reaffirm the "Christian" basis of the FOR while emphasizing "the militancy of our policy."[48] In 1923, the executive council tried just that, drafting a statement of purpose that was vetted by FOR members and introduced the "Fellowship principles" as "a worldwide family of men and women of different races, combinations and classes" bound by a common "desire to recognize this true unity and to find out more and more all that it implies." The FOR named as its guiding principle "love as disclosed in the Life, teachings and death of Jesus" and described the application of teachings from the life of Jesus to contemporary society as an "effective power for overcoming evil and accomplishing the purposes of God." Claiming that "reverence of personality" was central to "creating a world order" where no person "or race" is "exploited for the profit or pleasure of others," the FOR believed Jim Crow undermined the fundamental sanctity of Black life in America and named as a clear goal the ambition to "reconcile race and race." FOR leadership argued that social divisions like those engendered by "the color line" in the United States are the primary predicates for violent conflict, and they called on members to "take risks" in living these principles in "a world which does not yet accept it." The FOR encouraged its secretaries to begin approaching their work in a more "experimental way."[49]

Notably, the FOR rejected "theories of non-resistance" as useless in matching the tremendous violence wracking the United States and the world. In doing so, they tapped into a long-standing debate in Christian thought. Some pacifist Christians had believed for decades that a key component of Jesus' message from the Gospel of Matthew was to "resist not" evil—an interpretation that led directly to the pacifist position of noncooperation with war. "Resist not" was construed to mean "noncooperation," a refusal to support war or the use of "force" that allowed pacifists to preserve individual holiness. But this left many seeking a more proactive approach to social evil. In the United States, FOR members and leaders called this "prohibition on the use of force . . . insufficient . . . to cure social diseases or eradicate war," and they implored members to take action—actions of "humility, honor, and love," which were the "constructive" work of building a new world. The FOR rejected what it called "minor protest" and called instead for a focus on engaging in proactive domestic work in the areas of industrial conflict and racial violence. The FOR believed that the widespread "intolerance, hatred, and violence of the Ku Klux Klan," which had reemerged in the 1920s, would only be "combatted" by "going directly into the field with meetings of goodwill."[50] The "future of the movement" depended upon a small but committed group of people, it concluded, who "will give time individually and in groups to thinking out" the implications of this principled approach to violence.[51]

The FOR made a modest start in its attempt to move beyond a "simple prohibition of violence" and toward a "constructive approach" to nonviolence in the early 1920s by focusing on race and labor. At the fall 1924 national conference, FOR member Jerome Davis implored those gathered to explore how the "method of Fellowship" could be applied "in industrial [conflicts], internationalism, and racial relations."[52] The FOR began to engage more youth in integrated spaces, with 715 young people from thirty-four states joining more than 3,000 other FOR members by the summer of 1924.[53] When an aspiring young Black minister and graduate of Morehouse College joined the FOR's executive committee in the spring of 1925, Howard Thurman found in the FOR an organization with a unique approach to racial conflict in the United States—but one that still struggled to show forth the "Fellowship point of view" through social action.[54]

In the early 1920s, the FOR sent staff to the most heated conflict zones in the nation. Representatives traveled to "industrial" and "racial" "hot spots" across the United States—places where "difficulties" were acute in an effort "to demonstrate the Fellowship way in such situations."[55] A. Philip Randolph and Chandler Owen had continually implored such action in areas of labor and racial conflict, calling on "the organized labor movement of America [to] accord the Negro worker justice" and urging that "black workers should join white unions and white unions should organize black workers."[56] But before the Congress of Industrial Organizations (CIO) committed to interracial organizing in 1935, Black workers were the last hired and first fired and were used routinely as scabs in white-dominated workspaces. Randolph and Owen noted that the American Federation of Labor (AFL) perpetuated these "racially discriminatory practices" and exercised almost total dominance over organized labor in the period, including the "large railroad brotherhoods."[57]

The FOR entered these segregated and contentious labor spaces in the early 1920s seeking to apply a new kind of technique for resolving the violent conflicts between capital and labor. Jerome Davis and A. J. Muste both traveled to the bloody textile strike at the American Thread Company in Willimantic, Connecticut, in the fall of 1925, and the FOR sent staff to a cotton mill strike in Utica, New York, in December 1925.[58] National secretaries sent letters of appeal to their northeastern members in the areas surrounding these conflicts encouraging them to convene worker and employer councils in an effort to resolve the conflicts. They asked local members to discern together "how they could help . . . in expressing most fully our principles" and "act for the non-violent method of adjustment."[59] But these early experiments raised more questions than answers about "the type of action which would be most effective," and the FOR struggled to deploy effective nonviolent methods in bloody labor conflicts throughout the 1920s.[60]

The search for a forceful method that could replace violence in social conflicts led to the rise of George L. Collins and A. J. Muste as leaders in the FOR. Hired as a traveling industrial secretary by FOR in 1923, Collins traversed the United States in the 1920s seeking "conciliation" among "groups in conflict" and advocated for "non violent methods of adjusting such difficulties."[61] Muste urged the FOR to "define what nonviolent methods in such situations are," to which the FOR's national council responded, "[We have] not yet enough experience . . . to say just how we can best express the fellowship principles in the industrial struggle." The council urged Collins to organize a "small conference for the purpose of getting more light on the subject," and to "make a trip into the South" in an effort to survey the problems there and seek student contacts.[62]

Under Collins's leadership, "interracial principles" became a priority.[63] Citing "a special need for the development of organization in the labor ranks in the South," Collins focused on overcoming "the antagonism to colored groups in labor." The shift aligned with the socialists Randolph and Chandler.[64] The two Black labor intellectuals wrote in *The Messenger* that the capital class worked "to engender race hatred" among workers and, as a result, "keep both divided and enslaved."[65] Collins was deeply aware of the way race was exploited to create cleavages between Black and white workers, noting that as Black workers were brought in to replace striking white workers, these class divisions further fueled interracial conflict. While the FOR's national council "could not make definite recommendations as to the exact ways of handling this work," it expressed to Collins "the importance of the interracial work which he had been doing." Collins traveled extensively across the South in early 1928, visiting seventeen colleges and reporting on the formation of "new interracial groups and a greater readiness to receive the message" of nonviolent methods.[66] He focused on creating venues for experimentation with the "Fellowship Method," and established interracial spaces as a generative venue for discussion of nonviolent direct action.[67]

Randolph's call for interracial "mass action" was a call for an end to the exploitation of both Black and white workers. He decried the American Federation of Labor as the "American Separation of Labor," slamming the organization for its focus on organizing "skilled" laborers at the expense of those whose positions required less skill, and he pointed out that it was Black workers who were often consigned to these less-skilled positions.[68] Randolph advocated "one big union," skilled and unskilled, Black and white, and began working more closely with the Industrial Workers of the World (IWW) and its leader William "Big Bill" Haywood to organize at the intersection of race and class. If Black and white workers could recognize their shared class interests, Randolph maintained, then racial difference might no longer be used as a wedge to divide and exploit Black people. Randolph believed that "socialism would abolish poverty and its consequences" and "remove Negro workers from the base of the working world."[69]

In a monumental moment for Black labor organizing in the United States, Randolph became the president of the Brotherhood of Sleeping Car Porters (BSCP) in 1925—assuming the mantle of leadership for a mass of Black railcar workers. But when the FOR's National Executive Council was asked to endorse the BSCP in 1928, it declined.[70] The vote marked the beginning of a tenuous relationship between Randolph and the FOR, one that included skepticism on both sides.[71] The FOR was only just beginning to shift toward prioritizing interracial organizing in the mid-1920s, and this process would take decades as the FOR overhauled its field secretaries and staff.[72] For Randolph's part, he did not yet possess the massive organizational infrastructure he would later assemble for the March on Washington movement—a massive organizing infrastructure that the FOR found quite attractive.

As the FOR continued to ponder "the scope and function" of the organization with regard to "race" and "other areas of conflict," its leaders called for an increased focus on the South.[73] A committee on administration called for "a distinct and specialized branch of the work in the south," and ultimately a decision was made to create budget allowances for "an additional man" to take on work dealing with the South. Ironically, the FOR's "Man in the South" appointed to oversee "race relations" was not a man. It was the FOR's executive council member Amy Blanche Greene.[74] Most importantly, a young divinity student at Vanderbilt University named Howard Kester was hired to help with the FOR's rapidly growing youth section in the fall of 1927 at a salary of $2,800.[75] Kester worked part-time with YMCAs and YWCAs throughout the South in the late 1920s and told the FOR that they desperately needed a dedicated staffer to work on race issues.[76] With questions about the efficacy of pacifism swirling in a world that was no longer at war, it remained unclear how a focus on racism might contribute to a revitalization of pacifist politics.[77] In the end, Jim Crow became the proving ground for this politics of religious nonviolence.

"Techniques Which Are in Themselves Immediate Ends"

More than fifteen years removed from its founding and nearly a decade after the end of the Great War, the FOR undertook a fundamental reassessment of its charter and leadership. Much of this reconsideration was precipitated by the resignation of Quaker secretary Paul Jones in March 1929. "The Fellowship was born out of the war," Jones wrote to his colleagues, but found itself struggling to prove the "application of FOR principles to current problems." He called for a new kind of leadership in the organization, admitting honestly, "My experience gave me a good vantage point in meeting those who were up against the same situation. But for the best development in the future a different person is required."[78] In his departing letter, Jones urged the FOR to "make a more definite demonstration of inter-racial fellowship" and ranked this as a top priority for a pacifist movement that battled for relevance.

Incoming secretary John Nevin Sayre, an Episcopal priest and longtime FOR member, heeded Jones's call to make interracial organizing a key priority. In 1929's "Development of the Fellowship in the Next Ten Years," Sayre wrote that industrial secretary George L. Collins had "blazed a trail for our witness on race relations in the South," noting also that Howard Kester was "following" his trail. He quoted a recent editorial from C. F. Andrews in the FOR's recently renamed organ, *The World Tomorrow*, to make the case that much work remained to be done on this critical issue. "Race arrogance is the curse which destroys all that is simple and beautiful and natural in those divinely appointed human relationships which are called 'races.' This wonderful thing, race, which was meant by God to give Harmony in color to human life and to prevent uniformity, is turned into a vast and awful fanaticism leading to war, cruelty, loss . . . and every other evil."[79] Early Christians "stood out boldly for racial equality," Sayre wrote anachronistically, suggesting that nation and ethnicity were not barriers to ancient Christian fellowship. But just as contemporary Christians had abandoned their ancestors' pacifist position, so too had they abandoned their commitment to equality across the lines of nation, ethnicity, and now race.[80] Calling on the FOR to "lead a Christian Movement for the recovery of the Gospel made real in life and race relations," Sayre asked FOR members to "invade the South on this issue." He called for the appointment of "a special secretary" to work on the application of a FOR method to address the violence and discrimination of Jim Crow and cautioned against waiting "too long for slower educational processes." Sayre said the FOR must be willing to "dramatize the issue" of racial violence and injustice across the South, to be "witnessing in action" rather than just preaching a different way.

If Sayre echoed the later language of Martin Luther King Jr. and the Southern Christian Leadership Conference (SCLC), it's because the FOR's focus on race in the South marked a watershed moment in the evolution of nonviolence as a technique with the power to transform a Jim Crow society. FOR executive council member Amy Blanche Greene eloquently described the FOR's principles as "a way of life which binds people of many races and nations into the consciousness of a common purpose," calling this "application of the spirit of love to conflict situations" the "fundamental philosophy" that guides "techniques which are in themselves immediate ends." She argued that such a method was a "positive action rather than a negative emphasis," a constructive approach rather than only a protest. As the 1930s began, among the most consequential decades for radical politics in the twentieth century, Blanche Greene captured concisely what the FOR had been working toward since its founding: a politics that flowed from one's way of being in the world, an immediate claim on the right to be free that was itself an expression of the social world as it should be.[81]

But translating such principles into action in the South proved a stern test. While the first Great Migration of Black Americans led more than 1.6 million African Americans out of the South by 1930, nearly 80 percent of Black Americans still lived in the former Confederacy when Sayre took over the FOR. The vast majority of these Black Americans were relegated to agricultural jobs or domestic service roles that paid poverty wages and locked them into a dehumanizing system of Jim Crow laws and customs vouchsafed by vigilante violence. Yet it was in this southern context that the Episcopalian priest saw a unique opportunity to recruit new members, launching a "special effort" in the area of southern interracial work in the 1930s. Sayre created a Southern Advisory Committee in October 1930 with forty-three representatives from twelve states to plan the initiative, and among that group was Howard Thurman. Thurman had just completed a semester of study in the spring of 1929 with FOR cofounder and Quaker Rufus Jones at Haverford College. The young Black intellectual was beginning to think and write critically about pacifism through the prism of the Black experience in America, and Jones—a founding architect of the FOR's philosophy—became a critical interlocutor for Thurman's writing.

The FOR tasked its Southern Advisory Committee with supporting and advising the part-time work of Howard Kester, who had already begun his work by organizing the FOR's first interracial conference at LeMoyne College in Memphis in December 1929. With sixty-two registered participants from eleven states, thirty of them white and thirty-two of them Black, youth participants came from seventeen different colleges and universities. Luanna J. Bowles of Fisk University called the conference "a laboratory experiment from which one can draw many conclusions." Participants discussed "The Economic Status of the Negro" and "The Negro in

Industry" and debated "Suggested Techniques" for combatting white violence and discrimination in the South.[82]

In an essay called "The Meaning of LeMoyne," Bowles explored how a nonviolent method might be applied to Jim Crow violence and segregation. In her comments, she noted that "regardless of seeming differences we are all seeking the same thing, namely a way of life that surmounts outward barriers and frees the spirit to experience the richness and fullness of life." The students at LeMoyne envisioned a society free of discrimination and violence, and they believed this world might come through their way of being together in the world. Bowles suggested that each person had a distinct and complex personality, and that as Black Americans sought to live into this freedom of expression alongside white supporters, they might destabilize Jim Crow laws and mores. Bowles wrote that her own world was "made bigger" by the conference, which had given her the feeling that she was part of a "beloved community." FOR's industrial secretary, George L. Collins, described the conference as an effort to move beyond the "easy" and "sentimental" approaches to the "race question" by engaging tough issues through interracial conversation. That included questions like why Black Americans were "prohibited from joining the union" amid the grinding hardship of the deepening Great Depression. "Is the Negro coming in on the ground floor," he asked, "or is he going to be left out of the question of Labor?" Noting that communists were the "only political party which frankly faces the question of race" with a "straightforward program," participants explored alternatives to communism, asking, "[To] what extent has [the Communist Party] been able to carry its program out?"[83]

The interracial group's search for a transformational political paradigm found no easy answers in existing groups, parties, or initiatives. The group at LeMoyne searched for "a technique for a minority group" that is "quite willing to do something to right this injustice," but they struggled with the practical aspects of how to move forward—of how to turn the personal commitments of kindness, mercy, and interracial fellowship into an effective politics.

> What is the best way to meet such situations of the following: negro women not being allowed to try on hats and gloves, shoes and other wearing Apparel in stores, discrimination on public conveyances, discrimination in hospitals, stores, in newspapers Etc. An effort should be made in each Community to work out a technique that will meet their community's needs. A study should be made of attitudes

exhibited by various organizations, institutions, stores, companies, in order to work out such a technique.... We must find ways for carrying our ideals of Brotherhood into action.[84]

The conference report suggested that in "every community of any size a few people could be found who would be willing to follow such a technique," citing specifically Atlanta, Birmingham, and Nashville as places in addition to Memphis where it might be possible to "get a group of considerable size" to "struggle for interracial justice" in "various perplexing situations." Benjamin Mays, then a student completing his dissertation at the University of Chicago, presaged his later work as an institutional leader at Howard University and Morehouse College in calling for the creation of "machinery whereby our technique may be carried out." Mays also facilitated a discussion among participants about what tactics might be used.[85] Ideas included establishing a clipping service, additional conferences, an interracial speakers bureau, and a coordinated campaign to "insist on people respecting other people's personalities" by capitalizing the letter "N" in "negro" and by calling for all Black women and men to be referred to as "Mr.," "Miss," and "Mrs."

But at the conclusion of the 1929 conference, participants were still searching for that innovative technique capable of transforming both people and structures, a method that might bring about what Luanna Bowles called the "Beloved Community." In his final report from the conference, Kester told FOR leaders that it was of the utmost importance that white people be "willing to sacrifice many of their privileges in order to increase ... opposition to the many injustices."[86]

In February 1931, Kester organized another interracial, intercollegiate meeting at Birmingham's Black Masonic Temple.[87] With eighty-five people representing eighteen schools, the conference included fifty-three Black Americans and thirty-two whites.[88] H. W. Pope of the National YMCA Council called the conference "another epoch in the history of race relations in the South" and praised the "the leadership of [FOR] Southern Secretary Howard Kester." Calling it "one of the finest interracial programs that I have ever witnessed," Pope said the conference was "calculated to mould sentiment, provoke thought, and stimulate action on the part of those directly touched." Naming the goal of the conference as the creation of "right human relationships ... predicated upon understanding and goodwill," Kester said such a "goal for the South" would require "changes of attitudes on the part of both white and black."[89]

A young Howard Kester in the 1920s. Howard Kester Papers, Southern Historical Collection, Louis Round Wilson Library, University of North Carolina at Chapel Hill.

Kester's belief that "attitudes" were a significant structural support for white supremacy was central to the FOR's broader analysis and approach. The FOR believed that individual attitudes were the animating impulse for prejudice, and that together these attitudes and behaviors constituted larger social structures that produced laws and customs allowing widespread discrimination at lunch counters, discriminatory lending by banks, the systemic underfunding of Black schools, and ultimately the violence of lynching. The FOR believed that *being* differently—as individuals and through collective actions—was a powerful way to influence and transform these larger structures in U.S. society. Kester envisioned these interracial conferences not only as opportunities to debate political strategies but as demonstrations of racial egalitarianism, a counterballast to the violently segregated nation that surrounded the conference. The new attitudes required for "the building of a new social order" flowed from these specific "theories" about the relationship between individuals and larger social structures. It was this idea, the notion of demonstrating interracialism in segregated spaces, that underpinned the philosophy of nonviolence in the decades that followed. This theory of how to transform Jim Crow was connected to a more tangled root system of pure pacifist ideology, a set of ideas that suggested one's way of being in the world was itself the key to transforming broader and more complicated social structures. Refusing to participate in war was not only a choice to live one's personal convictions; it was also a strategy that, if deployed collectively, could actually interfere with the state's ability to carry out that war. Yet ironically, it was precisely the FOR's commitment to this pure personal pacifism that undermined Kester's efforts to organize a nonviolent battle against Jim Crow in the segregated South.

In the fall of 1931, Kester reported to his New York bosses that the Scottsboro trial had precipitated horrifying levels of white violence directed at Black men. During the trial, nine African American teenagers accused of raping two white women in a boxcar in northern Alabama were sentenced to death by an all-white jury in April 1931. Kester reported that an African American man had been killed and a Tallapoosa County sheriff "seriously wounded" when police broke up a meeting of "alleged Negro communists" seeking to organize a sharecroppers' union in the wake of the trial. Kester reported that these Black sharecroppers, whom he later organized as a field worker for the Southern Tenant Farmers Union (STFU), were living "a hair's breath away from slavery."[90] Thirty-four Black men awaited trial for their role in the armed resistance to the police siege in Tallapoosa County, and Kester reported that communist organizers were being "driven from cities," provoking "considerable unrest" in rural areas across Alabama. "Armed men are patrolling the district," Kester wrote, noting that sharecroppers were determined to fight back against the violent efforts of law enforcement to break up communist organizing.[91] To halt any outside support for these Black sharecroppers, 150 white men built a roadblock on Tallapoosa's main highway, urged on by an article in the *Birmingham Age Herald* entitled "Negro Reds Advancing" that suggested Black communists from Chattanooga were driving to Tallapoosa to assist the besieged sharecroppers.[92]

As the historian Robin D. G. Kelley writes, "Outraged middle-class black leaders, clergymen, and white liberals blamed white communities for the incident, asserting that armed resistance on the part of black sharecroppers and tenants was unnatural."[93] But as D. G. Kelley notes, armed self-defense against white law enforcement and vigilante violence had been a staple of Black southern life since the end of the Civil War. Kester warned his New York boss John Nevin Sayre that in this moment the communists were "making every effort to capture the Negro." Kester believed that in the process "the Communists are hurting themselves, hurting the Negroes, and hurting those of us who are trying to build interracial Goodwill and cooperation" by "trying to bulldoze the state and to turn the Negroes against everyone who is not lined up with them. . . . The NAACP and the interracial commission follow the only logical political method they could under the existing circumstances." But, he warned, the NAACP and the interracial commission were proving relatively weak in response to the violence in Tallapoosa.[94]

In an open letter to FOR members across the South, Kester called on people of goodwill to play a larger role. "We cannot pussyfoot," he wrote. "We must go on. That there will be serious troubles I haven't any doubt." But it was the communist vision of equity for Black Americans, not class warfare, that proved most frightening to white southerners: "It is not the economics of Communism that frightens the white Southerner," Kester wrote. "It is the racialism." He called the Scottsboro trial but "a moment in our drama" and implored the FOR to focus on winning "the respect, loyalty and affection of negroes and whites" to build an interracial movement that could compete with communism in the South.[95]

Privately, however, Kester confided to his supervisors in New York that he was concerned. "Conditions in the South are worse than they have been at any time since reconstruction," he wrote. He continued:

> The conditions under which Negroes live in the south are so severe that it is questionable whether they will continue to rely upon evolutionary methods in attempting to secure the rights and privileges guaranteed to them by the Constitution. It is clear that unless Negroes are convinced in no uncertain ways that the evolutionary method is best that they will turn to violent methods. It is, therefore, of Paramount importance that the fellowship insert every ounce of strength it possesses in demonstrating the effectiveness of aggressive pacifism for social and economic revolution.[96]

Kester's descriptions of an "evolutionary method" and "aggressive pacifism" reveal a continuing search for the language and tactics of nonviolence, ideas and methods that simply were not yet visible in the fight against Jim Crow. Kester also revealed his belief that there were very real limits to pacifist ideas and tactics in his organizing work in the South. The FOR would continue to have limited success organizing Black southerners around pacifism as long as white vigilantes used extralegal violence and political leaders used the law to persecute Black southerners with impunity. Communists were organizing effectively around the economic conditions that racism was enlisted to support: they were challenging the system of sharecropping, debt peonage, the crop-lien system—economic conditions that "tied Black people to the land" and perpetuated an antebellum social order.

Kester admitted that while communist tactics "have thus far been open to serious criticism, they have nevertheless succeeded in arousing many hitherto despondent and lethargic Spirits. It is a well-known fact that the Communists are bidding strongly for negro support," Kester warned, and "they are winning adherents everywhere." But, he reminded FOR leaders, both the communists and the FOR were joined by a commitment to "accept the negro and the white on the same bases, with no discrimination whatsoever." "The question," he continued, 20 "is which will win." Calling 1932 as "a year of testing," Kester wrote, "We are faced with a conflict situation the proportions of which one cannot imagine without being in it." He argued that "the future of The Fellowship depends upon how we meet this situation," and he implored the FOR to remain "as 'crazy' for our cause" of solutions which do not use violence "as the Communists [are] for theirs."[97] Without continued support for a dedicated program to organize Blacks and whites in the South, Kester wrote, "we are lost."[98]

Perhaps Howard Kester's greatest challenge in persuading both Black and white workers to a position of "aggressive pacifism" was the fact that most southern workers were armed regardless of race. It was unclear to most how pacifism might be enlisted to help poor people in the South as they fought to change the fundamental circumstances of their lives. Kester admitted personally that he was not "so emotionally wedded to the idea of pacifism that I'm blind to the positive benefits of violence in certain situations." But he was also grasping for something bigger, what he continued to call an "aggressive pacifism."

Kester later clarified that he was, in fact, "wedded" to an aggressive pacifism because "I am absolutely convinced that any attempt on the part of negroes to attain their rights through violence at this stage would be a colossal failure and the result suicidal." And he asked his bosses to walk a similarly fine line in understanding his work in the South, reminding them that the practice of armed self-defense among southerners was an issue steeped in the politics of race—that interracial organizing depended on organizing Black people with guns. He urged his bosses to understand that encouraging Black folks to give up guns aligned them with the forces of white supremacy in the South. "Negroes are being disarmed wholesale," Kester told them, stating that "hardware stores, pawnshops, and other dealers in firearms have been instructed not to sell firearms or ammunition to

Negroes," while "no attempt has been made to disarm whites."[99] A close friend told Kester, "We Negroes have taken all we can stand and we are determined to go down shooting." Kester wrote that "young [Black] intellectuals" are "increasingly sceptical [sic] of evolutionary methods and are thinking more and more of violence." He pleaded with the FOR to "improve and enlarge [its] tactics," describing its pacifist political techniques in late 1931 as "woefully inadequate."[100]

While Sayre urged the FOR to double down on its interracial organizing work in the South, in practice the FOR struggled mightily to advance a nonviolent method for transforming the white violence central to southern life. The FOR partnered with the American Friends Service Committee (AFSC) in 1931 to copublish an interracial newsletter edited by Sarah DuBois, and Kester traveled 4,500 miles across the South in 1931 speaking in Mississippi, Alabama, Tennessee, and Georgia. He planned additional interracial conferences in Memphis, Nashville, Montgomery, Atlanta, and Lynchburg, Virginia.[101] But late in 1931, Kester reported that a Mr. Boaz, a professor at State Teachers College in Huntsville, "was brutally murdered by white men on streets of Birmingham." The murder likely occurred as part of a wave of violence meted out against the Black Birmingham community in the wake of two white women being killed and a third being wounded, allegedly by a Black attacker.[102] Kester said the "beastly affair, of which no accounts ever appeared in the white press," had created another "great stir" across Alabama and led many African Americans to be "afraid to get out upon the Highway." The pacifist FOR's tepid response of conferences, dialogue, and interracial fellowship continued to prove an inept politics in the face of routine and barbaric white violence.[103]

Yet for all the FOR's challenges, Kester's work did begin to bear some fruit. He reported in March 1932 that the FOR was in a "stronger position" in the South than "it has ever been before." Letters from Montgomery, Durham, Chapel Hill, Memphis, Chattanooga, Montgomery, and Shreveport expressed "appreciation . . . for the organization of local FOR groups" and "its radical approach to the race issue, labor, and peace." Some suggested that the FOR's efforts in the South had "given heart to those who have grown cynical and despondent."[104] Sayre and the Black YMCA leader Ned Pope joined Kester in March 1932 for an "interracial tour" that "broke over Jim Crow restrictions all along the line." The group stayed in Black hotels and organized interracial FOR meetings in seven cities, and Pope spoke at a number of white institutions: Birmingham Southern College, Maryville College, the Lynchburg YMCA, Durham University, and Pullman Memorial.[105]

Sayre spoke at thirty-eight meetings, twenty in Black spaces and eighteen in white spaces, and reached more than 4,000 people directly. Kester, Pope, and Sayre garnered 750 new FOR members as a result of their tour, and new local chapters were organized in Montgomery, Durham, Atlanta, Lynchburg, Raleigh, Maryville, and Chattanooga.[106]

At the conclusion of the trip, Sayre called for the creation of "a youth group study course . . . on the interracial problems and specific suggestions of action and strategy that might be tried out by young people who were in earnest." The team also called for "action by the Fellowship stimulating churches throughout the country on the evil of segregation and the duty of the Christian Churches to take its stand for unity in interracial worship and fellowship."[107] With the Great Depression deepening, and with white violence in the South worsening, Sayre pressed the FOR to do more through "methods of social persuasion." Other political groups may excel at fomenting political pressure, Sayre argued, but the FOR should continue "experiments in persuasion" and develop a new kind of political method for transforming Jim Crow America.[108]

But the Wilder Coal Strike of 1932 again painfully exposed the inadequacies of pacifist "persuasion" in the South and led to the dismissal of Howard Kester by his pacifist bosses in New York. In the summer of 1932, miners and workers launched a strike at the Fentress Coal and Coke Company in Wilder, Tennessee. Worker pay had been reduced twice by ownership earlier in the year, and when wages were reduced yet a third time in the summer of that year, miners walked off the job. Fentress had operated as an open shop mine until workers struck during that summer of 1932, so when the mining company reopened amid the July 1932 strike, it decided to employ an exclusively nonunion scab workforce—locking out the previously unionized workers. A court injunction made illegal any attempts to interfere with the scab workers brought in by the company. Kester and his colleagues, seeing a humanitarian crisis among the locked-out workers, provided aid through the "Wilder Emergency Relief Committee," collecting food and clothes that were distributed to more than 300 families.[109] By the end of the labor conflict, Kester and the committee estimated that three tons of food and 6,000 pieces of clothing had been provided to the workers locked out at Wilder.

In the Wilder strike, Kester saw an opportunity to do what FOR had envisioned for decades—a chance "to discover the applicability of Christian principles to the settlement of violent situations."[110] When Wilder union leader Barney Graham was killed by local police, shot multiple times in the back, Kester stepped up his organizing efforts.[111] He told his bosses in

New York that he had been identified as one of six people who should be killed if he came near Fentress, and shared that because he was targeted he "was always guarded" when going into the striker's camp. He explained, "When going into the camp I was usually met by a group of the strikers who accompanied me until I left."[112] Kester explained further that he believed "the task of the fellowship is that of a revolutionary movement which must approach its work with the abandon, enthusiasm and realism of the Revolutionary," a none-too-subtle justification for his armed attaché. Seeing no more important venue for this work than the South, Kester wrote, "I dogmatically assert that no great change is possible in the status of the millions of peons and wage slaves in the South as long as the present economic system endures."[113] The FOR, he wrote boldly, was failing to address these larger structural questions:

> To attempt to emancipate the mass of white and Negro workers in the South, employed in mill, mine, farm and factory only through the methods of goodwill, moral suasion and education is to invite the continued exploitation, misery and suffering of generations not yet born. The extreme callousness of the white South to the brutalities of life in relation to the Negro and disinherited white dictates for us a policy of developing those social forces which will not only undermine its present position of power and authority but help usher in The Cooperative Commonwealth.[114]

Drawing on the story of Jesus, as the FOR's leaders had done since the organization's founding, Kester argued that the Nazarene carpenter had "defiantly recognized the class struggle" and worked "steadfastly against the oppressors of the poor, the weak, and the disinherited." Concluding his report somewhat cryptically, and forebodingly, Kester wrote, "Your Secretary has aligned himself with those forces making for a revolutionary change."[115]

Kester's report to the FOR offices in New York was marked up in red pen, presumably by Sayre, who immediately wrote Kester to register his concern with the young secretary's report. If Sayre's response was direct, it was also condescending:

> Although you do not say so, I presume that the strikers who guarded you had guns (of course for self defense). I must say that I consider it seriously wrong for a fellowship secretary to have to depend on the "private gunman" at his side to defend him. To admit the validity of such a procedure would come pretty close to sanction for self-defense.

It would not be what Jesus believed in when in the Garden of Gethsemane he commanded Peter to put his sword away. Therefore, I should feel that in the future no Fellowship secretary should go into situations of danger like those you describe *unless* he goes alone, unarmed, or with a group of friends who will go unarmed also and be prepared, like Gandhi's followers, to offer no violence themselves to opponents who may beat or shoot them down.[116]

Kester had also used spies to gather information from the Ku Klux Klan, to which Sayre responded, "I am dead against that practice. Unless the Fellowship can fight its battles by holding on to truth and refusing deception and undercover crookedness, and unless we can do our work without the support of armed guards, I think we are licked before we begin."[117]

In the FOR's 1933 annual report, Sayre strongly reiterated a commitment to pure pacifism—the absolute prohibition of violence—and he extended this prohibition to include organizing anyone who was armed. Taking up specifically "the question of violence in the class struggle," Sayre told members, "The fellowship should always advocate and have faith in methods of non-violence, persuasion and self-sacrificing love." He encouraged individual members to "pioneer and experiment increasingly with nonviolent ways of affecting social justice," stating that while he often sided with workers in violent struggles, these workers must remain nonviolent. "If this cannot be done or cooperation compromises the clear setting forth of our ideal," he wrote, "we should withdraw cooperation."[118]

Sayre was bound to the idea of pure pacifist nonresistance, a commitment to do nothing rather than become an accomplice to violence, and he remained unable to articulate how a politics of nonviolent direct action might be used as a positive and constructive force in the South. J. B. Matthews, the FOR's industrial secretary, said that whether to "hold to nonviolence in the class struggle as [FOR] did in international war" was a complicated one. "Is violence never curative," Matthews asked provocatively, "but always destructive in its effects? May not violence sometimes be protective and the failure to use it simply an acquiescence in the suffering of others by violence as when armed forces used to protect one from a mob bent on lynching?"[119] The issues faced by Kester on the ground in Alabama, at Wilder, and in his work across the South belonged to a larger question about how the FOR might organize interracial nonviolent campaigns.

In an effort to develop clarity around these issues, the FOR sent a referendum to members in November 1933 with a question about "your own position as to the struggles of workers and other underprivileged groups." The referendum asked members to weigh in on how far secretaries should go in creating a new social order where "no individual or groups" would be "exploited for the profit or pleasure of another."[120] Members were given six options, but the clear dividing line came between options 4 and 5. Option 4 asked if secretaries should be "dissociating themselves from any group that used armed violence," while option 5 asked if secretaries should "consent to the use of armed force if necessary to secure the advantage of the workers, but regretfully and only while the necessity for it continues."[121]

It was Kester's work in the South that precipitated this national debate. "I have never entered Wilder or any other dangerous situation possessing arms or in any way rely upon the arms of Associates or friends for protection," Kester told Sayre weeks before the issuing of the referendum, saying that "nonviolence is the only practical weapon for strikers to use, and in my conversations with individuals and when I talked before the unions I have repeatedly taken this position."[122] But, he added, "every man, woman and child in the mountains of Tennessee knows the use of firearms. The use of a rifle is as natural to them as the use of a knife and fork. The women are frequently as expert as the men." Pivoting to Sayre's admonition that he ought to look to Gandhi as an example, Kester wrote, "What you say about Gandhi and his mass following in India leaves me cold." Gandhi was certainly waging an admirable movement, Kester conceded, but "the problems confronting those who are working in violent situations are not greatly relieved by referring to Gandhi."

For Kester, it was a point of reference without meaning. He concluded his rebuttal to Sayre by addressing openly the issue of organizing Black and white people in the U.S. South. "I can't work with Negroes here in the South like you can in the East," Kester wrote. "To announce our work 'in the open' simply means that our work is terminated here," he wrote, referring to the fact that interracial organizing meetings were routinely ended by white violence—as had been the case in Tallapoosa. Kester told Sayre optimistically that the FOR in the South was seen as a real threat to the racial oligarchy. He wrote of his "wish to reach the strawberry pickers in Southern Tennessee and Mississippi this spring," groups that Kester described as "little better than chattel slaves," continuing: "If you know anything about southern life on the plantations, and you do, you will not wonder why it is necessary to work in secret."[123]

In his effort to "develop certain social forces to combat other social forces," Kester believed there are "no ready-made patterns upon which to work." Some pacifist "theories" might be used to "govern a perfect society," but "I am living in a society possessed of many devils who have their abode in this hell we call Earth. I'm trying to be intelligent and honest and working with the fellowship. I make mistakes often enough and will probably continue to make them. If anyone has a better way let him *demonstrate it* and I will be the first to follow."[124] Sayre's response was a continuing admonition to condemn violence and armed self-defense. "It is right for you to urge non-violence as the only practical weapon for Strikers," Sayre wrote, "[but] I hope you will also make clear that you, as a fellowship secretary are dead opposed to being defended by anybody's guns in any situation, that you are endeavoring to stand one hundred percent for a nonviolent way of life and that you would rather to be hurt and bearing witness to this principle than you would to escape but have your testimony be clouded."[125]

The Wilder affair ultimately cost Kester his job. He received news that he had been fired on the same day as an "atrocious lynching" in Tennessee.[126] Twenty-year-old Cord Cheek, accused of attacking an eleven-year-old white girl, was filled with bullets and hung from a tree in Columbia, Tennessee. Confronted once again with savage white brutality, and now fired for his work to organize people who practiced self-defense, Kester sardonically asked Sayre to "advise me regarding use of persuasive love" in the face of Cheek's brutal lynching.[127] "Appeal to newspapers and public opinion of city and state for cessation of further violence and upholding good name of state and peaceful support of process of law," Sayre wrote in a telegram, advice that rang hollow for Kester. The two men had reached an impasse.

Kester called his dismissal from FOR "a horrible mistake and one that will have far-reaching consequences." He told Sayre that he had strictly adhered to nonviolence in conflict situations but had remained open to working with people who owned guns. "My position was not achieved in a day nor was it born out of an emotional bias for the working class," he explained, "but was wrought from the furnace of Southern life."[128] He told Sayre that he was "sorry to be severed from the work of the fellowship here in the South. I feel that we were beginning to make a really effective and most worthwhile contribution in this area."[129]

Kester's wife and partner in work, Alice Kester, wrote Sayre to register her complaint that a group of New Yorkers had overreached into the efforts she and her husband had undertaken in the South. Calling Kester's dismissal another example of "the incapacity of a local committee" in New York "to direct a National Organization," Alice told Sayre that "one has to be a part of a scene to realize its needs." She and Howard had "thought, talked, and preached only non violent methods" in their time with FOR, but Howard had wrestled with how and whether to organize armed people for months. She noted her disappointment that "a so-called liberal group could be so intolerant," and likened the firing of Howard to the actions of "the old fashioned Church groups with which I worked as a young girl." She continued: "It is rather disillusioning to find that there is no freedom of thought even for a FOR secretary."[130] In closing, Alice lamented the loss of "the interracial side" of the work, which she believed had the capacity for "real success."[131] In his final letter to Sayre in 1934, Howard shared his continuing commitment to the work: "I shall stay in the South . . . unless starved out, and do a more vigorous job than I have ever done before. I can't quit because some people go haywire over the question of violence."[132]

The Color of Pacifism

FOR field secretary Claud Nelson took over much of Kester's responsibilities in the South. In 1935, he wrote a pamphlet provocatively titled "Can Guns Settle Strikes?"[133] The answer from the FOR was, of course, no. But the FOR did attempt to continue its organizing work in the South alongside the AFSC. Throughout the late 1930s, the two groups hosted a series of interracial institutes similar to the conferences Kester organized in the late 1920s and early 1930s.[134] "We were united," wrote AFSC industrial secretary Ray Newton, "in feeling that the institute is as concrete and promising a step in the development of the Fellowship program in the South as could be devised and carried out at present."[135] The institutes explored how "friendly relations," a type of social interaction intended to express reverence for personality and to nurture what the Quakers called the "inner light," might mitigate violence. These institutes became spaces where methods could be explored for "eliminating racial injustice using non-violent means."[136] Like the FOR, the AFSC envisioned these interracial institutes as the foundation for a better world, what the historian Allan Austin has called a "technique in interracialism" that was, itself, the goal.[137] The AFSC and the FOR both agreed on "a definite emphasis on the religious approach to race," and the institutes were designed to focus more on the "practical" questions of how to improve "race relations."[138] But as a method for battling Jim Crow violence and discrimination, being together in conference spaces across lines of difference attracted little interest among Black Americans in the interwar period. The color of pacifism was white, and with armed self-defense a survival imperative for most Black Americans, the lily-white and rigidly pacifist FOR struggled to take root in southern soil.

But in the late 1930s, there was a shift. Howard Thurman was elected to the FOR's executive council in December 1939, and by the end of 1940 he had become the council's vice chairman.[139] The elevation of the white labor radical and FOR cofounder A. J. Muste to executive secretary in the mid-1930s, after he had abandoned the FOR to work with armed labor activists in the early 1930s, pushed the FOR more aggressively toward piloting interracial nonviolent direct actions. Muste implored FOR members early in 1941 to move beyond what he called a "negative protest" toward a constructive nonviolent technique that would achieve "a new social order in the spirit and by the method of nonviolence." The FOR's executive council authorized "the setting up of a Committee on Nonviolent Techniques of the FOR" early in 1941 to focus explicitly on linking this "spirit" of nonviolence with the "method" of direct action.[140]

In its first report on the "application of nonviolent techniques to problems of race" in September 1941, the Committee on Nonviolent Techniques noted the tension between the "scarcity of negroes in the Fellowship and the urgency of the problem of racial reconciliation." FOR secretary and Unitarian minister John Haynes Holmes, a cofounder of the NAACP and the American Civil Liberties Union (ACLU), felt hopeful after his meetings with "younger members of Harlem churches. . . . An interest has been awakened in the study of the possibility of the application of the way of non-violent action to the real emancipation of the Negro," he wrote. "Who knows when and where an American Negro Gandhi may catch the vision!"[141]

Muste recruited Bayard Rustin, a Black Quaker raised in Pennsylvania, and James L. Farmer, a recent graduate of the Howard School of Religion, to work as FOR field secretaries in September 1941. Their appointments marked the establishment of the FOR's first Black leadership dedicated to thinking about how the spirit and method of nonviolence might transform Jim Crow America.[142] Nearly thirty years after the FOR's first secretary, the Quaker Edward Evans, called racial violence and lynching the "supreme test both of our democracy and our Christianity," the Fellowship of Reconciliation recruited Black board members and hired Black staff to focus on organizing a nonviolent movement to end Jim Crow. Their ultimate success would depend on their ability to develop a revolutionary nonviolent vision with the power to ignite the Black imagination.

2 From Mere Quietus to Prophetic Religion
Howard Thurman Imagining Nonviolence in America

....

Howard Thurman was intrigued by pacifism, but not convinced. The Morehouse valedictorian was one of only three students in the class of 1923 to describe himself as a pacifist, but he remained wary of embracing it as his life philosophy. The horror of the First World War with its gases and trenches and machine guns had inspired a global pacifist movement, but for Black Americans it was different. Wars had often paved the way for major advancements in Black life, and Thurman had no interest in the peace movement per se. More importantly, he found the idea of "passive resistance" problematic. Life was something to be lived actively, he thought, and Jim Crow—a system that prevented Black Americans from living fully and freely—must be transformed. But how?

As he puzzled over this question, Thurman joined the Fellowship of Reconciliation as a sophomore at Morehouse in 1921. It would take him years to locate the ethical core of pacifism, even as he worked to articulate a force more powerful than passive resistance, but he described his introduction to the FOR's philosophy as like learning "a secret." Another world is possible, he thought, and the commitment of the FOR to mend violent conflicts between U.S. social worlds—black and white, labor and capital—was making that world today, here and now, in the present. The FOR's work contrasted sharply with the white nativist currents fueling immigration restrictions, public lynching, and police violence directed at striking workers, and it all proved deeply appealing for the young Black intellectual. Years later, Thurman reflected that the FOR had given him the way he "should take to walk" through the world. He believed he had found a "place to stand" in the FOR's mission of hope and healing, an affirmation of "mind and personality" that was so deep he was "strengthened by a sense of immunity to the assaults of the white world of Atlanta."[1] In the organization's charter, Thurman came to see a vision for his own life: fellowship and reconciliation.

But if Howard Thurman was intrigued by the ethics of pacifism, he was not convinced it could speak to the problems of Black people in America. "It is a very simple matter," Thurman wrote in 1929, "for people who form the dominant group in society to develop what they call a philosophy of pacifism that makes few, if any, demands upon their ethical obligations to minority groups with which they may be having contacts." The color of pacifism was white, Thurman contended, and it was worth remembering that the FOR's pacifist inspiration had emerged from the mutual slaughter of Europeans in the trenches of the First World War. These were the same white Europeans who had practiced colonialism for centuries while their American counterparts colonized the "New World" and established a slave society. Who were these white pacifists, Thurman asked pointedly, to tell Black people they should be passive in the face of public lynching? Pacifism, he intoned, appeared to be "mere quietus to be put into the hands of the minority to keep them peaceful and controllable."[2]

By 1929, Howard Thurman was a nationally renowned public religious intellectual. He was invited to speak regularly at both Black and white colleges and churches across the United States, and his ideas were published regularly in Black and white religious journals. He had risen to tremendous heights from the rigidly segregated world of Daytona, Florida, where he was born in 1899—a place without a high school for Black children. And on the doorstep of thirty, Thurman had become a leading religious authority on the major issues of his time: the ethics of war and peace, the morality of race and violence. He came to believe that disenfranchised peoples in the United States and across the world would not find liberation in the dominant forms of politics endemic to the disfranchising powers themselves—whether violence, law, or passive resistance. He instead became a seeker of something different, something deeper, something more powerful. By the late 1920s, Howard Thurman began to imagine an innovative and revolutionary force for the liberation of Black Americans: nonviolence.

He began with the premise that, to be free, all people must be allowed to flourish and grow into the unlimited creative capacity that is the great promise of all humanity. He called this the development of individual personality, taking a cue from the Quaker idea that all people have an "inner light" that must be allowed to shine forth. Any social system that interferes with this must be actively resisted and ultimately changed.

In the historical figure Jesus of Nazareth, Thurman saw an excellent example of how personal actualization could produce world historical change. Carefully distinguishing Jesus of Nazareth from the Christian archetype "Jesus Christ," a political figure co-opted to march under Constantine's imperial banners in the fourth century, Thurman described the first-century Nazarene carpenter as a persecuted religious minority living amid the immoral demands of an imperial state, a monotheist Jew forced to conform to the immoral demands of a polytheistic empire under the threat of violence. In the life of Jesus of Nazareth, Thurman identified responses to this suffocating imperial context that were neither retreat nor violence. They were creative and transformative, actions made possible because this Palestinian Jew chose to live the highest ethical demands of his religion despite the violence it provoked. He refused to bend or contort himself to the narrow and immoral demands of an unjust state, and his life thus became an insurgent political action. In the story of Jesus, Thurman saw creative nonviolence—a "technique of survival for an underprivileged minority," with the power to generate individual and collective freedom.[3]

Understanding how Thurman arrived at this conclusion requires an excavation of the Black institutional spaces within which his intellectual work took place. Following his graduation first from Morehouse College and then from Rochester Theological Seminary, Thurman joined a distinguished faculty of Black religious scholars at the Howard School of Religion in 1932 that were dedicated to graduating Black women and men with "integrity of character and social imagination."[4] Just as Charles Hamilton Houston and Spottswood Robinson worked with Howard students to wage a legal assault on Jim Crow, Thurman and his students focused on mounting an ethical challenge to white supremacy in America. Their writing expanded significantly the Black religious imagination in the 1930s, and their work at Howard reveals an immutable link between intellectual activity and movement organizing in the early twentieth-century Black freedom struggle. Howard Thurman and his students of religion at Howard University enlarged the episteme of Black religious thought before 1941, imagining together how nonviolence might revolutionize the racial politics of the United States and transform the nation.

The Howard University School of Religion

Howard University was founded on 2 March 1867 when President Andrew Johnson signed the founding charter for the institution. Ironically, the notoriously anti-Black president signed the charter on the same day that Congress overrode his veto of the Reconstruction Act of 1867.[5] By that time, a dozen or so colleges and universities dedicated to the education of Black Americans were already operating—Shaw, Rust, and Fisk among them—and a larger shift in American life was taking place in this postbellum moment as Black Americans defined the meaning of freedom through education, associational life, and mutual aid.

Howard was originally envisaged as a seminary, one dedicated to preparing "preachers with a view to service among the freedmen," an idea borne from a special conference of mostly white Congregationalists held in Washington, D.C., on 20 November 1866.[6] The "School of Theology" at Howard was formally established in 1906, but students only began to pursue postbaccalaureate study in religion in 1918.[7] University-wide growth led to a new facility for the School of Religion (SOR) at 5460 Sixth Street NW in late 1928, and by 1931 the SOR counted more than 500 graduates.[8] "Who can estimate the influence which they have exerted," the School of Religion bulletin boasted that year, "in elevating the standards of the Christian ministry in serving the communities to which they have gone?"[9] But the SOR's best days lay ahead.

Born in Paris, Tennessee, in 1890, Mordecai W. Johnson rose to great educational heights after receiving primary and secondary education in Nashville and Memphis. He earned bachelor's degrees from Atlanta Baptist College (later Morehouse College), the University of Chicago, and Rochester Theological Seminary before earning a master's of sacred theology from Harvard University in 1922. Johnson turned down an initial offer to run Howard in the early 1920s, but ultimately agreed to take on the role as the university's first Black president in 1926, leaving his prestigious pastorate at the historic First Baptist Church in Charleston, West Virginia to do so. In his inaugural address on 10 June 1927, Johnson specified rigorous preparation for the ministry as a central task of his administration. Of the many groups capable of uniting Black Americans, Johnson argued, "there is no organization and no combination of organizations that can, at this stage in the history of the Negro race, begin to compare with the fundamental importance of the Negro church." "And yet," he continued, "we can see what is going to happen to that church if only sixty college men are preparing to enter the Negro pulpit."[10]

In his remarks, Johnson blended pride in what Black churches had accomplished since the end of the Civil War with a note of caution, asking pointedly what it would mean to continue to rely on ministers without formal academic training. Johnson believed that formal education was the surest path to both individual and collective growth for Black Americans, an idea that was widely shared among Black leaders in the late 1920s. But Johnson also struck a kind of middle path between the more famous figures W. E. B. Du Bois and Booker T. Washington. He did not maintain publicly that accommodation to segregation was acceptable, but as president of the nation's largest Black university—an institution whose very existence depended on the blessing of white congressmen—he remained extremely cautious about overt challenges to America's racial laws and mores.[11]

In the formal training of Black ministers, Johnson saw an important, if long-term, strategy for the growth and development of the Black community. He believed ministers should preach inspiring sermons but must also address the unique challenges of an increasingly complex "modern" world. "The religion of the Negro cannot continue to endure," Johnson told the thousands gathered in Washington for his inauguration on that day in early June, "unless it is reinterpreted over and over to him by men who have a fundamental and far reaching understanding of the significance of religion in its relations to the complexities of modern civilized life."[12] Johnson's emphasis on men in ministry is notable. Although the Congregationalists who had founded Howard ordained women as early as the late nineteenth century, Protestant denominations by and large reserved ministry for men. Pauli Murray, a talented student in the Howard School of Law during Johnson's tenure as president, would spend much of her life challenging the idea that the ministry was reserved for men. But as the young Baptist preacher Johnson set out to create a "great nonsectarian school of religion" at Howard dedicated to "seeking truth about the meaning of life without bias," the school's students would be almost exclusively men.[13]

The School of Religion sought to raise the bar for graduate training in the early 1930s by admitting only students with a bachelor's degree, and two critical hires were made in this period to strengthen the rigor of the curriculum: Howard Thurman was appointed associate professor of systematic theology and dean of Rankin Chapel in 1932, and Benjamin E. Mays was asked to serve as the SOR's eighth dean in 1934.[14] Mays, who had graduated from the University of Chicago with a Ph.D. in 1935, had academic and administrative acumen that proved essential to Johnson's goal of developing the highest quality graduate training in religion for Black Americans. By 1938, the SOR had "39 college graduates enrolled during the second semester," and by the end of 1939 Howard boasted more African American college graduates in master's-level religious training than any other institution in the United States. Forty-three students were enrolled at the SOR in the spring of 1939, and all of them had a bachelor's degree.[15]

The growth and professionalization of the Howard SOR was a watershed moment in the battle against Jim Crow. The School of Law at Howard set out to intentionally challenge de jure segregation by training a cadre of young lawyers to wage legal battles against racial discrimination under the leadership of Black Harvard Law graduate Charles Hamilton Houston.[16] Students in the School of Law examined the legal architecture undergirding racial violence and discrimination, and they used legal challenges to probe the laws of Jim Crow's underbelly searching for weaknesses. Similarly, faculty and students at the Howard SOR grappled with the role of religion in the perpetuation of Jim Crow, believing that laws flowed from ethics, and that to change the structure of society there must be a new and different ethic to guide the creation and enforcement of laws.

Segregation and discrimination were not simply legal problems, they believed, but also ethical problems to which religious people and religious institutions must address themselves. Changing laws, while essential, may have little effect on the deeper problem of how people thought about and related to one another in day-to-day life. It was the ethic of Black dehumanization which was, at bottom, the fundamental infrastructure of a Jim Crow society. This ethic of dehumanization made violence against Black Americans easier to perpetrate, and it naturalized legalized discrimination as a way of life. If a method might be devised that could be widely used to revolutionize this ethical infrastructure of American race relations, the thinking went, then American politics and society might be revolutionized.

In 1939, just as the SOR became fully accredited by the American Association of Theological Schools, it moved into the Carnegie Library building at the center of the Howard campus.[17] "The whole tone of religion will be raised to a new height and dignity when the University opens in the fall," Mays wrote of the move, adding that "school of religion alumni are rejoicing all over the nation."[18] Mays, like Johnson, believed in formally training Black ministers in rhetoric and preaching, especially amid the growing influence of what he called "anti-religious forces." Combatting the growing communist influence in the mid-1930s with a more "respectable" approach could pay dividends, Mays believed, as educated ministers might be more effective in their appeals to both Black and white people in the fight for Black freedom.[19]

Whether Mays's prescription was correct, his diagnosis was on target: communists were actively organizing Black Americans in the 1930s, particularly in the South where the majority of Black Americans still lived. The Communist Party offered an attractive alternative to the National Association for the Advancement of Colored People (NAACP) in the 1920s and 1930s as this nascent organization still struggled to find its footing in southern communities. The party provided legal aid, supported armed self-defense, and offered a viable option for Black Americans where few others existed. "In times like these," Mays wrote, "when anti-religious forces are rife even on our own campus, and when the status of religion is not high in the thinking of the average person in the university community, it is quite necessary to make religion *respectable in every particular*."[20] While the "politics of respectability" espoused by Mays can be viewed as an acquiescence to white culture and dominance, the historian Evelyn Higginbotham observed that such an approach also proved to be a "powerful weapon of resistance to gender and race subordination."[21]

As the Howard SOR worked to develop an academically trained ministerial class, it expanded its faculty ranks. By 1941, it had grown to four full-time professors and seven part-time faculty.[22] Its stated purpose was "to prepare men and women for Christian service," to train "ministers and Christian workers whose integrity of character and social imagination are superior to those of the average citizen." Continuing to emphasize training that allowed students to "interpret the Christian message in a convincing manner," the SOR fashioned itself as a site where ministers drew "no fundamental distinction between men," and they were urged to call out "the farce that caste built upon color, intellect, wealth or ancestry as both vicious and ungodly," and they were encouraged to focus their ministry on the growth and development of human "personality." Like their religious counterparts in the FOR, Howard SOR leaders viewed this flourishing of individual human personality as critical to collective liberation, naming their goal as making "religion an effective agency in developing personality and a vital force in perfecting social change."[23]

The language of personality was common not only to faculty and students at the SOR but also to a wider intellectual discourse in the early twentieth century. The emerging fields of psychology and sociology made critical contributions by clarifying the relationship between the individual mind and the social body, but a specific religious discourse on personality also circulated in this period, stemming in part from the Quaker religious tradition. Howard Thurman had a direct link to this Quaker discourse, having studied with the pacifist Rufus Jones at Haverford College in the spring of 1929. Thurman came to believe all humans were joined by the capacity for creative action and expression, despite Jim Crow's insistence that Black Americans follow restrictive and prescriptive social codes under the threat of violence. Thurman maintained that each individual nonetheless possessed a unique and distinct personality, and one's life journey was a continuing venue for creative human expression. Jones and the Quakers used the term "inner light" to capture this idea of personality as that unique aspect of being which lives within all people and which seeks free expression in the social world. Discovering ways to let inner light shine forth in the world, and learning to live from this unique expression, was the pathway to human freedom.

Thurman carried this vision for liberation to Howard at just the moment when the school was engaged in a major battle for relevance. Mays, Thurman, and other SOR leaders believed that this relevance would come in part from moving beyond fundamentalist religious interpretations to historical approaches to the Bible that reflected academic rigor in a positivist age of science and reason. "To what kind of fate are the five million negro church members being led," Howard administrator William Stuart Nelson wrote in 1941, calling this "the most vital and difficult problems of Negro life today." Nelson called for "a frank review" of Black ministerial training "and in some instances a thoroughgoing reconstruction of philosophy and techniques." Echoing Mays, Nelson said that "a spirit of secularization" was "running athwart the most powerful forces which religion has been able to develop during all of its history." The SOR must play a vital role in constructing the new class of educated Black clergy in America, and as religion can and must play a primary role in addressing the violence and discrimination facing Black Americans every day.[24]

Nelson was a distinguished scholar of religion and an extraordinary college leader, serving first as a special assistant to President Moredcai W. Johnson in the late 1930s before becoming dean of the SOR in 1940. Nelson was a graduate of Howard, having earned his bachelor of arts degree in 1920 before attending Yale University, where he earned a bachelor of divinity in 1924. Nelson became the first Black president of Shaw University in 1931 and became Dillard University's first Black president in 1936. He took over the deanship of the Howard SOR as Benjamin Mays transitioned to the presidency of Morehouse College in Atlanta, and Nelson continued the momentum of his predecessor in numerous ways. Nelson grew the SOR library from 1,443 to 46,527 volumes, and he increased the number of students enrolled in postgraduate religious study to an all-time high of fifty-four.[25] In a nod to President Johnson, Nelson wrote that he could "think of nothing for which we might reasonably have asked which you have not stood ready to provide."

Johnson named the development of a "great nonsectarian" School of Religion a top priority when he arrived almost fifteen years before, and the graduate school had grown and flourished under his leadership. Faculty in the SOR focused on religion as a force for social change in a secular age.

Emphasizing biblical historicism over biblical literalism, administrators highlighted the cultivation of personality—a social world that facilitated continuous and creative expression—as a pathway for Black liberation. Howard Thurman became a critical contributor in this intellectual space, and it was his work in the years before he came to Howard that prepared him to articulate the foundation of religious nonviolence in the Black freedom movement.

Howard Thurman and the Roots of Religious Nonviolence in America

By the time Howard Thurman came to the SOR in 1932, he had known Mordecai Johnson for nearly fifteen years. Thurman had first corresponded with Johnson in the spring of 1918. The eighteen-year-old Thurman sent Johnson a letter that said in the Baptist minister's life he saw a path that he himself might follow, a rarified road for a young Black man at Jim Crow's nadir. Thurman wrote about the daily grind of his life in the small town of Dayton, Florida, sharing that he had been raised by his mother alongside three other small children, proudly declaring that he was the first Black person from his county to receive a "Certificate of Promotion" from middle school. His town had no high school for Black children, and he was only able to attend secondary school in nearby Jacksonville because, miraculously, a stranger saw him forlorn on the train's boarding platform and provided him with the baggage fare he needed to travel. Now he wanted to go to college. "I want to be a minister of the gospel," Thurman told Johnson, "I feel the needs of my people, I see their distressing condition, and have offered myself upon the altar as a living sacrifice, in order that I may help the 'skinned and flung down' as you interpret." "God wants me," he continued in his elegant longhand, "and His precious love urges me to take up the cross and follow him. I want advice from you as to how to direct my efforts."[26]

Johnson's reply three weeks later marked the beginning of a lifelong friendship between the two men. He implored Thurman to "go on with your preparatory and college work," writing that "it will be far better for you to enter the ministry after you have completed a college course than to make a shortcut." Johnson, who carefully and effectively navigated a violently segregated society, had found success through formal education. Born among the first generations outside slavery, his grandparents were legally forbidden to read or write. And despite their many other differences, at one time all of the major Black leaders of his generation had served as formal educators in Black schools: Ida B. Wells, Booker T. Washington, W. E. B. Du Bois. Earning formal education, Johnson told the young Thurman, made it especially important to "keep in close touch with your people, especially those who need your service. Take every opportunity to think over all that you learn, in relation to them and to their needs. Make yourself believe that the humblest, most ignorant and most backward of them is worthy of the best prepared thought and life that you can give."[27] You have a responsibility to serve, Johnson told Thurman, to give back and to build up—a reminder that the nadir of Jim Crow was also the apex of Black associational life, a time of institution building as Black churches, schools, clubs, and businesses abounded in the United States.[28]

The early twentieth century was also a time when many churches both Black and white felt a responsibility to serve those in need. Some ministers came to believe that their churches were obligated to live and preach what Walter Rauschenbusch called the "Social Gospel." The insights of Rauschenbusch, a professor at Rochester Theological Seminary where both Mordecai Johnson and Howard Thurman studied, flowed from major changes to U.S. society in the early twentieth century. Improvements in transportation and communication networks and the growing concentration of Americans in cities led to what the historian Robert Wiebe called the end of "island communities." U.S. society became increasingly mobile and connected, and these changes had enormous implications for both Black and white people. Major corporations consolidated their power, often subjecting workers to miserable conditions on the job and in their neighborhoods, and the problems of the poor were typically left to churches or progressive organizations like Jane Addams's Hull House. The United States was riven by what Supreme Court Justice Louis Brandeis called "the curse of bigness," and Black Americans were especially vulnerable. As millions of Black Americans migrated from the rural South to cities in the West, Midwest, and North in search of opportunity, they were often the last to be hired and the first to be fired. And white violence was rampant: Black neighborhoods were attacked in dozens of cities during the Red Summer of 1919, and hundreds of African Americans were killed or injured. Millions of dollars of damage was done to property in Black neighborhoods across the United States.

In this context, Thurman's vocation to become a "minister of the gospel" went beyond the idea of the Social Gospel, which had little to say on the issue of race. Service to the poor and charity to those in need were important, but for Thurman the goal was something greater, something deeper.

Thurman envisioned a social transformation, and in the process he joined a broader religious movement in the early twentieth century that began to examine the structures of society, both past and present, by using a historical approach to study the Bible. Inspired in part by Albert Schweitzer's 1906 book *The Quest for the Historical Jesus*, many scholars and ministers began to treat the Bible as both a living document that required continual reinterpretation and as a historical text produced within a particular historical moment. Yet even amid these "modern" Protestant approaches to religion, Thurman went further. His approach more closely resembled the American pragmatists and Quakers of his day than that of his Protestant contemporaries. Thurman emphasized contemplation of ancient religious texts, a practice closer to Sufism than the Christianity of his day, and came to believe that such contemplation could produce what William James called "authentic religious experience." Thurman believed authentic religious experience culled an internal force—or power—that prepared a person to transform the social conditions structuring their lives. How to generate this spiritual power became a central preoccupation for Thurman in the 1920s, the foundation for what he called the "Christian way in race relations."

In the April 1924 edition of *Student Challenge*, Thurman described the Christian way in race relations as the "way of sympathetic understanding—which leads to respect for personality," establishing in a single sentence two ideas that would become central to religious nonviolence in the fight against Jim Crow.[29] In claiming that there was such a thing as a Christian way in race relations, Thurman joined a small but important group of people who believed that Christians living in the United States of the early twentieth century had an ethical obligation to deal with race. The early twentieth-century progressive Christian movement, which called loudly for temperance and outreach to the urban poor, was often short on Christian responsibility amid the routine violence and discrimination meted out against non-white people. In calling for a "Christian way in race relations," Thurman staked out intellectual territory for the development of an ethical framework to account for and address racism and violence in America, calling especially for an end to the silence of white Christian churches on this fundamental social problem.[30]

In emphasizing a "respect for personality," Thurman used the language of his Quaker mentor Rufus Jones and the discourse common to the Fellowship of Reconciliation. Racism "strangles personality and inhibits its highest growth and development," Thurman argued, and "any attitude, regardless of its basis," that prevents the full development of one's personality is not only "wrong" but "for a Christian believer to have that kind of attitude is a crime against God."[31] Segregation and Jim Crow warped the individual personalities of both Black and white people, Thurman suggested, preventing a "relationship of primary contact" between people and inhibiting the most authentic parts of oneself from engaging with the other. It is only through such primary contact "that the individual emerges," Thurman wrote, that both oneself and the other can become authentically who they are supposed to be in the world.[32] Because Jim Crow halted such "primary" interactions, it prevented both Black and white people the freedom of expression that was their birthright as humans and made impossible the foundation for a just society.

Thurman did not arrive at these ideas from study alone. They came also from experience—his first experiences living with white people. In September 1923, Thurman began graduate studies in religion at Rochester Theological Seminary in Rochester, New York. For the first time in his life, Thurman lived and worked among white people.[33] As one of only two Black students at Rochester, he came to understand that the ethics of both Black and white people in America were underwritten by race—whether or not they were conscious of this. These experiences led to a reshaping of Thurman's "magnetic field of ethical awareness," a recalibration that sought to account for the way Jim Crow distorted not just the life and personality of Black people but also those, as Thurman wrote, "other than my own people."[34] Working under the tutelage of the systematic theologian George Cross, himself a student of Walter Rauschenbusch, Thurman came to believe that a sound ethical framework could not be developed in the United States without accounting for the way race influenced the ethics of American society. He began to write about a new ethic in the 1920s, and his preaching and writing in this period led him to develop a national interracial following.

In a 1925 essay published in *Student Challenge*, Thurman wrote that ensuring the "sacredness of human personality" required both acknowledging "the interdependence of all men" and acting from a place of "passionate good-will or love." Acting in a spirit of goodwill can be difficult, Thurman conceded, but "the salvation of the world depends upon individuals who are willing to pay the debt they owe to their dignity as human beings by fighting out the battle within themselves until they possess their souls."[35] Thurman believed that the purpose of courageous action was the reclamation of personal integrity, a fullness of confidence and belief in oneself, and he emphasized that a path to liberation could open up if one shaped their way of being in the world around this way of being. Such a way of being went

Howard Thurman circa 1930. Howard Gotlieb Archival Research Center, Boston University Libraries.

beyond contemplation or praying. Thurman rejected "immature piety borne of platitudes" as "the presentation of words without the possession of the experience . . . superficial, ineffective, and incomplete," arguing that only individuals who claimed the integrity to act with courage and compassion would transform the ethical structure of this violently racist nation. "Jesus is still unknown in this land that is covered with churches erected in his honor," he wrote, calling the United States a nation "*absente Christo.*"[36]

Thurman's writings in the 1920s put him at the forefront of a broader intellectual movement focused on the "experiential basis of religion," a movement that emphasized not merely ideology or right thinking but active religious living. Yet Thurman pushed even the edges of this intellectual field by probing the metaphysics of religious experience, citing what he called "a realm that is above sense phenomena." Thurman certainly shared sensibilities with people rightly called "mystics," but such a characterization elides the well-trod relationship in Thurman's work between the ethereal and the concrete, the link between ideas and action that is evident throughout his writing and preaching.

In the fall of 1925, Thurman described a "unity of relationship" that exists between people and their experience, arguing that humans are uniquely endowed among animals with the ability to reflect on themselves and their experiences. Such reflection should account for the "Being" that permeates all life, a being that he described as "a creative spirit" rather than "a static infinite." He described a sound ethics as one that requires continual reinterpretation of how one ought to live in light of one's relationship to God and one's social experiences.[37] "If a normal individual has to stretch himself out of shape in order to be proper and acceptable to society," Thurman wrote, "then the standards of society are such that the individual becomes immoral in conforming to them. . . . It must be in relation to society that the individual discovers what is the criterion of conduct for him."[38] Thurman here again echoed William James, who nearly twenty years earlier had written that truth happens to an idea in the social world.[39]

But as a Black man in Jim Crow America, Thurman added a critical amendment: one might only come to understand the truth of oneself by acknowledging the creative impulse at the center of all human life, and by refusing also to cooperate with a social world that limits one's freedom to be. Arriving at the truth about one's full creative capacity in a restrictive social world generated the indisputable fact of one's power to transform that social world, Thurman believed, and it was this idea that became the foundation for a religious sensibility with the power to shatter the ethical infrastructure of Jim Crow in America.

Howard Thurman and the Politics of Nonviolence

When Mordecai Wyatt Johnson was appointed president of Howard University in 1926, his old friend Howard Thurman was among the first to know. Ten years after writing Johnson "seeking a kind word of encouragement," Thurman had emerged as a national voice among religious thinkers concerned with racial justice. "We are fed and clothed by a system built upon deceit and adulteration," Thurman wrote to Johnson in 1927, reflecting on how futile it was to "talk the talk about sincerity, about purity and honesty" while people are "eating, seeing, reacting to a mighty array of lies!" But the ever-hopeful Thurman wrote to Johnson, "Of course this is not the whole story. I believe with all my heart that our task is twofold—seek how we may release to the full our greatest spiritual forces that there may be such a ground swell of spiritual energy that existing systems will be upset from sheer dynamic—and make whatever temporary adjustments may prove helpful in relieving intolerable situations until there is a genuine uprooting." He called this a "new kind of education," and noted that it "has a very 'Jesus' contribution to make to this whole problem."[40]

In his intellectual work throughout the late 1920s and 1930s, Thurman focused on how to build that "ground swell of spiritual energy" to upset "existing systems." He began to sketch the outline of an ethical framework specifically for Black liberation, and his analysis led him to the premier theme of his later work—the "very Jesus contribution" he envisioned in his letter to Johnson.[41] "If the religion of Jesus cannot purify human relations," Thurman wrote in 1928, "if it cannot teach men reverence for life and personality, then one of two attitudes is forced upon us: men have misunderstood its genius and upon embracing it discover that it is impotent, or they have deluded themselves into believing that they have embraced it when they have not."[42] In claiming the "religion of Jesus" as distinct from Christianity, Thurman leveled a pointed critique at Christians broadly in 1920s America. His criticism flowed from their anemic response to the dire situation facing Black people in the United States. In quoting the words of Jesus, Thurman wrote:

> "In so far as ye did it to one of these brothers of mine, even to the least of them, you did it to me." This applies to all men, not to Nordics alone. God identified with human life! Who dares preach and teach and live such a revolutionary gospel? Do these words mean that every time a negro is lynched and burned that God is lynched and burned? Do they mean that God is held as a peon in certain parts of this land of "Liberty"? Do they mean that God is discriminated against, segregated and packed in Jim Crow cars?[43]

Many of these so-called Christians either misunderstood or ignored the core message of the religion of Jesus, Thurman argued, and Black ministers must "assert continually the ethical demands of the religion of Jesus upon those who would walk on the earth by the light in the sky."[44] Thurman insisted that taking seriously the religion of Jesus meant moving away from creedal proclamations and toward ways of being and living. "It may be a very strengthening exercise to be concerned about the Trinity and the Apostles' Creed," Thurman wrote sardonically, "but a precise theological statement of what is involved in these may make no ethical demands upon him who states it."[45]

Thurman called for a religion that made ethical demands of its practitioners, an insistence that led Thurman to his indictment of white Christian pacifism—a critical move in the shift from pacifism to nonviolence. Pacifism, the refusal to fight, had for too long been an excuse for a pious few to preserve their holiness at the expense of the expansion of great social evil. If one does not participate in war, the thinking went, then the stain of war is not upon oneself. But Thurman argued that "the man who *attends* to evil that he may not fall heir to it becomes like it."[46] Pointing directly to Jim Crow, Thurman argued that whites must acknowledge their role as a majority group in the United States and must recognize also the attendant social power that comes with this status. Whites possessed the power to legally control the behavior of Black people in America and maintain the ability to muster state and mob violence to perpetuate an unjust social order. If this very same white group develops "what they call a philosophy of pacifism that makes few, if any, demands upon their ethical obligations to minority groups with which they may be having contacts," then "such a philosophy becomes a mere quietus to be put into the hands of the minority to keep them peaceful and controllable."[47] To prescribe pacifism to Black Americans, Thurman argued, to ask Black Americans to subscribe to pacifism without acknowledging their perch of white supremacy means that white pacifists are simply replicating the same form of paternalist domination inherent to the United States since slavery.

But Thurman did not discard pacifism wholesale. Instead, he lauded what he called the "genius" of pacifist thinking as "the will to share joyfully the common life and the will to love all—healing and creatively." "I can never be the kind of person that I ought to be," he continued, "until everybody else is the kind of person that everybody else ought to be."[48] The flourishing of all people depends on this interdependency, Thurman contended, and pacifism rightly began with this premise. "There is something that each one has to say to me that will make my life what it cannot be unless that person says it," Thurman wrote, echoing the Jain religious teachings that suggested truth was something we could only know with and through others. A process of coming to understand truth is social, involving others, as the American pragmatists suggested. So to do violence against another person, then, was an assault on our ability to know the truth about our own lives and the world around us.[49]

Pacifism's genius also included an antidote to one of the more caustic elements of white supremacy: the false sense of superiority internalized by white people in a Jim Crow society. Pacifism, he wrote, "has its roots in a primary *self-estimate*, a self-awareness from which it gets its key to the life around it." Pacifists maintained a primary self-estimate borne not from the violent degradation of other people but from a deep source of internal security. Violence, on the other hand, "seems to spring out of a warped self-estimate," with one's own worth coming at the expense of others. To be great, someone else must be lowly, must be less than oneself.[50] The true genius of white pacifist thinking, Thurman suggested, was the rejection of this false premise of superiority and the complete abandonment of violence toward another. For white people, this was an especially healthy philosophy. "White people who make up the dominant majority in American life must relax their will to dominate and control the Negro minority," Thurman argued. If pacifism leads them to this place, it is ethical.

But the task for Black Americans is different, he wrote. Black Americans "must develop a minority technique, which I choose to call a technique of relaxation, sufficiently operating in group life to make for vast creativity with no corresponding loss in self-respect." This "minority technique" must begin with oneself, for "a man *ought* to love his neighbor as he *ought* to love himself." It begins internally, within oneself first, Thurman believed, not as a force directed outward at others for the purpose of change or conversion. It must not replicate the "will to dominate and control" that had proven so caustic to white people. It must be grounded in "spontaneous self-giving . . . sharing all gratuitously," as this is a "very positive and dynamic" force that will lead "a group so disposed" to find "its security in a new kind of relationship."[51] This new kind of relationship, this new set of social relations, could be built around mutuality, undiminished by the warped self-estimates Jim Crow cultivated in both Black and white people.[52] It must "spring out of the life of the minority group itself" through "individual creative experimentation along with the actual harnessing of social forces." Learning practices should be "formal and informal, direct and indirect, studied and spontaneous." And a "unique concept" of "indigenous" education was critical to cultivating this force, Thurman argued, a focus on training by and for Black Americans that was a key element in his choice to teach at Howard University.[53]

In August 1932, after Thurman accepted an invitation from Mordecai Johnson to serve at Howard, Dean D. Butler Pratt issued a letter to Thurman indicating that the faculty of religion at Howard sought to "avoid dogmatism." He noted that professors in the School of Religion are "distinctly modern" in their "attitude toward the Bible and theological questions," and he told Thurman that faculty at Howard see their roles as "searchers for the truth, rather than of the closed mind."⁵⁴ Citing the challenges faculty faced in teaching students who come from biblical literalist backgrounds, Pratt told Thurman that the Howard approach to theological education must be done "sympathetically to some who hold to the literal views of tradition." Emphasizing the "actual study of the facts" as the best strategy "to open their minds to the historical method of approach," Pratt officially welcomed Thurman to the university.⁵⁵

A historical approach to the study of the Bible, among the defining features of Protestant modernist sensibility in the early twentieth century, had become central to the academic training at Howard by the time of Thurman's arrival. Faculty and students at Howard grappled with the meaning of Jesus' life within the particular historical moment within which he lived, and they sought to apply these insights directly to the challenges facing Black Americans in the 1930s and 1940s. As one of the nation's oldest historically Black universities, Howard was a unique context for discerning what Thurman called "the basic spiritual issues of our generation [and] the points of great tension" that defined modern life for Black Americans. He sought to "discover a sound hypothesis with reference to our attack" on racial violence and discrimination, citing as imperative the need to "enlist the youth . . . in our enterprise." In his work as a professor in the SOR, Thurman saw the "machinery" required to prepare a class of Black ministers to transform the United States.⁵⁶

Within two years of being at Howard, and in part because of his work with students, Thurman began to more clearly articulate how the religion of Jesus might become a transformative way of being for Black Americans. In a 1935 essay entitled "Good News for the Underprivileged," Thurman returned again to the "social force" he first described in his 1928 indictment of pacifism, characterizing the life of Jesus of Nazareth as a series of courageous personal actions against an oppressive regime. Beginning with what he called the "historical facts" of the Nazarene as a "poor Jew" who was also "a member of a minority race, underprivileged and to a great degree disinherited," Thurman declared that Christianity was "in its social genesis . . . a technique of survival for a disinherited minority."⁵⁷ Rather than a balm for the pain of a persecuted race, Thurman argued that the religion of Jesus was a model of social insurgency, and he used Jesus' historical context to illustrate that the social and political forces of first-century Palestine were not dissimilar to those facing Black Americans in the twentieth century.

Thurman was careful to argue that Jesus' way of being in the world was not political by design, but instead provoked the political and religious authorities of his day because it was an expression of religious freedom against a backdrop of violent social control. Jesus of Nazareth's primary allegiance belonged to a power that transcended both state and religious authorities, Thurman wrote, and he lived from this "transcending basis of security which locates its center in the very nature of life." Jesus was able to act "as though his deeds were of the very essence of the eternal" by drawing on a deep well of internal security to confront "the hungry hound of hell that rarely ever leaves the track of the dispossessed."[58] Thurman called this hound of hell fear, noting it was the same one that had nipped at the heels of Black Americans since they had arrived on the shores of Virginia in 1619. Such fear, Thurman wrote, led to "self-deception," an "intricate" and "subtle defense mechanism" that was inspired by "the terror of . . . present existence" which urged some Black Americans to "become a candidate for a glorious to-morrow, under a different order of existence." Such an otherworldly religion, Thurman wrote, the idea that a better life might come after this lifetime, flowed from the fact that the average Black American was "having his hell now."[59]

But Thurman believed an honest confrontation with these horrifying conditions was the key to conquering fear and moving beyond self-deception, and he pointed to the life of Jesus to make his case.[60] Jesus came to see "the far-reaching significance of many of his simplest deeds," Thurman wrote, claiming personal power amid the seeming ubiquity of state violence and terror—a realization that led him to a "type of action [that] inspires courage and makes for genuineness at increasingly critical points." The reactionary behaviors that flowed from fear were replaced by a willingness to "absorb violence . . . by the exercise of love," a refusal to "compromise" with unjust power and violence through accommodation to unjust demands. Jesus' choice to respond in creative and ethical ways within this context, Thurman argued, led to his crucifixion at the hands of an empire. But that was far from the end of his story.

It was here that Thurman located "good news for the disinherited," evidence that the life of Jesus was itself "a technique of survival for a disinherited minority." He showed that accommodation or violence were not the only two ways to live beneath a violent and repressive regime. "Jesus was compelled to expand the boundaries of his citizenship out beyond the paltry political limitations of a passing Empire," Thurman wrote, claiming the identity "Son of God" and declaring his allegiance to that cosmic force which caused the "sun to shine upon Roman and Jew, free and bond."[61] The force of this witness proved far greater than "passing" state power, as the

Roman empire crumbled. And here was the good news for the "children of God." One could act from a place of deep security and infinite worth that could have world historical consequences that lasted well beyond one's own lifetime. The choice to act with mercy and kindness in the face of brutal violence—Jesus' willingness to do so beneath the yoke of Roman imperialism—flowed from the "healthy self-estimate" Thurman first wrote of in the late 1920s, and as a nonviolent religious expression these actions inspired generations of followers for centuries.

This healthy self-estimate emerged from "an inner-togetherness" that communicated a self-assurance of who Jesus was and to whom he belonged. This led to the "relaxation" Thurman wrote about in the late 1920s, a letting go that led Jesus of Nazareth to conclude that *"vengeance belongeth to God."* Severe judgment and punishment would come, and they would come in time, but we do not know when or how. Jesus forgave his killers from the cross, and not because he had pity or sympathy for them. He forgave because he chose to live the highest ethical commitment of his religion despite the brutal violence of a crucifying empire, a world historical demonstration of creative and social transformation that has, for centuries, outlasted Roman imperial rule.[62]

Thurman forcefully challenged narratives of the religion of Jesus as examples of patient suffering or pacifism unto death in the face of great social evil. He argued instead that Jesus was a persecuted religious minority, a nonviolent political insurgent who courageously and strategically defied the demands of an empire and permanently altered the course of human history. This thesis, produced while Thurman served as a professor and dean of Rankin Chapel at Howard, inspired a cohort of Black students to probe deeper into the relationship between the life of Jesus of Nazareth, nonviolence, and the African American experience. These students would go on to do important work in the Black freedom movement at both the local and national levels, and as students at Howard they advanced understandings of how the Judeo-Christian prophetic tradition of the first century spoke to the twentieth-century African American experience. They began to make visible what religious nonviolence might look like in the fight against Jim Crow.

Dialectics in Black Religious Education

Three students of religion at Howard grappled with major themes in Thurman's work, wrestling as ministers of practice with how a religious ethic of nonviolence might address the persistent problem of white violence and racial discrimination in the United States. James Russell Brown, who published his thesis in 1935, argued that an ethical way of being in the world ought not be grounded in reactions to oppressive regimes but motivated instead by adherence to the "highest ideals" of the Judeo-Christian tradition—citing Jesus of Nazareth as the leitmotif. In his 1939 thesis, Lee C. Phillip took a different approach by examining the possibility for converting others by using nonviolent tactics. The possibility for conversion of one's enemy was also of primary concern for Charles M. Campbell, whose 1941 thesis sought to square the religious dimensions of personal nonviolence with effective political techniques. Each student made the principle of personality central to his own work, agreeing with Thurman that the cultivation and growth of human personality was the anchor of ethical nonviolent action. These Howard students studied how religious ideas might inform political practice in the struggle against Jim Crow, imagining nonviolence as a force for transforming racial politics in America.

James Russell Brown arrived at Howard after completing his bachelor of arts degree at Friends University in Wichita, Kansas, a Quaker school. After he graduated from Howard, Brown integrated William and Mary College in 1944 as a member of its school for naval chaplains and became one of the first two Black chaplains in the navy. While he was studying at Howard, he produced a thesis entitled "An Examination of the Thesis That Christianity in Its Genesis Was a Technique of Survival for an Underprivileged Minority," testing Thurman's 1934 claim that Christianity was, in its origins, a politically insurgent way of being for a marginalized Jewish population in the Greco-Roman Empire. Brown highlighted the constant incursion of state power and economic forces into the religious and cultural life of the Jewish people, and argued that the Jewish prophets implored their people to find a way to live the highest ideals of Judaism amid these encroachments. This "prophetic tradition," Brown argued, included protest and self-sacrifice unto death for the cause of religious freedom.

This historical context was crucial for Brown. "Christ was a Jew," he wrote, and "his religion was Judaism." But making sense of this fact required Brown to dive deeply into the long history of Judaism in the centuries before the birth of Jesus. "For generations," Brown said, "the Jews found themselves the political pawns of the large civilizations surrounding them." This fledgling Jewish civilization was challenged to maintain "democratic ideals of living" amid the "dominating and 'crude' civilizations" in their midst.[63] Brown described "the political condition of Jews immediately before the birth of Jesus" as one where Jewish religious freedom was subservient to the economic considerations of a colonizing imperial power. So that by the time of Jesus' birth in the first century B.C.E., the Jewish people were "an underprivileged minority that had been politically, economically and religiously frustrated." "Without their religion they could not live," Brown continued, "[but] with their religion civilization would not let them live." Such oppression was both "psychological" and "material" in nature, forcing the Jewish people to align their religious life with a solution to the political problem they faced.[64]

By the time Jesus of Nazareth was born in Bethlehem between 7 and 3 B.C.E., Rome was dealing with a Jewish people that was "economically exploited and religiously persecuted." And yet a healthy contingent of the Jewish population simply refused to be "politically dominated." The Roman imperial state "was now dealing with the type of Jew who preferred death to Roman rule," Brown argued, suggesting that this "Jewish underclass" was receptive to the message that Jesus delivered "about the disinherited, the outcasts and the underprivileged." Quickly isolating "the inadequacy" of the "solutions" proposed by other Jewish leaders, Jesus argued that the "Jewish Ethic . . . necessitated an entirely new approach. The Jewish nation was facing utter annihilation at the hands of Rome during the first half of the first century, A.D.," Brown wrote, and it was in this context that Jesus developed "a technique of survival," a method that preserved their ability to survive and enabled their religious ethics to continue on through the ages.[65]

Brown believed that "the reactions of Jesus" in this situation were unique. It was not the "violence of the Zealots," nor was it "the asceticism of the Essenes." The Nazarene rejected "the cultural compromise and political intrigue of the Sadducees" and refused to mimic "the legalism, self-righteousness and hatred of the Pharisees." Instead, Brown argued, Jesus had a distinct "basis for his different reactions."[66] The "personality of Jesus," what Brown alternatively called the "mind of Jesus," was motivated by "a unique intellectual insight" to live the highest religious ideals of Judaism. Maintaining a commitment to live according to his deepest religious convictions, Jesus responded to Roman cruelty with creativity and fortitude.[67] Brown is worth quoting at length: "The interplay of the mind of Jesus motivated by the highest Jewish ethic upon the facts involved in the problem lifted him above the standardized organization of orthodoxy. Orthodoxy could not hold within its banks 'the rushing freshets' of a life quickened by admitting the facts in the Jewish-Roman situation, the conservatism of Judaism, and the urgency of the Jewish ideal to reach a transcending moral quality sufficient to invalidate and annul the Jewish response of bitterness and hatred toward the Romans."[68]

Animated by "the highest ethic" of the Jewish religion, the mind of Jesus of Nazareth "was cleared of the habitual responses" of anger and violence and the way was made for "new insights." Employing a psychological analysis of the mind of Jesus, and echoing Thurman's suggested technique of relaxation, Brown wrote that "Jesus was relieved . . . of the private forces of decay—orthodox nationalism and chauvinism, and thus his natural capacities—mind and emotions—then could be absorbed and utilized by the higher power of his ideal, God. It was in this state of humility and insight that Jesus perceived that the method employed by the Jews was absolutely the reverse of what it should have been." Jesus recognized that Jews, like their opponents, "were sinners and needed to repent." This admission of self-fault, Brown argued, led Jesus to approach Roman rulers with a mercy and forgiveness animated by humility.[69] Exhausted by the demands of an empire and contemplative before his God, Brown wrote that Jesus discovered "a principle by which the highest religious ideal could survive and be utilized by mankind," a breakthrough that served to "open the kingdom of heaven to those who would believe and use this principle."[70]

Like his professor Howard Thurman, Brown saw in the life of Jesus a way of nonviolent being amid state violence and political domination. He asked how and why this sensibility emerged, and Brown concluded that the majority's attempt to impose its will on a minority was not only unethical but raised the necessity for creative action among the minority. Neither violence nor retreat would suffice in these conditions, and Brown saw in the life of Jesus of Nazareth "the way" of creative action for a Jewish people who sought to "maintain their ideal" amid smothering oppression. This "method" that flowed from the "principle which morally tied man to God" and to one another "as brothers," a way of kindness, mercy, and forgiveness, which made "love the dominant working activity and principle," an embodiment of the "highest ethics possible" in Judaism.[71] The life of Jesus of Nazareth became an example of how to live the principle of agape love, what Brown called "a proposal to treat all men with this brotherly attitude," not simply an abstract notion of disembodied piety. This required nonviolence toward Rome, but perhaps more difficult was the deeper implication: "that the Jews should even love the Romans."[72]

Brown's work reflected the historical approach central to Protestant modernist analysis, but his thesis also reflected new insights developed among Black students at Howard as they considered the "peculiar position of the

Hebrew nation among other nations." It was this relative position in historical context, Brown argued, "that provoked Jesus' new insight." This focus on Jesus' minority status was a particularly salient point for Black Americans living in a violent nation defined by the politics of white supremacy. Aware of the failure of other religious strategies for dealing with the demands of an unjust empire, "the disinherited" Jews "were especially in need of a new integrating attitude and force," a point that resonated with some Black religious people in Jim Crow America.[73] Concluding his thesis by suggesting that Jesus' life and work was an effort "to validate the integrity of the Jewish nation in the face of vast political, social, economic and religious frustrations," Brown argued that Jesus' life ought to be understood as a "technique of survival" for a "disinherited religious minority"—a way of being that ensured survival of the physical body—but just as importantly, he added, this way of being preserved religious ideals that would persist for thousands of years. This, Brown argued, "became the genius of the Christian religion."[74]

Just four years after Brown completed his thesis, Lee C. Phillip wrote "A Critical Study of Two Minority Techniques in the Light of Christian Principles." Phillip had previously earned a degree from Howard in religion in 1931 before studying Christian ethics at Union Theological Seminary under Reinhold Niebuhr. He began a career as the chaplain at Prairie View A&M College where he taught classes in philosophy, psychology, and Black history before returning to Howard in 1937. Beginning his thesis with the observation that "the average minister feels that it is his duty to preach the Gospel and not bother with the social, economic, and political life of those to whom he ministers," Phillip set out to claim a wider vision for Black Christian ministry: "A minister is not preaching the Gospel if he pretends to look after men's souls and allows their bodies to go to hell."[75] Phillip interrogated the question of whether nonviolent resistance and nonviolent coercion might be ethical strategies for addressing this hell on earth for Black Americans, seeking to prove that "the dominant note in the teachings of Jesus was in favor of non-violent resistance."

Phillip's thesis contrasted significantly with the work of Brown in its tendency toward a strategy of acquiescence—rather than resistance—in thinking about a persecuted Jewish people.[76] Citing the parable of the Good Samaritan, Phillip argued that while Jewish law prohibited interaction between the Samaritan traveler and the gentile priest left for dead by the side of the road, Jesus' ethic required that "HUMANITY took precedence over race, which again demonstrated the value placed upon ANY personality." He continued: "ANYTHING which was contrary to man's freedom and fullest growth called forth his bitterest resentment."[77] Drawing on another story from the bible, Phillip argued that the parable of the Jewish man commanded to carry the load of a Roman sentry was a lesson from Jesus to "resist not" such commands from authority. Phillip wrote that the Jewish man's willingness to carry the load should be understood as an effective technique for "a minority group who actually had to live with a majority group who actually imposed tasks upon them."[78] There were few options available to the individual commanded to carry the sentry's pack, Phillip argued, suggesting that a "person who uses this method of defense"—nonresistance, or acquiescence—chooses not to "fight with violence" or "run away."[79] Phillip suggested that "going the extra mile" was a third way between violence and running away, arguing that it would "invoke a sense of justice in the aggressor" and "save the personality of the user of non-resistance."[80] Abiding by the command of the sentry and bearing the load was an ethical response, Phillip argued, a way of being merciful and kind in the face of unjust demands.

Yet Phillip was less clear about how this method of personal nonresistance could be used to transform the broader social and political conditions facing Jewish people as subjects in the Roman Empire. Throughout his work, Phillip's interpretation of Jesus' life tended toward acquiescence as a method of personal survival, a method of "nonresistance to evil" that remained disconnected from a broader explanation of how such personal action might transform the unjust structures of Roman political power. Persecuted minorities ought to do "something constructive in the place of the destructive," Phillip argued, but he continually emphasized the importance of provoking sympathy from an aggressor as that constructive action.[81]

While this notion that a nonviolent practitioner might convert an aggressor later emerged as a common trope in explanations of nonviolent direct action's intent, Brown and Thurman—in contrast to Phillip—emphasized how the nonviolent practitioners themselves were transformed by taking nonviolent action rather than the aggressors. This distinction is key in understanding the power of nonviolence as articulated by Brown and Thurman. For these two intellectuals, nonviolence was about the cultivation of courage and efficacy on the part of the practitioner, the ability to build and develop strength for sustained struggle over time. For Phillip, it was about the power of nonviolent tactics to assuage, appease, or convert an aggressor. Phillip's was not the vision of personally transformative nonviolence outlined by Thurman and Brown, which they articulated as personal adherence to one's highest ethical ideals that led not just to survival but to the creative capacity for transforming social structures over time.

Phillip, in emphasizing an "opponent's" conversion, located the center of transformation in the opponent.

These distinctions between Brown and Phillip reflect a major inflection point in religious approaches to white supremacy in America. Brown and Thurman, like their Quaker and pacifist counterparts, emphasized living one's highest religious ideals despite the restraints of the social and political world within which one lived. These ways of being were not a reaction to the world as it was but were instead an effort to live fully and freely one's most deeply held ethics, showing forth the world as it should be. The implications of this difference are stark. For Brown and Thurman, the starting place for social change was a personal commitment to a way of being in the world, a way of being that flowed from ancient practices of mercy, kindness, and forgiveness. This way of being built an internal well of strength and courage that allowed for sustained nonviolent actions. These group-based nonviolent actions, in time, proved powerful enough to transform a violent social order of white supremacy.

These politics were not only a "protest" against the existing social and political structures, as this way of being was not a reaction to one's immediate context. They were, instead, the expression of an ethics that existed prior to and which transcended the immediate context of imperial rule. Individual Romans were not the target of such expressions: the target was the unethical political context within which both Romans and Jews lived, a social world that demeaned the minority and created a false sense of superiority in the majority. The nonviolent claims of religious human freedom in the life of Jesus of Nazareth became a direct challenge to this context, challenging the imperial state and forcing the Roman authorities to decide how to respond. Brown and Thurman believed that the violence of colonial crucifixion proved less powerful, over centuries, than the creative nonviolent response of Jesus. It was this idea—the notion that the transformation of the structure of society must come from within, and that such change may come well after one's death—that became the foundation for religious nonviolence in the Black freedom movement.

In his 1941 thesis, Charles M. Campbell—who later served in the Hawaii state legislature—attempted to synthesize these ideas of personal religious nonviolence with nonviolent direct-action tactics. In "Educating Young People on the Philosophy and Technique of Nonviolence," Campbell called nonviolence "a social concept that has at its basic and paramount objective a social order without tanks, long-range guns, bombing planes, battleships; a social order that places supreme worth on human personality." Simply achieving power within existing social and political structures—and using nonviolent tactics to gain this power—was insufficient. The goal of nonviolence was a new society entirely, one built wholly on reverence for human personality. Calling for "the use of social pressure or moral force to settle a conflict," Campbell defined nonviolent methods as the practice of "humility, love, compassion and forgiveness."[82]

If nonviolence had to come through oneself and one's way of being in the world, teaching youth how to do this required making the methods plain.[83] Campbell pointed to historical examples of nonviolent action in outlining what a nonviolent curriculum could look like for Black youth in America. He credited pacifists with originating the idea that nonviolent politics must not be "divisive" and ought only include those things "consistent with spiritual unity," and he saw in the labor movement historic examples of successful nonviolent conflict. He noted that the boycott had been a consistently effective tactic but urgd caution, arguing that labor activists were often "retaliatory" in their use of the boycott.[84] Arbitration, civil disobedience, and noncooperation rounded out Campbell's typology of nonviolent methods as he sought to give "a comprehensive meaning" to nonviolence as a strategy for social transformation.[85]

Perhaps unsurprisingly, Campbell's foremost example was the work of Mohandas Karamchand Gandhi in South Africa and India. Quoting Gandhi, Campbell wrote, "Satyagraha excludes the use of violence because man is not capable of knowing absolute truth and therefore not competent to punish."[86] He lauded Gandhi's integration of religious living with nonviolent political action and wrote that the Mahatma's nonviolence grew from his belief that people depended on one another to understand truth. Truth is something people attain together, Gandhi argued, and it is only together that the truth of who we are might emerge. Respect for personality flows from this mutual understanding, and a new society might only burst forth from the old if social relations are grounded in this mutual reverence for personality. Charles Campbell joined the Mahatma and his fellow students Lee C. Phillip and James Russell Brown, along with their teacher Howard Thurman, in imagining how nonviolence might transform Jim Crow America.

The Christian Antithesis: American Christianity

In a 1941 thesis entitled "The Relation between Religion and Racism with Special Reference to the American Scene," James L. Farmer Jr. examined "the racial brotherhood idea by religion in general" with a dedicated focus on "Christianity with reference to the American scene." Like his classmates in the School of Religion at Howard, Farmer wrote about the relationship between social action and religion and asked whether "religion is eternally allied with the status quo." It is "not infrequently the case among oppressed peoples," Farmer argued, that if "their life values are of revolutionary content, then their religion tends to possess revolutionary character." Farmer accused Karl Marx of being "mistaken in his observation concerning religion," arguing that religion in general had not been a social opiate. If Marx had been "speaking to a specific situation and had no intention of declaring a universal principle," Farmer wrote, then perhaps he would have been right.

But Marx was speaking of religion in general—to which Farmer took exception, claiming that Judaism and Christianity were in their origins revolutionary systems of thought and action.[87] Like James Russell Brown, Farmer—whose thesis benefited from the criticism and input of Howard Thurman—drew on the Hebrew Bible to document how religion inspired social insurgency. "Had Marx forgotten about the revolutionary Jewish sect, the Zealots?" he asked rhetorically. "Had he forgotten about the radicalism of Jesus and the early Christians? Was he unaware of the Peasant Revolt, unmindful of the many utopian sects which were in [Marx's own] time tearing through the Old World and the New, proclaiming a fierce, millennialist communism which terrified the ruling classes?" Concluding pointedly, Farmer wrote, "Only the ridiculously obtuse will contend that they are mere exceptions to the rule."[88]

Farmer did concede, however, that it was possible that "the social role of religion has been to bridle the reactions of the people." But "its functional purpose," he argued, "has been to conserve the life values accepted by the dominant element within the religious group at any given time." Farmer acknowledged that in the United States a "priestly religion" had "maintained the racial values of the secular world which, in the American scene, is a rigid color caste system." But that meant this particular instantiation of a broader religious tradition, what he called "American Christianity," had accepted "the validity of racial distinctions and placed the stamp of God upon an enforced division of mankind."[89] Calling this American tendency fundamentally "opposed . . . to the teachings of Christ," Farmer suggested that the United States' racialized Christianity was the opposite of "the racelessness which [Jesus'] religion was designed to foster . . . the true purpose for the very existence of Christianity has now given way to its antithesis."[90] Farmer called for a prophetic religion to "drive the non-prophetic group onto the progressive requirements of a new age." Speaking specifically of "the masses of American Negroes, particularly in the South, despite many efforts to turn their eyes to radical secular movements," these Black southerners "continue to look to the church for leadership." But he cautioned: "Under the prevailing conditions, their loyalty cannot permanently endure; the bidders are too many, and the bidding too high."[91]

On the eve of the Second World War, as A. Philip Randolph called for a March on Washington and the *Pittsburgh Courier* called for a double victory—a victory over Jim Crow at home and fascism abroad—Farmer's call to head off "radical secular movements" echoed the earlier concerns of Howard administrators and the challenges Howard Kester faced on the ground. The appeal of communism may have diminished significantly following the 1939 nonaggression pact between the Soviet Union and fascist Germany, but the persistence of racial violence in the United States and the continued segregation of nearly all aspects of U.S. life meant Black Americans and their allies continued to search for an effective and ethical method to transform a Jim Crow society—a society Farmer condemned as the antithesis of Jesus' teachings. Randolph called for widespread experimentation with nonviolent direct action through his March on Washington Movement (MOWM), and with financial support from the Fellowship of Reconciliation, the two organizations supported the development of the interracial Congress of Racial Equality (CORE). It was through CORE that Farmer, Bayard Rustin, and interracial teams of youth activists across the nation began to experiment with nonviolent direct action in local communities.

But a national nonviolent movement for ending racial violence and discrimination had yet to materialize in the United States on the eve of the Second World War. Nonviolence as a set of ideas, as a religious philosophy, had begun to crystalize in the work of Howard Thurman and his students. But there were few examples of how this spirit of nonviolence might become a political method for transforming Jim Crow. A national nonviolent direct-action fight against Jim Crow remained elusive as Western Europe endured Nazi blitzkriegs, and turning this religious philosophy into a national movement strategy demanded dedicated learning and practice. It took time, it took dedicated local mobilization, and it took courageous and committed organizers in local communities.

An exceptional young student of law at Howard University, inspired by Gandhi's example and supported by pacifists from the Fellowship of Reconciliation, became a nonviolent leader in this wartime moment. Pauli Murray co-organized one of the first American nonviolent direct-action campaigns targeting Jim Crow, and in the process elevated the ethics of nonviolence to the national level. Murray and her fellow students urged the budding Black freedom movement to take nonviolent direct action seriously as a powerful strategy, and they provided an ethical defense for their insurgent political action. They expanded the boundaries of the burgeoning freedom movement to include student voices and, critically, made the voices of Black women central to local nonviolent campaigns. They showed both the nation and the nearly all male civil rights establishment that Jane Crow must also go.

Part II **Practicing Nonviolent Direct Action**

3 Jane Crow Must Also Go
Pauli Murray and Politics of Sex and Nonviolence in the Midcentury Freedom Movement

••

In the spring of 1944, after graduating from the Howard University School of Law, an aspiring Black lawyer submitted an application to continue and deepen their legal training at Harvard University. Pauli Murray had studied with Spottswood Robinson and Leon Ransom during her time at Howard. She studied at Howard during a time when Charles Hamilton Houston was preparing a generation of Black lawyers to systematically dismantle de jure Jim Crow segregation and discrimination. Murray worked closely with one of Howard Law's most distinguished alumni, Thurgood Marshall, and her final paper at Howard, "Should the Civil Rights Cases and *Plessy v. Ferguson* Be Overturned?," was later used by Marshall in the landmark *Brown v. Board of Education* case of 1954.[1] But by the time Murray graduated first in her class from Howard in the spring of 1944, her biographer Rosalind Rosenberg writes that Murray had grown "increasingly impatient with the incremental strategy for civil rights litigation championed by Howard."[2] She believed a more aggressive approach would be needed to end segregation and white violence directed at Black people in the United States, and she believed training at Harvard might be just what she needed.

In response to her application, the dean of the law school at Harvard sent Murray a letter with the following response: "In due course, your picture and the salutation on your college transcript indicate that you are not of the sex entitled to be admitted to Harvard Law School."[3] Incensed, Murray wrote her close friend Eleanor Roosevelt, first lady of the United States. Roosevelt persuaded her husband to write a letter directly to Harvard president James B. Comant supporting Murray's candidacy, but Comant was unmoved. Murray's response to the law school was typical of her writing style—clever and cutting. "Gentlemen, I would gladly change my sex to meet your requirements but since the way to such change has not been revealed to me, I have no recourse but to appeal to you to change your mind on this subject. Are you to tell me that one is as difficult as the other?"[4]

Murray's letter to the law school opens a window into a personal and political dilemma with which she grappled throughout her life, one that led her to push the boundaries of liberation in the midcentury Black freedom movement. By 1944, Murray was deeply frustrated by the bureaucratic structures that perpetuated sexism and racism, and she was coming to see the law and the legal profession as among those forces. Murray also grappled privately with her own sexuality in a period when such things were infrequently discussed. In the 1930s and 1940s, Murray wrote that she believed herself to be a Black man trapped inside the body of a Black woman. In a medical exam at Howard in the early 1940s, Murray told doctors that she believed there was "the presence of a male organ secreted in my abdominal cavity," speculating that perhaps there was a "possible division between one ovary and one testes." Rosenberg writes that Murray "admitted that this was the most radical theory, but she insisted that she would not consider any other diagnosis until this topic was quite thoroughly exhausted."[5] Pauli Murray might have found comfort in a nonbinary gender identity, but such language and categories remained elusive throughout most of her lifetime.

Over time, political freedom became indivisible from personal freedom for Pauli Murray. In the fall of 1943, as Allied forces landed in a town south of Naples called Salerno, Pauli Murray served in the avant garde of the nonviolent direct-action wing of the movement to topple Jim Crow. Like her contemporary Bayard Rustin, Murray could not ignore the way sex and gender intersected with the fight for freedom. And over the course of her life, Murray developed a vision for freedom that was wider and deeper than changes to the law. In the early 1940s, this vision pitted her against the legal flank of the freedom struggle—insulated as it was by the same sexism that pervaded the nation.

Yet Murray was intrepid in advancing innovative solutions to seemingly intractable problems, a tendency that flowed in part from her identity—the specific ways she experienced the world and the particular ways she sought to challenge it. Nonviolent direct action, an egalitarian freedom practice with dimensions of both personal and collective liberation, culled personal power through individual action and built collective strength through public demonstrations. In her work in the early 1940s, Pauli Murray came to believe that nonviolent direct action could fire people with the strength they needed to take risky action and steel them with the courage required to sustain the work of transforming America. Murray was among a group of intrepid women that became early adopters of nonviolent direct action, and they were animated by the commitment to be—fully and freely. Forty-five years before Kimberlé Crenshaw introduced the term "intersectionality," Murray and her fellow students organized to topple both Jim Crow and Jane Crow.[6]

Murray was a central figure in the Howard University NAACP Civil Rights Committee in the early 1940s, and this student group organized one of the first local nonviolent direct-action campaigns that successfully ended Jim Crow practices.[7] She undertook this work with fellow Howard students as part of the larger intellectual project at Howard to develop Black women and men with an expansive social imagination, young people who could not only reimagine America but who had the skills and experience to bring a new social order to life. Frustrated by the slow pace and limited scope of legal change, Murray and a group of young women organized a nonviolent direct-action campaign targeting Jim Crow practices in Washington, D.C.'s downtown restaurants. More than a decade before nonviolent sit-ins and pickets became a strategy of choice for students across the South, Murray and her fellow Howard students notched a significant victory against Jim Crow in the nation's capital. Their campaign stirred a national controversy, and led Murray and her peers to go toe to toe with Howard president Mordecai Wyatt Johnson.

With national Black papers focused squarely on her efforts, the young Black intellectual Murray made the ethical case for nonviolent direct action—echoing the ethics of Howard professor Howard Thurman in the process. The campaign marked a key moment in the shift from imagining nonviolence to practicing nonviolent direct action in the burgeoning Black freedom movement, and like much of the work Murray did throughout her life the Howard campaign proved to be well ahead of its time—demonstrating a method with the power to achieve a freedom that went beyond the law.

Just as Gandhi Did with the British Lion

In February 1940, Pauli Murray was traveling on an interstate bus from Washington, D.C., to Durham, North Carolina, with her friend Mac, whom Murray described as "a peppery, self-assertive young woman of West Indian parentage" when two young women abandoned the broken seats they were forced to occupy behind white passengers.[8] Murray asked the driver if they could move from the broken seats to better seats, remaining careful to position themselves behind the white passengers, but the driver said no and physically pushed Murray backward. After a stop in Petersburg, Virginia, Murray and Mac nevertheless moved one row up to avoid the broken seats while still being careful to stay behind every white passenger on the bus—thus maintaining strict compliance with the curious Jim Crow laws of Virginia.

The white bus driver perceived their action as one of outright defiance. He demanded that the two women move, to which Murray responded with a barrage of legal questions about his knowledge of segregation laws in Virginia. Refusing to answer the questions, the driver instead pulled over and called the police. As other passengers left the bus, Murray and Mac stayed on, opting, as the *Carolina Times* later reported, "to use Mahatma Gandhi's technique with the British lion. . . . . [They] just sat . . . and sat."[9] Remarkably, the two young women seemingly won using this nonviolent technique when police arrived and requested that the driver repair the broken seats. But Mac wanted an apology, one that was not forthcoming. When the driver passed out "accident report" cards to white passengers only, Murray cried foul again. Officers were called back to the scene, and both Mac and Murray were arrested for disorderly conduct.

"We did not plan arrest intentionally," Murray wrote later, but "the situation developed and, having developed, we applied what we knew of *satyagraha* on the spot."[10] Journalist Ted Poston published an account of this episode in the *Pittsburgh Courier*, noting that Virginia law did not, in fact, require Black people to fill the bus from the rear; they simply were required to remain behind all white passengers. Murray and Mac had followed the letter of the law all along. But when Dartmouth professor Herbert Garfinkel wrote about the encounter in *Opportunity Magazine* in May 1940, he made note of an interesting detail. Garfinkel wrote that Mac was accompanied by a young boy, "an arrogant young adolescent repeating by rote" a litany of legal questions about segregation in Virginia.[11] Pauli Murray had been dressed as a young boy during the episode, something she did often while traveling, both because it was how she felt most comfortable and because it boosted her personal sense of security to pass as a young man.

In 1940s America, being who she was proved to be an act of nonviolent resistance. "We did not force this fight," Murray wrote to NAACP secretary Walter White. "It was thrust upon us by the brutal discourtesy of the Greyhound Bus Driver." The issue was a deeply personal one for Murray, but one that was inseparable from the political context of midcentury America. The fundamental question, Murray told White, was whether they "would be bullied into doing something which was contrary to our rights under the law, or whether we would stand up for those rights and contest the long-time policy of rough, discourteous treatment to Negroes on the part of the Greyhound Bus Service."[12] For their willingness to stand up for those rights,

Murray and Mac were now caught up in "the southern penal system with all its attending contradictions and vagaries." Murray vowed not to "let this thing rest" and committed to "go all the way" to "the Supreme Court and back again if necessary." "We will live through it," Murray told White, "being strong of mind, body, and conviction."[13]

But it was white pacifists who seemed more interested in Murray and Mac's bus action than White and his team of Black lawyers at the NAACP. Candace Stone, a board member in the John Dewey Educational Society and a supporter of the Fellowship of Reconciliation, commended Murray and Mac for their actions and encouraged them not to pay their fines and to instead remain in jail as Gandhi would do. "In order to accomplish the *real* purpose as Gandhi would see it," Stone wrote, "the only way you can vindicate the principle at stake and really make a test case for yourselves and your friends is to pay the full penalty by serving the jail sentence. Paying the fine is an escape and the very resort that makes it so difficult, if not impossible, to put satyagraha into practice." Stone encouraged Murray to think about how "an experience like this can so enrich one's life or it can mean nothing at all or it can leave a lasting wound of bitterness and resentment that will gradually destroy you."[14]

Stone's letter retained echoes of the white pacifist paternalism that Howard Thurman indicted in the 1920s, but Murray nevertheless thought a lot about Gandhi's nonviolence and the Indian movement from her jail cell in Petersburg. Lacking the typewriter in her cell that had become a staple in her political battles, Murray scribbled out with pen and paper the key differences between the Indian and the U.S. contexts.[15] She recalled that Gandhi had been imprisoned seven times since the start of the Second World War and noted that the Indian civil disobedience campaigns had at their heart "a willingness to sacrifice for your ideal—to change [the] heart of [the] enemy." Murray wrote that India seemed to have a "well-disciplined movement" that grew from ancient religious traditions where a concern for the enemy was deeply rooted and sincere. Murray believed it was this spiritual discipline that led India to consistent and effective nonviolent direct actions, while the "lack of a well disciplined movement" grounded in spiritual principles in the United States had led to a "legalistic movement [with] NAACP [leadership]—through court tests."

From her musty jail cell, Murray began to imagine a different way—a nonviolent way—to transform Jim Crow America.[16] "We are most anxious to discuss with you the Satyagraha technique as applied to ourselves in this situation," Murray wrote to Candace Stone, whom she called "Pan."

"We believe that through it we were able to accomplish education among Negroes and whites wherever we came in contact with them through our arrest, imprisonment, and through our testimony at the trial." Murray noted that *Carolina Times* editor Lewis E. Austin was "begging us to stay here and help him fight this race battle by starting a Gandhi-type of movement among Negroes," but Murray admitted that she and Mac "are caught between the essential justification of his appeal and our own feeling that we may not be strong enough or sacrificial enough to give up our freedom for the South." Murray was deeply aware of the stakes of their critical nonviolent test of segregation laws in 1940. Arrested two years before the Congress of Racial Equality (CORE) began its tentative use of sit-ins against Jim Crow in Chicago, Murray—like other young Black people across the nation—was only beginning to realize that there might be national and international implications for their nonviolent action. "We read yesterday that a young Indian student is lecturing in the Southern Negro Colleges," she wrote to Pan. "We want to get in touch with him and let him know that already the technique of the Indian movement is being put into action as a test for its adaptability to the American minority struggle."[17]

But Pan was intent on testing the sincerity of Murray's personal commitment to nonviolence. She asked if Murray had violated the segregation law "by accident or by principle" and requested that Murray be "more explicit in showing how you applied Satyagraha to the situation."[18] Pan pushed Murray to make more clear how the action might become "an American version of non-violent direct action," expressing her eagerness to apply "the nonviolent direct action principle to a solution of the Negro and sharecropping problem."[19] Few Black Americans in the early 1940s beyond Howard Thurman and a smattering of his students of religion were invested in the idea of using nonviolent direct action to combat Jim Crow. White pacifists had, for decades, been searching for a test case where nonviolence might be successfully used to upend segregation, discrimination, and ongoing white violence. Thurman insisted that white pacifists eschew their paternalist admonition that Black people remain passive in the face of these mighty forces, but he noted also that the kernel of "genius" in pacifist thought might contain within it a powerful method for Black Americans seeking to transform the nation. Thurman remained clear, however, that such a method would only succeed if it came from Black Americans, what he called an "indigenous technique," not a white insistence that Black Americans remain passive in the face of white terror and violence.

As a result of her action on the bus, Murray began to think deeply about the importance of her sit-down, linking law and civil disobedience together in an intrepid way. Murray explored the link between personal discipline and political action, inspired by Gandhi's example and some of the religious people with whom she worked in the labor and antiwar movements. For a few short months, Murray had even lived in the "Harlem Ashram"—a New York analog to Gandhi's ascetic Indian communities.[20] We are "prepared to contest the segregation law as unjust and inhuman," she wrote to Stone, but "it is hardly likely that such law will be repealed unless some 'Civil Disobedience' movement catches the imagination of the Negro masses. . . . This movement cannot be effective unless years of preparation through discipline and through the technique of non-violence is established."[21] Murray's arrest drew tremendous national attention, pushing her to think critically about how a national nonviolent movement against Jim Crow might be mustered. Following Pan's probing, she drafted a ten-point outline articulating "our strict application of satyagraha" on the bus and reflected on what might be required to launch what she called "a satyagraha movement" against Jim Crow.[22] She called for "an organ of interpretation" that could make sense of the technique in an American context and suggested that a "tried-and-tested organization, an organization which had made an interpretation of the American scene" was required to bring together "existing pacifist, negro, labor and other organizations for social and economic justice."[23]

But for all her work to envision this national nonviolent movement, Murray was troubled and, perhaps, a bit overwhelmed by the challenges involved in such a venture. "Mac and I cannot seem to develop sufficient energy to rise above the South and its complexities," she wrote. "We are truly alien souls. Both of us are living from day to day. Trying to develop resistance against the numerous anxieties which plague us."[24] Murray felt hers was a voice in the wilderness, and she was right: a national nonviolent movement was still decades away, and there was no indication in 1940 that such a movement might emerge. A. Philip Randolph would soon issue his call for a massive march on Washington, D.C., using the language of nonviolent direct action, but the march never materialized, as President Franklin Roosevelt conceded to his demands.

Yet like Randolph Murray sensed the time was right for a widespread nonviolent direct-action movement, but with no clear antecedent she and Mac staged their sit-in on the bus in Petersburg as a claim on their personal freedom in the face of the bus driver's aggression. They did not have, as later generations of student activists would, the benefit of looking to other communities across the South who were taking similar actions—or training schools for such actions such as the Highlander Folk School. For Murray and Mac, they simply refused the dehumanizing demands of Jim Crow. They chose to revolt, to be who they were, and in the process tilted at the seemingly monolithic system of Jim Crow. In hindsight, their action was a visionary turning point—a critical moment in the process of practicing nonviolent direct action in the fight against Jim Crow.

Prominent Black attorneys in charge of the NAACP's fight against Jim Crow on interstate travel—William Hastie, Link Johnson, and Thurgood Marshall—saw in Murray's case a possible legal challenge to Jim Crow laws on interstate travel. But as Rosenberg has suggested, Garfinkel's description of Murray as being dressed like a boy—a persona Murray sometimes described as "the dude"—may have led Hastie and the other Black lawyers to conclude that because of the "cross-dressing" Murray was not the ideal candidate for a successful court challenge to Jim Crow on interstate travel.[25] Hastie instead later chose a case that originated with another young Black woman, Irene Morgan. Hastie also told Murray and Mac that the NAACP would not pay the $300 fee required to appeal their case to a higher court. So the two young women were forced to return to jail to serve out their sentences until the Workers Defense League (WDL) raised money to bail them out.

If Murray could not easily change her sex in 1940, she could change her gender. Presenting as male was, for Murray, a way of being in the world that ran contrary to the demands of a Jane Crow nation.[26] Murray never believed that her presentation as a young boy would be nationally broadcast, but when it was, the national press garnered by the Petersburg saga put her at odds both with customs of segregation and an exclusively male civil rights legal establishment. In a letter to her aunt, Murray wrote that "this little boy girl personality as you jokingly call it sometimes gets me in trouble. . . . Where you and a few people understand, the world does not accept my pattern of life. And when I try to live by society's standards it always causes me such inner conflict that at times it's almost unbearable. I don't know whether I'm right or whether Society (or some medical Authority) is right; I only know how I feel and what makes me happy."[27] As with subsequent cases used to "test" the law, there was a fear that Murray's intersectional identity might diminish the efficacy of a case designed to challenge Jim Crow laws.

Another issue at the heart of the Petersburg bus saga was a question about the degree to which the law could alter deeply rooted social behaviors. Laws flowed from ethics, both individual ethics and the group ethics of a legislative body. These ethics were, across the nation, demeaning and dehumanizing Black people in the United States and, most especially, Black women. "Law is a tedious method of fighting social issues," Murray wrote at the time, as "the fundamental issues themselves may be lost through quips and quirks of the judge with the way the case is filed for the time given in which to file an appeal." This certainly proved true in the Petersburg case, as the NAACP ultimately did not carry it forward—not only because Murray was dressed like a boy, but because the local courts did not, in the end, charge Murray and Mac with a violation of Virginia's Jim Crow laws. This point is not insignificant; Murray's "girl-boy" qualities certainly played a role in the NAACP's refusal to take the case, but the Petersburg court's refusal to prosecute the two women under the segregation laws made the case seem less viable for the NAACP's ultimate goal of testing and ending interstate segregation laws.[28] Despite the clear fact that Murray and Mac were arrested for violating the norms of segregation, prosecutors were careful to avoid any charges that could be seen as direct violations of segregation law.

The bus saga brought into sharp focus how Murray's way of being in the world came into direct conflict with the nation's social order. The case also revealed that the law, while a powerful tool that Murray would dedicate much of her life to using and understanding, could not encompass the greater vision for freedom Murray developed over the course of her life. The NAACP's refusal to carry the case forward was initially disappointing, but Murray responded in a fashion that was typical throughout her life: she became deeply motivated to pursue a more intrepid and revolutionary vision for human freedom, one that was egalitarian and inclusive, seeking with others to collectively transform the nation's politics not through the law alone but through nonviolent direct action.

Building a Local Nonviolent Movement: Organizing Students at Howard

When Murray entered the Howard University School of Law in the fall of 1941, it was almost exclusively male. Despite performing at the highest levels while at Howard, graduating as valedictorian in 1944, Murray was initially denied admission to the court of peers based on her sex. More than an impediment to professional advancement, for Murray sex and gender were never far from the front of her mind, and both intersected with her public activism. In a journal entry from her time at Howard, Murray somewhat sardonically analyzed herself as if from the vantage point of a doctor, revealing the internal and external challenges prompted by the misalignment between her gender identity and her sex. "Terrific mental conflict on the point of wearing dresses or pants," she wrote. "In pants, it is difficult to make persons believe she is not a boy; in dresses her awkwardness is the object of hilarious comment on the part of her closest friends. . . . Consistent emotional attraction toward the female sex, consistent attraction of apparently bisexual women."[29] For both personal and professional reasons, sex and gender were not something Pauli Murray had the luxury of ignoring.

Murray's journey through the Howard law school progressed on parallel tracks. On the one hand, she labored to find the political tools needed to battle the social forces of racism and sexism in a Jane Crow nation. On the other, she sought the personal freedom to be fully and freely who she was. Over the course of her life, Murray labored to integrate these visions of personal and political freedom, and the Indian independence movement became an important touchstone in that process. Murray likened the American mantra "Give me liberty or give me death" to the "Do or die" mantra heralded by the movement for Indian independence. She believed that Indian leader Jawaharlal Nehru's words could have been the words of March on Washington Movement (MOWM) organizer A. Philip Randolph as Nehru called on London and Washington to abandon "the doctrine of racial superiority which is no monopoly of the Nazis and which we in India have known in its most intense form for many generations." For her part, Murray argued that "the recognition of Indian independence . . . will not only release the suppressed and pent up energies of a great nation but will be symbolic of a new freedom all over the world."[30] Calling the Second World War "Democracy's Acid Test," Murray reminded the nation that "the eyes of the colored peoples of the world, including our own national minority of Negroes, are fixed upon India today."[31] Murray was convinced, as were many Black Americans across the nation, that the Second World War and the attendant movement for Indian independence made the time right for a concerted, militant, and nonviolent attack on Jim Crow in the United States.

Murray focused her efforts on organizing Howard students in a nonviolent direct-action campaign against Jim Crow practices in downtown Washington, D.C., businesses. She later wrote that "ideas about the use of nonviolent direct action . . . were in the air" late in 1942, noting that she was a "contributing member" of the Fellowship of Reconciliation (FOR) and had "studied its literature on nonviolent direct action."[32] Murray was aware of the FOR's long history with advancing nonviolence as a political philosophy, including its attempt to mobilize Black activists and white pacifists in a nonviolent struggle against Jim Crow. Her classmate and confidant, Ruth Powell, had encountered the harsh reality of Jim Crow after moving to D.C. from Milton, Massachusetts. While Powell later recalled the difficulty in doing "anything concrete to revolutionize conditions . . . I also knew that I had to do something to preserve what remained of my self-respect."[33]

As the historian Paula Giddings has written of Black women who both preceded and succeeded this moment, Powell was committed to "do what had to be done" to build a better world.[34] She began sitting-in at drugstores in downtown D.C. as an individual, challenging the social custom—if not the law—of refusing service to Black people. Murray later recalled Powell's action a kind of invasion of "forbidden territory." For her efforts, Ruth Powell was arrested along with two other Black women from Howard, Marianne Musgrave and Juanita Morrow.[35] The three women were initially refused counter service at Washington, D.C.'s United Cigar Store, but after persisting they were served hot chocolates and overcharged: the three women were asked to pay a quarter per cup instead of the customary dime. The women left thirty-five cents total, ten cents for each hot chocolate plus a five-cent tip, but they were met by six police officers as they left the store. They were placed in a holding cell by police and ultimately dismissed to the dean of women at Howard, but as Murray wrote of the women's arrest, "the flood of resentment against the whole system of segregation broke loose. These young women of Howard were determined" to fight.[36]

Throughout the spring of 1943, the Howard women organized what they called "chocolate hours" in the dormitory at Howard to think through how to proceed with the campaign.[37] "The men had spent hours in their 'bull sessions' discussing attack and counter-attack upon jim crow," Murray reflected, noting that fellow student "William Rainse had agitated for months for what he called 'the stool sitting' technique."[38] But Murray and her ad hoc committee sought to gain a wider understanding of student sentiment around a public direct-action campaign, particularly amid the war. In early 1943, the students issued a campus survey asking whether Black Americans should "suspend [the] struggle for equal rights until the end of the war" or "actively participate in the struggle during the war." More to the point, the survey asked, "Will you join?" If the respondent replied no, the survey asked whether the respondent would support or disapprove of others who did join.[39]

The student survey netted 292 responses, with 97 percent communicating that they did *not* believe in suspending the struggle amid the war. The survey also showed that 218 of the students said they would join a campaign, while thirty-eight said they wouldn't join but would support others in the struggle. Murray and her peers moved swiftly to organize five subcommittees to carry forward the campaign, hosting pep rallies and town halls to build momentum across campus. They also established a "direct action subcommittee" to oversee a series of planned public demonstrations.[40] In articulating their purpose, they cited passage of a long dormant Civil Rights Bill as their key objective:

> The Howard chapter of the NAACP is sponsoring a civil rights committee for the purpose of uniting the entire student body of Howard University in a drive to urge the passage of the Civil Rights bill for Washington DC. The committee is to be composed of all organizations on the campus. Already Kappa Sigma, the court of peers, the association of interns and medical students, and Zeta Phi Beta have pledged their support. You are asked to send five members of your organization to the next meeting of the civil rights committee on Thursday April 1st 1943.[41]

The students assembled a leadership committee composed of representatives from all campus organizations and lobbied for a bill that would outlaw segregation in the nation's capital once and for all. They urged students to write letters to senators and congressional representatives, and stated that "vigorous demonstrations should be made against discrimination." The committee on direct action was charged "to enroll students who will participate in small, carefully planned demonstrations for equal rights in the district that include

   a) Weekly visits to certain downtown restaurants. Sitting quietly. Requesting service.
   b) Securing tickets to National Theater and attempting to go.
   c) Other Demonstrations which can be worked out.[42]

The students launched their first formal action on Saturday, 17 April 1943 at the Little Palace Cafeteria on Northwest U Street. The *Chicago Defender* reported that the "action was a planned part of their 'direct action' campaign to bring civil rights to the D of C." The students organized a daily broadcast to be dispatched from "the university tower" to encourage students to join the campaign, and the direct-action committee offered classes "in the study of the disorderly conduct laws in the D of C and of the civil liberties law, in order that they may conduct their campaign within the framework of legality." The students all pledged to "avoid violence," and as the *Pittsburgh Courier* reported, "They are determined. . . . They believe that negro students throughout the country could take this type of intelligent action to batter down discrimination in a shorter time."[43]

Twelve students challenged the practice of racial discrimination at the Little Palace Café through nonviolent direct action. In addition to the sit-ins, students carried placards asking the question, "Our boys, our bonds, our brothers are fighting for you. Why can't we eat here? There's no segregation law in Washington, D.C." Other signs read, "What's your story, Little Palace?" The owner of the café, a Mr. Chaconas, told the *Defender*, "I lost money, but I'd rather close up than practice democracy this way. The time is not yet ripe."[44] Raymond Sarnes, a white baker originally from Charlotte, North Carolina, who was interviewed on the street during the demonstration, told the *Defender*, "I eat here regularly, and I don't care who else eats here. All I want is to eat. I want the place to stay open. After all, we're all human." Another white bystander called the students' action "reasonable," saying, "Negroes are fighting for democracy just like the whites. If it had to come to a vote, it would get my vote!" Perhaps most notable is that the majority of the participants in the initial Little Palace action were women, among them Murray, Ruth Powell, Juanita Morrow, and Marianne Musgrave.[45] The students' grassroots effort to organize and facilitate a nonviolent direct-action campaign was almost completely novel. With the exception of smaller groups of Congress of Racial Equality (CORE) activists in Chicago, there were few analogs to the Howard nonviolent direct-action campaign in 1943—and perhaps no analog led primarily by women. While their demonstrations contrasted sharply with the national NAACP's effort to lead with litigation, the students likely gained support from the NAACP's director of branches, Ella Jo Baker.[46]

Even as Murray formally studied the law as a method for social change at Howard, her relationship to legal strategies for personal and social liberation remained fraught. She was frustrated by the slow pace of legal change for Black Americans, but perhaps more importantly she believed that every person, especially young people and women, should have the opportunity to participate in the struggle for freedom. She did not see freedom only as something others won for you in a courtroom. It was also a personal practice, what Ruth Powell described as an effort to preserve one's self-respect. Such practices cultivated individual esteem and personal power, and when organized collectively, they could also produce changes to the structure of society. Murray maintained an egalitarian view of the movement to end Jim Crow, and legal battles almost always meant limited community participation as cases fought in the rarified space of courtrooms required people trained in law. In the 1940s, as seen in Murray's exchange with Harvard, that meant an almost exclusively male "freedom" struggle.

Murray envisioned liberation as a process that was collective and political, but also one that was deeply personal. These ideas flowed in part from the fact that Murray did not have the freedom to express the fullness of her sex identity in the 1940s. She lived in a nation that was openly hostile and sometimes violent toward such expressions. Murray wrote that during this period the struggle over her gender identity "causes me such inner conflict that at times it's almost unbearable."[47] The internal conflict was one element, but another was the bittersweet feeling that accompanied the social advances she did achieve through collective action against Jim Crow. "This conflict rises up to knock me down at every apex I reach in my career and because the laws of society do not protect me," she wrote, noting that even amid their accomplishments in the battle against segregation, Murray felt "exposed to any enemy or person who may or may not want to hurt me."[48]

Murray and her peers did, in fact, achieve success at the Little Palace Café—one of those apex moments in her life. Within forty-eight hours of the student direct actions, the owners of the Little Palace capitulated and served Black and white people equally in the restaurant. The students at Howard were among the first to successfully use nonviolent direct action to end the custom of racial segregation in the United States in a local business, and they did so not in the rarified spaces of courtrooms but at the lunch counters and dining halls of the nation's capital. Their work was all the more remarkable because they achieved this without a clear template or precedent. In fact, theirs would become an outline for the nonviolent direct-action campaigns that would follow, a revolutionary example of how to transform the social fabric of American political culture.[49]

Arguing the Case for Nonviolent Direct Action

In the spring of 1944, the Howard civil rights student committee "decided to renew" its direct-action campaign at Thompson's restaurant on Fourteenth Street and New York Avenue NW.[50] They initially sent two scouts to test the policy of discrimination before the committee made a decision to "sit in and picket." Before beginning the action, students were asked to sign a pledge "to conduct themselves in the most inoffensive manner and to observe all laws which might have led to our arrest." The students were careful to note that it was custom, not law, that perpetuated segregation in D.C., and they

Pauli Murray in 1946. Photographer unknown. Pauli Murray Papers, Arthur Schlesinger Jr. Library, Harvard University.

named transforming this custom of discrimination and segregation as a goal around which they could all organize.

The students concluded the best way to raise the issue was to place themselves in spaces where Black Americans were restricted by practice, seating themselves "about the cafeteria while the pickets commenced their activities on the outside." They strategically added "several white friends" to the outside picket lines and gained "expressions of sympathy by some whites and others in the observing public." The group was also strategic in sending Black servicemen to further test the practice of discrimination at Thompson's. The Black servicemen were initially denied food alongside the other students, but after four hours the students reported, "The management said that it had received orders to serve us which was done."[51] Murray recalled, "It is difficult to describe the exhilaration of that brief moment of victory," adding "nothing like it had ever happened in the city of Washington."⁵²

The student civil rights committee at Howard anchored its direct action in ideas. "I conceive one of the most precious of all human rights to be the right of equal privileges in all places of public accommodation," the students wrote, calling the "effort to eliminate discrimination against any person because of race or color to be a patriotic duty and an act of faith in the American boys fighting for the Four Freedoms in foreign lands." They shared these ideas with the student body and asked their fellow students to "devote as much time as possible each week to the purposes of the campaign." Students pledged "to do nothing to antagonize members of the public with the management of public places" and made a commitment "to look my best whenever I act as a representative of the committee, to use dignity and restraint at all times; to refrain from any boisterous or offensive language or conducts no matter what the provocation, and not to do or say nothing that will embarrass the committee or the University." By the time of the Thompson's demonstration, more than 200 Howard students had signed the pledge.⁵³

The students were aware that they were doing something new and significant, and they tried to capture it in the way they spoke publicly about the campaign. "Howard University students are demonstrating a new technique in the breaking down of Jim Crow in public accommodations in the nation's capital," the group proclaimed, calling their technique "nonviolent direct action." The committee publicly outlined its methods, noting that the "refusal" of service by a business led students "to take seats at tables, open newspapers and books and quietly read." Picketers arrived shortly after "with embarrassing signs such as 'Are you for Hitler's way (race supremacy) or the American way (equality)? Make up your mind!'" The students argued that their campaign put pressure on management to negotiate, and that if negotiations led to "a change of policy on the part of management," students would immediately "withdrawal the picket signs which have created crowds on the outside."⁵⁴ The students believed "such demonstrations dramatized the issue of equality for all American citizens, and appeals to the sense of fair play which is inherent in American thinking."⁵⁵

The Howard students relied on what they called "intelligent showmanship and an attitude of Goodwill on the part of the demonstrators," noting that their efforts were strategically "calculated to minimize antagonism and to 'swing the crowd on our side.'"⁵⁶ Echoing an argument that became common during the peak years of nonviolent direct-action campaigns in the early 1960s, the students sought "to make it clear" that their purpose was not to foment any racial conflict. Any disturbance, they argued, came "from undisciplined members of the public." Every student who participated was required to go through "a process of training and discipline" before participating in the demonstrations, including the signing of the pledge of conduct and the commitment "to sit all day if necessary." Pointing directly to the personal discipline required to practice such techniques, the committee noted that during the Thompson's demonstration "many students sat the entire 4 hours until management capitulated."[57]

In practicing nonviolent direct action, the students were among the first in the nation to articulate the vision of nonviolence as a political philosophy. The students described their actions as a way of transforming the ethical structure of racism in the United States. "With this technique," a spokesman of the committee said, "we hope to tear down some of the stereotype impressions in the minds of our white fellow citizens and to invoke their respect. We want to demonstrate our Goodwill, but at the same time we are equally determined to secure our rights." Challenging stereotypes was important, but just as important was the determination to make a claim on freedom through nonviolent direct action.

Since the nation's founding, the politics of race in the United States had been predicated on Black dehumanization—the idea that Black people were inherently less human than white people and were thus not afforded the same rights or respect as white Americans. The three-fifths clause of the Constitution codified this subjugation, but Black dehumanization remained a hallmark of American life following enslavement. The ethics of the 1896 *Plessy v. Ferguson* decision were not dissimilar to those of the 1852 Dred Scott decision: whites were not bound to respect the life or liberty of Black Americans. There was no more gut-wrenching evidence of the depth of Black dehumanization in the United States than the lynching of more than 4,400 Black men, women, and children over the course of a century.

Through the technique of nonviolent direct action, the Black students at Howard would "tear down some of the stereotypes" by sitting down in spaces reserved for whites, looking their white counterparts in the eye. They were cultivating self-respect and respect from others by expressing their right to be free, and the effect was powerful. Through these demonstrations, Black students penetrated the "veil" of Jim Crow that separated Black and white people in America, forcing whites to deal directly with the human being in front of them. Direct action was just that, direct; it was a way of achieving a proximity that Jim Crow was designed to preclude. Black and white people often interacted amid Jim Crow, and sometimes in intimate ways. But these interactions were maligned by white supremacy because they did not occur within a social or political context where Black life was respected or safe. The students at Howard believed that nonviolent direct action forced whites to recognize the individual humanity, the distinct and complex personality of individual Black people, through the practice of active mercy in the face of these white attempts to humiliate and dehumanize. The students described the "experience and knowledge acquired through such activities" as "a vital part of the education of minority students in a democracy," noting that it had a profound effect on "the public conscience and opinion both here and abroad."[58]

The national press also noted the novelty and potential promise of their approach. "There is much talk about how the Negro can get his case before the American public in a dramatic fashion," Horace Clayton wrote in the *Pittsburgh Courier*. "White people don't know about all the things that negroes have to put up with," he continued, noting specifically the daily humiliation of Jim Crow. "They don't know because the newspapers don't tell them, the radio doesn't tell them, the motion picture doesn't tell them." Gesturing to the power of nonviolent direct action, Clayton argued, "White people have to learn about the Negro problem in spite of themselves. This means Negroes have got to present it in dramatic fashion." He pointed to "a group of young idealistic white students" associated with the Fellowship of Reconciliation who began "talking about using the passive resistance techniques developed by the Indians."

But Clayton also noted the widespread reticence toward nonviolent direct action among Black Americans in the mid-1940s, arguing, "We're not going to try any of that Gandhi stuff" as civil disobedience often led to jail. A 1943 survey the *Courier* circulated among its Black readers showed that 70.6 percent of Black Americans opposed the use of a "non-violent civil disobedience campaign" in the fight against Jim Crow.[59] Some noncooperation techniques could be appealing though, Clayton wrote, suggesting, "Anyone in America has the right to quit work and window shop, even a Negro in Georgia, doesn't he?" Clayton concluded his editorial noting that nonviolent direct action "demonstrates simply and profoundly the feeling of Negroes," capturing two key elements of nonviolent direct action's power: a demonstration of the world as it might be, and an immediate claim on the right to be—fully and freely.[60]

Articles in national press outlets like Horace Clayton's became more common as the stakes grew higher for the students' actions. The stakes grew higher not simply for the students themselves, but for the historic institution they represented. "Students at Howard, the famous negro university here, are not out 'to turn 100 years upside down in a minute,' but they think the start must be made," reported the *PM* newspaper in New York.[61] With national attention growing and external pressure mounting, Howard president Mordecai Johnson was forced to respond publicly to the students' actions. The *Pittsburgh Courier* published an editorial criticizing the Howard president, an editorial hailing satirically from the "We Ain't Ready DEPT." The editorial noted that Johnson "has banned such a 'direct action' against food establishments . . . on the ground that 'the present policy and regulation of the board of trustees do not provide the authority or approval for an officially recognized student organization to engage in a program of direct action in the city of Washington for the purpose of accomplishing social reform affecting institutions other than the university itself.'"[62] The editorial intoned that Johnson "is apparently completely out of tune with the temper of the New Negro," arguing that "the good prexy wants the students to endure indignities and discrimination until some millennium date." The *Courier* claimed that the "New Negro doesn't think (OR ACT) that way . . . not in the midst of a war against fascistic practices, anyway."[63]

Johnson's response created pressure for the students to argue the ethical case for nonviolent direct action, including the values that underpinned their actions and goals. In a letter to President Johnson, Ruth Powell and Pauli Murray wrote, "We are not unaware of the grave responsibilities under which you labour as head of a large university, and the natural concern you may have for the sets of members of the university community." "At the same time," they continued, "we believe in the principle of freedom of action for student groups within the democratic framework of this institution so long as such action is taken in a lawful, proper, and dignified manner." They asked Johnson, What would you do "if you were a student in our position?" They noted the "wide publicity" Johnson had earned "for his militant speeches on behalf of the rights of minority groups" across the United States and asked, "Is it surprising or unwise that his own students should be the most inspired to put into practice through their own considered method some of the philosophies he has outlined in pulpit, platform and over the radio?"[64]

In his response, Johnson clarified the problem as being that of an official student organization of the university being "engaged in a program of direct action in the city of Washington, designed to accomplish social reform affecting institutions other than Howard University itself." He made clear that Howard University "does not provide authority or approval for an officially recognized student organization, and Howard University, to engage in a program of direct action in the city of Washington for the purpose of accomplishing social reform affecting institutions other than Howard University itself." The president called on the students "to desist from [their] program of direct action in the city of Washington, until such time as their proposed program shall receive the voted approval of the Board of Trustees of Howard University."[65] Murray and Powell carried this response back to the members of the civil rights committee, and made clear their own position: "In a full membership meeting of the Howard chapter NAACP," they wrote, "it was unanimously decided that we are unwilling to discontinue our campaign as it is now outlined."[66] The students would not be turned around.

Pauli Murray and the Intellectual Foundations of Nonviolent Direct Action in America

The Howard campaign was significant in being among the first in the nation to center nonviolent direct action as a strategy against Jim Crow. The fact that it was led completely by students made it even more unique. Pauli Murray and her peers were deft organizers, demonstrating the collective power of nonviolent direct action to the nation, but Murray also articulated the ethics of nonviolence as students justified their use of direct action. She tied these political and ethical issues together, and in the Howard demonstrations the philosophy of nonviolence was bound to the practice of nonviolent direct action in visible ways. Pauli Murray placed a significant role in the shift from imagining nonviolence to practicing nonviolent direct action, and in making the case for nonviolent direct action she turned to someone who had become a mentor to her over the years.

In a lengthy exchange with First Lady Eleanor Roosevelt, Murray made the case for why nonviolent direct action was the best path for Black Americans seeking freedom in the United States. She centered her argument in the idea that nonviolent direct-action campaigns were egalitarian movements with the power to transform individuals and the structure of America's racial politics, not simply a method designed to produce more "advantages for a mere talented tenth." She told the first lady that nonviolent direct action had the potential to "break through on a level where all Negroes might be free to seek accommodation." Murray argued that nonviolent direct action was a more democratic method for battling segregation than legal cases. With proper preparation and discipline, preparation and discipline magnitudes lower than earning a law degree and passing the bar, everyone can participate in a nonviolent direct-action campaign.

Murray noted that the groundwork for such actions must emerge from a group of people committed to such preparation and discipline. She also made the point that "a student group would receive far more favorable opinion from even potentially hostile sources than a group of students indiscriminately diffuse with adult members from the population."[67]

Murray explained that the students' work was a "demonstration on the part of the student sector of the NAACP to show community groups how it could be done with careful planning and intelligent creative execution." She believed the students had provided an example to the nation of what an effective technique might look like for challenging Jim Crow, steeling a commitment to ongoing struggle among students and showing forth what a new America—a nation not bound to Jim Crow ethics—might be. Remaining aware that nonviolent direct action was still a novelty for much of the Black community, Murray argued that Howard students had taken a critical first step in the growth and evolution of this "strategy." She told the first lady they had used "intelligent showmanship" in their work, calling their theatrics a "technique of mass education" and a "catchy advertisement," a process of engaging the public that went beyond "the traditional protest placards" and in which "everything was to have an educational value." Murray honed in on the indivisible link between individual action, collective mobilization, and structural changes to America's racial politics.[68] She gestured to how a new politics might come through the students' way of being in making their claim on freedom in a Jim Crow city.

In her correspondence with Roosevelt, Murray offered a powerful assessment of nonviolent direct action more than a decade before it became a widespread strategy in the freedom movement. Just as Murray was a trailblazer in her legal work, she also became an intellectual trailblazer advancing the strategy and rationale for nonviolent direct action in the United States. She expanded the vision of what the struggle for Black freedom looked like, arguing it was not enough to simply win concessions from the Little Palace Café or Thompson's restaurant, and noting the real question was how Black Americans could claim freedom in a Jim Crow nation long committed to Black dehumanization. She recalled a visit from Max Lerner to Howard during which he argued that "the negro should act on the assumption they were Americans," to live from a place of understanding that, as Langston Hughes wrote and A. Philip Randolph echoed, "I am an American, too." Murray argued that she and the students were making a claim on their birthright, embodying the creative capacity to be fully and freely, and refusing to shrink or contort in the face Jim Crow humiliation.

Nonviolent direct action had a powerful impact on the students who undertook such actions, but Murray also pointed out that "such demonstrations would dramatize the issue of equality for all American citizens, and would appeal to the sense of fair play which is inherent in Americans today." She cited Gunnar Myrdal's argument that "the American creed" was defined by an "internal conflict" as white Americans grappled with "the color question," and Murray believed that nonviolent direct action would "swing the crowd to our side." Perhaps most critically, Murray told the first lady that if "the technique proved successful it would give hope and encouragement to negro youth and displace some of the poison of retaliation." Pauli Murray described nonviolent direct action as "an alternative to mass riots, destruction and actual internecine warfare." If effective, Murray wrote, "we prayed that it might be one answer (not the answer) to Detroit, Los Angeles, Harlem, etc."

Murray was clear in her theory of what nonviolent direct action was and where it came from. "What we needed to do was to extract some of the techniques which labor uses and its struggle," she wrote, "and combine them with the 'nonviolent (cooperative where possible, non-cooperative if we're forced to it) direct action.'" Murray noted such nonviolent direct-action "techniques" had "buzzed about" but were not "carefully defined in terms of mass education" to "produce an American product of social pressure which worked." She believed that members of the Howard civil rights committee "might be sympathetic toward the Gandhian way," but in echoing Howard Thurman's call for an "indigenous" technique, Murray concluded that the students' task was to "find a technique which was uniquely American even though it might have other elements within it." Noting the particular benefits of discerning what such a method might look like within a college community, Murray argued, "The very close life of the college community, their proximity to one another, would give them opportunity to meet and discuss the problem frequently, to analyze their mistakes, to evaluate their methods, to correct errors, and to evolve the technique and get it into a scientific form."[69] Pauli Murray and the Howard NAACP students committed themselves to ongoing experimentation with nonviolent direct action, a process of collective learning that defined successful nonviolent direct-action campaigns in the years that followed.

Murray was in a unique position to draw broadly on a number of intellectual and organizing traditions in her letter to the first lady. She was a contributing member of the Fellowship of Reconciliation, had reviewed all of its literature on nonviolence, and had worked closely with former FOR staffer Howard Kester in organizing National Sharecroppers Awareness Week. Murray was an intrepid organizer and an intellectual. She joined the ethics of nonviolence that Thurman and his students were writing about with the direct-action tactics used so effectively by labor activists. The networks she maintained no doubt contributed to Murray's innovative approach to thinking about and practicing nonviolent direct action. She maintained close connections to pacifist women like Pan throughout the 1940s, worked for the socialist Worker's Defense League (WDL), and sought advice continually from Howard Thurman in his capacity as Dean of Rankin Chapel at Howard. Murray's impatience with the limited pace, scope, and inclusion of legal change, combined with her refusal to bow or bend to the daily indignities of Jim Crow, propelled her to experiment with new ideas and tactics in the fight against Jim Crow.

Murray offered the first lady "the rationale behind the whole project" in her letter, noting that "the entire campaign was student inspired, student executed," and that "faculty members were only for advice and criticism." She pointed to the opening salvo of the campaign, the denial of service to three young Black women, and noted that "the technique evolved from three individual students, who acting in an individual capacity, were arrested and embarrassed with consequent embarrassment to the university to an organized, disciplined, informed, democratic group in which practically no plan of action was followed until the decision was unanimous." While the Student Nonviolent Coordinating Committee (SNCC) was still a decade and a half from being born, the similarity to SNCC's group-based deliberation and decision-making is notable. Ella Baker, the NAACP's director of branches and a mentor to SNCC students in the early 1960s, likely advised the students on the Howard civil rights committee.

Murray noted that the campaign had subjected students to "a rigid and exacting process of trained leadership" as students tried out actions, evaluated them in group settings, made refinements and improvements, and tried them again. Murray called the leadership that emerged from this process "a most vital byproduct" of the campaign, noting that among the larger challenges facing local communities is leadership which "does not know how to go through the channels of democratic procedure to reach its objective." In their work at Howard, students centered collective democratic deliberation in their process to arrive at the intrepid method of nonviolent direct action. Murray believed that in doing so, they had found that "a philosophy was in the process of developing" in their work, a philosophy of nonviolence where freedom could not be divorced from individual and group practices. Murray and her fellow students at Howard demonstrated what the philosophy of nonviolence looked like in practice against Jim Crow a decade and a half before such practices became widespread: a reflective, collective, nonviolent direct-action campaign.

Concluding her letter to Roosevelt by returning to the conflict with President Johnson, Murray admitted to the first lady that the students were asked by the administration to desist, but they refused. "I was placed in the position of fighting our own Administration to preserve intact a method some of us are convinced is worth keeping even if [it leads to] the expulsion or suspension of those of us who have taken such a stand." Murray wrote that she loved Howard and would never want to see it harmed publicly. But she also believed that what the students were doing was of vital importance—showing forth the power of nonviolent direct action—and that she was willing to suffer the consequences to raise up this intrepid technique. She believed Howard should support the students given the importance of their example. "We believe we have given some open encouragement to the masses of frustrated Negroes who resort to violence because they have seen no effective alternative," she told the first lady. That alternative was on full display in the work of Murray and her fellow students: in the streets of D.C. and in the pages of the *Pittsburgh Courier*, the *Chicago Defender*, and scores of other Black papers there was a new and effective method, one with the potential to steel individual commitment to collective nonviolent actions and transform the nation's racial politics. Murray concluded, "We are therefore caught between our responsibility as potential leaders not to repudiate this leadership we hope we have demonstrated and our responsibilities as members of the university community not to hurt the reputation of the University."[70]

The day after sending her letter to Eleanor Roosevelt, Murray organized a meeting focused on a "formulation of principles" in response to the challenge from President Johnson. The students codified these principles in an "Instruction Sheet to Picketers" document that was circulated widely across campus. The students turned to Howard Thurman for "spiritual guidance in the midst of the campus crisis," and he assisted the students in developing a clear articulation of the deeper vision animating the demonstrators' actions.[71] The students encouraged one another to "adopt the conviction that you are first an American and [to] act upon that assumption in all public and private situations."[72] Beginning with this "assumption that you are an American," the students wrote, seek constantly to "raise the issue in the minds of other Americans with whom you come into contact." In doing so, the students were shifting the moral dilemma from the demonstrator to the antagonizer. The demonstrators had already made their decision about how to be when they asked for service just like any other American. The antagonizer was forced to respond. "You cannot decide that issue. . . . Your job, your main job," according to the students, "is to raise the issue."

The Howard civil rights committee presaged the Nashville student movement organized in 1960 and foreshadowed the teachings offered by FOR organizer James Lawson.[73] Lawson followed the lead of these Howard demonstrators fifteen years later in reminding his students that they always had a choice about how to be in the world: accommodate Jim Crow or live your highest ethical ideals, claim the freedom to be free, and refuse cooperation with Jim Crow. Such choices would determine the life or death of Jim Crow. As the Howard students wrote in 1944,

> So long as your thinking is "negroes are not allowed to do this" or "they don't want us here" or "may we come in here" you are denying with your conduct the very principle that you want applied to you—that you are an American and have inherited all the traditions and rights which other Americans lay claim to. . . . You must, in your own mind, believe that you are a part of the whole of American culture, and have both the right and the obligation to participate equally and fully in every phase of this culture. You must enlargen [sic] your social horizons and your social visions. You must widen your dreams. You must believe that some day you may be a Justice of the Supreme Court, President of the United States, Ambassador to China, a member of the President's Cabinet, or whatever position you are best fitted for. And with your dream and goal set, you must fit yourself for such a position.[74]

The students at Howard captured the deeper vision at the heart of nonviolence as a politics of being—a method to bring forth the world as it should be by demonstrating the world as though it were so. The students were clear: Their demonstrations were not simply a protest of the existing order, a criticism hurtled at the daily injustice of Jim Crow. Their demonstrations were an embodied claim on the belief that Black Americans have the same humanity as all Americans and are thus guaranteed the same civil rights, liberties, responsibilities, and protections from violence and discrimination. They encouraged one another to act from this deeper understanding of freedom, and their nonviolent demonstrations became a testament to the world of this vital truth. In challenging segregation and discrimination in public spaces, the Howard students remade their world—in their moment and in the decades that would follow—according to principles of fairness and justice, through strategic and public nonviolent direct actions.

The students at Howard articulated a clear relationship between their collective actions and the larger social structures they sought to transform. Pointing to law and custom, the students argued that this "technique of democratic procedure must be applied to each of these structures." They implored students to see even frustrations as part of a productive process, writing that they should "exhaust every step of democratic procedure" as they move steadily but firmly toward the goal of changing Jim Crow customs in local establishments. Success will not come quickly, but "despite the apparent waste of time, the red tape involved, and the constant frustration that it entails," the students believed that each action "will give you a knowledge of the internal workings of procedure, it will show you the weaknesses in the strong points of the government which regulate both your personal and public life, and it will suggest to you the direction in which changes must be made and some of the instruments and techniques of change."[75]

With preparation and collective support, and by participating in these actions, the students argued, "You will discover for yourself . . . that you are now ready to participate in the social conflict whenever it confronts you. It may be on a bus, a streetcar, a governmental office, riding in a car in traffic, a mixed cafeteria, or on the street." Pauli Murray knew this firsthand. She had done just this on the bus in Virginia. Courage came from taking courageous action, and this courage could be used day in and day out. Used collectively, it might prove to be a powerful strategy for Jim Crow's complete demise. "You must develop your own personal code of conduct in your philosophy," the students argued, urging one another to stay out of restaurants that did not serve Black Americans "unless you're prepared to be ejected by the police or even to suffer physical violence."

The students had a clear theory of social change: "Try to imagine the consequences of your attitudes and your conduct upon other people . . . every individual with whom you come in contact as a small world unto himself." The type of person one encounters every day, whether a waitress or fire fighter or street cleaner, "is part of the social structure which regulates your life as a member of a minority group." For the students, this was an empowering insight. They argued that an individual such as this "can help your cause . . . depending upon the way in which you handle him or her." Echoing their chaplain and spiritual advisor, Howard Thurman, the students argued, "You must recognize his personality, his shortcomings and limitations, and his potentiality. You must respect those aspects of his personality."[76] Urging one another to remember that "no matter what happens to you temporarily, whether you are served in a restaurant, or go to prison, or get slapped down, the resources of human history are behind you and the future of human society is on your side, if there is to be any human society at all in the future. You have nothing to lose and everything to gain."[77]

Looking back on the work of the civil rights committee at Howard, Murray remembered that "the most abiding gain" of the demonstrations in 1943 and 1944 "was in our own self-respect."[78] Nonviolent direct action steeled a commitment to struggle and sacrifice among the students. It both required and built personal courage. It replaced hope with evidence that a better world is possible as their nonviolent actions changed Washington, D.C. Through their demonstrations in 1943 and 1944, the students at Howard University set forward a critical template for nonviolent direct action in the American struggle for Black freedom. They aligned the ethics of nonviolence, the idea that all people should be allowed to grow in their creative potential and not be disfigured by a sinister social system of Jim Crow, with the long-standing political tradition of using direct-action tactics, picketing, and sit-downs. And it worked.

Ruth Powell later wrote that "they had achieved a nearly perfect demonstration based on Gandhi's methods. . . . Non-violent resistance awaited only a mass following."[79] It would take a special organizing talent to build that mass following, and a widespread articulation of the ethical principles at stake, and Bayard Rustin achieved just that in bringing this collective practice to communities across the nation during the Second World War. It was Pauli Murray and her fellow students at Howard who established a clear template for collective ethical action against Jim Crow, an "indigenous" technique widely reported in the national Black press. The national attention that their effort garnered led to a compelling defense of a method with the power to dismantle Jim Crow—city by city, town by town. As Powell later wrote, the Howard campaign was among the avant garde of nonviolent direct-action campaigns, a "daring" effort that went to "the very heart of racism."[80]

Change Your Sex or Change America?

As the spring of 1944 turned to summer, the students' campaign lurched toward a conclusion. The *Washington Tribune* reported that President Johnson "expressed a sympathetic attitude for what the students have been endeavoring to accomplish with some success, but feels that the same result can be achieved without making it appear to be a program of Howard University." The paper reported that Johnson was worried that his support of the students "would open the university to attack by reactionary congressmen in whose hands Howard's appropriations rest from year to year." The students had grown their efforts from twelve participants in the Little Palace Café action in the spring of 1943 to more than fifty-six (including six from the armed forces) in the Thompson's action in the spring of 1944. In the process, the *Tribune* reported that the students "achieved a moral victory for student-administration-faculty relationships. They . . . learned that Howard University is a beacon light to the Negro community and a significant contribution to the total community, and that everything done there is watched with intense interest."[81]

But the students had done something else. They created evidence, a successful example of nonviolent direct action, proof that this method might make true the American promise of life and liberty for all people. A D.C. paper reported that some Americans believed "the energy and the dynamics of social change must originate in democratic institutions," such as colleges and universities, "which form test tubes of democracy." The paper called for "a realistic relation of one's activities in the community to one's studies in the classroom." How could students learn the richness of Black life, work, and culture in the classroom while abiding by the degradation of Jim Crow segregation in their day-to-day life? There were people, the paper continued, who believed that Howard should shut down the demonstrations because they see education as "a static affair" that "must not be related to the community at large." "Between these two points of view Howard University must make a choice," the article stated. "Whatever the final outcome, Howard may be proud of those students who have led the way toward a new, and perhaps successful technique to achieve first class citizenship in one area of life in these United States."[82]

For Pauli Murray, this new technique was deeply promising. It was a collective freedom practice, an egalitarian tactic with space for everyone to participate. It recognized the power that each individual possessed to take direct action against the social evil of segregation. But for Murray, "first class citizenship" was never just about ending Jim Crow. There was a greater freedom at stake. Describing herself as "a representative of a blended humanity, carrying in my bloodstream the three great races of man—caucasian, negroid and mongoloid . . . I will refuse every attempt to categorize me, to place me in some caste, or to assign me to some segregated pigeonhole."[83] The prejudices and violence so entrenched in American life at midcentury were very real, and Pauli Murray understood them intimately because of her direct experiences with them. But she refused to let demeaning social practices determine the boundaries of her vision for freedom. Recalling the generations of people who came before her, Murray began to think and write critically about her own complex identity and the changes to U.S. society required to live this identity in a world that seemed to respond to her violently at every turn. "I am determined that my country shall take her place among nations as a moral leader of mankind," she wrote, and "no law which imprisons my body or custom which wounds my spirit can stop me."[84]

Returning to the idea that her way of being in the world could itself be a powerful politics, Murray argued, "I would bring shame and disgrace upon the United States' flag if I tolerated for one moment any practice of discrimination, segregation, or prejudice against any human being because of an accident of birth which has determined race, color, sex, or nationality and helped to shape his or her creed."[85] Murray's refusal to cooperate with discrimination and prejudice, a commitment on vivid display on that Greyhound bus in February 1940, was both a duty and an inheritance from her ancestors, who "left for me and my contemporaries of the 20th century the task of destroying the incidents of slavery—segregation, discrimination, and prejudice."[86] Striking a tone of racial nationalism, Murray pointed to the history of the United States not to cast aspersions on the nation at present but to call it back to its most fundamental values. "With my feet rooted firmly in the moral precepts of the Declaration of Independence and the Constitution of the United States and all the preachments of humanitarian tradition throughout the history of man," Murray wrote. "I take my stand against the institution of segregation and all of its incidents. For segregation is a monster, dividing peoples, thwarting personalities, breeding civil wars."[87]

Pauli Murray articulated the ways that both sexism and segregation interfered with both personal and collective freedom, and she sought a method that might reshape the ethical structures of the United States: "Force is not the way. Bloodshed is not the answer. We deserve to go down in history as the most bankrupt generation ever produced, if with the total cultural and spiritual resources of the globe at our disposal, we cannot fashion superior instruments to those of civil war, or riots, or personal retaliation. We must span the chasms of internecine strife, we must heal the wounds even while removing the cancerous growth."[88] To reconcile a nation whose ambitions of egalitarian democracy remained stifled by the reality of racial and sexual discrimination, Muray maintained, required a method sufficient to the task.

As the Quakers in the Fellowship of Reconciliation had done decades before, Pauli Murray envisioned a means which was itself the end—a technique to demonstrate the world as it should be. "The evolutionary law of survival teaches me I must be an integrated personality," she wrote, not a personality divided against itself but a full and whole human.[89] Murray committed to attack "the constitutionality" of segregation laws where they existed, but as importantly, she vowed, "where confronted with these laws in person, I shall resist them. If the refusal to abide by segregation statutes means imprisonment, I shall choose prison. If it means death, I can say only that my brothers and cousins are facing death every day. . . . For me there can be no compromise with segregation and discrimination."[90]

Calling this "a power greater than all the robot bombs and explosives of human creation," Murray wrote, "I do not intend to destroy segregation by physical force. I hope to see it destroyed by a power of the spirit . . . a laying hold of the creative and dynamic impulses within the minds of men. . . . The great poets and prophets have heralded this method; Christ, Thoreau, and Gandhi have demonstrated it." She committed "to do my part through the power of persuasion, by spiritual resistance, by the power of my pen, and by inviting the violence upon my own body. For what is life itself without the freedom to walk proudly before God and man and to glorify creation through the genius of self-expression?"[91]

The irony of history is that when Bayard Rustin and the pacifist Fellowship of Reconciliation sought to test the law that banned segregation on interstate travel in 1947, Murray—the original freedom rider in 1940—was denied participation based on her sex. Both Ella Baker and Juanita Morrow were also denied participation because of their sex.[92] Rustin, whose sexuality became an unavoidable topic in his movement work during the 1940s and 1950s, agreed with the other men in arguing that it was too dangerous for women to participate. The "Journey of Reconciliation" ended up composed of sixteen men.[93] Her response to Harvard Law School could have constituted her response to Rustin: "I would gladly change my sex to meet your requirements but since the way to such change has not been revealed to me, I have no recourse but to appeal to you to change your mind on this subject. Are you to tell me that one is as difficult as the other?"[94]

4 From Pacifism to Resistance
Bayard Rustin and the Roots of National Nonviolent Direct Action in Wartime America

∙∙

When the Quaker activist Bayard Rustin was called up to serve in the Second World War, he refused to go. "I came to the firm and immovable conviction," Rustin wrote, "that war was wrong and opposed directly to the Christian ideal."[1] Returning his draft classification cards to the U.S. attorney's office in Manhattan just before Thanksgiving 1943, Rustin included an "interracial primer" he had written earlier in the year. For Rustin, the "refusal to conform" to federal conscription laws was inseparable from his refusal to comply with Jim Crow. In both cases, he felt his ethics were distorted by the state—his freedom to act in accordance with his conscience was impinged. For his refusal to participate in the "good war," Rustin was arrested on 12 January 1944 and ordered to report to the lower Manhattan federal detention facility, where he began a twenty-seven-month prison sentence as a draft resister. His mentor, the Black trade unionist A. Philip Randolph, told him on the eve of his arrest, "Your action will give hope and spirit even to those who may disagree with your philosophy."[2]

Throughout the Second World War, one in six federal prisoners was a conscientious objector (CO).[3] But very few of them were Black. The lily-white American pacifist movement was facing its greatest trial to date in a moment of total global war. Pushed to the left by socialists and communists in the 1930s, American pacifists were forced to defend the efficacy of their political ethics amid a global war against fascism. COs were crowded into detention facilities across the country or placed in Civilian Public Service (CPS) camps where they undertook New Deal–like work projects. In these camps and prisons, the COs held workshops on pacifism, seeking to educate and then convert their fellow prisoners to a philosophy of noncooperation with war. Rustin did his part at the Ashland Federal Penitentiary in Kentucky, the prison where he was initially assigned to serve out his sentence. He taught workshops on nonviolence and incorporated direct-action projects into his prison seminars. For his efforts, the warden at Ashland recommended Rustin's transfer to a new facility. "This man will be a constant trouble maker," he told his bosses.[4]

By the time he went to prison for resisting the draft, Rustin had earned the ardent support of America's most prominent pacifist, a white minister who had dreamed of a national nonviolent movement in America for decades.[5] Abraham Johannes (A. J.) Muste corresponded regularly with Rustin during his time in jail, mentoring the thirty-two-year-old Black organizer in part because he saw in Rustin the single greatest hope for a nonviolent movement in his lifetime. But Muste also saw in Rustin what he believed was a grave vulnerability, one that might undermine the great promise of the young organizer. Rustin was gay, a fact that many in the pacifist movement were well aware of—even if it wasn't discussed. But when inmates at Ashland charged that Rustin had engaged in sexual acts with other men at the prison, he was pulled aside and questioned by prison officials. Rustin vehemently denied the charges, but prison authorities nonetheless placed him in solitary confinement for more than two weeks. After learning of the events, Muste wrote to his mentee, "My love for you has suffered no change." And yet, he continued, "this does not mean that I have not suffered some deep disappointment and that I am not greatly troubled."[6]

Muste and his pacifist colleagues worried that Rustin's sexuality would compromise his ability to work in the wartime pacifist movement. Rustin worried about it as well. In a letter to Muste after his isolation at Ashland, Rustin wrote, "I want you to know that I love you. . . . I feared facing the reality of the ugly facts. I feared the humiliation and dishonor. . . . I have misused the confidence the negroes here had in my leader-ship; I have caused them to question the moral basis of non-violence; I have hurt and let down my friends over the country and caused people like you . . . to grieve."[7] The historian John D'Emilio writes that Rustin "contemplated the possibility of becoming, through an exercise of will, heterosexual and even speculated about his capacity for celibacy."[8]

But that was not who Rustin was, and it was not who he would be. Muste admonished Rustin and told him that he must choose between his "promiscuous" sexual activity and his role with the Fellowship of Reconciliation. "There cannot be the slightest question as to what this means for your participation in the pacifist or any other social movement which has any ethical implications," Muste wrote, focusing his scorn on Rustin's personhood. "The thing to me goes a lot deeper than any question about your role in any movement. It has to do with you as a person. Don't you see that with your indiscipline, deceit . . . arrogance . . . you are—in one sense—running away from yourself and—in another—destroying yourself?"[9] In anguish over the ire he had provoked from his mentor, Rustin searched for the solace of understanding amid the unrelenting physical and emotional grind of life in prison. But the two men found no common ground in their correspondence, and their letters ended abruptly late in the summer of 1945. Rustin served out the balance of his prison sentence well into 1946—months after the surrender of the Axis powers to the Allies on 7 May 1945.

Rustin's marginalization, a prominent feature throughout his decades of public life, points to the sharp limits of movements for freedom in wartime America. Just as Pauli Murray's identity limited her access to the highest echelons of civil rights leadership and led to conflicts with the legal flank of the largely male civil rights establishment, as an intrepid gay organizer Bayard Rustin also faced challenges from movement leaders reluctant to make space for him in their ranks. But by the end of the 1940s, the deeply resilient Rustin emerged as one of the most effective and well-respected national organizers in the push for a nonviolent movement against Jim Crow. He advocated for a move "forward from pacifism," and not only because "pure pacifism" had little appeal for Black Americans.[10]

Nonviolent direct action was an egalitarian and inclusive freedom practice not bound by the narrowness and insularities, the rigidity and dogmatism, of pure pacifism. In the wartime effort to transpose the philosophy of nonviolence into a strategy of nonviolent direct action, there was no more important figure than Bayard Rustin. He organized Black and white people in local communities across the nation around the philosophy of nonviolence in the fight against Jim Crow, leading local experiments with nonviolent direct-action tactics through "interracial and interchurch" institutes in cities and towns from the East Coast to the West Coast. Like Murray, Rustin worked hard to fuse the philosophy of nonviolence with the tactics of nonviolent direct action. But he took this work a step further in creating spaces for local people to experiment with joining nonviolent ideas to direct action in dozens of local communities across the nation. For the first time, while a global war raged overseas, it became clear that a nonviolent direct-action movement might transform the structure of American racial politics.

Rustin was supported in this work by two mentors—Muste and Randolph.[11] He became the key link in a partnership between the vast movement infrastructure of Randolph's all-Black March on Washington Movement (MOWM) and Muste's white pacifists in the Fellowship of Reconciliation (FOR). Through voice and drama, and using experiential methods for teaching and learning, Rustin introduced hundreds of Black and white people to the idea of nonviolence in nonviolent institutes across the country. He encouraged individuals to live this ethical philosophy through personal practice and to enact it collectively through local direct-action campaigns.[12] Organized around a blend of instruction, debate, and active experimentation with direct-action tactics in local contexts, the institutes were "movement schools"—places where new ideas and practices were learned and enlisted in the fight against Jim Crow.[13] Rustin's work in these liminal spaces between Black and white organizations, within and between religious traditions, speaks to the depth of his acumen as an organizer. But just as importantly, Rustin's work speaks to the wider vision of freedom at the heart of nonviolence. Freedom meant honoring what Howard Thurman and the Quakers had cited as the deep promise of nonviolence since the 1920s: the fullest and freest expression of one's most authentic self, the thriving and flourishing of one's personality despite the severe and often violent limitations of the social world.

Rustin was far from perfect—succumbing to sexism at key moments in his movement work—but he was incredibly effective in teaching nonviolence and in organizing communities around the egalitarian freedom practice of nonviolent direct action. Rustin organized in communities across the country during the Second World War, teaching a method with the power to advance both individual and collective liberation. And in these spaces it became clear how nonviolent direct action might become a national strategy for revolutionizing a nation founded on white violence and racial discrimination.

Making Sense of Gandhi

Mohandas Gandhi was key inspiration for the nonviolent insurgency against Jim Crow in America, belonging as he did to a larger "colored cosmopolitanism" in the mid-twentieth century as ideas about resistance to racial empires flowed across national lines and old European empires fell between two world wars. Within these massive global ruptures, pan-African conferences and transnational networks brought people and organizations together routinely in their fight against racialized empires across the world, and Black nationalist women played an especially important role in the process.[14] A particular interest in Gandhi's nonviolence among African Americans began as early as the 1920s, with the *Pittsburgh Courier* and *Chicago Defender* routinely sharing Gandhi's image and ideas with Black Americans around the United States.[15] Black religious thinkers in particular began writing regularly of the political power generated by the ascetic man as early as 1921, while in the 1930s Black religious intellectuals traveled to meet the Mahatma to understand what he called nonviolence—Howard University School of Religion leaders Howard Thurman and Benjamin Mays among them.[16] These men spoke regularly to large Black audiences upon their return to the United States and contributed directly to what A. J. Muste called the "Gandhian Moment" of 1941.

But hearing about Gandhi in a sermon or seeing his picture in the newspaper was only one factor in the development of a national nonviolent movement against Jim Crow, and not the most significant one.[17] Efforts to discern how to ethically and effectively transform a Jim Crow society rose concurrently with the hardening of the U.S. racial order, and nonviolent referents in Black political culture often originated with stories of Jesus as often as Gandhi. The Mahatma became a critical conceptualizer for the ethical principles of political nonviolence, as well as an inspiring contemporary embodiment of the politics of being for the nonwhite world. But even Gandhi pointed to the Sermon on the Mount as the highest expression of what he believed to be humanity's most essential religious ethics, ethics far from prominence in a world defined by violent global conflicts claiming the lives of tens of millions of people.

In the U.S. Black freedom movement, nonviolence had more direct domestic intellectual sources than Gandhi—Howard Thurman foremost among these. And the direct-action tactics of the boycott, sit-down, and mass mobilization were deeply familiar to U.S. activists fighting in the labor movement or challenging segregation in buses and public places in the American struggle for Black freedom. The challenge in wartime America was articulating nonviolence as an appealing political ethic and then linking this ethic to direct-action tactics on a national scale. It was the problem of making nonviolent direct action a visible strategy for firing up individuals to enlist in a risky national freedom movement with the power to transform the nation's racial politics.

In a surprising alliance, the lily-white pacifist FOR and the all-Black MOWM united to address exactly this problem. Their shared work was forged in no small part by Gandhi's militant call to "Quit India" in the summer of 1942, a stunning rebuke of British colonial authority that captured the attention of the world.[18] Unplacated by British promises of Indian independence at the conclusion of the Second World War, Gandhi and the All-India Congress Committee demanded immediate independence from Britain and threatened a national campaign of civil disobedience if British authorities refused. The call to "Quit India" featured noncooperation campaigns with British laws, taxes, and policies in hundreds of communities across the subcontinent, a phenomenon the historian Judith Brown has characterized as "a flotilla of rafts colliding with a battleship."[19] More than 90,000 were arrested as Indians made salt, boycotted British courts and schools, avoided the use of foreign cloth and liquor, and refused to pay taxes or rent to British authorities.[20]

The Quit India campaign energized MOWM chairman A. Philip Randolph's long-standing interest in the politics of mass mobilization. In 1941, Randolph threatened to bring hundreds of thousands of African Americans to march on Washington, a proposed action that led President Franklin D. Roosevelt to issue Executive Order 8802 on 25 June 1941 just as Germany invaded the Soviet Union and the Second World War entered a new phase. Roosevelt's order required any military contractor doing business with the federal government to desegregate its workforce immediately, and it created the Fair Employment Practice Committee to ensure compliance. Randolph responded by canceling the proposed march in 1941, but he channeled the energy of his well-established network of activists into mass meetings across the United States throughout 1942.

The largest of these meetings took place in June 1942 as more than 18,000 people gathered in Madison Square Garden to demand an end to "all discriminatory practices in jobs, housing or otherwise."[21] In his address to the crowd, Randolph cited specifically the spiritual fortitude of Gandhi, imploring the assembled group to "fight, sacrifice, go to jail and, if need be, die" to win freedom from ongoing racial violence and discrimination. He called on Black Americans to recognize their "moral obligation . . . to demand . . . civil and political rights," and cited India as proof that "the Negro people are not the only oppressed section of mankind. . . . India's fight is the Negro's fight."[22] The mobilization of tens of thousands of Indians in the Quit India campaign illuminated a new possibility for Randolph and his national network of local delegates. The Black labor leader had the key ingredient for a similar campaign in the United States, a tool that no other African American organizer of his generation possessed: mass-movement infrastructure.

Meanwhile, FOR pacifists had for decades sought a "method" that might square means and end—a nonviolent strategy that could bring forth a less violent world. In Gandhi's example, these American pacifists saw a militant and religious nonviolence that was a proof of concept.[23] Gandhi's "do or die" approach resonated deeply with a militant American pacifist class that had long sought a national movement with the power to displace violence as the United States' predominant political method.[24] But this wartime interest in Gandhi divided American pacifists from their British counterparts in an earlier generation, many of whom disagreed with the approach Gandhi patented in the 1920s and 1930s. Earlier British pacifists, allied to colonial benefits if not the imperial sensibility of war, claimed that Gandhi had used coercive tactics during his 1930 "salt satyagraha" to bend imperial authorities to his will. These British pacifists believed the New Testament message was one of "nonresistance," and they argued that Jesus called for the complete denunciation of any kind of force—including nonviolent "coercion." They argued that Gandhi's forceful deployment of satyagraha was not "pacifism in the Christian sense. . . . His is not the way of Christ as we have seen it."[25]

And yet the Black religious intellectual Howard Thurman had spent the better part of the 1920s and 1930s envisioning the way of Jesus in a forceful and revolutionary way. He described the Nazarene carpenter's life as a series of creative and insurgent nonviolent actions against an unjust empire, courageous acts which steeled his internal strength and left an example that outlasted the violence and brutality of the Roman Empire by centuries. This characterization of Jesus as a nonviolent insurgent aligned well with the labor leader Randolph's own thinking on the matter.[26] Local Black churches were critical to Randolph's effort to organize the Brotherhood of Sleeping Car Porters (BSCP), the nation's "first successful black trade union," and as the historian Cynthia Taylor argues, Randolph "never strayed far from his African Methodist roots" throughout his public life.[27] In the life of Jesus, Taylor argued, Randolph saw a "revolutionary ministry of the brotherhood of man." Randolph himself used the same language as Thurman and the Quakers to describe African Methodist Episcopal (AME) Church founder Richard Allen's belief that "the dignity of human personality was sacred." He called Allen's walkout during a segregated Methodist church service in 1787 the first step in bringing down the "iniquitous partition wall of racial proscription and segregation in the Christian Church."[28]

Randolph's religious sensibilities overlapped with the socialist Christian left in the 1930s, including America's most notorious pacifist on the eve of the Second World War, A. J. Muste. Like Randolph, Muste spent much of his life involved in the labor movement. The white Congregationalist minister grappled routinely with the ethics of political activism throughout life. As a cofounder of the U.S. FOR in 1918, Muste initially believed that all social conflicts should be resolved without violence. But as a firsthand witness to the bloody labor battles of the early twentieth century, Muste grew wary of pacifist strategies. He watched as state-sanctioned violence was used time and again to crush labor strikes, drifting toward a "qualified defense of labor violence" as a Trotskyist before a "return to pacifism" in 1936.[29] This return to pacifism marked a turning point for the FOR, which he co-led alongside the Methodist minister John Swomley starting in the late 1930s. Muste pushed the FOR toward a politics that was more than mere abstinence from war, and in the factory occupations by industrial workers in the mid-1930s Muste saw great potential for the new way forward. He expressed trepidation with the relatively new tactic of "sit-downs and lie-downs" in the United States, but he lauded "the spiritual qualities of men who will subject themselves for over forty days to the stern rigors of a sit-down."[30]

The widespread use of the sit-down strike in the mid-1930s became a turning point in the effort to build a nonviolent direct-action movement against Jim Crow. Following a strike at the Akron Rubber Plant in February 1936, sit-downs, lie-downs, and stay-ins increased rapidly, and by the end of 1938 the "sit-down strike" had been used in more than 500 labor conflicts across the United States. This tactical innovation aligned well with Randolph's call for the "weapon of Negro mass power."[31] Speaking at the national NAACP convention in 1941, Randolph argued that "the old weapon of the conference" must be replaced by "some other technique of action." This sit-down technique, it appeared, was an excellent candidate.[32] Muste called the sit-down strikes "a glorious opportunity for those of us who believe in the way of love and nonviolence," and against the backdrop of Gandhi's Quit India campaign, Randolph's MOWM and Muste's FOR formed an unlikely alliance dedicated to advancing nonviolent direct action as a keystone strategy in the fight against Jim Crow.[33]

In the pacifists, Randolph saw the staffing power he did not possess within his nascent MOWM. The FOR also possessed decades of experience with an innovative "technique of action," including reams of literature on the subject and a bevy of materials for local workshops and trainings. In Randolph and the MOWM, Muste and the pacifists saw the political operation necessary to launch the nonviolent movement they had long envisioned. Together, and under the leadership of Bayard Rustin, these two organizations built a mass-movement infrastructure around a political philosophy of nonviolent direct action that proved essential to the 1950s and 1960s revolt against Jim Crow.

An Interracial Alliance

As early as 1941, the FOR began "study and experimentation" with nonviolence as a method of tackling "social issues" by commissioning a nonviolent direct-action committee.[34] But it quickly became clear that an exclusively pacifist movement would be impossible to build if the FOR envisioned a fight against Jim Crow in alliance with African Americans. The FOR's newly hired race relations secretary, Howard School of Religion graduate James Farmer, was charged with giving "very special consideration to the race relations field" in his work with the FOR early in 1942. Muste believed race would be "one of those fields" in which the FOR could "play some such role as Gandhi and his Satyagraha volunteers have played in the India National Congress." Muste envisioned "a nonviolence movement . . . in which the masses can have real faith, and to which they can therefore turn whenever they no longer have any confidence in any of the elements that believe in war and violence." Muste and his colleagues in the FOR believed that the Second World War afforded them the best chance for "the [nonviolent] revolution" to "really get somewhere."[35]

The Black organizer Farmer agreed with Muste that a concerted focus on Jim Crow segregation during the war might lead to such a national nonviolent movement. But Farmer was clear in arguing that pacifism must not be the basis of such a movement. In his visionary sketch for such an effort, "Provisional Plans for Brotherhood Mobilization," Farmer advocated individual and local experimentation with "relentless non-cooperation, economic boycott," and "civil disobedience," emphasizing that such tactics enabled people to be "thrown into swing wherever and whenever necessary." Building a mass movement around such tactics is possible, Farmer told Muste, but the key was making it egalitarian rather than ideological— "to 'mobilize' all persons who want to see an end to racial discrimination in America, and are willing to commit themselves to a disciplined nonviolence in working toward that goal."

Farmer agreed with Muste that a personal nonviolence must precede the successful use of direct-action tactics, that individuals must prepare themselves to maintain discipline if such a nonviolent movement hoped to transform America's racial politics. And Black Americans might join such a nonviolent movement, Farmer told Muste, especially if special attention were given to "specifically Negro channels" like Black churches, fraternal organizations, and schools. But Farmer was clear: the mass movement could not be avowedly "pacifist." The vision must be broader than simply abstaining from war and violence. It must be grounded in a wider understanding of what freedom was and how this particular method would allow Black Americans to strive toward freedom together. It must be based in an ethic that made sense to Black Americans, and the narrow conception of moral pacifism, the moral ideology Howard Thurman had scathingly critiqued in 1929, would not suffice.[36]

Randolph, meanwhile, began taking major steps to prepare his national network for nonviolent mobilization. He announced that the MOWM would host its first official national meeting in Chicago in July 1943, and he called on "every militant Negro with pride of race" to make the claim "I am an American, too"—echoing the poet Langston Hughes and Pauli Murray's band of student activists at Howard.[37] Delegates to the conference debated "a broad national program of non-violent civil disobedience and non-cooperation," with a special focus on using nonviolent action in "the interest of abolishing jim-crowism in America."[38] The pacifist Muste wrote Randolph to offer his "personal word of congratulations at the vision, intelligence and courage" represented by the call for a national program of nonviolent civil disobedience. "I should only be too glad to render any help possible in the achievement of your goal," Muste wrote to Randolph, seeing in Randolph's work the very thing he had sought for years.[39] Randolph's response was brief but cautious: "Brother Muste . . . I appreciate your interest in this problem and suggested cooperation."[40]

Randolph subsequently invited Muste to offer a keynote address at the conference themed around a "strategy of non-violent techniques for mass action" that might "awaken the consciousness of America to this whole problem of Jim-Crowism." He told the white pacifist Muste that he was uniquely equipped to speak on the topic of "race and non-violent solutions" at the massive national meeting of the MOWM.[41] While Muste was unable to appear at the conference, the Rev. E. Stanley Jones—who had previously met with Gandhi in India—spoke in his place. Most importantly, Muste deployed FOR staffers Bayard Rustin and James Farmer to assist Randolph and the MOWM in the months leading up to the conference.[42] Rustin, a Quaker born in Pennsylvania in 1912, had developed a very strong relationship with both Randolph and Muste by the early 1940s. Rustin told Muste that Randolph "is really concerned to develop an understanding and use of non-violence by the American Negro," and noted that Randolph seemed "anxious" to work more closely with Muste and FOR.[43]

But in a press release issued by FOR's executive committee, the pacifist organization offered only muted public praise for Randolph's effort. "Such a program is . . . a serious undertaking," the press release stated, and "much thought needs to be given at the very outset and through the period of preparation and execution to Gandhi's clear and insistent teaching that nonviolent action requires the most careful training and severe discipline, including spiritual discipline." The pacifists seemed outwardly skeptical that Randolph believed that personal nonviolence was an essential predicate to effective collective nonviolent direct action. They were not convinced that Randolph believed, as they did, that social change starts from within, as a personal practice that flows outward to impact the world.

And yet Randolph had written eloquently about the sacredness of human personality, noting the political challenge and personal freedom expressed in Richard Allen's 1787 walkout. And he arrived at his perspective on Jesus as a transformational figure through the prism of his African Methodist Episcopal roots. This, combined with his faith in Gandhi, makes it likely that Randolph did, in fact, understand that a disciplined mass movement predicated on direct action—one that would invite violence onto its practitioners—must be grounded in a discipline of personal nonviolence. Randolph's decades of experience in the labor movement taught him the critical importance of preparation for action, but the paternalist moralizing of the white pacifists seemed to leave little room for the ideas and experience that Randolph brought to a national nonviolent movement. The FOR's deep desire to play a *leading* role in an American nonviolent movement, a desire that flowed from decades of failure in this exact area, combined with the organization's general lack of experience in working with Black communities, prevented the FOR's white pacifist leadership from recognizing the depth of Randolph's contributions to the effort—at least initially.

But in appointing Farmer and Rustin to work with the MOWM, whether this was to keep a close eye on Randolph's efforts or ultimately to claim credit for what followed, Muste made an important decision. Allowing the two young men to lead the FOR's efforts in this area was a recognition of the pacifist organization's historical shortcomings, its longstanding struggle to build bridges to the Black community, and an acknowledgment that the pacifist movement must expand to survive amid a "Good War" to halt fascism. Muste's decision to appoint Rustin and Farmer as partners with the MOWM paid quick dividends. In 1943, the MOWM and the FOR began to cohost nonviolent institutes in local communities across the country, building a common space for white pacifists and Black Americans to engage the long history of religious ideas about nonviolent resistance as they prepared to use nonviolent direct action against Jim Crow.[44] These institutes represent the first concerted national effort in the United States to teach nonviolence in local communities in preparation for nonviolent direct action in the Black freedom movement.

The idea for the institutes came from the Quaker pacifist Rustin. He introduced the notion at the MOWM's national meeting in Chicago in July 1943, which included 109 delegates from fourteen states. Among the delegates were FOR activists and representatives from the Congress of Industrial Organizations (CIO), the national Young Men's Christian Association (YMCA), the United Mine Workers (UMW), and the Brotherhood of Sleeping Car Porters (BSCP).[45] On the final day of the meeting, before singing "The Star-Spangled Banner" and attending an "inter-denominational, inter-racial service" themed "We Shall Not Fail Our Boys," the 109 national delegates approved the "adoption of the method of non-violent, good will direct action to be developed in specific areas of injustice in protest against employment, transportation discrimination, civil rights violations, armed forces segregation and constitutional injustices." They called also for "local institutes in various localities to educate people to this program."[46]

For Rustin, the significance of the MOWM going "on record to use NVDA [nonviolent direct action] in its struggle for racial justice" could not be overestimated. He saw in Randolph's national network the mass-movement infrastructure needed to launch nonviolent campaigns "in the grass roots of the organization." And now, he could see a practical path forward for teaching personal nonviolence, utilizing Randolph's well-established local labor and church networks and the teaching materials developed by the FOR. Rustin saw in these spaces an opportunity to link the personal discipline of nonviolence with the direct-action tactics familiar to those with experience in the labor struggle. He introduced local leaders to the religious and philosophical bases of nonviolence in these institutes and argued that nonviolent direct action must emerge from a personal commitment to nonviolence.

He built his lessons around the direct-action legacy of the labor movement, but added a religious dimension that may have been new to many. Rustin introduced participants to the "various segments of negro thinking in facing this problem" of Jim Crow, but only because "the conclusion will, of course, be that NVDA is the most applicable and logical answer."[47] It was both ethical and effective, Rustin believed, arguing that so many other past strategies, whether legal or otherwise, had fallen short both in effectively building widespread participation and in transforming the deeper structural elements of America's racial politics. Nonviolent direct action would be different, he suggested. It would be different because it allowed everyone to participate in movement work and had the power to transform the ethics undergirding the unjust laws and violent social practices endemic to the United States since its founding.[48]

Rustin advertised the interracial institutes as an opportunity for local people to "live racial justice," a politics of being, and he began to organize them across the country in 1943.[49] The "Institute on Race Relations and Non-Violent Solutions" at Bethel AME Church in Detroit in mid-April 1943 was followed by a "Conference on Creative Non-violence as an Aid to Racial Understanding" at Avalon Boulevard Christian Church in Los Angeles in early May.[50] The Los Angeles conference was described as "not just a study, but an experience in race relations," arguing this way of being in the world was essential to the broader mission of transforming U.S. society through nonviolence. Participants debated the question of whether "the church is serious in its race relations program" and conducted a workshop on how to create interracial fellowships. The Los Angeles weekend also included a panel on the labor movement and nonviolence, as well as a workshop on the specific use of "non-violent techniques in the West."[51]

Institutes throughout the late spring and early summer of 1943 were held in industrial cities in the Midwest, and local pacifists partnered with African American civic organizations and churches. Local action projects became a focus. At the institute in Indianapolis on 12 June 1943, Henry Richardson—one of the first two African Americans elected to the Indiana legislature in the twentieth century—called those attending the institute "friends of liberty" who were "willing to shoulder their responsibilities . . . to the cause . . . of true liberty for all citizens."[52] Days later, 125 people attended the FOR-sponsored "Dayton Inter-Racial Institute" at the Bethel Baptist Church in Dayton, Ohio. Alfred Emerson from the University of Chicago addressed the crowd on "what science has to say about race," and James Farmer outlined the "race situation today in the US and abroad." *Dayton Herald* editor Michael Bradshaw and *Ohio Express* editor William Dunn explored "the race problem in Dayton," and FOR secretary John Swomley offered a talk on "nonviolent techniques for the US."[53] The Saturday program included a "work project" focused on "experimental non-violent direct action in conflict situations in Dayton . . . under the leadership of Bayard Rustin, special field secretary, FOR."[54]

On 16 June 1943, an institute was held in Columbus, Ohio, at the Second Baptist Church.[55] The format was similar to that of the Dayton Institute, but in addition to national speakers—among them MOWM executive secretary Pauline Meyers—local speakers also appeared. A worship service "arranged and conducted by Mr. Bayard Rustin" was a core part of the institute, and inside the program was an introduction to the institute concept. "No issue before mankind today is more important than that of the

A flier for a race relations institute organized by Bayard Rustin. Library of Congress.

relations between the white and the colored peoples," it read. The program text juxtaposed escalating global violence with the rise in white violence in the United States, stating both were the result of nonwhite populations remaining "in a status of inferiority" while supposedly "democratic" nation-states battled fascism abroad. This contradiction would lead to a "major crisis" in the United States, the program warned, a crisis the institutes hoped to mitigate by acquainting "people of both races with the work that is already being done, and to study the possible application of non-violent methods in the United States."[56]

The warning in the Columbus institute program proved prescient. In late June 1943, a white mob in Detroit doled out an unrelenting wave of violence against Black Detroiters. Twenty-five African Americans were killed, along with five white people, and more than 700 were injured before 6,000 national guard troops arrived to quell the violence.[57] In "A Statement on the Race Relations Crisis," Rustin joined Muste and Randolph and dozens of other leaders in calling for Americans to "open wide the doors of all churches, all schools, all unions, all fraternal bodies and all businesses to people of every race and color." In their statement, the leaders emphasized "working, playing and worshipping together, day by day" in order to "wipe out the misunderstandings which are fertile soil for race hatred."[58] The letter envisioned the kind of "authentic" interactions between Black and white people Howard Thurman wrote about in the 1920s and 1930s, and the organizer Rustin "immediately set about" the continued "formation of interracial fellowships." Rustin made clear that there would not be a "strict emphasis upon pacifist membership," and he directed white organizations to aid "such groups as the MOW . . . by identification with them in their cause," just as the FOR had done by appointing him to this work.[59]

A powerful symbol of the united efforts of the MOWM and the FOR came as Muste appeared alongside Randolph at the nonviolent institute held at Lincoln Congregational Church in Washington, D.C., in August 1943—the same semester that the Howard students launched their nonviolent direct-action campaign against Thompson's restaurant and the Little Palace Café in the nation's capital. The institute included addresses from Randolph, Rustin, FOR youth secretary James Farmer, and Muste's co-executive secretary, John Swomley.[60] Muste spoke on "the spiritual basis of non-violence," while Randolph made the case for nonviolent action as a practical "program for today." Their joint addresses showcased the unique contributions each group brought to the partnership.[61] Muste's emphasis on personal nonviolence was incomplete without Randolph's explanation of how such a philosophy might be operationalized through direct action.

It was Rustin who joined these discrete pieces in practice by linking local FOR chapters with MOWM affiliates across the country. In each instance, he brought together Black and white people with a common interest in nonviolent action. Participants grappled with the religious and humanist philosophies that undergirded nonviolence but remained focused on how to fuse these ideas into an insurgent politics through local direct-action campaigns. Rustin's institutes became spaces for interracial thinking, planning, and execution of small-scale direct-action campaigns, affording participants the opportunity to assess the promise and pitfalls of nonviolent direct action in practice.

In September 1943, a local activist in D.C. named W. Astor Kirk reported that Washingtonians had "formed a non-violent direct-action institute on

Race Relations to further work on problems of discrimination and segregation in our city." Emerging from the institute held at Lincoln Congregational Church in August, the group began to meet weekly at 5:30 on Saturday evenings. The agenda began with an interracial meal at the Lucy Slowe Dormitory at Howard University on Third and U Streets NW, followed at 6:45 with a gathering to "study the theories and applications and examples of non-violence and direct action," including reflection on "what techniques we should try and what changes we should make." At 8:00, separate groups flanked out to local institutions where racial discrimination was a routine part of business. A half-dozen drugstores and dime stores were targeted by the local activists in September, and Kirk reported the results:

> All racial barriers have been broken down at the People's Drug Store at 14th and U Sts., and colored people are served at the counter without discrimination. A mixed group has also been serviced without trouble at the Thompson's restaurant, but the manager said later that he had been unaware of the incident and that it is not the policy of the chain to serve colored people. All the other places refuse to serve colored people. . . . Through direct action, we are trying to show people, instead of merely preaching it at them, that the brotherhood of man is real and present now.[62]

Kirk saluted the work of Pauli Murray and the Howard students at Thompson's in his report, but he also emphasized the lived expression—the demonstration of Black and white people being together in public space—that was articulated through the collective actions of the demonstrators. The D.C. activists confronted the hostile and segregated city in which they lived with the nonviolent, interracial world they envisioned. They believed that a deeper change to the structures and ethics of D.C. might flow from their collective demonstration of interracial fellowship.

By October 1943, the *New York Amsterdam News* reported that the race relations institute in D.C. had coalesced into a number of neighborhood cells planning "a concerted attack" against Jim Crow in local restaurants. Navy serviceman Clyde Ashby said groups of thirty-five people were occupying segregated restaurants until they were either served or the restaurant closed its doors. Occupying restaurants would, according to Ashby, reduce the number of paying customers and place pressure on the restaurants to "adopt a more liberal policy." D.C.'s local police chief admitted he was powerless under the law to stop the "sit-down," as segregation was custom rather than ordinance in the city, but he nonetheless discouraged the interracial teams of demonstrators from acting for fear they would provoke violence from white bystanders. Congress of Racial Equality (CORE) activist Bernice Fisher, however, argued that such nonviolent methods were preferable to more traditional tactics like court battles, despite the risk of violence from white bystanders. In a legal battle, winning a favorable legal decision was the goal. But with nonviolence, by contrast, a more lasting change was sought through a "voluntary capitulation" by whites. Through a combination of personal kindness and political pressure, nonviolence afforded white people the opportunity to relax the reflexive practice of racial prejudice—just as Howard Thurman had written in the late 1920s.[63]

The D.C. efforts belonged to a larger national campaign coordinated by Rustin focused on establishing and sustaining local nonviolent movements in "several northern industrial areas and at least one southern city." The industrial cities of the Midwest were of particular importance, wrote Rustin, seeing in them "a wide variety of soils on which to plant our nonviolent experimental seed." Moreover, he added, "each of these cities has a FOR group, and MOW group, or both." The unique geography and history of these places enabled Rustin to link local FOR chapters with "Negro Church groups," MOWM affiliates, and burgeoning committees of CORE activists to experiment concertedly with nonviolence in local communities. Midwestern cities had been home to dozens of sit-down strikes throughout the 1930s, and the organized labor infrastructure proved key to Rustin's success in organizing local nonviolent direct-action campaigns. He remained insistent on discipline and "preparation in the local community" as a critical predicate to the "action programs," including an orientation to the ideas of nonviolence before the implementation of direct-action campaigns. He often relied on "the use of art, music, and drama in African American churches" to effectively seed "the message of nonviolence" in the hearts and minds of participants.[64]

Rustin's institutes are vivid examples of what the sociologist Larry Isaac has called "movement schools," spaces where specific ideas and tactics are transferred between different kinds of groups. New ideas and political tactics often emerge through dialogue across difference, and learning can happen as actions are planned, implemented, and assessed by diverse groups. Collective learning in these diverse spaces often relies on "key individuals," and that was certainly true of Bayard Rustin in the early 1940s. Rustin became that key individual, the bridge between white FOR pacifists and Black Americans.[65] Rustin illustrated the connection between religious nonviolence and direct-action tactics by using examples from Christian parables and the labor movement. He often used hymns, litanies, and songs to engage participants in enacting past dramas of nonviolence, drawing on his talents as a performer to involve participants in the pageantry of the past while imparting critical lessons about how to take nonviolent action in the present.

But facilitating interracial collaboration on nonviolent solutions remained difficult, especially for white pacifists. Eleanor Perry Moore, an employee of the War Relocation Authority in Washington who attended the institute in Washington, D.C., recalled that Bayard Rustin "conducted a symposium" and "sang several hymns beautifully." She remembered Swomley's speech but recollected also that A. Philip Randolph addressed the group, adding that the March on Washington Movement "scares me to death." Moore expressed fear that the MOWM "will be so misunderstood as to strike the white population here with horror. It may even be the worst race riot the country has ever had." Striking the tone of paternalism so common among "sympathetic" whites in the decades leading up to this moment, Moore suggested that "a white man's March on Washington in behalf of the negro" might be more prudent than a Black march on the capital. Otherwise, any "concerted effort to disrupt Washington at this time," in combination with the summer heat and the racial tension surfacing from the forced relocation of Japanese Americans, "could well be called sabotage."[66]

Long-standing paternalism among white groups seemingly sympathetic to the Black freedom movement made building an interracial nonviolent movement a struggle. In October 1943, Rustin organized a monthlong workshop in San Francisco to deal precisely with the difficulties of interracial organizing. In one of his many addresses to the San Francisco institute, Rustin told the interracial group that the MOWM must be understood as the most recent response to a long-standing question at the heart of the African American experience: "How can we win freedom?" Rustin argued that the unifying theme of strategies for Black advancement since slavery, from electoral success during Reconstruction to Marcus Garvey's Universal Negro Improvement Association (UNIA) to W. E. B. Du Bois's work in founding the National Association for the Advancement of Colored People (NAACP), was the creation of "strong pressure groups" through which African Americans might "obtain their rights." Recalling that "many objected" to Randolph's initial call for "non-violence and civil disobedience" in 1941, Rustin cited the Detroit uprisings of 1943 in claiming that Randolph's nonviolence proposal had become "the only sound one." The current difficulty, he continued, "is that Negroes do not believe in it or support it because they do not understand it." Rustin echoed Howard Thurman in cautioning white pacifist "talking groups" to avoid attempts to show African Americans the way forward on the issue. "If pacifists and socialists were concerned enough and live enough to take a lending part in the MOWM, they might do so. But at this point, they are not ready for it," Rustin concluded. Whites should instead support Black efforts at organizing, not try to take over and lead.

In addition to a smattering of pacifists, Rustin argued that the majority of whites fighting Jim Crow in the 1930s had been communists. Often, Rustin argued, these whites sought to usurp Black leadership. Rustin believed that white communists in particular sought leadership because they had a "fear [that] a movement of non-violence" might be successful and thus "would do their best to oppose it and change it."[67] Rustin's words likely rang true for Howard Kester, who dealt with exactly this issue in his interracial attempts to organize sharecroppers and workers in the 1920s and 1930s. Rustin's words also recall the challenge articulated by Howard School of Religion leaders Benjamin Mays and William Stuart Nelson in the 1930s as their graduates battled for the hearts and minds of Black southerners. In citing this recent history, Rustin implored whites to become partners with Black Americans, not "leaders" in a national nonviolent movement against Jim Crow.

Rustin's mentor A. Philip Randolph was all too familiar with this recent history. The fear of communist co-optation had been, in fact, key to his decision to make the MOWM an avowedly all-Black movement.[68] But Rustin hoped the interracial nonviolence institutes might become sites where a positive collaboration, not a paternalistic one, could lead to a formidable interracial movement against Jim Crow. "The discipline of non-violence cannot be talked about," Rustin implored. "It can be learned only by doing. Nonviolence believes in action. It says that the question of whether you will act or not act is academic. You *will* act in certain situations because you are forced to act when confronted with social issues. . . . In the past non-violence has been too close to non-resistance with its fear of action. Now the element of resistance in nonviolence is daring to come to the fore, with its challenges to action."[69] In his denunciation of passive resistance, Rustin joined both Howard Thurman and Gandhi. Thurman had condemned pacifism as "mere quietus" used to control an oppressed minority, and Gandhi argued that pacifism is to nonviolence as north is to south: utter opposites. Rustin also presaged his successor James M. Lawson Jr. in arguing that people facing oppressive social demands always had a choice about how to be, capturing succinctly the political ethic at the heart of the politics of being in the Black freedom struggle.

In his "Lesson Plan on Nonviolent Action," Rustin named five necessary steps as antecedent to nonviolent direct action: investigation, negotiation, education, ultimatum, and self-examination. Nonviolent direct action could not be practiced devoid of personal discipline, he argued. It must flow from a personal commitment, even if this personal commitment to remain nonviolent in the face of white aggression was strategic so as not to provoke more deadly force from state authorities. Rustin put this methodical process to work with local people in San Francisco in experimental action projects at the Hasting's Clothing Store, the Ambassador Skating Rink, the Crystal Baths, Woolworth's, the Recreation Department at the City of San Francisco, and a number of restaurants in the Bay Area.[70] Six months after Rustin's monthlong visit, local activist Peg Deuel reported to Rustin that a San Francisco CORE chapter had notched twenty-two pledged members with a regular attendance of twenty-five total people at weekly meetings.[71]

During his time in San Francisco, Rustin formalized an extensive curriculum for how to teach nonviolence in interracial spaces.[72] He wrote, "One must bear in mind that non-violence is more than direct action—boycott, etc.—it is made up of preceding steps which can be carried out in millions of ways and which have always been going on throughout the course of history."[73] He echoed Howard School of Religion student James Russell Brown and his professor Howard Thurman in writing that practitioners of nonviolence must "have no fear, tell the truth, admit [their] own share of guilt, behave creatively." Moreover, like the students at Howard, Rustin argued that nonviolence practitioners must "raise the struggle from a physical to a moral plane." In his "Lesson Plan on Faith, Discipline, Action," Rustin emphasized personal practices in preparation for nonviolent direct action, including praying for "at least one-half hour daily," joining a community (a "cell or group"), and making a commitment to "simplifying" one's life to focus on fellowship and authentic actions with other people rather than on material things.[74]

Pointing to these practices in the life of Jesus, Rustin both cited and expanded upon the work of Howard Thurman. He outlined the "five kinds of nonviolent direct actions Jesus used," including defiance of the Sabbath laws as acts of civil disobedience, noncooperation in refusing to answer King Herod's census, a mass march when Jesus entered Jerusalem with a "large procession of his followers," and the "nonviolent direct action" used to drive the money changers from the temple. Beginning with a disposition of personal nonviolence, Rustin argued, Jesus attracted individuals to the public practice of nonviolent direct action. It started with courage, truth telling, and humility—ways of being in the world that provided strength and power for strategic nonviolent direct-action tactics such as the "non-violent strike, economic boycott, picketing, non-payment of taxes . . . non-cooperation," and "civil disobedience."[75]

Simply using these tactics in a quest for power, Rustin warned, would mimic the ethics of white supremacy and leave the structure of U.S. politics unchanged. Rustin envisioned nonviolence as a different kind of tool, one more powerful than the laws, customs, or violence used to perpetuate Jim Crow. Rustin cited historical examples to prove that such a method worked, going beyond the well-trod campaigns of Gandhi to illustrate how it might be done. He cited resistance by "Norwegian and Finnish governments" to Nazi occupation and held up specific examples from "the labor movement in America" to argue that individuals committed to nonviolence as personal discipline mustered the power to effectively use nonviolent direct action to transform political realities.[76]

In his primer "The American Racial Scene Today," Rustin linked the U.S. struggle against Jim Crow to the many battles waged against racial superiority around the globe. Pointing to what he called "colored allies in the fight against fascism," he cited "Japanese propaganda to the darker races" in the Second World War and "India's demand for freedom" as part of the global discourse around colonialism and white supremacy. Pointing to "colored allies" in India specifically, Rustin described these nonwhite activists as a hopeful analog for Black Americans seeking to rectify the "disparity between our democratic aims and our undemocratic treatment of the Negro." He pointed to a "failure by all to set up a program to meet present revolutionary social change" and outlined an extensive list of suggestions to better prepare Black Americans to build on these international efforts.[77] His suggestions included the organization of an interracial ministerial alliance, the use of radio and press by clergy, the organization of workshops in churches, an educational program designed specifically for whites, and use of the arts, such as "modeling in clay, painting, singing, dancing" so that "people of all ages can find and enjoy special interests" across racial lines.[78] Rustin also included worksheets in his curriculum that offered practical suggestions on what to do in specific instances of discrimination or aggression, including how to respond nonviolently if served a drink in a rusty cup or when being overcharged for coffee.[79]

Forward from Pacifism

Rustin ramped up his seminars on nonviolence after being imprisoned in February 1944 for refusing to comply with the National Selective Services Act. He continued his workshops in the federal penitentiary in Ashland, Kentucky, and in defiance of the prison's segregation policy, he maintained the interracial composition of these workshops.[80] In prison, Rustin called for a move "forward from pacifism," recalling "the strikes, boycotts and sit-down strikes of American labor," but arguing that "our strikes and battles will always be conducted with full respect for our opponents, and without violence or terrorism of any kind."[81] Rustin wrote of a "moral force" built around "positive activities," a constructive program centered in an ethic that transcended segregation and violence.[82] He envisioned a "flesh and blood program which deals with physical realities and social relationships" rather than the "perverted pietism" that "preaches disembodied spiritualism." He encouraged study and action together, like other COs in prisons and work camps around the country, and he believed that cells across the country committed to the study of nonviolence and experimentation with nonviolent direct action might produce "a network of moral force to promote that which . . . is best for all."[83]

But Rustin did not envision nonviolence as simply a momentary disruptive force or a protest of the world as it is. He did not, in fact, limit his writing and teaching to ending Jim Crow only. Rustin envisioned liberation as an active and ongoing process that flowed from his way of being in the world, a set of freedom practices that could be a routine part of his day-to-day life. Rustin saw nonviolence as the process of making the world as it should be through the free and full expression of his most authentic self in the face of social and political structures that placed sharp restrictions on his ability to be free. Yes, nonviolence included a refusal to abide by Jim Crow custom and law, a noncooperation with state coercion toward wartime violence. But it was also a firmness of courage, kindness and mercy, forgiveness and openness, honesty and authenticity—constructive actions that came through one's way of being in the world and which showed forth the world as it should be. It was reverence for personality, both one's own and the other, practices that embodied the pursuit of a greater freedom.

Experimenting with these politics of being in prison, Rustin was attacked with a mop handle by a white prisoner named Huddleston as he sat among his cohort of white conscientious objectors (COs) in the prison's typically segregated recreational hall. When other inmates tried to stop the attack on Rustin, he asked them to step away and let the man beat him. A white CO named Bronson Clark recalled Rustin's actions as "a perfect example of what Richard Gregg described in his *Power of Nonviolence*. Huddleston was completely defeated and unnerved by the display of non-violence and began shaking all over and sat down."[84] The COs requested that Huddleston not be punished—an act of forgiveness that earned them good standing with the administration and allowed Rustin to earn a regular spot in the prison's education program.[85]

Rustin refined his workshops on nonviolence in these interracial prison seminars, but he also began cultivating a deeper vision of nonviolence by exploring the relationship between the structures of society and human behavior. "How universal in every individual heart is the quality of mercy," Rustin wrote in his personal journal. "This is the strange riddle of the individual versus society, of the conscience of the individual versus that of society, and of the action of the individual and that of society."[86] Homing in on the relationship between individual behavior and the broader process of social change, Rustin pondered, "What method of change is necessary to do away with exploitative oppressive measures of national and international economics and politics?"[87] Pacifists had failed to create this more fundamental revolution in U.S. society, Rustin argued, concerned as they were "with denunciations of war and the causes of war" rather than developing what William James called the "moral equivalent of war." How, Rustin puzzled, can individuals create "fundamental change which does not necessarily involve violent methods"?[88]

Rustin's denunciation of pacifism, his call for something deeper and more durable than pacifist politics, is notable. Rustin was in prison because he refused to fight in the Second World War. He was a pacifist who refused to participate in the "Good War" against fascism due to his religious beliefs. But Rustin also sought something more, recognizing the very real limits of pacifism. In a time of tremendous trial, while a world war raged, Rustin came to see pacifism as a limited philosophy that kept a select few individuals from the stain of war while the terror of violence continued to wreak havoc on the many. Pacifism would not stop the war, he concluded, and pacifism would not stop the white violence meted out routinely against Black Americans in the United States. Pacifism would not stop the violence directed at labor activists or anyone else suffering violent oppression. Rustin envisioned a broader liberation, a greater freedom, and believed the greatest expression of this ethic was nonviolence—an opportunity for each person to make a stride toward this greater freedom through nonviolent direct action.

In the months before his imprisonment, Rustin had organized spaces for "living" this vision of nonviolence institutes around the country. In prison, he continued this work through careful study, teaching, and demonstration. But his efforts to bring forth the world as it should be continually ran aground the limitations of the world as it was. As a gay Black man in a sexually conservative epoch, Rustin bumped into the sharp corners of respectability politics routinely. And the boundaries of such respectability politics were policed most vigorously not by Rustin's prison guards at Ashland but by the mentors and leaders he relied upon for support in the pacifist and Black freedom movements.

A. J. Muste was almost certainly aware that Rustin was gay even before he entered prison. The historian John D'Emilio writes that every pacifist he interviewed in his biography of Rustin "said that they knew he was gay, even while saying that, at the time, no one spoke about it."[89] Rustin maintained an active and open relationship with a man who became his partner for decades, Davis Platt, whom he met at Bryn Mawr College on a FOR speaking engagement.[90] But how Rustin's pacifist colleagues came to know about his sexuality, D'Emilio writes, and what exactly they knew remained elusive. Doris Grotewahl, Rustin's primary correspondent in prison, knew about Platt. But she wrote about Platt and Rustin's sexuality only in coded terms to protect Rustin from the prison guards, who reviewed every piece of his mail.

Muste directed his scorn at what he called "the issue of promiscuity" in his correspondence with Rustin rather than directly condemning Rustin's homosexuality. But because homosexuality and promiscuity were often conflated throughout much of the twentieth century, it is possible that Rustin's homosexuality—and how it was perceived by the political forces opposing the budding freedom movement against Jim Crow—was the true source of Muste's frustration. Characterizing true love as the "exchange of spiritual life [and] . . . an understanding above the ordinary between two persons," Muste asked Rustin, "How can this happen with an indefinite number of people?" He characterized Rustin's sexual encounters in jail as "an impulse to use and exploit rather than to understand and nourish . . . the opposite of love."[91] Decades later, Platt recalled that Muste was "ambivalent" toward him:

> Muste knew we were lovers, he tried to get me to desist, to leave Bayard and try to get Bayard to give it up. . . . He tried to give me the impression that it was an unsatisfactory lifestyle that wouldn't work. It wasn't that it was wrong or evil, but it was not viable and if Bayard continued this way it could destroy him and the movement. . . . Bayard never promised [Muste] that he would give up homosexuality or give me up. He would be careful. That's my recollection. . . .

I never had any sense at all that Bayard felt any shame or guilt about his homosexuality. And that was rare in those days. Rare.[92]

In a letter to Rustin in mid-June 1945, Muste unleashed the full force of his ire in what D'Emilio calls "tough words written with the passion of a moralist arguing his case who, finally, could not imagine homosexual love."[93] Muste called for a "decisive parting of the ways," but Rustin would not give up so easily—on Muste, on the FOR, on himself, or on his partner Platt. He refused to give up on the search for his most authentic self, believing—as did so many who surrounded him—that he must play a profound role in the nonviolent transformation of America.

Rustin's time in prison was not simply a test of his moral purity to lead a nonviolent movement. It belonged to Rustin's deeper search for his truest self. "I had not really had exchanges of the little things that make life grow," he wrote to Platt from prison, noting the severe limits on his ability to interact meaningfully with the people he loved while imprisoned. He committed to becoming more disciplined in his correspondence with Platt. He referred to Platt as "her," and used the third person when writing to disguise Platt's identity. Rustin wrote of "reading little lists I know she would want to hear, copying little poems I write that she would laugh with me over, collecting material on race that she would find interesting, making notes of what to say in the next letter." He continued: "I know that I need to give myself to build (as you have analyzed) a beautiful and sincere relationship—to overcome that disbalance between adventure and emotional security you so excellently and accurately described. To find beauty and peace with another for only in this way can love flow back toward humanity."[94] Finding and building internal peace and personal well-being were essential for Rustin's service to the movement, hard and painful as it was from prison, and this process of learning to love himself ranked high among the contributions Rustin made from Ashland. That Rustin's most authentic expressions came not with the nonviolent moralist Muste but with his gay lover Platt suggests that the limits of liberation were very real in the moral movements seeking to transform a nation that fell short on its ethics.

Nonviolent Direct Action: A More Durable Weapon

When Rustin was released from prison on 11 June 1946, he found that the work he had started in the nonviolence institutes had continued. Kansas City held its second nonviolence institute in April 1945, and Toledo organized its first in February 1946.⁹⁵ Toronto hosted a "Race Relations Institute Emphasizing Democratic and Non-violent Solutions of Present Day Race Problems" in May 1947, and having patched up his relationship with Muste, Rustin facilitated a monthlong interracial workshop in Washington, D.C., in July 1947 similar to his San Francisco workshop.⁹⁶ The monthlong D.C. workshop required participants to live in interracial housing and share meals in addition to doing seminars on nonviolence and sustained direct-action projects across the city. Thirty-one people participated in the D.C. institute from New York, Canada, California, Florida, New Jersey, Ohio, Illinois, Pennsylvania, Virginia, and Kansas.⁹⁷

Reflecting on the D.C. workshop, Rustin identified three women—Lynn Seitter, Sydney Irwin, and Emily Josif—who were "seriously concerned with remaining in Washington to help provide the kind of leadership which is so necessary for effective nonviolent action." These three women came to believe that segregation produced a profound ignorance of the other, and that a lack of authentic engagement between communities was the root cause of violence. The violence directed at Black Detroiters and the Nazi drive to conquer and annihilate nations overseas were vivid examples of this phenomena. Frank Kavjka of Illinois, a veteran of the Second World War, concurred. He came away from the D.C. workshop with "very great experiences in the use of non-violent direct action. . . . [I am] now convinced that such methods are very effective. My whole thinking pattern has been challenged." Margaret Boos of Canada reflected on the lived interracial experiences at the heart of the institutes. She deeply "appreciated the opportunity of living for a couple of weeks with an interracial group." While previously she had "contended that it was possible, now I *know* it can be done."⁹⁸

In early 1948, the FOR hosted an "All Ohio Collegiate Workshop in Minority Problems." Rustin assembled an exhaustive list of more than a hundred contacts from a dozen colleges and universities across Ohio, among them a first-year student at Baldwin Wallace College in Berea named James M. Lawson Jr. The stated goal of the youth workshops was stimulating "college students to take an active role in eradicating injustice to minority groups" through the "study [of] positive non-violent techniques." The Ohio workshop reflected the general approach to nonviolence institutes since they were first organized in 1943. Participants would study "methods and programs for breaking down discrimination in housing, theaters, restaurants, jobs, barber shops on and off the campus" and would examine "the principles of non-violence in preparation for the afternoon action projects." The afternoon action projects would be "determined by the conditions in the community where the workshop is being held," would be directed by local leaders, and could serve as "just a beginning" or "a campaign of duration." The ultimate decisions about target locations and methodologies were to be "made by student representatives in cooperation with local leadership." At the conclusion of these nonviolent workshops, participants would provide "a report to the community of the unique aspects of the workshop—the action program," a process of reflection and refinement that was intended to sustain local campaigns of nonviolent direct action.[99]

Following the Ohio workshop, as a second-year student at Baldwin Wallace College, Lawson staged his first nonviolent direct action in a downtown barbershop. There were no integrated facilities in Berea, and Lawson recalled that "after several complaints, particularly from an Ethiopian student, two of us finally decided 'Well, why don't we begin?'" With no real plan other than to challenge the reality that Black people could not get a haircut downtown, Lawson recalled, "Our tactic was very simple. I would walk in first and take a seat. Then the white fellow walked in behind me, so we went in that order. And that would give us the certainty I was ahead of him; if I were not asked if I wanted a chair by the barber and [the white student] was instead, he would decline and say 'he was ahead of me.' Well, the first shop we went to we were summarily thrown out. That was our introduction to it."[100] Lawson and his fellow students persisted. They tried three more times with other barbers in Berea until at last they discovered someone in town that would cut the hair of Black students. The barber was an usher at the local Congregational church where Lawson attended services throughout college, and he wondered, Could the white barber seat him in the pews at worship but then refuse to cut his hair at the barbershop? As Lawson put it, their nonviolent action "was a simple, moral confrontation" of the white barber, one "he answered . . . positively."[101]

In the wartime nonviolent institutes, the political philosophy of nonviolence crystallized into a lived expression of an America transformed through local direct-action campaigns. People in cities and towns brought to life this vision through direct-action campaigns in communities across the country, a major turning point in the growth and evolution of local Black freedom movements. Inspired by Gandhi, the all-Black MOWM allied with the lily-white FOR, and their collaboration laid the groundwork for interracial nonviolent movements in cities across the country. In living together, sharing meals, singing together, listening to each other, and taking shared action, institute activists integrated the typically segregated spaces of U.S. social life and, in the process, made interracialism a visible movement goal in the nonviolent fight against Jim Crow. Integration was a challenge to a rigidly segregated nation, but it also expressed America as they believed it should be—a Jim Crow nation transformed by local nonviolent movements. In their expression these nonviolent activists, perhaps ironically, became part of an emerging Cold War strategy to craft a new racial image abroad through desegregation at home, an image often eclipsed by the reality of ongoing white violence and Jim Crow discrimination. And the ideas that underpinned the nonviolence institutes, which were organized in American churches, were decidedly Christian—a feature that likely preserved the political philosophy in a nation with rapidly rising religious sensibilities.[102]

But the wartime work's deeper importance was to cement nonviolent direct action as the centerpiece of a postwar revolution in American racial politics.[103] The institutes belonged to an enduring quest among religious Americans to develop a method for revolutionizing the nation's politics by revolutionizing its ethics. Their work belonged to the longer effort to advance this quest that included the work of Howard Kester, who in 1929 brought together an interracial group of students at LeMoyne College in Memphis to figure out how to nonviolently fight Jim Crow. The ethics and ideas flowed from the writings and sermons of Howard Thurman and the pacifist Quakers, who encouraged the dissolution of any social system that interfered with the ability of people to fully express their most authentic selves. The action projects were attempts to make more widespread the nonviolent example put forth by Pauli Murray and the students at Howard as the Second World War raged overseas.

The wartime institutes organized by Bayard Rustin sought to make the discipline of nonviolence a predicate to nonviolent direct action, an ethical and durable weapon that might transform the structure of American politics by revolutionizing the nation's ethics. James M. Lawson Jr. was the most important figure in carrying forward this tradition of nonviolent institutes in communities across the South and Midwest in the years immediately before the major nonviolent campaigns of the 1960s Black freedom struggle. Thirty years after Howard Kester's attempt to mount a nonviolent battle in the Jim Crow South, James Lawson became the FOR's southern field secretary—planting seeds that would sprout in communities across the South the sit-in revolution of 1960 changed America forever.

Part III Building a Movement

The Politics of Being

5 Disrupting the Calculation of Violence

James M. Lawson Jr. and the Religious Politics of Nonviolent Direct Action

....

On a cold Saturday morning in late February 1960, Bernard Lafayette and Solomon Gort walked side by side on their way to downtown Nashville's department stores. Over the last ten days the sit-in movement had transformed the city. Wave after wave of Black students, alongside a few white supporters, had filled the city's segregated lunch counters to challenge Jim Crow discrimination. Hundreds of students had been arrested for their efforts. And while most of the students had been arrested peacefully, these two young men from American Baptist Theological Seminary were prepared for violence. Their teacher, James M. Lawson Jr., had trained them to anticipate such violence—had, in fact, facilitated drills to hone and test their responses. But as they marched to Woolworth's on that Saturday morning, a day later remembered as "Big Saturday," Bernard Lafayette worried he might return a punch for a punch.[1]

The two young men belonged to a pair of massive columns of students marching from their headquarters at First Baptist Church Capitol Hill to Nashville's downtown business district. By the end of the day, more than 400 would participate in the sit-ins—the largest demonstrations in Nashville to date.[2] As one wave of students was arrested and packed into Nashville paddy wagons, another came right behind them to fill the stools. But before the students could arrive downtown to take their place at the lunch counters, they had to pass by small groups of young white men who taunted them and called them names. The students ignored the heckling and name calling, just as they had been trained to do, but upon seeing the end of the line, one of the white men leapt onto Solomon Gort and began to assault him. *Love your enemies and pray for those who persecute you.* Bernard Lafayette knew the Sermon on the Mount well. He had grown up Baptist, and his father had been a deeply religious man. The young seminarian had been taught that refusing to respond to violence with violence was among the highest expressions of Christian love—that to give your life for a friend was, in fact, the greatest act of love. But in the melee that erupted before him

Lafayette had no time to think. He simply reacted, throwing his body onto his friend Solomon to protect him from the blows.

James Lawson was alert to the situation and walked calmly—almost casually—to the young men in a scrum on the ground before him. He politely asked the white man to stop beating his colleagues. Looking up only long enough to spit in Lawson's face, the attacker continued to pummel Gort and Lafayette. But when Lawson asked the white man for a handkerchief to wipe his face, the assailant obliged. Cleaning the spit off his face, Lawson noticed the young man's leather jacket and ducktail haircut. He asked if the man owned a motorcycle or a hot rod. A motorcycle, the young white man replied. Was it modified? Well, yes, it was. What kind of engine? As the white man began to describe the engine on his customized motorcycle to the Black Methodist seminarian, Gort and Lafayette picked themselves up off the ground and scrambled to rejoin the students marching downtown.[3]

James Lawson's response to the young white man in Nashville was a careful one, an intentional act animated by the ethic of nonviolence. Lawson sought in that moment to bind himself to his "enemy" by creating a connection around a shared interest. The feat was brave, given the circumstances, but it was not an accident. His response flowed from a conception of what nonviolence was and how to practice it, an understanding gleaned through years of study and experimentation, insights which he shared with a generation of students that went on to play an outsized role in the revolt against Jim Crow.[4]

Lawson saw his way of being in Jim Crow America as a spiritual discipline. He sought always to protect his intellectual and emotional interior from racist attacks in order to preserve the possibility of a creative response to Jim Crow's constant caustic demands. Such a mindset was redolent of what Howard Thurman described as the "psychology of Jesus." His intervention in the beating of Bernard Lafayette and Solomon Gort was an example of the politics of being par excellence: a merciful act of human fellowship in the face of a violent white attack that transformed the effort to diminish and dehumanize Black people with an act of human connection and fellowship. As importantly, his response was strategic: a well-calibrated intervention designed to expose the weakness of white supremacy—violence—while powerfully elevating Black humanity. This ethic of nonviolence was centered in the belief that all people should be allowed full and free expression of their unique personality, the idea that engagement with others should build connections across the lines of racial segregation patrolled vigilantly by violence.

Thousands of students were inspired to struggle using nonviolent direct action in the early 1960s, even if the philosophy of nonviolence was not their core motivation. They mobilized in massive numbers across the South in local nonviolent direct-action campaigns, and the net result of their collective efforts was the draining of power from Jim Crow violence in America.

The Rev. James M. Lawson Jr. became the most important teacher of nonviolence in this period, a philosophy that often—if not always—undergirded local direct-action campaigns in cities and towns across America.[5] Lawson illuminated how the politics of nonviolent direct action flowed from the ethics of nonviolence, a way of being that was not only a protestation against Jim Crow but also a personal expression of the will to be free—an act of courage both borne from and contributing to the fortifying of one's inner life from the violent and insidious mandates of a Jim Crow nation. This ethic of nonviolence in the Black freedom movement flowed in part from Howard Thurman's reconciling of the "genius" of pacifism with the reality of Black life in America. It was an ethic that was insistent on the full and free expression of all humans, grounded in the idea that all people possessed boundless creative potential, and that this birthright must not be interfered with by any social system of race or caste. But the ethic of nonviolence was also about seeking truth and understanding in the world, grappling with the nature of the world as it was, who we are in this world, and how the world might be differently. More than any other figure, Lawson brought this Gandhian perspective to the forefront of nonviolent direct-action politics in the Black freedom movement.

Lawson drew on ancient Jain ideas central to Gandhi's own nonviolence, but he taught these ideas to his Black students as an "indigenous" method of religious being by grounding these lessons in stories from the Bible and a diverse set of analogs from across the human past. For Lawson, nonviolent direct action was a political force that could challenge Jim Crow—but it was also one that had the additional benefits of producing internal security and creating a deeper understanding of who we are both as individuals and as a society. The most powerful tactical expression of this nonviolent approach was borne from the crucible of the Black experience in the United States: the sit-in, a direct-action tactic most commonly practiced in the labor movement before the 1950s, became the tactic of choice for Black Americans because it was an egalitarian assertion of the right to be—fully and freely, creatively and publicly—in spaces long preserved for whites by violence. The sit-in became a nonviolent direct-action technique that was ethical, egalitarian, and effective, a freedom practice that often was the introduction for many to a lifelong struggle for justice.

Pauli Murray and Bayard Rustin had both done essential work to advance nonviolent direct action as a strategy for political success in the struggle against Jim Crow. Neither had the privileges or the social access afforded the straight male legal leadership of the movement. So instead of a primary focus on litigation, Murray and Rustin advanced insurgent political tactics instead. In so doing, they projected a vision of personal and collective freedom perhaps deeper than anything that could be accomplished through changes to the law alone.[6] Lawson was deeply aware of their work to advance nonviolent direct action, as well as that of A. Philip Randolph, A. J. Muste, and the others that preceded him in the effort to elevate nonviolent direct action as a freedom practice in the struggle against Jim Crow.

At a key moment in the emerging Black freedom movement, working within the same networks his predecessors had established—white pacifist communities, Black student groups, church-based entities, and organized labor affiliates—Lawson added a compelling philosophical dimension to the nonviolent struggle against Jim Crow. He taught that when practiced collectively, nonviolent direct action could transform the structure of America's racial ethics. Describing nonviolence as a form of power uncommon to American politics, neither violence nor law, and as a method rarely tried in serious violent conflicts throughout the nation's history, Lawson argued that white supremacy turned Black people into subjects and required them to manipulate their behavior under the constant threat of violence. He suggested that the choice to be—fully and freely—was a powerful personal expression of freedom with deep political implications for the racial politics of the nation. The strategic refusal to sit at a Jim Crow counter or use a Jim Crow toilet could be a powerful act of political insurgency when practiced collectively, a freedom practice wherein Black Americans courageously asserted their humanity and forcefully challenged the Black dehumanization so central to the nation's social and political life. And in the burgeoning age of television, these assertions of Black humanity took on new power as the clash of Black humanity against white violence was beamed into individual homes via television sets across the nation. A society long built around the conflicting ideals of freedom for all and Black dehumanization was forced to confront the dissonant reality of its own brutality.

Lawson understood that the choice to be fully and freely in segregated public spaces was a risky one for his students, one that often provoked violence. But he convinced them to take risky action by framing nonviolence as an ethical form of ancient religious power. He trained an influential cohort of young Black students to use this ethical politics, demonstrating that mercy, kindness, and forgiveness in the face of white violence was a way of practicing the highest ideals of their religion—just as Jesus did—a practice that exposed as immoral the violence long used to intimidate, marginalize, and dehumanize African Americans. Lawson's teachings proved deeply appealing to a generation of students eager to forcefully challenge Jim Crow, a cohort of students in search of a revolutionary form of political power amid near complete electoral disenfranchisement. Their collective nonviolent witness turned the violence long used by whites to enforce Jim Crow in on itself, exposing the nation's immorality through acts of forgiveness, kindness, and mercy and, in the process, transforming both themselves and the United States.[7]

Preparing the Soil: Nonviolence Workshops and White Violence in the U.S. South

Lawson was hired as the Fellowship of Reconciliation's first southern secretary in the late 1950s to build on the national work of organizing nonviolence workshops and action projects in local communities across the nation. Rustin continued organizing in the years before Lawson was hired by the FOR, and he was joined in this effort by Congress of Racial Equality (CORE) cofounder George Houser, a Methodist minister who—like Rustin—refused to fight in the Second World War and served a year in jail. The two led a weeklong institute on race relations in Toledo, Ohio, in late February 1947 that was sponsored by Toledo's First Baptist Church and the YMCA. The institute included action projects each day at 2:30 P.M. and 8:00 P.M. in addition to study groups, banquets, and interracial worship services.

In their 1947 report to the FOR national council, Houser and Rustin wrote, "Our specific job within the area of race relations is to emphasize the importance of the nonviolent approach in both attitude and action. Therefore in everything which we have done . . . our unique contribution has been considered to the nonviolent emphasis." They noted that six interracial nonviolence institutes had been held since November 1946, as well as the "Journey of Reconciliation," which led to the arrests of twelve men in six cities across North Carolina. Rustin and Houser continued: "The service which has been rendered through the Institute and Workshops should be expanded. It is our belief that both a valuable educational and an action job can be done through these instrumentalities."[8]

The FOR heeded their counsel and expanded its workshops in the mold of the 1947 D.C. nonviolence institute, making future institutes a full month in duration. The FOR hosted two monthlong interracial workshops in July 1948, one in Washington, D.C., and one in Southern California, stating that "these projects will combine an interracial non-violent action program of combatting discrimination in the communities where they are located with a studies program on both the race problem and methods for successfully meeting it." Participants also participated in the "experience of [interracial] group living and fellowship." Emphasizing "the Negro's struggle for freedom and the part in it played by nonviolence" as central to the institute's mission, FOR and CORE continued these monthlong programs the following year. They announced a "race relations institute on action techniques" in Cambridge, Massachusetts, for May 1949, and in a bulletin published for participants the FOR cited its 1918 founding charter to battle racial violence and discrimination.[9] "The F.O.R., founded during the First World War," the bulletin read, "bands together those who feel that division in human society can be bridged by reconciliatory methods and yet without appeasement, and who feel that war is utterly the wrong way to attempt solutions to the problems that exist. FOR members are working to eliminate the causes of war found in such problems as racial discrimination."[10]

By the end of 1949, the FOR had designated a "racial-industrial department" and appointed Houser and Rustin as co-secretaries. Rustin, who had organized nonviolence institutes for the better part of the last decade, noted the need for "more Negroes" in the workshops and institutes, calling for "at least 1/3 the total number of members." While the FOR still struggled to organize in the grassroots of the Black community, those who did attend the interracial institutes noted a positive impact. One person wrote, "I learned and was convinced of the effectiveness of nonviolent direct action techniques," highlighting "the feeling one acquires" through such action programs as a result of deploying "the proper method of attacking a discrimination situation." This person concluded, "I think the most of what I learned was by actually doing, which of course is the best way, and you don't forget very quickly."[11]

In July 1951, the FOR began to strategically push a bit farther south with its workshops, hosting its now-typical summertime interracial workshop in D.C. but extending also to St. Louis. "Washington and St. Louis," the bulletin proclaimed, "the capital of our nation and one of our biggest industrial centers, both at the gateway to southern jimcrow country. What more strategic localities could be chosen for an interracial nonviolent action program of combatting discrimination?" The D.C. workshops continued through 1953 and 1954 as the FOR prepared to spend more time and resources to advance nonviolent direct-action trainings in local communities across the South. Looking back at the FOR's efforts across the decade in a 1959 report, the FOR's national field secretary Glenn Smiley wrote, "Race relations continue to occupy a substantial portion of the energies of the F.O.R., nationally, regionally, and locally." In particular, he noted, "the National Field Secretary has spent considerable time in the South and in the fall and early winter at institutes and workshops on nonviolence in Montgomery, Birmingham and elsewhere. The regional offices have made an emphasis in almost all cases. This is especially true with regard to Jim Lawson, who continues to travel half time for the F.O.R. out of Nashville, Tenn."[12]

Lawson's success in cultivating interest in and experience with nonviolent direct action in the late 1950s came against a backdrop of routine and barbaric violence meted out against Black women, men, and children in the decades since Reconstruction.[13] At least 4,400 Black Americans were lynched between 1877 and 1945, and more than half of these lynchings are estimated to have taken place in the South between 1885 and 1903. The historian Andrew Zimmerman writes that such white violence took place with stunning regularity: "White mobs, often with the consent of police and other local authorities, lynched two or three black southerners every *week* in the period between 1890–1917."[14] The horrific reality of racial terror was among the most routinely deployed forms of social control utilized to keep Black people politically disenfranchised, tied to the land, and socially segregated in the decades following Reconstruction.[15] As the historian and sociologist Charles Payne sardonically assessed, when it came to such violence "the point was there didn't have to be a point; Black life could be snuffed out on a whim, you could be killed because some ignorant white man didn't like the color of your shirt or the way you drove a wagon."[16] Indeed, the ever-present possibility of white violence in the late nineteenth and early twentieth centuries had the effect of creating an atmosphere of constant intimidation for perceived Black transgressions of the racial order.

Despite decades of effort, the United States failed to pass federal legislation that would explicitly end lynching and white violence in the United States.[17] But law was far from the most common arena of resistance to white supremacy for most Black Americans, even amid the concerted push among the legal flank of the civil rights establishment to create a better social order through court challenges. Individual acts of noncooperation, organized acts of collective direct action, and armed resistance to white violence were routine among Black people throughout the late nineteenth and early twentieth centuries. And among Black religious people, the search for an ethical politics of defense and freedom led, as early 1919, to India. Two years after spectacle lynching reached its height in the Red Summer of 1919, the African Methodist Episcopal minister Reverdy C. Ransom wrote an article about an "Indian Messiah and Saint" in the *A.M.E Church Review*. Ransom suggested that the skinny leader in colonized India might deliver his shackled nation from British imperial rule "through the peaceful method of non-cooperation."[18] Ransom called this "awakening of Asia . . . one of the great historic movements of our time," noting the Indian struggle "deserves the sympathetic understanding of every man who waits for a new birth of freedom in every land."[19]

Ransom was one among many in a generation of Black religious intellectuals looking to Mohandas Karamchand Gandhi for an ethical form of political resistance to white political rule. The School of Religion at Howard University became a critical site for these religious intellectuals to work out this ethical methodology for challenging Jim Crow.[20] Foremost among this group was Howard Thurman, a professor of religion and dean of Rankin Chapel, who arrived at Howard in 1932. Thurman and his wife, Sue Bailey Thurman, led more than a dozen associates to India on a "Pilgrimage of Friendship" in 1935 with the support of the Federation of Student Christian Movements, and the 1935 delegation marked the first of many trips to India by a cadre of African American religious leaders in the years before the civil rights movement: Benjamin Mays, Mordecai Johnson, and William Stuart Nelson—all Thurman's colleagues at Howard—traveled to India in the years that followed.[21]

On his 1935 trip, Thurman lectured and learned at more than forty institutions across the South Asian subcontinent over two months. On Thurman's first night in India, the chairman of the Law Club at the Law College of Ceylon interrogated Thurman about the long history of racial violence in the United States. His query was pointed: How could Thurman call himself a Christian when it was Christians who sold Black people into slavery and sought to preserve the "peculiar institution" through a bloody civil war? The young man asked the Baptist minister Thurman, "How can you account for yourself being in this unfortunate and humiliating position?" Thurman responded, "My judgment about slavery and racial prejudice relative to Christianity is far more devastating than yours could ever be.... From my investigation and study, the religion of Jesus projected a creative solution to the pressing problem of survival for the minority of which He was a part in the Greco Roman world. When Christianity became an imperial and world religion, it marched under banners other than that of the teacher and prophet of Galilee."[22]

Thurman's response flowed from ideas he worked out in detail in his 1935 article "Good News for the Underprivileged," ideas he worked through with his student James Russell Brown. There is a difference, Thurman argued, between the "Religion of Jesus" and "American Christianity." This distinction became the hallmark of his 1949 book *Jesus and the Disinherited*, which proved deeply influential to generations of advocates of nonviolence. Thurman described Jesus "as a religious subject rather than religious object."[23] He wrote of the historical Jesus, the poor Jew living in a region recently annexed by Syria for Roman rule, and suggested—as his student James Russell Brown had done years before—that Jesus' Jewishness made him a target of the powerful Roman military state, which sought to impose its own religion on local people. In this context, the Jewish carpenter became an enemy of the state, provoking its violent legal power. The religion of Jesus, Thurman argued, the response of Jesus to this dehumanizing historical context, contained within it creative methodologies for responding to violent and oppressive state forces.[24]

In *Jesus and the Disinherited*, Thurman likened Jesus' political environment to the one facing Black Americans in modern America, arguing that in the responses of Jesus we can see both politically insurgent and spiritually fortifying practices. Both Black Americans and first-century Jews faced "the problem of creative survival" as a persecuted minority with no protection from violence—whether state sanctioned or extralegal—and were forced to think creatively about how their bodies and traditions might endure. Violence was futile, and flight was impossible. As in Rome, the United States used a host of methods to exercise control over its population: taxation and registration, regulation of land ownership, limited access to education, and control over labor. But what lay behind all of these was violence. In such a climate of "deep insecurity," and "faced with so narrow a margin of civil guarantees," Jesus belonged to the disinherited class—a class forced "to find some other basis upon which to establish a sense of well-being."[25]

Jesus and the disinherited to whom he spoke were scorned and threatened with no protection from the state. Security and power must come from somewhere else.[26] Thurman argued that violence could not be that source of security for Jesus and the disinherited, primarily because a minority was unlikely to successfully overpower the state using violence. But Thurman went further in his critique of violence, arguing that violence would not alter the core of mistrust borne from separation, the crux of oppressive human relations. Constant group separation bred ignorance and distrust, which fortified hatred of the other and guaranteed what Thurman called a "final isolation from one's fellow." This isolation became the predicate to do violence.

But Thurman also argued that the alienation from the other borne of hatred and fear had the caustic effect of obliterating the "creative residue" needed to give rise to "great ideas," creative ideas that might bring human beings closer together and transform the violence, fear, and hatred at the heart of oppressive social orders.[27] Fr Thurman, violence limited creative thinking about how to effectively transform human relationships, and for those with their backs against the wall, survival of their bodies and religious traditions depended not on violence or flight but on a creative response. A creative response depended on courage, on the mastering of fear, and that required individuals to act from a deep sense of internal security.[28]

The twin influences of Gandhi and Thurman were critical to the development of James Lawson's political philosophy of religious nonviolence, which he taught to hundreds of students across the South and Midwest in the two years prior to the sit-in revolution of 1960. In the interwar period, Gandhi became an important example for religious Black Americans seeking a solution to the problem of creative survival for the disinherited, and his allure came, in part, from his Christ-like asceticism and, perhaps most importantly, his identity as a nonwhite person developing an ethical politics that effectively challenged white imperial power.[29] Jesus of Nazareth was an inspiration for Gandhi's religious activism. Gandhi wrote that in the life and teachings of the Jewish Jesus was the Hindu principle of *ahimsā*—literally "no violence"—and he interpreted Jesus' counsel in Matthew 5:40, "If any man take away thy coat, let him have thy cloak also," as an illustration of how one might actively and nonviolently "disarm" an aggressor by giving "your opponent all in the place of just what he needs."[30] Jesus' parable resembled for Gandhi the Hindu practice of *dharna*, an action by which a person attempts to shame a debtor by sitting nearly naked on his stoop. Both acts were intended to have "a wholesome effect upon evildoers," and Gandhi interpreted the life of Jesus as "a picturesque" and "telling" example of "the great non-violent doctrine of non-cooperation."[31]

Both Gandhi and Howard Thurman saw in the life of Jesus an example of creative ethical being that posed a powerful challenge to state power.

Each saw in Jesus a life lived without violence, one that transformed history through nonviolence in response to state violence. It was a life that drew its strength from a relationship with God rather than the diminution of other people or creatures. In Jesus, Thurman and Gandhi saw a way of being that proved more powerful than physical violence. And in claiming the story of Jesus central to his nonviolent politics, Gandhi was cemented alongside Jesus of Nazareth as a model for Black religious activists searching for an insurgent and ethical force in the fight against Jim Crow.[32] But Gandhian ideas required a critical process of translation for importation to the United States, and James M. Lawson Jr. became this key translator in a critical moment of the Black freedom struggle.

"A Complete Denial of the Meaning of Freedom"

From major local campaigns in Nashville and Memphis to large-scale Southern Christian Leadership Conference campaigns in Birmingham and Selma, James M. Lawson Jr. indelibly influenced the politics of the 1960s Black freedom movement.[33] But before these moments of high drama in the peak years of the movement, Lawson traveled across the South and Midwest teaching nonviolence as a politics of being, working through ideas and tactics in dozens of communities with hundreds of local people.[34] Building on the work of Rustin and Houser, he used nonviolence workshops to teach students in colleges and churches across the Midwest and South how Gandhian politics and what Thurman called the "psychology of Jesus" might become methods for transforming the ethical infrastructure of America's Jim Crow politics. Often a footnote to larger stories of Black resistance, Lawson was in fact the most important figure in the development and diffusion of nonviolent direct action in the Black freedom movement in the years immediately before and after the sit-in revolution of 1960. A major reason for his impact was the depth and strength of his philosophy of nonviolence.[35]

From an early age, Lawson was taught by his parents that he would be forced to choose how to respond to white supremacy and racism in the United States. He grew up on heroic stories of his great-grandparents' flight from slavery in the South, and Lawson's father—a Canadian-born African Methodist Episcopal Zion preacher—continued the tradition of resistance to white supremacy by founding an NAACP chapter in every town he pastored. The Rev. James M. Lawson Sr. encouraged his son Jimmy to fight, to stand up for himself, and to never back down if challenged. The elder Lawson carried a .38-caliber pistol on his hip and made clear he would not acquiesce if challenged. Lawson's mother, Philane May Cover Lawson, was born in St. Anne's Parish, Jamaica, and migrated to the United States as a teenager. She proved to be the counterballast to her husband. She believed Christian love prohibited physical and verbal violence, and when Jimmy smacked a white child in elementary school after being called a "nigger," his mother asked him, "Jimmy, what good did that do?" Lawson remembers it this way: "She went on talking quietly in that vein, among other things mentioning the love of God, the love in our family, Jesus and our commitment as Christian people. In the process of this conversation, I remember only the two sentences: 'Jimmy, what good did that do?' and 'Jimmy, there must be a better way.'" Lawson called this "a numinous experience," the moment his life became an "experiment with finding the better way."[36]

In the fall of 1947, as a first-semester student at Baldwin Wallace College in Ohio, Lawson heard FOR executive secretary A. J. Muste lecture on the history of pacifism and nonviolence. Muste introduced the nineteen-year-old Lawson to Reinhold Niebuhr, John Paul Sartre, Leo Tolstoy, and Mohandas Gandhi. Lawson was inspired by these examples of the "other way" to engage in political resistance at the advent of his college career, and he dedicated much of his college coursework to understanding the long global history of noncooperation and nonviolent action. Muste, known nationally as "America's number one pacifist" in the 1940s, was a Dutch-born immigrant who cofounded the American affiliate of the FOR with sixty-seven other U.S. pacifists in 1916.[37]

Radicalized by the Lawrence Textile Strike of 1919, Muste consistently positioned himself to the left of the American Federation of Labor (AFL) throughout the 1920s. Like his ministerial counterpart Reinhold Niebuhr, Muste was active with the FOR throughout the 1920s and, like Niebuhr, ultimately grew frustrated with Christian passivity in the face of state violence against workers in the 1930s.[38] Muste became a follower of Trotsky during the Popular Front era, but unlike Niebuhr he did not ultimately abandon his pacifist principles for a "just war theory." Instead, on the doorstep of the Second World War, Muste devoted himself to advancing "non-violence in an aggressive world."[39] He became FOR's executive secretary in the 1940s, and with Howard Thurman on his executive council, Muste financially supported the formation of the Congress of Racial Equality (CORE) in 1942 and actively counseled CORE students as they experimented with the sit-in as a method of nonviolent social change. The FOR was at the leading edge of nonviolent theory and practice in this 1940s period, with Bayard Rustin and CORE cofounder James Farmer working as the FOR staff members to nurture the rise of nonviolent leadership in the struggle against Jim Crow.[40]

Muste's 1947 talk at Baldwin Wallace College tapped into Lawson's childhood commitment to avoid violence, yet militantly resist oppression, in a moment of stern personal testing.[41] At the end of his senior year in college, Lawson refused to register for the draft. He consulted with Muste, as Bayard Rustin had done before him during the Second World War, before sending back all his federal draft materials with a letter explaining why he could not cooperate. "I felt that the free man must maintain his right to determine those laws that are absolutely contrary to the meaning of freedom and justice," Lawson recalled, concluding that both conscription laws and segregation laws were "a complete denial of the meaning of freedom."[42]

Lawson's parents had taught him that he would have to decide how he would respond to the social evil of segregation, and Lawson carried the lesson forward to the unjust law of conscription. On 25 April 1951, just weeks before he was to receive his degree from Baldwin Wallace College, Lawson was sentenced to three years in a federal prison for violating the Conscription Act of 1947.[43] Muste wrote to Lawson after he returned his draft card, saying, "I pray that God will give you grace and strength, and I am grateful to you for your prayers for myself and the other members of the FOR staff."[44] Lawson spent fourteen months in two federal penitentiaries, serving a partial sentence before being paroled and traveling to Nagpur, India, to coach sports and mentor youth at Hislop College.[45] In 1952, Muste described Lawson as "one of our most dedicated and active young FOR members. . . . Anything that can be done to enable him to reach an understanding of the problems of India, to meet those who are active in the Gandhian movement, etc., will constitute a contribution to the cause of peace in the United States."[46]

While in India, Lawson read about the Montgomery Bus Boycott on the front page of the *Nagpur Times*. He did "some jumping up and dancing and shouting" as he believed the seeds of a nonviolent movement were finally taking root in the United States.[47] When he returned to the United States in the fall of 1956, he enrolled at the Oberlin School of Theology, where less than a month into his studies he met Martin Luther King Jr. The two men—King twenty-six and Lawson twenty-seven—sat beside each other at dinner after King's speech, and as Vincent Harding wrote, "When King realized that Lawson had spent three years in India absorbing the teachings of the Mahatma, King knew that he had met his soul brother."[48] Lawson believed that nonviolence had failed "to impress the Negro" until the Montgomery Bus Boycott of 1955, and he saw in King a dedicated student and spokesperson for religious nonviolence.[49] Lawson called Montgomery "the cauldron" within which Gandhian politics and the Black Christian tradition "conjoined to make nonviolence a serious alternative for the Negro."[50] Most importantly, Lawson believed the bus boycott made it much harder for African Americans who, in the past, dismissed nonviolence. Black Americans now had a successful example of a nonviolent campaign and a once-in-a-generation spokesperson for this political philosophy of religious nonviolence.

After a decade of study and experimentation, Lawson decided he was ready to focus full time on applying nonviolence to the problem of white supremacy in the South. In January 1958, after some urging from King, Lawson moved to Nashville and began working for the Fellowship of Reconciliation. As the FOR's southern secretary, a title earlier held by Howard Kester, Lawson reported to the FOR's national field secretary, Glenn Smiley, a figure who, alongside Bayard Rustin, was critical in convincing King to commit to nonviolent action in the Montgomery Bus Boycott.[51] Lawson transferred to Vanderbilt Divinity School in 1958 and began to deepen his inquiry into religious nonviolence. The "concrete and persistent" role of the "Christian faith remains the internal emancipation of the Negro," he wrote during this period, citing A. Philip Randolph and Rustin as invaluable to the advancement of nonviolence in the United States. Rustin, in particular, he described as "the foremost teacher and practitioner of nonviolence," but he contended that Rustin and Randolph's work had a "limited effect" for a host of reasons.[52]

First, Lawson believed there had not been enough attention to disseminating nonviolence widely through workshops and teachings specifically to Black people, arguing that where such workshops had been undertaken the efforts had been sporadic and that ultimately "the Negro was generally untouched by them." Lawson's sentiment was largely confirmed by Houser and Rustin's 1949 report on FOR's nonviolence workshops throughout the 1940s: the FOR struggled mightily to organize in the grassroots of the Black community. Lawson also criticized high profile African American leaders without naming names, arguing that many were "by and large uninterested" in nonviolence because most were not interested in transforming power structures so much as preserving the limited power they maintained within those existing structures. Lawson's observation seemed to align with the experiences of Pauli Murray in the 1940s, whose efforts to advance nonviolent direct action were intended to widen participation in the freedom movement beyond a select few powerful Black attorneys. Lawson believed that by and large, many Black leaders rejected nonviolence because of its uniquely revolutionary character—the idea that it represented not an effort to gain power within existing structures like the law but that it was a new kind of power which represented a threat to the lawyers and established ministers at the very top of Black economic and political life.[53] These views led Lawson into high profile conflicts with national leaders in well-established organizations like the NAACP throughout the 1960s.

But Lawson articulated a vision of nonviolence and direct action that proved persuasive, particularly for Black religious students. He became the first figure to systemically share this vision in communities across the South. "Non-violence is first a way of life," he argued, "a religious faith, steeped in the religious traditions of the world."[54] Gandhi offered a model of "moral resistance," he taught, and pacifists had produced "reams of evidence that a largely theoretical approach had actual technical content." But Lawson pointed to the New Testament as "its own matrix for nonviolence," cautioning against the tendency to "stress" dependency on Gandhi in a search for nonviolent analogs to the Black freedom movement.[55] Lawson shared Gandhi's own view that all the "great living religions" counseled a life of nonviolence in order to know God, and like Gandhi, Lawson used the Hindu notion of *ahimsā*—doing no violence as a way of being the world—in arguing that prohibitions against violence were endemic to major religious philosophies in Asia: Taoism, Mohism, Buddhism, and Sufi mysticism.[56] In an unpublished manuscript on nonviolence Lawson wrote in the late 1950s, he described the Hindu concept of truth—Gandhi's *satya*—in this way: "Truth [is] transcendency [sic] which beckons man beyond himself to a truthful self-understanding."[57] Knowing oneself depended on knowing others, Lawson argued, and this teaching precluded doing violence against another.

Lawson's understanding of how to pursue *satya* is akin to what religious scholar Jeffery Long calls the "Jain path" to spiritual knowledge. In Gandhi's life, Lawson saw a way of being geared toward understanding truth. Gandhi was a Vaisnava Hindu who wholly embraced the theistic model of Hinduism throughout his entire life, but in his late teens and early twenties Gandhi became convinced that different religions offered equally significant—though distinct—ways of knowing truth and connecting with God. "Religions are different roads converging upon the same point," Gandhi argued. "What does it matter that we take different roads so long as we reach the same goal?"[58] Subscribing to the Hindu notion of *advaita*, literally "not two" in Sanskrit, Gandhi came to believe that religious ways of knowing are bound together, even in their distinctions, because all human understanding flows from the distinctly human capacity to be, fully and freely.

This principle of nonduality at the level of being explains why *ahimsā*, or "nonviolence," was so important to Gandhi.[59]

Ahimsā is literally translated as the opposite of striking or doing harm, and Gandhi described this ancient principle as "the basis of the search for truth." "I am realizing every day," he wrote, "that the search is vain unless it is founded on ahimsā as the basis."[60] Gandhi reasoned it this way: "It is quite proper to resist and attack a system, but to resist and attack its author is tantamount to resisting and attacking oneself. For we are all tarred with the same brush, and are children of one and the same Creator, and as such the divine powers within us are infinite. To slight a single human being is to slight those divine powers, and thus to harm not only that being but with him the whole world."[61]

Lawson described this idea of unity at the level of being as part of the core Christian mandate to do no violence, but he went a step further in arguing that it required active love toward one another. Lawson took this critical next step of grounding a religious teaching in action by showing his students that living this way of *ahimsā* had the potential to transform unjust social systems. He was very careful not to describe nonviolence as simply "the Gandhian method," a political technique to be used and adopted and then later discarded. It was, rather, a way of being that leads to knowledge of oneself and the world around us—a way of moving through the world which strengthens one's bond with God.[62] Echoing Howard Thurman, Lawson argued that nonviolence was a powerful religious discipline that could undo "both the inferiority complex of the Negro and the superiority complex of the white," not simply "a technique" that gave Black people an edge within existing systems of social power.[63] He believed that *ahimsā* was the path to a "new creation," a new truth about the world ushered in by "the new heart and spirit" of nonviolent practitioners—that came through their way of being in the world.[64]

Lawson believed that a "Christian revolutionary" sect practicing nonviolence would lead to a complete "restructuring" of American society.[65] Distinguishing this nonviolent Christian revolution from what he called "counterfeit revolutions," Lawson singled out the Bolsheviks of 1917 in arguing that they sought only to "manipulate social machinery" and "eliminate former injustices to the extent of eliminating persons." Likewise, the American, French, and Cuban revolutions—in fact any revolution achieved through violence—were counterfeit to Lawson because they were "a shortcut to complex problems." Lawson emphasized that such political revolutions failed to build social and political structures that were humane and inclusive of all peoples. Like legal decisions, such "counterfeit revolutions" did little to address the roots of injustice, what Lawson described as "the moral and spiritual sources of evil" in a society.[66]

By contrast, a nonviolent revolution, a "real and total revolution," would "transform human life in both private and public forms." Lawson believed that *people* must be changed for a culture or society to be changed, and only when people act differently might society itself be "turned upside down." A nonviolent revolution in the United States, Lawson wrote, "will be measured not so much by its ability to manipulate the machinery of society or push human beings about; but by its capacity to transform the internality of human life in such a fashion that assumptions and methods of the social order are altered as well."[67] Lawson envisioned a new kind of power in the United States. It was not a power of law or violence, but an ethical power that revolutionized social structures because the originators of these social structures—individuals—were themselves transformed and oriented toward justice and care for all. They were able to see with new eyes, the core notion at the heart of the idea of "repentance." It was this message that Lawson carried to dozens of Black Christian churches and colleges in the late 1950s, teaching a nonviolent politics capable of generating real political power for a population locked out of electoral politics in the United States.[68]

A recurring theme in the history of how nonviolence and nonviolent direct action evolved in the twentieth century is the limit of the law in bringing durable change to Black life in America. Lawson's views reflect this sharp critique of law as a process for lasting social transformation in the United States. While a series of legal shifts seemed to remove chinks from the armor of Jim Crow, Lawson suggested that the limits of legal change for Black people in America were real and acute.[69] Law had proven to be a slow and limited method of ending discrimination, and rigid segregation in schools remained a fact of life despite the 1954 *Brown* decision. The widely publicized lynching of Emmett Till in 1954 was a reminder that abrupt, lethal, and unchecked white violence against Black people remained a constant threat in the United States. The Montgomery Bus Boycott, a strong local movement defined by a nonviolent ethic, resulted in yet another largely unenforced Supreme Court decision and sowed doubt about the NAACP's strategy of litigation to achieve equality. Despite the *Smith v. Allwright* (1944) decision outlawing the white primary, the *Shelley v. Kramer* (1948) decision striking down racially restrictive housing covenants, and both the *Brown* (1954) and *Browder* (1956) decisions issuing blows to Jim Crow segregation, white supremacists continued to evade the law, engage in campaigns of massive resistance to legal changes, and use violence to control

Black labor and politics. Lawson argued, controversially, that only in going "beyond the law" to confront "the public mind with the necessity" of ending Jim Crow would genuine progress be possible.[70]

Changing laws was, for Lawson, a secondary project to the creation of a new ethic in the United States. "We do not have the atmosphere in which the constitutional or democratic framework has relevancy," Lawson told a group of students at Penn State in 1960.[71] Debated by elite actors in insulated courtrooms, the law was not for Lawson the democratic form of change for disenfranchised Black Americans that nonviolence was. Echoing Pauli Murray, Lawson suggested that nonviolence is a more effective and egalitarian form of engagement because it is "involving many, encountering all."[72] Nonviolence could bring about the "radical reversal of perspective" needed to confront and transform the ethical rot of white supremacy at the core of much legislation in the United States.[73] Lawson described this perspective as repentance, *metanoia* in the biblical Greek, which means to see with new eyes, and he called the "present openness" to the politics of nonviolence he encountered as he traveled across the South in the late 1950s as borne, in part, from the seemingly slow progress of legal reform compared with the relatively rapid success of nationalist revolutionary movements in nonwhite nations—particularly across the African continent.[74]

In his first full year of work as a FOR field secretary, Lawson made trips to colleges and churches in every former Confederate state but Florida.[75] In his first three months, he traveled through Mississippi, Kentucky, West Virginia, North Carolina, Maryland, Arkansas, and Ohio.[76] A hunger for different models of social change was confirmed on his first trip to Memphis in early 1958. Meeting with a group of "highly respected" leaders in the Black community, Lawson learned that Church of God in Christ founder Charles H. Mason had had a cross burned in his front yard, that his church sanctuary had been torched, and that his newly built home had also been set to flame. Hollis Price of LeMoyne College in Memphis told Lawson that such incidents indicated the need to "change the entire nature of" activism in the city to focus on "stiffening the will to resist evil" and "effectively overcoming fear."[77] Racial terror in Memphis led Price to suggest "a different and newly oriented leadership" for challenging white supremacy.[78]

By the spring of 1958, sensing weariness in the young seminarian, FOR Secretary Glenn Smiley told Lawson, "We feel a great confidence in your work in the South," urging him to keep up his feverish schedule in the faith that it would pay off.[79] But Lawson wasn't so sure. He reported to Smiley that his trip through Virginia in early May 1958 was vastly underwhelming, noting

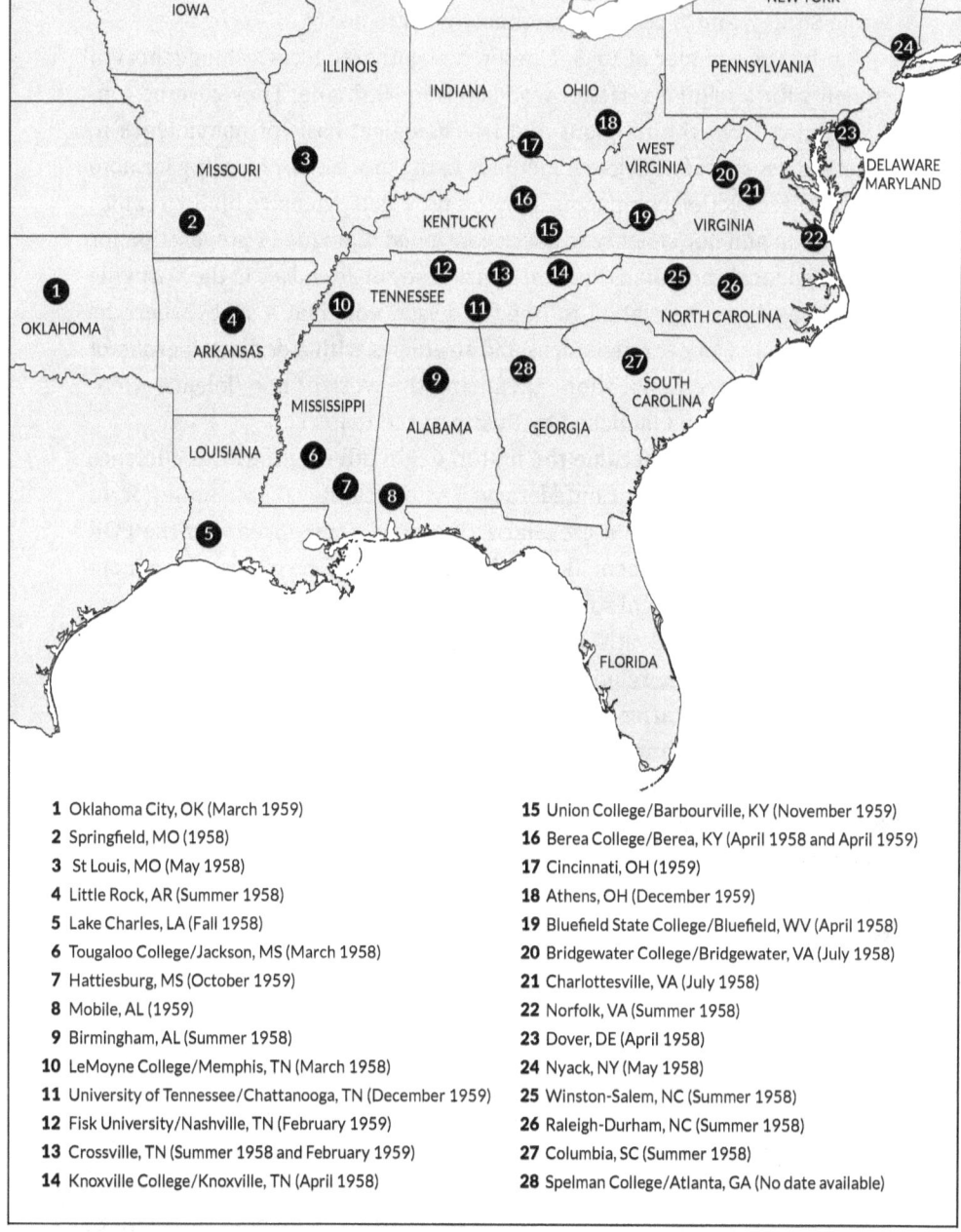

1 Oklahoma City, OK (March 1959)
2 Springfield, MO (1958)
3 St Louis, MO (May 1958)
4 Little Rock, AR (Summer 1958)
5 Lake Charles, LA (Fall 1958)
6 Tougaloo College/Jackson, MS (March 1958)
7 Hattiesburg, MS (October 1959)
8 Mobile, AL (1959)
9 Birmingham, AL (Summer 1958)
10 LeMoyne College/Memphis, TN (March 1958)
11 University of Tennessee/Chattanooga, TN (December 1959)
12 Fisk University/Nashville, TN (February 1959)
13 Crossville, TN (Summer 1958 and February 1959)
14 Knoxville College/Knoxville, TN (April 1958)
15 Union College/Barbourville, KY (November 1959)
16 Berea College/Berea, KY (April 1958 and April 1959)
17 Cincinnati, OH (1959)
18 Athens, OH (December 1959)
19 Bluefield State College/Bluefield, WV (April 1958)
20 Bridgewater College/Bridgewater, VA (July 1958)
21 Charlottesville, VA (July 1958)
22 Norfolk, VA (Summer 1958)
23 Dover, DE (April 1958)
24 Nyack, NY (May 1958)
25 Winston-Salem, NC (Summer 1958)
26 Raleigh-Durham, NC (Summer 1958)
27 Columbia, SC (Summer 1958)
28 Spelman College/Atlanta, GA (No date available)

This map documents James M. Lawson Jr.'s travel itinerary in 1958 and 1959 as the Fellowship of Reconciliation's southern secretary. Lawson taught workshops on nonviolence and offered talks, primarily to Black youth at colleges across the South, Midwest, and East Coast in the months leading up to the sit-down revolution of 1960.

that Richmond had "fallen flat." "The Nashville group still lags behind," he wrote Smiley, and "I really do not know what to do."[80]

But by the summer of 1958, Lawson had gathered a consistent cohort of students for a regular series of workshops in Nashville. They covered topics ranging from the religious and psychological basis of nonviolence to practical aspects of nonviolent methods to the process of preparing for nonviolent direct-action campaigns. Lawson provided extensive bibliographies on religion and nonviolence to spark continued dialogue in preparation for sustained local campaigns, and the consistency of attendees in the Nashville workshops was a revelation to him.[81] Lawson now had a space where he could actively work through ideas and strategies with a dedicated group of students in a specific location, advancing the work of nonviolence workshops developed and launched by Rustin in the 1940s.

Critically, Lawson became the first to begin offering these nonviolence workshops in the former Confederacy.[82] As he told Rev. S. M. Smiley Jr. of Cory Methodist Church in Cleveland, "I am now convinced that the FOR has been born for a moment like this." His belief that the philosophy of nonviolence and the political strategy of nonviolent direct action could address "the problems of the South" was growing stronger, despite the hardships of travel and the FOR's relatively small southern following. In his first six months as a FOR staffer in the South, Lawson nevertheless became convinced that nonviolent direct action might become the force capable of transforming the ethic of white supremacy in the United States.[83] His faith in direct action came from a belief in the philosophy of nonviolence, that the discipline and practice of nonviolence could transform people, both practitioners and witnesses. For practitioners, taking nonviolent direct action could steel a commitment to justice work. For witnesses, it could lead to seeing themselves as well as demonstrators and the society they belonged to differently.

If nonviolent direct action became an answer to how a Jim Crow society might be transformed, nonviolence became the answer to why some demonstrators pursued change in that way. Combined, the vision was one of how the social structure of the United States might be altered through collective direct action, in local campaigns, one at a time, in cities and towns across the nation. This remaking of the social structure through nonviolent direct action inspired a critical contingent of Black students to move "from idea to action" and build authentic political power in a time of almost complete Black electoral disenfranchisement.[84]

Nonviolence and Black Being

James Lawson taught that the New Testament was a counsel to actively resist violence and oppression through nonviolent means. Echoing the fiery language of Thurman and Rustin before him, Lawson castigated continuing counsels to Christian passivity in the face of racial oppression as "theologies of realism" that made God "anemic" and "defenseless" in the face of great evil.[85] Religious nonviolence "stands opposed" to the "status quo because it stands in dialogue with Holy God who of necessity drives history towards his Kingdom."[86] Lawson rejected interpretations of Jesus' teachings as "impossible ideals," calling instead on Christians to see that Jesus did "on the cross . . . what he says in the Sermon on the Mount"—that is, he showed how strategic personal suffering was a more powerful force than state violence.[87] Jesus' suffering on the cross was "always impinging on man—forcing revolution," Lawson argued, and it is only when human beings match the level of violence at the heart of such evil with their own suffering—as Jesus did—that personal *and* social transformation might occur.[88] Christian love meant suffering, Lawson argued, and to love as Christ loved meant that we "must bear atonement in our very own bodies."[89]

Lawson described such suffering as the "power-force method of salvation," an opportunity to use oneself and one's own body to transform the pain so deeply present in the world.[90] But it was not just suffering for the sake of suffering. Black people had suffered since the forced migration of millions of enslaved people were brought to the Americas across the middle passage. The suffering Lawson located in the story of Jesus was strategic suffering, a taking of violence into one's own body that was designed to challenge the ethics which underpinned the systems, structures, and individuals central to the maintenance of Jim Crow. And such strategic suffering included going to jail. Lawson argued that nonviolence "does not debate" whether to go to jail and stay there, he wrote. "Jail going and staying symbolizes the cross," he told his students, it "represents [the] cheerful suffering" at the "heart" of nonviolence. "Accepting jail sentences tests the fiber of love," which Lawson called "the root law and sustaining spirit of insistent resistance." He explained: "Cut out jail-occupation and you of necessity cut out suffering—cut out suffering and you no longer have [nonviolence]."[91] In Lawson's view, through abandoning the status quo religious politics of comfort to embrace the pain and suffering of Jesus, Christians could recover the cross as good news for the disinherited.[92] The suffering

Rev. James M. Lawson Jr. being arrested in Nashville in March 1960. Photographer unknown. Vanderbilt University Special Collections.

Jesus became a vivid illustration of how the ascetic practice of individual suffering might strategically engage and transform the relatively weak ethical frameworks of a violent Jim Crow society.

Reframing suffering through the lens of Jesus' crucifixion was crucial, as Lawson implored his students to refuse compliance with Jim Crow while understanding that such actions would provoke personal violent attacks on them. But Lawson argued the personal demands that Jim Crow made of both Black and white people were worse. Segregation attempted to condition and warp how one was in the world, what he called "spiritual violence." Howard Thurman described such spiritual violence as a false sense of inflated self-worth for white people and a caustic and dehumanizing diminishment of self-worth among Black people. Refusing to cooperate with such social conditioning was the first step in abandoning these externally imposed but often individually internalized "emotional complexes," which for Black Americans, Thurman argued, often played out as internalized fear, hatred, and inferiority.

Refusing to abide by the demands of segregation was, for Lawson, a refusal to internalize this externally imposed inferiority. "Oppression always requires the participation of the oppressed," his student Diane Nash remembered Lawson teaching, as Lawson taught that one could not "deny consciously" one's inferiority while simultaneously "testifying" to such inferiority in abiding by Jim Crow laws.[93] Simply put, political resistance to Jim Crow required Black Americans to be, fully and freely. "The real violence of segregation," he wrote, is "not the lynching of Emmett Till— but the lynching of genuine selfhood (white and Negro). . . . The Negro has been violent towards himself and passive towards segregation."[94]

The political philosophy of religious nonviolence was grounded in the freedom to be. For Black Americans, in a social structure ordered by white violence, this way of being was one that was both personal and political. It was political because a refusal to obey Jim Crow laws was a public rebuke of Jim Crow in both law and custom. But it was personal because it was a rejection of inferiority and a claim on the human birthright to grow fully into the creative capacity afforded all people. No person or law could make a person inferior, Lawson argued, despite the attempts of people and laws to do just that, because individuals always retained a choice about how to be. When confronted with "colored" restrooms, segregated pools, and divided lunch counters, refusing to use these facilities was an act of political noncooperation—an act of political resistance—but it was also a choice to fortify oneself against the "emotional and spiritual violence" of Jim Crow in claiming the courage to be.[95]

Lawson taught his students that they always had this choice, and thus they always maintained tremendous power: perpetuate white supremacy and one's own inferiority by cooperating with Jim Crow, or claim the freedom to be by refusing to cooperate with segregation. For the Black students Lawson taught, nonviolently placing themselves in spaces restricted for white bodies became a powerful challenge to the Black dehumanization central to U.S. life since the nation's founding. It became an opportunity to develop a "force more powerful" than either law or violence, an effort to demonstrate to the nation the world as it should be.

The response of demonstrators to the white violence these acts of being provoked mattered greatly. Lawson recalled, "Howard Thurman in his 1949 book, *Jesus and the Disinherited*, [described] the gospel as a survival kit for those whose backs are against the wall. You didn't have any control over the hostility, but Jesus taught that you can have control over the way you responded to it. You do not need to respond with an eye for an eye. . . . You could make a decision, you have the power of choice, not to imitate the evil, the hostility. Thurman points out that anger, fear, deception and hatred are the four hounds of hell, often . . . nipping at the heels of the oppressed."[96] Like Thurman, Lawson argued that mastering fear was the first step in refusing to accommodate Jim Crow—a profound act of courage that allowed for creativity rather than reactivity. He taught his students that refusing to bow or accommodate, especially in the face of white violence, was their choice.

But he taught also that taking such courageous action built a well of strength to continually practice mercy, kindness, and forgiveness throughout their lives—acts of compassion that were often impossible to muster without the "creative residue" built up through courageous direct actions. This courage allowed students to act in ways that aligned with the highest ethical mandates of their religious sensibilities. Lawson called this entire process of preparing for and taking nonviolent action as the "serious and concrete alterations of persons in the social order" that was, itself, the remaking of the social order. It was not just the observers of nonviolent direct action who were remade. It was, critically, the demonstrators themselves who were also transformed by taking nonviolent action. And this internal fortification was requisite to maintaining a struggle for justice well beyond an afternoon of action.

In his formulation of nonviolence, James Lawson narrowed the distance between self and structure, between individuals and social systems, as he argued that every Black student had the power to make a change in the United States.[97] "The important thing about nonviolence is not the action taken," he wrote, "but the basic relationship with God out of which or because of which the action is necessary." Lawson taught that all people were beloved of the creator, and restoring this reality required actively loving oneself and loving others. It required taking loving action. "The action itself," he argued, had "little power or no merit or worth; it derives its character from Truth. It has force, power and meaning merely because . . . it is the natural outgrowth of truth seeking." In the late 1950s and early 1960s, Black students demonstrated to the nation the truth that the United States must be better. They also demonstrated to the nation how it could be better through interracial nonviolent direct actions defined by practices of mercy, kindness, and forgiveness.[98]

Lawson's religious philosophy of nonviolence reflects what the Jain scholar Bimal Krishna Matilal calls "the anekānta doctrine," the notion of radical toleration which Jain philosophers transformed from "respect for the life of others (*ahimsā*) . . . into respect for the view[s] of others."[99] *Anekāntavāda*, which translates as "the doctrine of the multifaceted character of reality," suggests that truth is not a single thing but a complicated milieu of many realities, all with distinct sides.[100] This many-sided nature of truth means "that anything may be known from a variety of *nayas*, or perspectives."[101] Gandhi often illustrated the concept of truth's many sides through the parable of the blind men all grasping different parts of an elephant: "The seven blind men who gave seven different descriptions of the elephant were all right from their respective points of view, and wrong from the point of view of one another, and right and wrong from the point of view of the man who knew the elephant. I very much like this doctrine of the manyness of reality."[102] Jain intellectuals joined the doctrine of *anekānta*, which means literally "manifoldness," with *ahimsā*—the way of being nonviolent—to argue that only through nonviolent being might one effectively see the many-sided truth of life.

Black nonviolent demonstrators, in claiming the freedom to be in segregated public spaces, injected a new side of truth into Jim Crow's ideological monopoly: nonviolence established dialogue amid white supremacy's monologue. Demonstrator and aggressor participated together in revealing truth's many sides, a "synthesis of opposites" that was a core concept in Lawson's political philosophy of religious nonviolence. By provoking conflict and engaging its seeming opposite in public spaces, nonviolent direct action enabled both nonviolent practitioner and aggressor to join together in revealing truth. Being nonviolent (*ahimsā*) and following the doctrine of the truth of many sides (*anekāntavāda*) made possible a disposition of nonpossessive and selfless action captured by the Sanskrit terms *aparigraha* and *Nishkam Karma*.

Describing Jesus on the doorstep of his death as exhausted and contemplative, in a state of selflessness before his God, Howard Thurman's student James Russell Brown claimed that in this state Jesus had discovered "a principle by which the highest religious ideal could survive and be utilized by mankind," a breakthrough that served to "open the kingdom of heaven to those who would believe and use this principle."[103] Selfless action was possible only once an exclusive claim to truth was relinquished. Militant nonviolence was predicated on such profound uncertainty—the idea that truth could only by sought through open engagement with the opposite. The principle of nonpossession, *aparigraha*, springs precisely from the nonviolent toleration of many perspectives, as even attackers may hold some important clue about the nature of reality. Nonviolent being allows one to hear and see these clues, which might lead both attacker and the attacked to uncover the ethical depravity of a Jim Crow society, as the truth that all beings are linked at the level of existence is revealed. Such knowledge was, both for James Lawson and Gandhi, the key to lasting social transformation.

Lawson articulated an innovative form of spiritual power grounded in the ancient Jain principles of *ahimsā, anekāntavāda,* and *aparigraha*, and he did so in a compelling fashion for Black students in the United States by linking the doctrine of the cross and moral atonement to nonviolent being in segregated spaces. Because violence had been directed at Black Americans across the United States for centuries, Lawson's ability to carefully distinguish this path of active nonviolence and suffering from the passive acceptance of suffering through white violence was crucial. Lawson believed, as did Thurman before him, that Black Americans stood with their backs against a wall. Segregation forced African Americans to make a choice: obey and participate in segregation, or refuse and resist through being who God made you to be, fully and freely. This is what Lawson's parents taught him as a young man. Doing nothing was not an option. Pointing to Gandhi as a religious analog, and drawing specifically on Jain ideas central to Gandhi's religious politics, Lawson used the example of Jesus to suggest that active nonviolent being could challenge the structure of white supremacy without harming the enforcers of Jim Crow. "We have [a] choice to share [the] load" of pain, Lawson argued, "or increase [the] burden [of pain] on others." Citing Jesus' crucifixion as an example of a world-changing event brought about by radical nonviolent selflessness, Lawson illuminated for his students the possibilities precipitated by this path of nonviolent being.[104]

Lawson's religious theory of social change cannot be disentangled from a set of strategic political calculations. As evidenced in the opening anecdote of this chapter, the politics of being were an effort by demonstrators to use violent encounters as a moment for individual and social transformation. Lawson showed little fear in approaching the man who attacked Solomon Gort, even if he was actually afraid, and Lawson's personal discipline allowed him creative control even with spit on his face. This self-mastery enabled him to take control over a violent encounter, and it was this kind of personal control that Lawson believed groups of demonstrators might possess if they could be nonviolent, together, as wave after wave of demonstrators filled segregated spaces in department stores, public pools, and skating rinks. If in their commitment to be free in public spaces demonstrators responded to violence with acts of mercy, kindness, and forgiveness, they might destabilize the calculation of violence that had been central to the control of Black people—and to U.S. politics—since the nation's founding. They were demonstrating a new political ethic and form of power for the United States.[105]

For Lawson, such strategic considerations about power and politics were inseparable from a personal commitment to being nonviolent. Violating Jim Crow strictures in public places was an intentional confrontation with the deep memory of racial trauma and violence built into the social structure of the United States. In those places where violence had been most intense and the threat of violence most imminent for Black Americans, the politics of nonviolent being seemed to do the most work. Embodied kindness and humility by nonviolent demonstrators was a strategic move to expose the weakness of white violence. As Black people refused to shrink from the fullness of their being in these public spaces, whether covered with spit or cigarette ash or ice cream, their acts of mercy and forgiveness became weapons to be used against a culture of white violence. They forced the United States to confront this hypocritical violence, and in the decades after the Holocaust changed forever the relationship between race and violence this strategy proved powerful. The students' actions became the "moral equivalent of war" Rustin had written about from prison, the "means which are themselves immediate ends" envisioned by the FOR in the early 1920s.

In the late 1950s, Rev. James M. Lawson Jr. articulated these politics of being by drawing on stories of Gandhi and Jesus. Like Rustin and Thurman had done before him, Lawson rejected notions of Christian "nonresistance" and pacifism, but went a step further in articulating how nonviolence could be an active form of ethical politics that simultaneously provided internal protection to oneself while proving "forceful" in challenging the ethics of white supremacy.[106] In the postwar Jim Crow South, the politics of being proved an effective weapon for curbing the gambit of fear central to the American racial order, and groups of students established a political advantage by courageously using nonviolent direct action in communities across the South. Lawson called the sit-in an opportunity to "challenge the life of a nation," a chance to give nonviolence "a hearing in a world of violence."[107] At work in the years between the Montgomery Bus Boycott and the sit-in revolution of 1960, Lawson became the architect for a forceful and novel form of ethical power that would sweep across the nation and transform the politics of race both at home and abroad.

Building a Nonviolent Army

In his 1961 keynote address at the Southern Christian Leadership Conference (SCLC) annual retreat, "The Deep South in Social Revolution," James Lawson forcefully indicted "the American way of life." He charged the United States with affording "structural support" to both segregation and slavery, and he implored the ministers gathered in Nashville to apply "moral, spiritual, and political pressure" to political and social institutions in the United States to make Jim Crow an issue "the president, nation, and world cannot ignore." Lawson called for the organization of "a non-violent army" made up of local cells, and he envisioned dozens of platoons and thousands of volunteers participating regularly in mass meetings, practicing the disciplines of fasting and prayer, and staffing work camps for the continued training of nonviolent soldiers.[108] Like Gandhi's satyagrahis, these nonviolent soldiers would engage in collective acts of civil disobedience across the United States and would go to jail and stay there until their demands were met.[109] "We can stand it in here for as long as you can stand it out there," Lawson often reminded his students.[110] He told the group assembled at Clark Memorial Methodist Church in Nashville that only "healthy minded citizens" prepared to enter prison instead of acquiescing to "forms of political evil" could bring about a "democratic society."[111]

By the time of his 1961 speech, Lawson was a nationally recognized "troublemaker" whose organizing and teaching around nonviolence had led to a major shift in U.S. politics. In February and March 1960, student-led nonviolent sit-ins had been launched against Jim Crow segregation in more than seventy cities across the South. Historian William Chafe called this the "civil rights revolution," a two-month period that permanently changed the trajectory of modern U.S. history. Lawson was ultimately expelled from Vanderbilt University for his role in the Nashville sit-down movement in March—an explusion gained widespread national attention. His old friend A. J. Muste delivered the sad news that SCLC president Martin Luther King Jr. could not offer him a job, despite King's desperate longing to do just that, because NAACP national director Roy Wilkins threatened to withdraw support from the SCLC if King hired Lawson or Rev. Douglass Moore, Lawson's friend from Greensboro.

Pauli Murray and Bayard Rustin would have been sympathetic, recognizing the limitations of "freedom dreams" among the established legal leadership in the Black freedom struggle.[112] But rather than retreat from his radical posture, in his speech at the SCLC retreat Lawson doubled down on his reputation as a firebrand and told the clergy gathered to seize the political moment and assemble a nonviolent army in twelve months. "The Deep South can scream rape and invasion if it wishes," he told the SCLC leadership, "but the moment of truth is not far off." Lawson believed this nonviolent army could precipitate "a world wide crisis" that would overshadow the recent standoff between Russia and the United States over missiles in Cuba. It might shift attention from the "distractions" in Berlin or Moscow to focus attention on "the cancer at home." With "jails . . . full of free men refusing to back down," Lawson told SCLC leadership, the world would shift its eyes to a racial revolution in the United States.[113]

This moment in September 1961, while steeped in the urgency of the student sit-down revolution, was the product of decades of intellectual work on nonviolence and experimentation with nonviolent direct action. As a FOR staff member, Lawson worked in the movement spaces Howard Kester navigated in the early 1930s. His philosophy of nonviolence was influenced by Howard Thurman and the work he had undertaken with students at Howard in the interwar period. Lawson had the benefit of precedents for his work, the demonstrations piloted by Pauli Murray and the students at Howard in the 1940s, and he was a direct inheritor of the FOR's nonviolent institute format devised and advanced by Bayard Rustin in the 1940s and 1950s. Lawson was positioned to play a key role in the nonviolent struggle against white supremacy in the former Confederacy in the early 1960s, a wider postcolonial moment defined by the nationalist revolts of nonwhite peoples across the globe against European imperial powers.

As Howard Thurman had shown with his analysis of the historical Jesus, and as Gandhi had done with his life, Lawson argued that ethical self-governance was borne from personal disciplines—a refusal to acquiesce to the immoral demands of state or society and a commitment to actively demonstrate a better way to build social and political worlds through one's way of being in the world. Lawson and his students claimed and demonstrated this freedom to be. They willfully broke segregation laws; responded to violence with acts of mercy, kindness, and forgiveness; went to jail to strategically challenge the system of punishment designed to perpetuate Jim Crow; and envisioned their work as a way of living the highest principles of the Judeo-Christian tradition. These politics of being generated significant political power for Black students in a critical moment of the Black freedom struggle.

This Black insurgency, often waged by well-dressed students carrying books, should not be dismissed as simply a politics of respectability. The politics of being were a direct claim on the right to be free by Black people in the United States. They were courageous acts strategically designed to challenge Black dehumanization. The result was also a demonstration of new possibilities for racial politics, new possibilities for the politics of the disinherited in America. As the historians Leon Litwack and Glenda Gilmore have suggested, the students' example redefined politics in the modern United States.[114] They jettisoned the typical pattern of aggression and retaliation common to courts, elections, and mob violence in favor of a direct action that brought Black Americans face-to-face with segregationists. These student actions forced the nation to confront Black life in America, centering Black humanity in U.S. politics and disrupting the long-standing commitment to Jim Crow in the United States.

James Lawson—a religious intellectual and political innovator—was the most important teacher of these politics. His was not a messianic leadership characteristic of the now-sprawling legacy of Martin Luther King in both literature and life, but neither was it the radical egalitarian leadership of Ella Baker that proved so powerful to so many. Lawson was instead a religious instructor who sought to convince his students that their way of being in the world could be a powerful form of politics. His was a method that was demanding, perhaps too demanding, but that for a time in the early 1960s made the biblical vision of a "new creation" ushered in by "the new heart and spirit" of nonviolent practitioners no longer a dream. He drew on the world's "great living religions" to convince them that nonviolent being could be an effective way to live the highest ideals of their religion, that nonviolent direct action might steel them in preparation for a battle for justice that would last a lifetime.[115]

As the 1960s wore on—what Todd Gitlin calls "years of hope and days of rage"—nonviolence would fall from grace among the very generation of students that found it so attractive. Yet the legacy of Lawson's work—along with that of Thurman, Rustin, and Murray—would endure.[116]

Epilogue
Of Agnostic Nonviolent Technicians and the
Conscience of the Congress

• •

On 17 July 2020, John Robert Lewis passed from this world at the age of eighty after fighting his final battle against pancreatic cancer. Lewis had been brutally beaten on the Edmund Pettus Bridge in Selma, Alabama, while leading a march for the right to vote in 1965. He went on to serve thirty-three years in the U.S. Congress as Georgia's representative from the Fifth District. He passed away on the same day as C. T. Vivian, a ninety-five-year-old minister that the *New York Times* described as "a paladin of nonviolence on the front lines of bloody confrontations" during the 1960s Black freedom movement. John Lewis and C. T. Vivian were both students at American Baptist College (ABC) in Nashville in 1957, and they both were introduced to the political philosophy of religious nonviolence by James M. Lawson Jr.

John Lewis was only the second Black lawmaker to lie in state at the Capitol rotunda, following Elijah E. Cummings in the fall of 2019. At his funeral, four U.S. presidents eulogized the man who was known by his colleagues as "the conscience of the Congress." Barack Obama, George W. Bush, and Bill Clinton offered remarks at Atlanta's historic Ebenezer Baptist Church while Jimmy Carter prepared comments that were read by a surrogate. Alongside these four men was another: the Rev. James M. Lawson, Jr. "I've read many of the so-called civil rights books over the last fifty or sixty years about the period between 1953 and 1973," Lawson intoned as he began his eulogy, "[and] most of the books are wrong about John Lewis." On the sixtieth anniversary of the sit-ins—"which swept into every state of the union, largely manned by students because we recruited students"—Lawson told those gathered that "the nonviolent struggle begun in Montgomery, Alabama, was not an accident." Instead, it was an intentional effort to show that "Christian love has power that we have never tapped, and if we use it we can transform not only our own lives but the earth in which we live."[1]

Lawson remembered that his students in Nashville, Lewis and Vivian among them, "determined that if there is to be a second major campaign that will demonstrate the efficacy of satyagraha, of soul force, of love truth, that we would have to do it in Nashville." Calling it "providential" that so many key people were brought together in one place for this purpose, Lawson remembered that it was with "great fear and anticipation" that the group decided to desegregate downtown Nashville. He pointed to local people as the driving force behind the decision to take on the "rapaciousness of a segregated system . . . people like Kelly Miller Smith and Andrew White, Janetta Hayes and Helen Roberts and Dolores Wilkerson, and John Lewis. And Diane Nash, C. T. Vivian, Marion Berry, Jim Bevel, Bernard Lafayette, Paulina Knight, Angela Butler. . . . We were all led there." We were committed to "tearing down the signs," he remembered, to "renovating the waiting rooms, [and to] taking the immoral signs off of drinking fountains." "It was black women who made that decision for us in Nashville," Lawson continued, saying, "I was scared to death when we made that decision. I knew nothing about how we were going to do this."

Returning to his main point about the aspiring preacher from Alabama, Lawson said, "John Lewis did not stumble in on that campaign. Kelly Miller Smith, his teacher at ABC, invited John to attend the workshops in the fall of 1959 as we prepared ourselves to face violence and to do direct action." The goal was "to put on the map the issue that the racism and segregation of the nation had to end," and Lawson called the Nashville movement "the second major campaign of the nonviolent movement of America." "Those are not my words," he reminded the millions live streaming the funeral through their computers during the Covid-19 crisis. "John Lewis called what we did between 1953 and 1973 the 'nonviolent movement of America.'"

Peering out upon the dignitaries behind his wire spectacles, quite Gandhi-like in appearance, the ninety-one-year-old Lawson's credibility flowed from a lifetime of service to nonviolent social movements. He told the friends and family of John Lewis gathered before him at the historic church, "John Lewis had no choice in the matter. . . . John saw the malignancy of racism in Troy, Alabama, [and] there formed in him a sensibility that he had to do something about it. He did not know what that was, but he was convinced that he was called, indeed, to do whatever he could do. Get in good trouble—but stop the horror that so many folk lived through in this country in that part of the twentieth century." John Lewis was not alone, Lawson said. "C. T. Vivian had the same experience. I maintain that many of us had no choice but to do as we tried to do, primarily because at an early age we recognized the wrong under which we were forced to live. And we swore to God that by God's grace we would do whatever God called us to do in order to put on the table of the nation's agenda 'This must end. Black lives matter.'"

In the summer of 2020, exactly sixty years after what Lewis called the "nonviolent movement of America" forced Black life to the center of U.S. politics, Americans are engaged in street demonstrations in numbers not seen since the late 1960s. They are demanding, once again, that the nation let Black people *be*, simply be, that African Americans are afforded the most fundamental human right: the right to live. In order to grow into the fullness of one's creative potential, as Howard Thurman and the Quakers implored, one must first have the security to *be*. It is impossible for people to grow into the full expression of their potential when they are face down on the pavement with a boot on their neck. Bayard Rustin and Pauli Murray envisioned a greater freedom, one wider and deeper than changes to the law alone. James Lawson, John Lewis, Angeline Butler, and Diane Nash claimed the fundamental right to be Black in America. They would not allow the racist forces of Jim Crow to distort and disfigure their character through law, custom, policy, or violence as they grew into their profound potential. And yet what Howard Thurman called the "problem of creative survival for a disinherited minority" remains the sorry inheritance of our generation six decades after the sit-in revolution swept over the nation. The United States still struggles to demonstrate, in policy and practice, that Black life matters.

Is it possible that the continuing struggle to make Black life matter in 2021 is, in part, a reflection of the limits of nonviolence—this central motif of the early 1960s freedom struggle? The immediate results of student nonviolent direct action are clear enough. Students undertaking nonviolent direct action created pressure sufficient to end de jure segregation through the Civil Rights Act of 1964—the most sweeping civil rights legislation in American history. But is it possible that, as Charles Payne has written of the ongoing work to build racial equity in education, there has been "so much reform and so little change"?

The nonviolence advanced by Lawson, Lewis, and others was under fire as early as 1964 as more than 650 college volunteers traveled to Western College for Women in Oxford, Ohio, to prepare for the Mississippi Freedom Summer.[2] On the morning of 17 June, Lawson was the featured speaker. As he had done since the late 1950s, he implored the students in Oxford to claim nonviolence as their way of being amid the hatred and violence of the Deep South. Ellen Barnes, a white volunteer in her early twenties attending the Oxford Conference, described Lawson as "a young Negro pastor from Memphis" who was "well dressed, good looking, and had a very commanding speaking voice. He began to speak, and I immediately knew there would be some fireworks today."[3]

Calling nonviolence "a fundamental organizing principle of life," Lawson told the students at Oxford that to practice nonviolence required "a fundamental belief in God." Such belief did not have to be in the Judeo-Christian God, Lawson stated, "[so] long as the possibility of transcendence is present through the object of your faith." Lawson argued that this faith prevents us from seeing a human being as a means to an end; it urges us to see that "one's goals are wrapped up in the methods used." Lawson reminded the students that religious nonviolence was not new to the Black freedom struggle. Groups such as the Fellowship of Reconciliation had been advocating the use of nonviolence for more than fifty years, he pointed out. Citing the interracial character of the students gathered at Oxford, Lawson argued that "the New Negro and the New Caucasian have both been born within the achievements of the Movement," and that this movement had been forged by nonviolence. Concluding his comments pointedly, Lawson called those who "advocate the use of violence" both "intellectually and spiritually dishonest."[4]

Just as Barnes suspected, Lawson's comments led to fireworks. After a ten-minute break of shared singing, participants regrouped and began to interrogate Lawson. One student challenged his use of "religious terms." The student saw his own purpose as "challenging and bringing change to the political, the institutional, and economic structure of the society," which, the student observed, often included religious authority. The reason he accepted nonviolent direct action, he told Lawson, was simple: "It seems to work. But I don't see the need for making an absolute commitment in order to accomplish my intent. It seems to me that this thing has its limitations, a point beyond which nonviolence won't work anymore."

In his response, Lawson rejected the premise that nonviolence was simply a tactic that could be used sometimes and discarded at other times. The problem with this approach, Lawson said, is that "if non-violence is only employed because of its pragmatic virtues then it is implied that there is a point at which you will be willing to switch to violence because now it is successful." Pivoting to the student's concern with changing the "structures of society," Lawson explained that the freedom struggle was about "the creation of a different order." "We accept non-violence because it has the power to move in a CONstructive, a creative fashion to persuade, to influence, to resolve conflict, to bring change."[5]

Nonviolence, Lawson insisted, was the only path to a real revolution. And he doubled down on the notion that one's way of being in the world was the essential content of nonviolent revolution. He told the student that one's behavior must itself be prefigurative of the world to come—that in acting a certain way you express a manifestation of the new order. Kindness, mercy, and forgiveness—practices that themselves constituted the new order—were also acts of political insurgency because they were a revolt against the meanness, violence, and prejudice that were the pillars of American attitudes toward nonwhite peoples. And the impact of such nonviolent direct actions, strategically and collectively deployed, would challenge the systems and structures—jail, the courts, law, customs, and culture—central to the maintenance of Jim Crow. Such courageous, nonviolent actions might also forge a deep well of internal security that could sustain activism for years to come.

Now came the real fireworks. Barnes remembers that "an uproar" followed Lawson's response. Only the well-respected activist Bob Zellner could quiet the crowd: "I can understand how difficult it is today to buy a thing like non-violence, but we're in grave danger of losing sight of something important." He asked the students to remember one thing, an "idea expressed into equations:

$$\text{politics minus morality} = \text{destruction}$$
$$\text{morality minus politics} = \text{irrelevance.}^6$$

With this simple explanation, Zellner succinctly captured what white pacifists, Black religious intellectuals, and activists in the Black freedom struggle had sought for decades: an ethical-politics capable of generating real power in an era when Black Americans faced near-universal electoral disenfranchisement.

While the morning workshop in Oxford concluded amicably, there was more drama still to come. In the evening, Lawson was scheduled to present practical strategies for running a nonviolent campaign to students, and this time Stokely Carmichael delivered a response to Lawson's evening talk. As Barnes recalled, Carmichael's point was a simple one. "There were very practical reasons why the movement succeeded with nonviolence and equally practical reasons now why nonviolence was losing its hold," Carmichael explained. "Success was certainly not due to any great transformation in the minds and hearts of men!"

As the evening session began to border on bedlam, another well-respected Mississippi activist, Bob Moses, restored order. Barnes remembered that

Moses stood before the group and addressed them slowly and methodically. "No human being could have been less dynamic," Barnes observed. "Yet as he spoke—slowly, gently—a subtle and, I believe permanent change came over the room." She called Moses "the Ultimate Reality and ultimate possibility," and remembers that he responded to Carmichael this way: "In Mississippi we have two ground rules: 1) no weapons are to be carried or kept in your room. 2) if you feel tempted to retaliate, please leave."[7]

Bob Moses had the last word in the Ohio conflict between Lawson and Carmichael, but the debate about the role of nonviolence in the Black freedom movement raged throughout the Freedom Summer of 1964. The contours of the debate followed the major themes in the Oxford workshop: What are the fundamental goals of the movement, and what is the relationship between these goals and the tactics used to achieve them? Is personal transformation a requisite for social transformation? Is transformation of a white society long committed to the domination and subjugation of Black people a reasonable goal? What is the role of white people, including their ideas and institutions, in the Black freedom movement? But a much older question was also driving these discussions in the 1960s, a question that the Fellowship of Reconciliation had struggled with in the years following the First World War. It was a question that Howard Thurman, Pauli Murray, and Bayard Rustin grappled with also. It was a question stated succinctly by Bob Zellner: How to wage an effective *and* ethical-political struggle that might revolutionize a white supremacy society?

Carmichael later said that while Martin Luther King had gotten many things right in his nonviolent crusade against white supremacy, "he only made one fallacious assumption: In order for nonviolence to work, your opponent has to have a conscience. The United States has no conscience."[8] But perhaps it was Carmichael who, despite emerging as one of the most dedicated nonviolent activists in the early 1960s, landed on a false assumption. From Howard Thurman through to James Lawson, the central idea at the heart of nonviolence in the Black freedom movement was social power generated through personal transformation. Love of the enemy was essential, but not because one expected a conversion or immediate affection. Love was not transactional: it was the right thing to do—a choice to courageously live according to the highest ideals of one's ethics—and when used strategically Lawson and others believed this collective power could transform the cruel systems and structures that dehumanized Black people in America. Such a revolution may take generations. But the personal resiliency to remain engaged in the struggle was among the most critical by-products of taking nonviolent direct action.

In the Black freedom movement, the politics of being were about making an immediate claim on the right to be free and, in the process, strategically forcing a society committed to white supremacy to confront this profound expression of Black humanity. It was about disrupting the calculation of white violence with expressions of kindness, mercy, and forgiveness. It was about ending the monologue of violent white supremacy by placing Black bodies in segregated public spaces patrolled by violence. It was about shifting the choice of how to be in a Jim Crow society from Black people back to segregationists. The animating impulse of personal nonviolence was a refusal to back down, a will to be free. "Now," the demonstrators asked, "how will you respond?" The political philosophy of religious nonviolence in the Black freedom movement was not motivated primarily by the idea that whites might be converted to love and respect them. The power of nonviolence came from shifting the moral burden of how to respond from Black people back onto white people. And this burden was shifted through massive collective expressions of Black being in public spaces.

"Nonviolence had been successful in the South because the South had been unprepared, and because there had been a hard core of well-disciplined workers," Carmichael told the students in Oxford. "Now the movement is assuming a mass character," he intoned, suggesting that the broadening of participants corresponded to both a diversity of thought and difficulty in training people in the discipline of nonviolence.[9] But this "mass character" of the movement's expansion included a significant influx of white students from northern universities who decided to travel south and join the freedom movement in majority Black communities. In this moment, the philosophy of nonviolence seemed to grow significantly less important. As white-led movements around the country such as the Berkeley Free Speech movement or Students for a Democratic Society (SDS) saw the political advantage they might achieve through nonviolent direct action, the core insight of nonviolence in the Black freedom struggle was missing.[10] Living one's highest ethical ideals through acts of mercy, kindness, and forgiveness as a prefigurative politics gave way to the utilitarian use of nonviolent direct action as a pressure tactic deployed for the purpose of developing and wielding power using tools endemic to that unjust political system.

The particular power that emerged from Black being in a nation founded on Black dehumanization could not be ethically or effectively replicated by Mario Savio or Tom Hayden. For these white activists, and for many that followed them in the New Left, nonviolent direct action simply became another useful tactic in the "repertoire of contentious politics."[11] It was divorced from the experience of being Black in America that led Thurman and his students at Howard to search for a "creative method of survival for a disinherited minority," an ethical quest that led dozens of Black Americans to journey across the sea to query the Mahatma about his battle against colonialism. For these white activists, nonviolent direct action was not a politics of being. It was just politics.

But Lawson and Lewis, Nash and Butler were fired by the promise of growing into the fullness of their being as Black Americans. Their demonstrations were bold and effective challenges to the disfiguring demands of Jim Crow. Lawson called this dealing with racism "not from the external side but from the internal spirituality," noting that resiliency borne from a deep sense of self-worth amid dehumanizing conditions is a very old idea in the history of Africans brought to America against their will. "There are stories of the ancient slave preacher who went into the darkness of the plantation . . . and that was one of the essential messages, you were not born to be a slave . . . you are somebody."[12] Lawson, like Thurman before him, challenged the notion that "you are somebody" was a novel idea emerging only in the Black Power movement of the late 1960s.

To be sure, the Black pride ushered in by the Black Power movement of the late 1960s had a profound impact on the nation. And there were obvious differences between activists in the Black Power wing of the movement and the apostles of nonviolence around the use of revolutionary violence and self-defense. But these two distinct flanks of the freedom movement were also joined in celebrating and asserting the sacredness of Black life. Both maintained that being Black was beautiful—that Black life mattered.

As the movement grew wider in the mid-1960s and more whites joined the struggle, there was less interest in the tremendous sacrifices that were the hallmark of the first four years of the 1960s. Some of this had to do with privilege. Unlike Black Americans, the white students who joined the Freedom Summer of 1964 did not have their backs against the wall. Participation in the freedom movement was one option among many for them, not a fight for their lives. They did not grapple with, as a central tenet of their day-to-day being, the problem of the disinherited: How to transform an unjust society when one had so few good options, with flight untenable and revolutionary violence meaning certain death? It was the experience of being Black in America, or in the case of Murray and Rustin being queer or gay, that contributed to the quest for a third way in America's politics—the way of nonviolence and direct action. The problem was not that demonstrators had lost the element of surprise by the 1960s. The problem was that as the movement widened and became more diverse, fewer people embraced the religious conviction that personal suffering might be a gateway to sustained political revolution.

Carmichael became a prominent spokesperson for the limits of nonviolent direct action after giving a speech at Broad Street Park in Greenwood, Mississippi, on 16 June 1966 on the Meredith March against Fear.[13] "This is the twenty-seventh time that I've been arrested," Carmichael told supporters. "I ain't going to jail no more," he continued, arguing that "all we've been doing is begging the federal government," and now "the only thing we can do is take over."[14] Carmichael was clear what he meant by "take over." He meant that Black people, particularly in majority Black counties in the rural South, should have the electoral power to take rightful control over elected offices.

John Lewis, especially the twenty-five-year-old John Lewis who assumed the helm of SNCC in 1965, concurred. The most significant rift between Carmichael and advocates of nonviolence was not whether Black people should develop and use political power. The question centered on what constituted revolutionary political power. For advocates of nonviolence, there was a belief that suffering as Jesus did could lead to a profound personal transformation that could, in turn, provide the strength required to produce a deep rupture in human society—the kind of rupture that separated time in two. They saw in the life and work of Gandhi a religious figure and contemporary example of such leadership. Such suffering could steel one's commitment to a lifetime of struggle.

Or you could be deeply traumatized and ultimately killed for your efforts. Such suffering and death was not uncommon in the peak years of the movement, and for Carmichael and many of those he inspired, such religious asceticism was unconvincing and, at worst, just flat out harmful. This was difference at the level of strategy, to be sure, but it was also a difference of belief in the most effective kind of work for producing change to America's racial politics—a distinction that flowed primarily from religious convictions. Carmichael's leadership and orientation to movement work was quite different from that of the Quakers, Methodists, Episcopalians, Baptists, Congregationalists, and Unitarians who were essential to the development of nonviolence in twentieth-century U.S. politics. It was different from the Hindu and Jain traditions that proved central to many participants in the movements inspired by Gandhi. An ecumenical band of religious people was at the heart of organizing and sustaining the Fellowship of Reconciliation, and it was the FOR that dedicated itself to creating space for nonviolent institutes and movement workshops over the decades.

Carmichael may have practiced nonviolent direct action—and in the process been radicalized for a lifetime of struggle—but it was not because he was motivated by the philosophy of nonviolence.

James Lawson, on the other hand, was a Christian minister committed to building a movement around the philosophy of nonviolence well beyond the peak years of the early 1960s. He approached his leadership from the perspective of a church leader, from the perspective of someone who sought to follow in the way of the Nazarene carpenter—a life that led to the cross. Lawson was committed to the idea that nonviolent ways of being were *the* source of profound power, and he pointed to Jesus and Gandhi as proof. And he wasn't alone. John Lewis and many others maintained a belief in nonviolence as the egalitarian principle around which to build ethical and effective movements for justice.

Martin Luther King was so inspired by Lawson's ability to persist in organizing massive nonviolent demonstrations that—against the advice of his closest advisors—he traveled to Memphis to ally with striking sanitation workers in 1968. On his first trip to Memphis on 18 March 1968, King opened his remarks to the massive crowd gathered at the Charles Mason Church of God in Christ Temple by saying, "As I came in tonight, I turned around and said to Ralph Abernathy, 'They really have a great movement here in Memphis.'" He told the thousands gathered, "You are demonstrating something here that needs to be demonstrated all over our country. You are demonstrating that we can stick together and you are demonstrating that we are all tied in a single garment of destiny, and that if one black person suffers, if one black person is down, we are all down." The movement in Memphis was a rare combination of labor and church groups, which King noted in his remarks. "We have Baptists, Methodists, Presbyterians, Episcopalians, members of the Church of God in Christ, we are all together, and all of the other denominations and religious bodies that I have not mentioned."[15]

In this late 1960s moment, Lawson worked hard to keep alive the egalitarian spirit of religious nonviolence so central to the early 1960s movement. "In Memphis," Lawson said in the wake of the strike, "you had something you could do. Not only could you support the strike, but you could fail to go downtown. You could proceed to boycott the stores downtown and you could proceed to support the relief effort of the strikers. You could go to mass meetings. You could get on the marches. You could start spreading the word. . . . There were things you could get people to line up behind."[16] Rank-and-file Memphians were afforded the opportunity to make their claim on freedom.

Lawson approached this work from the perspective of the Judeo-Christian prophetic tradition. "The main role [of the local church] is to try to develop the kinds of moments that will help reconciliation to take place, and this doesn't take place by pretending problems aren't there," Lawson stated in 1968. Reconciliation, he argued, "takes place in confrontation, and of course, I think very clearly non-violent confrontation." "I take this very seriously from the prophetic tradition," Lawson wrote. "The word doesn't precede the demonstrations, the word follows the demonstrations."[17] The word that Black demonstrators shared with the whole world through their demonstrations in Memphis in 1968 was *being*. It was the power to be, fully and freely, the "am" in "I am a man." We *are* Black and human, those sanitation workers said to the nation, with a profound capacity for creative expression despite living in a nation that dehumanizes us with starvation wages.

There is perhaps no better example of how the politics of being continued in the lives of movement activists well after the "heroic" years of the Black freedom movement than Pauli Murray. Murray was not just an intrepid nonviolent organizer in a key moment in the mid-1940s. By the 1970s, Murray had become an influential Black religious intellectual like Thurman, Rustin, and Lawson. She belonged to a tradition of Black religious thinkers advancing a politics of being, and in Murray's life and words we find a praxis for liberation that was both deeper and more holistic than a legal strategy for ending discrimination.

Over the course of her seventy-five years, Murray encountered sexist and racist social structures that sought continually to shrink her from her ability to be herself. As Lawson noted about Jim Crow, such racist and sexist mores forced Murray to continually decide how to respond. Murray drew on these personal experiences to make sense of what structural racism and sexism looked like, how they intertwine, and to explain with stunning clarity what the effect is on the lives of Black people who don't conform to race, sex, or gender norms.

Murray's effort to make sense of her lived experience through writing and preaching, her intellectual activity, paved the way for thinking about structural racism and sexism as similar, if not the same, phenomena. Her life and writing influenced deeply a generation of womanist theologians— Joanne Terrell, Katie G. Cannon, and Jackie Grant among them—who critiqued James Cone's Black political theology for not taking seriously the experience and liberation of Black women.[18] Experience became the foundation for her theorization about the relationship between gender and race, and ultimately a formulation for her praxis of liberation, the foundation of what Katie Cannon has called "a moral wisdom."[19]

Like Jim Crow or conscription, sexism and homophobia infringe on an individual's ability to be, attempting to distort the individual personality and group character of women and nonstraight people. As with racism, the fundamental burden of sexism and homophobia is that they demand women and nonstraight people contort themselves and their ways of being to accommodate external demands. To refuse the demands of a sexist society; to reject the admonition to be pretty, pious, pure, and private by dressing like a man when you were born biologically as a woman; to speak "out of turn" or fraternize intimately with women rather than men—these were not simply socially transgressive acts; they were political acts. Refusing cooperation with racism and sexism served to shift the burden of choice back to the dominant groups. Such bold confrontations of sexist expectations, just like the refusal to concede the sidewalk to whites, to eat at a segregated lunch counter, or to use a Black-only toilet were about to claim the right to be—fully and freely—and these politics of being became powerful insurgent acts when deployed collectively.

Near the end of her life, Murray's vision for liberation became inseparable from her religious identity. On 8 January 1977, 172 years after Absalom Jones became the first Black man ordained in the Episcopal Church, Pauli Murray became the first Black woman. Less than five feet tall, Murray struggled to find a clerical robe that fit her properly as she prepare for her ordination. As her biographer Rosalind Rosenberg has written, "Murray found a solution, the same one she had been using since she was eight years old: boys' clothes. She found a choirboy robe, size 14, perfect for this 'E-pixie-pailion,' as she jokingly referred to herself."[20] After a lifetime of struggle, Murray proudly and boldly claimed her identity from the pulpit as a duly ordained minister of the gospel:

> It was my destiny to be the descendent of slaveowners as well as slaves, to be of mixed ancestry, to be biologically and psychologically integrated in a world where the separation of the races was upheld by the Supreme Court of the United States as the fundamental law of the Southland. My entire life's quest has led me ultimately to Christ in whom there is no East or West, no North or South, no Black or White, no Red or Yellow, no Jew or Gentile, no Islam or Buddha, no Baptist, Methodist, Episcopalian, or Roman Catholic, no male or female. There is not Black Christ nor White Christ nor Red Christ—

Pauli Murray in her clerical robes in the 1970s. Photo © Susan Mullally.

although these images may have transitory cultural value. There is only Christ, the Spirit of love and reconciliation, the Healer of deep pychic [sic] wounds, drawing us all closer to that Goal of perfection which links us to God our creator and to eternity.[21]

After decades of struggle and discernment, it is likely that Murray felt like another rebel, Martin Luther, who stated at the Diet of Worms, "I am bound by the Scriptures I have quoted, and my conscience is captive to the Word of God. I cannot and will not recant anything, since it is neither safe nor right to go against conscience. May God help me."[22]

At the end of her life, Murray described herself as the "pixie priest . . . getting into people's hair, raising people's blood pressure." When a new parishioner called her "father," Rosenberg writes that Murray likely took "secret delight," given her "close cropped hair, slacks, and clerical collar."[23] Murray's commitment to being, fully and freely, and her vocation to search for innovative nonviolent methods to transform a cruel society, belonged to the same religious sensibilities that led to her ordination as a minister of the Christian gospel: a belief that freedom is something we practice, something that takes daily vigilance, something on which we can make a direct claim. Murray's journey offers guideposts to those today who are seeking pathways of nonviolent liberation from the disfiguring structures of sexism, racism, and homophobia. Her way of being in the world was itself an insurgent and confrontational force for transforming the dehumanizing structures of racism and sexism. But Murray knew that the structures must be transformed also. She organized to end Jim Crow practices in wartime Washington, and her ordination transformed the Episcopal Church—among so many other accomplishments. At the intersection of individual and collective freedom, Murray located liberation.

When it comes to liberation, we should be careful not to constrain our imaginations. The cost of certainty, or ideology, is being robbed of the ability to think creatively about how the world might be different. In the case of Black liberation, such a dearth of vision can be deadly. The history of nonviolence in the Black freedom struggle started here deserves continued dedicated study not because it was the most sensible or pragmatic politics for our nation. To resign ourselves to grapple with nonviolent direct action "because it works" within existing structures of unjust power is to give way to an insidious cynicism in a neoliberal age dominated by increased efficiency. Such cynicism often greets those of us out on the road imagining together how we might co-create the world as it should be.

We should dedicate ourselves to the study of nonviolence—as it evolved in the United States through Thurman, Rustin, Murray, and Lawson and others—because it is a politics that takes seriously the full potential of every one of us as humans. Nonviolence is grounded in an intentional effort to link our identity with our actions, to organize at those intersections. It is about claiming the power to be, together, and toppling those things that interfere with this liberty. Nonviolence is a choice to live our highest ideals, even if it means deep suffering, in a political context that can reward pettiness, cruelty, and meanness. Nonviolence is a choice to be transformed, and it is a faith in the belief that the new world can and must come through us—each and every one of us.

Notes

Introduction

1. Walter Fluker writes, "Thurman emphasizes the relevance of the spirituals as religious documents, the product of the subtle and sophisticated search of antebellum slaves for sacred wisdom amidst extraordinarily distressful circumstances. Thurman illustrates how the primacy of religious experience provides the basis of hope and the tools for survival in an otherwise hopeless situation." *The Papers of Howard Washington Thurman* [hereafter PHWT], vol. 1, *My People Need Me, June 1918–March 1936*, ed. Walter Earl Fluker (Columbia: University of South Carolina Press, 2009), 127.

2. Thurman, PHWT, 1:128–29. Building a well of internal security, and protecting this internal security from the outside world, emerged as a major theme in Thurman's thought.

3. On the link between Black enslavement in the United States and Christianity, Albert J. Raboteau notes that by the eve of the Civil War, "Christianity had pervaded the slave community," and that by 1905 "a black population of more than 8.3 million contained 2.7 million church members." Albert J. Raboteau, *Slave Religion: The "Invisible Institution" in the Antebellum South*, updated ed. (Oxford: Oxford University Press, 2004), 209. Thurman drew on and extended this tradition of syncretizing Christian teachings with the Black experience in the United States by focusing on the similarities between the enslaved Hebrew people and Black Americans. Later, Thurman would make similar connections between the persecuted religious minority figure Jesus suffering beneath the yoke of the Roman Empire and African Americans living in a Jim Crow society. But this process of syncretizing Christian ideas and practices with the Black experience of enslavement in the United States was one that took centuries. Raboteau argues that linking Christian ideas and practices with the reality of Black life during enslavement was "a long process spanning almost two hundred and fifty years, by which slaves came to accept the Gospel of Christianity and at the same time made it their own. It is important to remember that it was a dual process. The slaves did not simply become Christians; they creatively fashioned a Christian tradition to fit their own peculiar experience of enslavement in America" (209).

Raboteau's argument builds on the work of Mellville J. Herskovits, who suggested that Africans brought much of their previous culture from their homelands across the Atlantic, and E. Franklin Frazier, who argued for a kind of cultural erasure as a result of the Middle Passage. Raboteau suggests that both Frazier and Herskovits were right to varying degrees (44–55). John Thornton has similarly argued for a similar model of cultural syncretism in the broader context of the Caribbean and South America in "African Religions and Christianity in the Atlantic World," in *Africa and Africans in the Making of the Atlantic World, 1400–1800* (Cambridge: Cambridge University Press, 1998), 235–72. Stephanie Smallwood has more recently argued that the commodification of enslaved Africans as chattel shipped across the Atlantic and sold in the Americas served to strip these human beings of a vital source of social power: connections to others in community and shared traditions and practices within these communities. Smallwood notes that stripping the enslaved of their connections to Africa made them more attractive products to slave traders, and Smallwood characterizes this commodification process as an attempt to inflict a "social death" among the enslaved. Stephanie Smallwood, *Saltwater Slavery: A Middle Passage from Africa to American Diaspora* (Cambridge, MA: Harvard University Press, 2008), 63. However, new social life was forged among enslaved Africans in the United States, and religion was a key element of this process of developing African American culture. As Stephanie Camp has argued, clandestine practices within slave religion "inspired spiritual strength and rapture, and it demanded autonomy (and mystery) of movement." Stephanie M. H. Camp, *Closer to Freedom: Enslaved Women and Everyday Resistance in the Plantation South* (Chapel Hill: University of North Carolina Press, 2004), 19.

Raboteau shows that while the conversion of Black Africans to Christianity functioned as a key justification for the enslavement of Africans in the seventeenth and eighteenth centuries, the ideas and rituals at the heart of the Christian religion—such as the egalitarian idea of oneness in Christ and the emancipatory notions at the heart of baptism—required that Christian practice and preaching among the enslaved be carefully monitored by plantation overseers. "To urge the slave's humanity was one thing," he writes of the thinking at the time, but "to declare his 'equal Right *with other men, to the* Exercises and Privileges *of Religion*,' was another" (101–2). Raboteau notes that as early as 1725 in South Carolina, "the clerical argument that Christianity made slaves more docile was weakened . . . when some slaves who had embraced Christianity participated in 'secret poisoning and bloody insurrection'" (124). For a host of reasons, Christian ideas and practices became a force in inspiring rebellion among the enslaved. Raboteau cites another example showing that "a majority of the slaves executed for conspiring to revolt in Charleston, South Carolina, in 1822 were members of the city's African Methodist Church. Two of the conspirators were class leaders, and several witnesses implicated Morris Brown, pastor of the church and later assistant bishop to Richard Allen. It was alleged that Denmark Vesey, the plot's leader, used scriptural texts to win supporters for the insurrection" (163). Raboteau also notes that Nat Turner, who organized the bloodiest slave rebellion in U.S. history in Southampton, Virginia, claimed "he had been directed to act by an omen from God" (164).

The preponderance of egalitarian ideas and an ethic of liberation, even insurrection, among the Christian Black enslaved led white theologians to invest deeply in a biblical justification for slavery. Benjamin J. Palmer, a southern Presbyterian minister, was perhaps foremost among intellectuals advancing what came to be called "Noah's curse," the notion that what the religious historian Stephen Haynes calls "the Hamitic myth" led "race and slavery" to be "consciously combined" in theological discourse (7). Palmer rose to fame by advancing an interpretation of the story of the tribe of Ham in Genesis 9 that suggested Black people were destined by biblical teaching to be "servants." Palmer wrote in 1863 of his hope that the Civil War would "teach mankind that the allotment of God, in the original distribution of destinies to the songs of Noah, must continue," calling the Hamites' "native condition" one "of fetishism and barbarism," and arguing that Black people "have never been stimulated to become a self supporting people, under well regulated institutions and law," arguing for the invariable descent among Black people to "their origin state of degradation and imbecility." Palmer continued: "All the attributes of the negro character, and . . . the whole history of God's dealings towards him, and . . . all the light shed upon his destiny from the sacred Scriptures" suggest that the "true normal position" of Black Americans is that of slave. Haynes writes, "This reference to Genesis 9 indicates that, at least through 1863, Noah's curse and its satellite texts remained the foundation for Palmer's theological superstructure of race, history, and destiny." Stephen R. Haynes, *Noah's Curse: The Biblical Justification of American Slavery* (Oxford: Oxford University Press, 2007), 136.

4. Thurman, PHWT, 1:132–33. Raboteau argues, "The most serious obstacle to the missionary's access to the slaves was the slaveholder's vague awareness that a Christian slave would have some claim to fellowship, a claim that threatened the security of the master-slave hierarchy," as "slaveholders feared that Christianity would make their slaves not only proud but ungovernable." The egalitarian impulse at the heart of much Christian thinking was especially threatening to the institution of slavery. Raboteau notes a fear among slaveholding society that "Christian fellowship between master and slave, unless very carefully regulated, would corrode the proper social hierarchy—the essential inferiority of blacks and superiority of whites—upon which the system rested. Slave conversion had to be measured by the rule of slave control, and a plantation manager would be dangerously remiss if he allowed anyone other than himself to do the measuring." Raboteau, *Slave Religion*, 102–3.

5. Blackmon writes of the shift from chattel slavery to criminal justice procedures in the effort to subjugate and expropriate labor from Black Americans, arguing, "By 1900, the South's judicial system had been wholly reconfigured to make one of its primary purposes the coercion of African Americans to comply with the social customs and demands of whites." Douglas A. Blackmon, *Slavery by Another Name: The Re-Enslavement of Black Americans from the Civil War to World War II* (New York: Anchor Books, 2008), 8. While a legal architecture was crucial to the long-term maintenance of Jim Crow, it was violence that served as seemingly the most durable vouchsafe of white supremacy in the United States. Individuals who adopted the political philosophy of nonviolence sought to engage and expose this white violence as immoral, unjust, and ultimately the great weakness of Jim Crow.

6. Equal Justice Initiative, *Lynching in America: Confronting the Legacy of Racial Terror*, 3rd ed., 29 January 2020, https://lynchinginamerica.eji.org/report/. Following the Civil War, the United States seemed poised for a profound transformation in social relations. African Americans, 179,000 of whom had fought for the Union to end slavery, sought and gained full citizenship with the passage of the Fourteenth

Amendment. The Thirteenth Amendment banned involuntary servitude except, problematically, in the case of crime—and ended the system of Black bondage that had been a hallmark of U.S. life since the nation's founding. The Fifteenth Amendment brought the promise of enfranchisement for Black men. Black families separated during slavery were reunited in cities and towns across the country by the Freedmen's Bureau in the years following the war, and Black men were elected to city councils, state legislatures, and even the U.S. Congress in the period between 1865 and the end of Reconstruction in 1877. But at every turn, these efforts among Black women and men to live as fully self-governing citizens were contested and, by the late nineteenth century, stymied in the transition from slavery to freedom. The "Black codes" became an early effort to use the law to restore the social order of slavery as so-called vagrancy laws were used to punish Blacks not employed as sharecroppers by southern planters—efforts to keep Black Americans "tied to the land." And while a Republican Congress in Reconstruction attempted to prohibit such legal persecution of Blacks by passing the Civil Rights Acts of 1866 and 1875—the first over a presidential veto from Tennessean Andrew Johnson—the U.S. Supreme Court in 1883 ultimately invalidated the Civil Rights Act of 1875's federal protection of Black civil rights and paved the way for the legal discrimination and segregation of African Americans in public spaces. These legal efforts to establish nonwhite Americans as second-class citizens were codified in the infamous 1896 *Plessy v. Ferguson* Supreme Court decision, whose majority opinion gave us the language "separate but equal" and made segregation the law of the land for nearly seventy years. But the law worked in tandem with violence, and in particular extralegal violence in the form of lynching, as many whites sought to restore American social relations to the days of chattel slavery and plantation capitalism. Black Americans were killed by whites without a trial—and often in public spaces using spectacle violence. Lynching was used to prevent Black economic advancement, intimidate Black men and women into complying with Jim Crow, and suppress political efforts aimed at enfranchising Black leaders through electoral processes. Although lynching was not the exclusive method used to achieve these goals, it did emerge as a tragically common practice in the late nineteenth and early twentieth centuries as ideas about what whiteness was were shifting from a complex tapestry of ethnic-national identities into a singular, cogent, sociopolitical identity, a phenomenon that emerging colonial powers, including the United States, took note of as they sought to build power over nonwhite populations across the globe.

7. There was usually a place for everyone in nonviolent direct actions, an idea captured perhaps most vividly in the 1963 "Children's Crusade" organized by the Southern Christian Leadership Conference (SCLC) as hundreds of school-age children faced off with Sheriff Eugene "Bull" Connor's dogs and fire hoses in Birmingham, Alabama. Taking direct action—making the individual or group choice to engage, challenge, and seek to transform individuals and structures central to the maintenance of white supremacy—was for many Black Americans a concrete and immediate claim on the right to be free. More specifically, nonviolent direct action was often a strategic choice to highlight and expose publicly two crucial weak points of white supremacy. First, nonviolent demonstrators exposed Jim

Crow's ethic of discrimination as running counter to the nation's stated founding charter of equality, often committing themselves to being arrested and jailed in numbers that could overwhelm the nation's "justice" systems. But perhaps more importantly, nonviolent demonstrators often exposed what appeared to be Jim Crow's most durable guarantor, violence—a force which ran contrary to the nation's civic impulse of social change and personal protection through law and parliamentary process. In the burgeoning age of television in the early 1960s, nonviolent demonstrators time and again successfully exposed the violent underbelly of white supremacy to millions of Americans. Richard S. Newman has described Richard Allen's 1787 walkout of a segregated Methodist church in Philadelphia as a "nonviolent protest," although the actual term "nonviolence" did not emerge until the twentieth century. See Newman, *Freedom's Prophet: Bishop Richard Allen, the AME Church, and the Black Founding Fathers* (New York: New York University Press, 2009), 10.

Black women in particular have strategically utilized direct-action tactics throughout the African American experience to challenge white supremacy. Stephanie Camp argues that "theft, foot dragging, short-term flight, and feigning illness were commonplace acts in the Old South and are widely understood to be everyday forms of resistance—hidden or indirect expressions of dissent, quiet ways of reclaiming a measure of control over goods, time, or parts of one's life." Camp, *Closer to Freedom*, 2. In the wake of enslavement, direct action against Black codes and ultimately Jim Crow began in earnest. Tera W. Hunter has written about the strikes organized by Black washerwomen in Jackson in 1866, in Galveston in 1877, and in Atlanta in 1881. See *To 'Joy My Freedom: Southern Black Women's Lives and Labors after the Civil War* (Cambridge, MA: Harvard University Press, 1997). In 1883, Ida B. Wells refused to leave the white "ladies car" on a C&O train in Memphis and lost her job as a school teacher in Memphis as a consequence. See Paula J. Giddings, *Ida: A Sword among Lions* (New York: Amistad, 2008), 62–63. Glenda Elizabeth Gilmore argues that Black women and men had to "invent" a politics that "decentered polls and parties," and notes in particular the way the "Organization of Colored Women" challenged violent white supremacists at the polls using direct action in the 1896 election in Wilmington, North Carolina. See Gilmore, *Gender and Jim Crow: Women and the Politics of White Supremacy in North Carolina. 1896-1920* (Chapel Hill: University of North Carolina Press, 1996), 120. And it was African American women who sparked a concerted nonviolent rebellion against Jim Crow for refusing cooperation with segregated seating policies on buses. Rosa Parks's story is well known, but Claudette Colvin—a fifteen-year-old Black girl, challenged segregated seating on Montgomery buses nine months before Rosa Parks and emerged as a key plaintiff in the *Gayle v. Browder* case that led to the end of legalized segregation on buses in Alabama. See Ellen S. Levine, *Freedom's Children: Young Civil Rights Activists Tell Their Own Stories* (New York: Puffin Books, 2000), 19–26.

8. Paula Giddings, *When and Where I Enter: The Impact of Black Women on Race and Sex in America*, 2nd ed. (New York: Amistad Publishing, 2006), 279.

9. Charles M. Payne, *I've Got the Light of Freedom: The Organizing Tradition and the Mississippi Freedom Struggle* (Berkeley: University of California Press, 1995),

68. As Ella Baker noted, "The movement of the fifties and sixties was carried largely by women," making it no surprise that tactics which both required and contributed to a sense of self-reliance were connected to the movement philosophies of powerful Black women. Quoted in Giddings, *When and Where I Enter*, 259. Septima Clark, who cofounded the first Citizenship Schools on Johns Island, South Carolina, in the late 1940s, described the purpose of the Freedom Schools—the successor to the Citizenship Schools—as "discovering local community leaders" on the belief "that creative leadership is present in any community and only awaits discovery and development." Clark believed in meeting people where they are, working with the strengths, skills, and sensibilities that each individual brings to the table. Oral History Interview with Septima Poinsette Clark, 25 July 1976, interview G-0016, Southern Oral History Program Collection (#4007), Southern Historical Collection, Wilson Library, University of North Carolina at Chapel Hill. See also Septima Clark, *Ready from Within: A First Person Narrative* (Trenton, NJ: Africa World Press, 1990), and Katherine Mellen Charron, *Freedom's Teacher: The Life of Septima Clark* (Chapel Hill: University of North Carolina Press, 2012).

10. Ella Baker, a cofounder of the Student Nonviolent Coordinating Committee (SNCC), was deeply committed to supporting self-reliance among local people in Black communities. Baker noted that such self-reliance was often undermined when national leaders entered into local spaces to give rousing speeches daring people to put their lives and bodies on the line, only to quickly leave for the next town. "My basic sense of it has always been to get people to understand that in the long run they themselves are the only protection they have against violence or injustice," Baker said. "People have to be made to understand that they cannot look for salvation anywhere but to themselves." Payne, *I've Got the Light of Freedom*, 93. As the historian Barbara Ransby has written, Martin Luther King Jr.'s "sudden fame" from the Montgomery Bus Boycott, for example, "did not sit right with Baker, especially given his youth and inexperience." Baker grew concerned that "the focus on King drained the masses of confidence in themselves," as "people often marveled at the things King could do that they could not." Ransby writes that King's "eloquent speeches overwhelmed as well as inspired," noting that "this disturbed Baker." Barbara Ransby, *Ella Baker and the Black Freedom Movement: A Radical Democratic Vision* (Chapel Hill: University of North Carolina Press, 2003), 190.

11. Angeline Butler, "What We Were Talking about Was Our Future," in *Hands on the Freedom Plow: Personal Accounts by Women in SNCC*, ed. Faith S. Holsaert et al. (Urbana: University of Illinois Press, 2010), 41.

12. James Lartey, "Diane Nash: 'Non-violent Protest Was the Most Important Invention of the 20th Century,'" *The Guardian*, 6 April 2017. As the historian Giddings has written, "Many of the Black women coming of age in the sixties . . . were encouraged to be independent, to do what had to be done, regardless of prescribed gender roles." Giddings, *When and Where I Enter*, 278.

13. Stokely Carmichael famously criticized King for believing that "unearned suffering is redemptive," arguing that King "only made one fallacious assumption: In order for nonviolence to work, your opponent has to have a conscience. The United States has no conscience." Carmichael believed that King and other advo-

cates of nonviolence believed, as Gandhi did with the Hindu practice of *dharna* discussed in chapter 5, that whites would be moved to change their racist practices and policies once they saw the public suffering of Black people caused by Jim Crow and white supremacy in the United States. But this seems to misconstrue the animating impulse of nonviolence, which was grounded in the idea that suffering is redemptive internally for the individual—not just an effort to force a society to confront its conscience. King argued that suffering brought him "closer to God" rather than the explicitly external purpose of redeeming a racist society. This is a very old idea tied to practices of religious asceticism for thousands of years across myriad traditions. As King wrote in "Suffering and Faith," an essay published in the *Christian Century* on 27 April 1960, "My personal trials have also taught me the value of unmerited suffering. As my sufferings mounted I soon realized that there were two ways that I could respond to my situation: either to react with bitterness or seek to transform the suffering into a creative force. I decided to follow the latter course. Recognizing the necessity for suffering I have tried to make of it a virtue. If only to save myself from bitterness, I have attempted to see my personal ordeals as an opportunity to transform myself and heal the people involved in the tragic situation which now obtains. I have lived these last few years with the conviction that unearned suffering is redemptive. There are some who still find the cross a stumbling block, and others consider it foolishness, but I am more convinced than ever before that it is the power of God unto social and individual salvation. So like the Apostle Paul I can now humbly yet proudly say, 'I bear in my body the marks of the Lord Jesus.' The suffering and agonizing moments through which I have passed over the last few years have also drawn me closer to God. More than ever before I am convinced of the reality of a personal God."

14. In his 1925 collection *The New Negro*, editor Alain Locke—using gendered language despite numerous entries from Black women—cites the idea of "personality" and points to the internality of change among younger African Americans. "So for generations in the mind of America, the Negro has been more of a formula than a human being—a something to be argued about, condemned or defended, to be 'kept down,' or 'in his place,' or 'helped up,' to be worried with or worried over, harassed or patronized, a social bogey or a social burden. . . . His shadow, so to speak, has been more real to him than his personality." But Locke notes what he calls a "renewed self-respect and self-dependence" among Black Americans amid the nadir, writing that "the life of the Negro community is bound to enter a new dynamic phase, the buoyancy from within compensating for whatever pressure there may be of conditions without. The migrant masses, shifting from countryside to city, hurdle several generations at a leap, but more important, the same thing happens spiritually in the life-attitudes and self-expression of the Young Negro, in his poetry, his art, his education and his new outlook, with the additional advantage, of course, of the poise and greater certainty of knowing what it is all about. From this comes the promise and warrant of a new leadership." Alain Locke, *The New Negro* (repr., New York: Touchstone Press, 1997), 3–5. In his seminal work *The Black Atlantic*, Black cultural theorist Paul Gilroy challenged what he called "absolutist conceptions of cultural difference allied to a culturalist understanding of 'race' and ethnicity," arguing for

the Atlantic as a category that produces a "single complex unit of analysis . . . of the modern world," a category that might "produce an explicitly transnational and intercultural perspective." Gilroy effectively complicated and destabilized the unstatic category of "Black" by challenging what he calls "nationalist or ethnically absolute" approaches to conceptualizing Blackness. Similarly, I suggest that nonviolent activists were seeking to engage and destabilize the pernicious stereotypes of Blackness in the United States to challenge and redefine the dehumanizing notions of Blackness perpetuated by a white majority in a Jim Crow society. Paul Gilroy, *The Black Atlantic: Modernity and Double Consciousness* (Cambridge, MA: Harvard University Press, 1993), 15. Part of this destabilization of stereotypes included the strategic use of respectability politics, but as Rhonda Williams has written of Black women seeking to improve public housing, nonviolent demonstrators "expanded as well as departed from earlier arguments for respectability which linked citizenship to the enactment of bourgeois behaviors." Rhonda Y. Williams, *The Politics of Public Housing: Black Women's Struggle against Urban Inequality* (Oxford: Oxford University Press, 2004), 10.

15. Legislative failure, injury, and death were far more common than legislative success for Black people throughout American history. It is also worth remembering that the landmark civil rights legislation of the nineteenth century—the passage of the Thirteenth, Fourteenth, and Fifteenth Amendments as well as the Civil Rights Acts of 1866, 1871, and 1875—all preceded one of the darkest eras in African American history, what Rayford Logan called the "nadir" of Black life in the United States. The durability of positive social change for Black people has always been and remains in question; progress is not linear, and the central state has often been a primary perpetrator of Black oppression—not a catalyst for liberation. There is a clear understanding among Black activists that just laws can quickly be reverted back to unjust laws. There is perhaps no better example than the 2012 gutting of the jurisdiction requirements in the Voting Rights Act of 1965. This is why I conceptualize freedom as an ongoing process defined by vigilant practices, not an endpoint achieved with the passage of federal legislation.

16. Walter Johnson, "On Agency," *Journal of Social History* 37, no. 1, special issue (Autumn 2003): 114.

17. "The condition of enslaved humanity," Johnson writes, "was a condition that was at once thoroughly determined and insistently transcendent." Johnson, "On Agency," 116.

18. The issue of how slavery was a "total" system of social domination, and the degree to which Black life and culture was or was not determined by white supremacy, has long been a source of fruitful scholarship. Literature on this issue in slavery, for example, has shifted. Orland Patterson has expressed a notion of slavery as an "extreme form of the relation of domination" wherein "the slavemaster's power over his slave was total." Orland Patterson, *Slavery and Social Death: A Comparative Study* (Cambridge, MA: Harvard University Press, 1982), 1 and 26. More recently, scholars have explored a kind of radical agency among the enslaved as seen in the work of Stephanie Camp. Camp writes, "Every day resistance occupied, as political scientist James Scott has argued, the wide terrain between consent, on

one hand, and open, organized opposition, on the other." Camp, *Closer to Freedom*, 2. For a much earlier work that engages the issue of the agency of the enslaved, see Eugene D. Genovese, *Roll, Jordan, Roll: The World the Slaves Made* (New York: Pantheon Books, 1974). Most recently, Ashon Crawley has examined the tension between the violence meted out against Black Americans from the late nineteenth through the twentieth centuries and the free expression of identity and culture in this period from an ethical perspective. Crawley calls for "an ethics project that recognizes the violence of white supremacist capitalist patriarchy as a response to the ongoing refusal of black life, of otherwise possibility." Ashon T. Crowley, *Blackpentecostal Breath: The Aesthetics of Possibility* (New York: Fordham University Press, 2017), 72. All of this work points to the complex relationship between Black being and political agency in the decades following slavery, amid what Douglas Blackmon has called "slavery by another name." See Blackmon, *Slavery by Another Name*.

19. This book is not an exhaustive chronicle of nonviolent direct-action protests aimed at toppling Jim Crow, and it is not an examination of all ideas related to nonviolence. Instead, it seeks to uncover the connections between ideas about nonviolence and the practice of nonviolent direct action, joining together these two often discrete areas of historical inquiry—social history and intellectual history—to show how nonviolence became the ethical foundation for the powerful political force of nonviolent direct action in the peak years of the Black freedom movement. I argue that this was the result of deliberative, conscious, thinking people who made informed choices grounded in religious ideas and humanist ethics over a period of decades. There is no study that approaches the topic in this way, and as I show below, this is the result of a major problem in the literature borne from the continuing replication of the Manichean notion that nonviolence was a tactic for most but a way of life for a few. My goal with this book is to establish a better understanding of how nonviolence as an ethic, a set of ideas about how people and the world ought to be, became the foundation for a widespread nonviolent direct-action movement. I argue there is a clear and coherent lineage of Black thinkers and activists who developed this innovative ethical politics, and this contrasts sharply with the most influential literature from scholars in the 1970s, 1980s, and 1990s.

In their seminal volume *Along the Color Line: Explorations in the Black Experience*, August Meier and Elliot Rudwick wrote three essays that outlined their thinking on the history of nonviolent direct action: "On the History of Nonviolent Direct Action," "The Boycott Movement against Jim Crow Streetcars in the South 1900–1906," and most importantly, "The Origins of Nonviolent Direct Action in Afro American Protest: A Note on Historical Discontinuities." In the rather lengthy latter essay, which originally appeared in David Garrow's *We Shall Overcome: The Civil Rights Movement in the United States in the 1950s and 1960s* (Brooklyn: Carlson Publishing, 1989), Meier and Rudwick excavated more thoroughly than any other scholars to date nonviolent direct-action campaigns undertaken by Black Americans in a diversity of regions and time periods between 1877 and 1941. Their focus was protest and nonviolent direct-action tactic campaigns, and they did not portend to grapple in any significant way with the philosophical underpinnings of nonviolence. This focus on direct-action tactics led directly to their conclusion that there was a "discontinuity" in the "protest" tradition that belies any kind of coherent philosophical lineage for nonviolence in the civil rights movement. They argued instead that nonviolent direct action was simply a tactic used sporadically—across time and space between 1877 and 1941. "Later activists were rarely aware of what their predecessors had done or attempted," they wrote. August Meier and Elliot Rudwick, *Along the Color Line: Explorations in the Black Experience*, 1st paperback ed. (Urbana: University of Illinois Press, 2002), 265.

Much of the literature produced before and after shared this assumption: nonviolent direct-action tactics were used routinely by Black folks across the decades as a tool for battling social, economic, and political oppression, but there is little evidence of a long developing commitment to nonviolence as a life philosophy among Black Americans. The literature on social movement organizations (SMOs) in the Black freedom movement, originally developed in the 1970s and 1980s, cleaved quite tightly to the assumption that nonviolent direct action was a tactic to be used for its political utility, and as a result these studies focused almost exclusively on the highly diffuse local nonviolent direct-action campaigns carried out under the aegis of these SMOs. Meier and Rudwick's 1973 text on the Congress of Racial Equality (CORE) became an early landmark work in the field, attending to the power that ordinary people built through direct action, organizational structures, and social networks from CORE's founding in 1941. See August Meier and Elliot Rudwick, *CORE: A Study in the Civil Rights Movement, 1942–1968* (New York: Oxford University Press, 1973).

In his 1981 book on the Student Nonviolent Coordinating Committee (SNCC), Clayborne Carson notes that the early SNCC philosophy was "eclectically adopting ideas from the Gandhian independence movement and Christian idealism," but Carson spends little time digging into these broad categories. Clayborne Carson, *In Struggle: SNCC and the Black Awakening of the 1960s* (Cambridge, MA: Harvard University Press, 1995), 2. For most of the book, Carson's analysis focuses on what he calls "the nonviolent protest strategy" of SNCC, again emphasizing nonviolent direct action as a protest tactic rather than examining the ethics or religious philosophy that underwrote these direct actions (304). Aldon Morris's landmark 1986 book on the origins of the civil rights movement focus on how SMOs used social networks and enterprise tools to support robust mass mobilization, providing excellent information on how churches especially became hubs where nonviolent direct-action tactics could be safely taught and nonviolent direct-action campaigns planned. See Aldon D. Morris, *The Origins of the Civil Rights Movement: Black Communities Organizing for Change* (New York: Free Press, 1986). Doug McAdam's 1982 book *Political Process and the Development of Black Insurgency, 1930–1970* contextualized these nonviolent direct-action tactics within a geopolitical context that he argued created a new "political opportunity" for Black mobilization in the postwar United States, one that built on the organizing structures established in the 1930s. See Doug McAdam, *Political Process and the Development of Black Insurgency, 1930–1970*, 2nd ed. (Chicago: University of Chicago Press, 1999). Perhaps more than any other text in this era, Harvard Sitkoff's 1981 *The Struggle for Black Equality* does a good job of citing the religious ethics that, when combined with direct-action tactics, propelled the emerging Black freedom movement to early successes. Sitkoff writes, "The Montgomery movement had been explicitly Christian. King had quoted Jesus—not Gandhi." But he notes that nonviolence was initially a hard sell: "Not surprisingly, King's strategy of nonviolent resistance struck many African Americans as unproductive, unbearable, even suicidal." But over time King "clothed the consequences of racial change in the garb of reconciliation and the creation of a beloved community." Sitkoff argues for King's seminal importance in encouraging "large numbers of African Americans to march under King's banner and to court beatings, jailings, even death, certain in the faith that their martyrdom would hasten the victory of their cause, firm in their belief that we shall overcome." Harvard Sitkoff, *The Struggle for Black Equality, 1954–1980*, rev. ed. (New York: Hill and Wang, 2008), 52–53, 57–58. Carson and Sitkoff hinted at a whole set of ethical ideas that raised the curiosity of some historians, but the die was cast: much of the historical literature that followed focused on nonviolent direct-action tactics, gesturing casually to the idea that for some, nonviolence was a way of life. This trope emerged as a common explainer in historical literature and became accepted wisdom in most literature on the movement. For rank-and-file Black activists, the thinking went, nonviolent direct action was a tactic to be used insofar as it was effective, while for a small band of religious radicals, nonviolence was a way of life. I do not dispute this point, but argue instead that we have missed a deeper vision for social transformation among this deeply influential cohort of thinkers and activists for whom nonviolence was the requisite ethic for the practice of nonviolent direct action.

20. To be clear, white supremacy guided the economic, political, and social development of the United States since its founding—an intrepid mission that Marilyn Lake and Henry Reynolds have shown to be an inspiration for the creation of "white men's countries" across the globe. But the advocates of the political philosophy of nonviolence claimed ancient origins for their political approach to Jim Crow in America. Marilyn Lake and Henry Reynolds, *Drawing the Global Colour Line: White Men's Countries and the International Challenge of Racial Equality* (Cambridge: Cambridge University Press, 2008).

21. Charles W. McKinney Jr., *Greater Freedom: The Evolution of the Civil Rights Struggle in Wilson, North Carolina* (Lanham, MD: University Press of America, 2010). In his study of the Black freedom movement in Wilson, McKinney writes of a "greater freedom to refer to the mindset that black activists employed as they confronted white supremacy." He argues that Black people in Wilson sought not simply to change the law, though this was important, but most importantly these activists "struggled for a greater freedom symbolized by a new phase of the quest for respect, equality, and civic, political, and economic inclusion," calling his rendering "a conception that redefines traditional notions of movement success, and significantly expands the traditional parameters of the movement" (xx). Here, I take a similarly capacious approach to understanding the Black freedom movement in chronicling the wider vision of freedom articulated in idea and action in this history of nonviolence. Similarly, in analyzing the variegated ways in which Black women thought about and worked toward freedom, Rhonda Williams has written

that by the late 1960s, "Black freedom struggles were increasingly being fought in neighborhoods around consumption as well as political issues. In addition to struggles for voting rights, school desegregation, and the opportunity to eat, swim, and play tennis wherever one liked, activists in northern and southern cities began to tackle a range of issues equally central to the achievement of full citizenship: the right to adequate housing, income, medical care, food, and clothing. These efforts, led largely by black women in the 1960s, represented another phase of the black freedom struggle—one that has now begun to be chronicled." In their quest for what Williams calls "neither pity nor handouts," these women "fought for decent lives and self-respect," and they are joined in their pursuits with the activists I examine in this book. Williams, *Politics of Public Housing*, 14, 8.

22. As Charles Cobb writes, "Simply put: because nonviolence worked so well as a tactic for effecting change and was demonstrably improving their lives, some black people chose to use weapons to defend the nonviolent Freedom Movement. Although it is counterintuitive, any discussion of guns in the movement must therefore also include substantial discussion of nonviolence, and vice versa. This book does that." Charles E. Cobb, *This Nonviolent Stuff'll Get You Killed: How Guns Made the Civil Rights Movement Possible* (New York: Basic Books, 2014), 2. Yet any substantive discussion of nonviolence, and in particular the history of how an expansive and revolutionary vision for nonviolence emerged in the Black freedom movement, is missing from Cobb's otherwise exemplary study. Cobb admits as much later, writing that among other things the book is not about nonviolence. He suggests instead that the book is about people—"especially the young people—who participated in a nonviolent movement without having much commitment to nonviolence beyond agreeing to use it as a tactic" (11). Cobb's otherwise astounding study does little to interrogate the development of the philosophy of nonviolence before 1955, especially among those widely influential figures for whom nonviolence can be understood as a religious commitment. For earlier works that chronicle the role of self-defense and armed resistance in the twentieth-century Black freedom struggles, see Timothy B. Tyson, *Radio Free Dixie: Robert F. Williams and the Roots of Black Power* (Chapel Hill: University of North Carolina Press, 1999); Charles M. Payne, *I've Got the Light of Freedom: The Organizing Tradition and the Mississippi Freedom Struggle* (Berkeley: University of California Press, 1995); Christopher Strain, *Pure Fire: Self-Defense as Activism in the Civil Rights Era* (Athens: University of Georgia Press, 2005); Wesley C. Hogan, *Many Minds, One Heart: SNCC's Dream for a New America* (Chapel Hill: University of North Carolina Press, 2007); Lance Hill, *The Deacons for Defense: Armed Resistance and the Civil Rights Movement* (Chapel Hill: University of North Carolina Press, 2006).

More recently, a cohort of scholars has directly engaged the questions of armed self-defense relative to nonviolence both during the civil rights era and in the years before, but as Akinyele Omowale Umoja writes, there is no question about the significance of nonviolence to the emerging freedom movement in 1960. And within grassroots movement organizations, there was little debate—at least at first—about the importance and efficacy of nonviolence. "SCLC, CORE, and FOR were all represented" at the founding of SNCC, Umoja writes, and "James Lawson, a committed

Gandhian and nonviolent activist, made convincing arguments for protests based on moral and spiritual foundations.... Lawson's influence was critical to the adoption of a nonviolent philosophy based on Christian principles." *Nonviolence before King* is largely about making sense of how the long struggle for Black freedom in the United States arrived at this consequential moment in early 1960 when activists would state that "we affirm the philosophical or religious ideal of nonviolence as the foundation of our purpose, the presupposition of our belief, and the manner of our action. Nonviolence, as it grows from the Judeo-Christian tradition, seeks a social order of justice permeated by love.... Nonviolence nurtures the atmosphere in which reconciliation and justice become actual possibilities." Umoja writes that John Lewis, Diane Nash, and James Bevel joined Lawson in advocating for "philosophical nonviolence as a way of life." On the other hand, Chuck McDew, Tim Jenkins, Charles Jones, and later Bob Moses "believed that SNCC's priority should be the massive registration of voters in southern states in which the voting rights of African descendants were denied. This group view nonviolence as a tactical weapon to be used by organizers for protections. These activists, similar to the leadership of SCLC, believe that the perception of armed Black organizers would not encourage federal intervention or garner support from White liberals for the Civil Rights Movement." Umoja continues: "In SNCC's early years, no debate took place within the national leadership over embracing nonviolence. While it is possible that some SNCC workers carried weapons in the early years of the organization, armed self-defense was not overly advocated. In local chapters, some young activists were indifferent to nonviolence; others openly challenged the concept as a strategy and philosophy. In Nashville, where philosophical nonviolence was reputed to be most entrenched, student activists debated the methods of nonviolence versus self-defense. The 'young Turks' of the Nashville student movement protected nonviolent demonstrators from White attackers in that city. On a few occasions in the early years, some SNCC workers were armed or advocated the use of force for self-defense." Akinyele Omowale Umoja, *We Will Shoot Back: Armed Resistance in the Mississippi Freedom Movement* (New York: New York University Press, 2013), 52–53.

Simon Wendt writes that "ironically, by the time CORE and SNCC officially embraced self-defense, armed protection was becoming increasingly irrelevant to the southern freedom movement." He argues that "while armed resistance during the black power era was intended to be a revolutionary alternative to nonviolence, it functioned primarily as a vehicle of psychological liberation.... Self-defense strategies during the Black power era proved self-defeating, [as] what may be considered a tactical innovation obscured the social, cultural, and political core of their programs." Wendt suggests that "the movement's ultimate success depended both on the spirit and the shotgun" but concludes there is little evidence that "actual, rather than rhetorical" violence aided the nonviolent wing of the movement. Simon Wendt, *The Spirit and the Shotgun: Armed Resistance and the Struggle for Civil Rights* (Gainesville: University Press of Florida, 2007), 6–7, 198. See also Nicholas Johnson, *Negroes and the Gun: The Black Tradition of Arms* (Amherst, NY: Prometheus Books, 2014).

23. As Glenda Gilmore has written, Black women and men were forced to invent an innovative politics that "decentered polls and parties." Locked out of electoral politics before 1965—banished from city councils, state legislatures, the U.S. Congress, and the White House—the political reality of Black disfranchisement before 1965 led many people to take up new ways of generating political power. Gilmore, *Gender and Jim Crow*, 120. Doug Rossinow has written of the student organizing efforts of the 1940s and 1950s, because "cultural meanings and possibilities are bounded by political realities," the "dialectics of politics and culture, structure and dissent, are the real objects of this study." Douglass Rossinow, *The Politics of Authenticity: Liberalism, Christianity, and the New Left in America* (New York: Columbia University Press, 1998), 20. I take a similar approach in analyzing the interplay between the boundaries of political and cultural freedom and the expansive vision maintained by nonviolent intellectuals and activists.

24. PHWT, 1:145.

25. Clarence Taylor, *Black Religious Intellectuals: The Fight for Equality from Jim Crow to the 21st Century* (New York: Routledge Publishing, 2002), 4. Resurgent interest in African American intellectual history in recent years has meant that the writings of Du Bois, Garvey, Fanon, and Angela Davis have been revisited, while new queries on transnational Black Atlantic thought have been situated alongside work on Black nationalism in nineteenth-century Haiti and the evolution of Black political ideologies in the twentieth century. The African American Intellectual History Society blog has featured much of this important work, but Laurie F. Maffly-Kipp, *Setting Down the Sacred Past: African-American Race Histories* (Cambridge, MA: Harvard University Press, 2010), is a notable exception that breaks this mold. Among studies of the Black church, W. E. B. Du Bois assessed quantitatively and qualitatively the significance of the Black churches in 1903. See W. E. B. Du Bois, *The Negro Church Report of a Social Study Made under the Direction of Atlanta University: Together with the Proceedings of the Eighth Conference for the Study of the Negro Problems* (Atlanta: Atlanta University Press, 1903). This intrepid social study was soon followed by Carter G. Woodson's *History of the Negro Church*, which built on and expanded the work of Du Bois to understand the rise and expansion of Black churches in the United States. Carter Godwin Woodson, *The History of the Negro Church* (Washington, DC: Associated Publishers, 1921). Benjamin E. Mays and Joseph W. Nicholson did a further study of this period, again quantifying the Black churches in America and examining their leadership. Benjamin E. Mays and Joseph William Nicholson, *The Negro's Church* (New York: Institute of Social and Religious Research, 1933). E. Franklin Frazier continued this work in *The Negro Church in America* (New York: Schocken Books, 1964). C. Eric Lincoln built on this long tradition of Black church history in two works: *The Negro Church since Frazier* (New York: Schocken Books, 1974), and *The Black Church in the African-American Experience* (Durham, NC: Duke University Press, 1990). Scholars of social movements like Aldon Morris have emphasized the very practical nature of Black church support for Black organizing through the provision of "enterprise tools"—phones, safe meeting spaces, and later mimeographs, fax machines, and other basic tools needed to organize. See Aldon D. Morris, *The Origins of the Civil Rights Movement:*

Black Communities Organizing for Change (New York: Free Press, 1986). See also Aldon D. Morris, "A Retrospective on the Civil Rights Movement: Political and Intellectual Landmarks," *Annual Review of Sociology* 25 (1999): 517–39.

The work of Black theologians on the ethical imperatives of challenging segregation and racism has been concurrent with much of this historical scholarship, but this work has tended to focus more on the normative than the empirical—the ethics of how society ought to be given the historical nature of racism and its ongoing legacy—but less attention has been given to the intersection of the ethical and the strategic, and the robust vision of liberation that lies at this nexus. For a good introduction to this work in Black ethics, see James Cone, *A Black Theology of Liberation* (Maryknoll, NY: Orbis Books, 1986), and Katie Cannon, *Black Womanist Ethics* (Eugene, OR: Wipf and Stock, 1988). For a more recent text, see J. Kameron Carter, *Race: A Theological Account* (Oxford: Oxford University Press, 2008).

26. Whenever historians did explain what was meant by calling nonviolence a way of life, the focus almost always turned to Martin Luther King Jr. In much movement literature from the 1970s, 1980s, and 1990s, explaining what was meant by nonviolence a "way of life" meant detailing the intellectual journey of King. This literature did a phenomenal job in explaining the role King played as a herald for nonviolence in the Black freedom movement, a mobilizer who inspired people to take risky action through soaring rhetoric in communities across the nation. King's theological work at Boston University in the early 1950s is cited, alongside his critique of classical liberalism, his trip to India in March 1957, and his writings on love, law, and civil disobedience. David Levering Lewis's 1970 *King: A Biography*, 3rd ed. (Urbana: University of Illinois Press, 2012); David Garrow, *Bearing the Cross: Martin Luther King Jr. and the Southern Christian Leadership Conference*, collector's ed. (Norwalk, CT: Easton Press, 1989); Adam Fairclough, *To Redeem the Soul of America: The Southern Christian Leadership Conference and Martin Luther King, Jr.* (Athens: University of Georgia Press, 1987); and of course Taylor Branch's three-part series *America in the King Years* (New York: Simon and Schuster, 1988, 1998, 2007) constitute a select portion of this literature—but there is much more. There are some good volumes on King and his theology, notably James Cone, *Martin and Malcolm and America: A Dream or a Nightmare?*, 20th anniversary ed. (New York: Orbis Books, 2012), but we miss the mark in our understanding of how nonviolence developed in the freedom struggle by focusing so heavily on King.

King inherited a religious intellectual tradition, ultimately becoming its greatest herald, but he did not play a significant role as an innovator or developer of the ideas in this nonviolent tradition. This is true not simply in the realm of ideas about nonviolence but also for the practice of nonviolent direct action: King followed the lead of SNCC students and others in participating in the sit-ins only by April 1960. This is not to discredit King but rather to situate King in a historical lineage of thinkers that preceded him, outlining the critical contributions of other figures in the decades before his rise to prominence, figures who have in fact been marginalized in the literature. It is clear that King's conversation to nonviolence as a "way of life" came relatively late in the story told in this book. In his March 1955 report to the national office of the pacifist Fellowship of Reconciliation (FOR), field secretary

Glenn Smiley told his bosses in New York that Martin Luther King Jr. wanted to "do it right" but that King was "too young" and "some of his close help is violent." Smiley reported that King's entourage of bodyguards had recently sought a "permit . . . to carry guns," and he described King's home as "an arsenal." Smiley told his New York bosses that "King sees the inconsistency" between his nonviolent ideals and the armed reality of the situation, "but not enough. He believes and yet he doesn't believe. The whole movement is armed in a sense, and this is what I must convince him to see as the greatest evil." Concluding his report without acknowledging the irony in his final statement, Smiley wrote "this stuff on arms is deadly. Treat it in the strictest confidence." Glenn Smiley, Letter to John and Al, 29 February 1956, Fellowship of Reconciliation (FOR) Papers, Series E, Box 17, Folder Correspondence Martin King 1954–1967; see also Christopher Strain, *Purefire: Self-Defense as Activism in the Civil Rights Era* (Athens: University of Georgia Press, 2005), 40.

King inherited a tradition of nonviolent thought and action made possible by the contributions of Thurman, Murray, Rustin, and Lawson—contributions that are vastly underrepresented in the literature as compared to King, and without their crucial contributions to nonviolence it is unclear what King's "pilgrimage to nonviolence" would have looked like. All four of these figures were linked to the FOR, as was King, and the FOR's staff and supporters were central architects of the nonviolent tradition King inherited. It is no accident that King published his "Pilgrimage to Nonviolence" essay in 1957 in the FOR's organ, *Fellowship Magazine*. King credits his introduction to nonviolence to the FOR executive secretary A. J. Muste, who supervised James Farmer and Bayard Rustin as staff members in the early 1940s, and King notes that he was deeply influenced by Mordecai Wyatt Johnson, the man who hired Howard Thurman as a professor of religion at Howard University. King's ideas were, through King's own attribution, directly and deeply shaped by the FOR and the Black thinkers affiliated with the group. Rustin, in particular, was a critical interlocutor for King. As Rustin's biographer John D'Emilio writes, "For the rest of the [1950s], Rustin applied himself to King's emergence as a national leader. He made himself useful in all sorts of ways. He introduced King to labor leaders, like Ralph Helstein of the Packinghouse Workers, who then became financial supporters of the SCLC. He drafted speeches and articles for King and provided line editing for King's own writing. Rustin helped prepare *Stride toward Freedom*, King's account of the Montgomery bus boycott, offering comments on chapters and working with King's agent and publisher to help with the book's promotion. When King had important meetings, such as the conference with Nixon, Rustin advised him about how to proceed. Rustin pushed the inexperienced young minister always to see the broader context for the fight against Jim Crow." John D'Emilio, *Lost Prophet: The Life and Times of Bayard Rustin*, 2nd ed. (Chicago: University of Chicago Press, 2004), 266. James M. Lawson Jr. was King's primary confidant and advisor on nonviolence beginning in the late 1950s until King's death in Memphis, where Lawson invited the Baptist minister to ally with striking sanitation workers in early 1968. Lawson originally came south from Oberlin Theological School in 1957 to work with King to advance nonviolence as a paid field secretary of the FOR. Lawson's contributions to nonviolence are detailed—for the first time, using new research from the recently opened Lawson files—in chapter 5. The FOR is at the heart of this story, and its staff and supporters were hard at work for decades experimenting with how the ethic of nonviolence could be applied to mass mobilization centered in nonviolent direct action. King became the greatest spokesperson for this ethic of nonviolence and the tactics that flowed from this ethic, but he built on ideas and tactics that were under development for decades among the FOR staff. Aside from passing references, none of the literature on King explores the FOR and its history in depth. This book fills that gap.

27. Sean Chabot, *Transnational Roots of the Civil Rights Movement: African American Explorations of the Gandhian Repertoire* (Lanham, MD: Lexington Books, 2012). Sean Scalmer has linked Gandhian ideals and their importance to domestic activists to the rise and fall of the New Left, while Quinton Dixie and Peter Eisenstadt have also examined Howard Thurman and the so-called Negro Delegation to India in 1934. See Sean Scalmer, *Gandhi in the West: The Mahatma and the Rise of Radical Protest* (Cambridge: Cambridge University Press, 2011); Quinton Hosford Dixie and Peter R. Eisenstadt, *Visions of a Better World: Howard Thurman's Pilgrimage to India and the Origins of African American Nonviolence* (Boston: Beacon Press, 2011).

28. Sudarshan Kapur, *Raising Up a Prophet: The African-American Encounter with Gandhi* (Boston: Beacon Press, 1992); Scalmer, *Gandhi in the West*; Sarah Azaransky, *This Worldwide Struggle: Religion and the International Roots of the Civil Rights Movement* (Oxford: Oxford University Press, 2017); Leilah C. Danielson, "'In My Extremity I Turned to Gandhi': American Pacifists, Christianity, and Gandhian Nonviolence, 1915–1941," *Church History* 72, no. 2 (2003): 361–88; Leilah C. Danielson, *American Gandhi: A. J. Muste and the History of Radicalism in the Twentieth Century* (Philadelphia: University of Pennsylvania Press, 2014); Dennis C. Dickerson, "African American Religious Intellectuals and the Theological Foundations of the Civil Rights Movement, 1930–55," *Church History* 74, no. 2 (2005): 217–35; Dennis C. Dickerson, "Gandhi's India and Beyond: Black Women's Religious and Secular Internationalism, 1935–1952," *Journal of African American History* 104, no. 1 (2019): 59–83; Randal Maurice Jelks, *Benjamin Elijah Mays: Schoolmaster of the Movement* (Chapel Hill: University of North Carolina Press, 2012); Nico Slate, "From Colored Cosmopolitanism to Human Rights: A Historical Overview of the Transnational Black Freedom Struggle," *Journal of Civil and Human Rights* 1, no. 1 (2015): 3–24; Nico Slate, *Colored Cosmopolitanism: The Shared Struggle for Freedom in the United States and India* (Cambridge, MA: Harvard University Press, 2012); Gerald Horne, *The End of Empires: African Americans and India* (Philadelphia: Temple University Press, 2008); Dixie and Eisenstadt, *Visions of a Better World*.

29. An emerging cohort of scholars is paying particular attention to the way religious sensibilities and ethics informed action for activists on the left in the United States. See Taylor, *Black Religious Intellectuals*; Dickerson, "African American Religious Intellectuals"; David Chappell, *A Stone of Hope: Prophetic Religion and the Death of Jim Crow* (Chapel Hill: University of North Carolina Press, 2004); Sarah Azaransky, *The Dream Is Freedom: Pauli Murray and American Democratic Faith* (New York: Oxford University Press, 2011); Azaransky, *This Worldwide Struggle*;

Joseph Kip Kosek, *Acts of Conscience: Christian Nonviolence and Modern American Democracy* (New York: Columbia University Press, 2011); Leilah Danielson, Marian Mollin, and Doug Rossinow, eds., *The Religious Left in America: Doorkeepers of a Radical Faith* (New York: Palgrave Macmillan, 2018).

30. Brittney C. Cooper has done important work in explicating the complex intersections of identity for Murray, arguing, "Murray's own struggle to both inhabit the bounds of middle-class racial respectability and to embrace her gender nonconformity to accepted ideals of Black femininity, challenge the terms upon which the conception of the race woman proceeds into the latter half of the century. More precisely, her failure, indeed her refusal, to inhabit the category of respectable womanhood in socially accepted terms exposed her to a mode of institutionalized gender disciplining and discrimination that she came to name 'Jane Crow.'" Brittney C. Cooper, *Beyond Respectability: The Intellectual Thought of Race Women* (Urbana: University of Illinois Press, 2017), 88.

Chapter 1

1. Fellowship of Reconciliation (FOR) Minutes of National Council and Executive Committee (hereafter FOR Minutes), 1916, FOR Records, Series A, Subseries A-2, 2 reels, Swarthmore College Peace Collection (SCPC), Reel 102.01, Minutes, 1915–32.

2. FOR Minutes, 13 February 1923.

3. Jill Wallis, *Valiant for Peace: History of the Fellowship of Reconciliation, 1914–89* (London: Fellowship of Reconciliation, 1991), 4.

4. Henry Hodgkin, "Quakers and Peace," in *Publications: Texts for Students of International Law* (London: Sweet, 1921), 41.

5. FOR Minutes, 1916. The U.S. chapter joined a global group of about 4,000 members in 1916.

6. FOR Minutes, 16 April 1916, SCPC.

7. FOR Minutes, 16 April 1916, SCPC.

8. FOR Minutes, 16 April 1916, SCPC.

9. FOR Minutes, 16 April 1916, SCPC.

10. FOR Minutes, 16 April 1916, SCPC.

11. FOR Minutes, 19 February 1916; FOR Minutes, 5 February 1918.

12. See Alan Gilbert, *Black Patriots and Loyalists: Fighting for Emancipation in the War for Independence* (repr., Chicago: University of Chicago Press, 2013).

13. Frederick Douglass, "An Appeal to Congress for Impartial Suffrage," in *Foundations of American Political Thought*, ed. Constance Polin and Raymond Polin (New York: Peter Lang, 2006), 428. See also Joseph T. Wilson, *The Black Phalanx: African American Soldiers in the War of Independence, the War of 1812, and the Civil War* (New York: Da Capo Press, 1994); Dudley Taylor Cornish, *The Sable Arm: Black Troops in the Union Army, 1861–1865* (repr., Lawrence: University Press of Kansas, 1987); James M. McPherson, *The Negro's Civil War: How American Blacks Felt and Acted during the War for the Union* (New York: Vintage Books, 2003).

14. See Gary Gerstle, "Theodore Roosevelt and the Divided Character of American Nationalism," *Journal of American History* 86, no. 3 (1999): 1280–1307; Gary Gerstle, *American Crucible: Race and Nation in the Twentieth Century* (Princeton, NJ: Princeton University Press, 2001).

15. David L. Lewis, *W. E. B. Du Bois: Biography of a Race, 1868–1919* (New York: Henry Holt, 1993); David L. Lewis, *W. E. B. Du Bois: The Fight for Equality and the American Century, 1919–1963* (New York: Henry Holt, 2000).

16. Cornelius L. Bynum, *A. Philip Randolph and the Struggle for Civil Rights* (Urbana: University of Illinois Press, 2010), 90.

17. Leon F. Litwack, *Trouble in Mind: Black Southerners in the Age of Jim Crow* (New York: Knopf, 1998), 322.

18. Quoted in Litwack, *Trouble in Mind*, 439.

19. As Isabel Wilkerson has written, "Estimates vary for the number of blacks who left the South during the Great Migration," a phenomenon typically separated into a first migration before 1940 and a second migration after 1940. Wilkerson suggests that between 1910 and 1970, more than 5.5 million Black Americans left the former Confederacy for the Northeast, Midwest, and West Coast. Isabel Wilkerson, *The Warmth of Other Suns: The Epic Story of America's Great Migration* (repr., New York: Vintage, 2011), 556.

20. Much work remains to be done in chronicling the rise of associational and institutional life among Black Americans. For examples of local studies that chart the growth of Black institutions, see St. Clair Drake, Horace R. Cayton, and Mary Pattillo, *Black Metropolis: A Study of Negro Life in a Northern City*, enlarged ed. (Chicago: University of Chicago Press, 2015); Preston Lauterbach, *Beale Street Dynasty: Sex, Song, and the Struggle for the Soul of Memphis* (New York: W. W. Norton, 2015); Otis L. Sanford, *From Boss Crump to King Willie: How Race Changed Memphis Politics* (Knoxville: University of Tennessee Press, 2017). For the rise of Black newspapers in Jim Crow, see August Meier, *Negro Thought in America, 1880–1915: Racial Ideologies in the Age of Booker T. Washington* (Ann Arbor: University of Michigan Press, 1963). More recently, Imani Perry has traced the rise of Black associational life in the twentieth century through the Black national anthem, "Lift Every Voice." See Imani Perry, *May We Forever Stand: A History of the Black National Anthem* (Chapel Hill: University of North Carolina Press, 2018).

21. See Colin Grant, *Negro with a Hat: The Rise and Fall of Marcus Garvey* (New York: Oxford University Press, 2010); Adam Ewing, *The Age of Garvey: How a Jamaican Activist Created a Mass Movement and Changed Global Black Politics* (Princeton, NJ: Princeton University Press, 2014). Black socialists Owen and Randolph, despite supporting Garvey earlier, ultimately became advocates of the "Garvey Must Go" campaign among Black leaders in Harlem. Randolph in particular believed in this period that interracial class-based solidarity was the only way to effectively organize against the racist and imperialist forces. "White and black workingmen . . . still fight over racial prejudice," he wrote in 1919, which leaves "rich white plutocrats [to] pick the pockets of both." Bynum, *A. Philip Randolph and the Struggle for Civil Rights*, 81.

22. Johnson, *Negroes and the Gun*, 105.

23. Johnson, 151.

24. Johnson, 157.

25. Bynum, *A. Philip Randolph and the Struggle for Civil Rights*, 95–96. Bynum explains that "though nonviolence became a central component of his subsequent activism, in the aftermath of the war and in the face of the rising racial tensions that exploded in the Red Summer of 1919, Randolph's take on black self defense is not surprising. . . . One can only really see Randolph's later embrace of nonviolence as part of a philosophical evolution on his part" (96). Randolph was critical to the process of imagining nonviolence and of pioneering nonviolent direct action in the struggle against Jim Crow, and both philosophical and practical impulses drove his shift in that direction. Randolph was, at heart, a reformer—someone who wanted to increase Black access to good jobs, affordable housing, and safe communities. But he recognized that the intertwined forces of racism and capitalism meant that these things would only be possible if there was a fundamental transformation in the structure of American society and politics. By the start of the Second World War, after decades of political organizing, Randolph came to believe that nonviolent direct action was the most effective tool to do this, and the ethical underpinnings of the tactic appealed to both his humanist and religious sensibilities.

26. The Black population in Detroit, for example, exploded from 5,000 in 1910 to 660,000 in 1970. Thomas J. Sugrue, *The Origins of the Urban Crisis: Race and Inequality in Postwar Detroit* (Princeton, NJ: Princeton University Press, 2005), 23.

27. For the authoritative study of the 1917 massacre in East St. Louis, see Elliott Rudwick, *Race Riot at East St. Louis, July 2, 1917* (Urbana: University of Illinois Press, 1964). Chapter 5, "The July Riot," deals specifically with the violence of July 2, including approximate death tolls and the difficulty of determining an exact death count. Rudwick notes that many "East St Louisans disputing the Congressional figures [of 39 dead] claimed that the true number of Negro fatalities would never be known because many corpses were not recovered" (50).

28. Robert V. Haynes, *A Night of Violence: The Houston Riot of 1917* (Baton Rouge: Louisiana State University Press, 1976).

29. Genna Rae McNeil, "Before Brown: Reflections on Historical Context and Vision," *American University Law Review* 52, no. 6 (2003): 1431.

30. Robert Whitaker, *On the Laps of Gods: The Red Summer of 1919 and the Struggle for Justice That Remade a Nation* (New York: Broadway Books, 2009).

31. Bynum, *A. Philip Randolph and the Struggle for Civil Rights*, 92.

32. FOR Minutes, 22 September 1918. The Federal Council of Churches created its own division to deal with issues related to race in 1920.

33. Wood was a dynamic figure who cofounded the American Civil Liberties Union, the Quaker American Friends Service Committee, and the National Urban League. FOR Minutes, 22 September 1918.

34. Edward W. Evans, "Christianity and the Race Problem," 1919, FOR Papers, Series E, Box 16, Folder Race Relations Misc. 1920s and 1930s, SCPC, 2. For a global analysis of Wilsonian rhetoric related to self-government and civilization, see Erez Manela, *The Wilsonian Moment: Self-Determination and the International Origins of Anticolonial Nationalism* (Oxford: Oxford University Press, 2009).

35. Evans, "Christianity and the Race Problem," 2–3.
36. Evans, 3.
37. Evans, 4.
38. Evans, 5.
39. FOR Minutes, 26 April 1918.
40. Cedric Long, "From Chairman Morningside Heights FOR Group NYC," FOR Papers, Early Records from Local Groups Pt. I.
41. FOR Philadelphia District Meeting, 31 May 1917, FOR Papers, Series A, Section III, Box I, Folder Early Records from Local Groups Pt. II, SCPC.
42. "Religious Forums," 1920, FOR Papers, Series A, Section III, Box I, Folder Early Records from Local Groups Pt. II, SCPC.
43. From Rev. Clarence V. Howell to members of FOR at Belmar Conference, 16 September 1921, FOR Papers, Folder Early Records from Local Groups Pt. II. In 1923, Howell featured an anarchist lecturer, a communist, a socialist, and an International Workers of the World representative from the marine transport workers union. "Religious Forum Flier," 17 February 1923, FOR Papers.
44. FOR Minutes, 8 March 1917.
45. FOR Minutes, 13 April 1917.
46. This discourse belonged to a larger set of important intellectual currents in the early twentieth century. The emerging field of psychology, with its emphasis on individual behavior and how these behaviors might be understood and changed, was an important driver of FOR thinking. Another influence was the emerging social science fields—especially anthropology and sociology—and in particular the focus on how groups of people thought about and organized themselves. The work of Franz Boas and Ruth Benedict was cited regularly and distributed widely by FOR in an effort to break apart what it saw as the debunked social science of race superiority. Perhaps most important was American pragmatism, defined concisely by William James as the notion that truth is not a priori but instead *"happens* to an idea." See Louis Menand, *The Metaphysical Club: A Story of Ideas in America* (repr., New York: Farrar, Straus and Giroux, 2002), 353. These intellectual undercurrents fueled the search for a nonviolent "method" that could express "supreme reverence for human personality." In this search, FOR emphasized trial and error and continuing experimentation in social conflicts throughout the late 1920s and early 1930s. For an introduction to the rise of psychology, see Daniel N. Robinson, *An Intellectual History of Psychology*, 3rd ed. (Madison: University of Wisconsin Press, 1995). For works on the relationship between the ideas of Boaz and Benedict and the fight against racism, see Gail Bederman, *Manliness and Civilization: A Cultural History of Gender and Race in the United States, 1880–1917*, Women in Culture and Society ed. (Chicago: University of Chicago Press, 1996). For an excellent intellectual history on the rise of American pragmatism, which also outlines the broader intellectual terrain for the emerging fields of psychology and anthropology in the United States, see Menand, *Metaphysical Club*.
47. FOR Minutes, 9–13 February 1923. The War Resisters League was discussed as being "distinct from the Fellowship" in an Executive Committee meeting on March 1923. FOR Minutes, 15 March 1923.

48. FOR Minutes, 3 November 1923.

49. "Revised Committee of FOR Statement," FOR Minutes, 3 November 1923.

50. FOR Minutes, "Appendix to the Report of the Committee Dealing with Pacifist Strategy of the FOR," 1923. For an excellent treatment of the rise of the "second" Ku Klux Klan, see Nancy K. McLean, *Behind the Mask of Chivalry: The Making of the Second Ku Klux Klan* (Oxford: Oxford University Press, 1995).

51. "Proposed Revised Committee of FOR Statement," FOR Minutes, November 1923.

52. FOR Minutes, 7 February 1924; FOR Minutes, 20 February 1924.

53. FOR Minutes, 7 June 1924.

54. FOR Minutes, 14 May 1925. Howard Thurman was present at this meeting at Bible House in New York City. FOR Minutes, 18 February 1926. Kirby Page also noted that he had persuaded Reinhold Niebuhr to dedicate all his time to FOR, speaking, writing, counseling, and carrying out missions in Europe.

55. FOR Minutes, 3 November 1925.

56. Bynum, *A. Philip Randolph and the Struggle for Civil Rights*, 104.

57. Bynum, 105. The AFL's continuing practice of racial segregation forced the almost exclusively Black sleeping-car porters to seek new outlets for organizing, the key factor that led to Randolph organizing the Brotherhood of Sleeping Car Porters. Randolph noted that "Negro unions would stand helpless before such economic juggernauts," suggesting that both capital and white unions would always be an inhibition to Black organizing. As his biographer Bynum writes, he thus saw organizing the sleeping car porters as "one key step in the process of drawing black workers more deeply into the American labor movement" (104–5).

58. FOR Minutes, 19 November 1925; FOR Minutes, 17 December 1925.

59. FOR Minutes, 23 December 1925.

60. FOR Minutes, 23 December 1925. Nathaniel Parker was also writing about "the Religious Basis of the Movement" for the International Fellowship of Reconciliation.

61. FOR Minutes, 9 November 1926. It's possible that Collins also completed duties related to the position of FOR youth secretary.

62. FOR Minutes, 9 November 1926.

63. FOR Minutes, 21 May 1927. As with similar efforts in the past, FOR cooperated with the Federal Council of Churches in these efforts.

64. FOR Minutes, 21 May 1927.

65. Bynum, *A. Philip Randolph and the Struggle for Civil Rights*, 106.

66. FOR Minutes, 8 March 1928.

67. FOR Minutes, August 1930.

68. Bynum, *A. Philip Randolph and the Struggle for Civil Rights*, 113.

69. Bynum, 114. Like FOR leaders, Randolph remained concerned about the root cause of lynching in the United States, but in a slight departure from the FOR Randolph suggested it was not simply a lack of authentic engagement between the races that led to such violence. It was "industrial capitalism," a system built around what Bynum describes as "peonage, the crop-lien system, tenant farming, and peasantry." Bynum, *A. Philip Randolph and the Struggle for Civil Rights*, 113.

70. FOR Minutes, 21 May 1927; FOR Minutes, 8 March 1928. Bynum suggests that Randolph was moving toward a race-first mentality in the late 1920s, but the evidence he cites is from 1940 and 1952. In a 1952 letter, Randolph wrote, "The only movement I would be interested in developing would be an all-Negro movement fighting for all our civil rights for first-class citizenship but with absolute dependence upon Negroes to furnish the money, the brains, and the direction." "As I see it," Randolph continued, overcoming Jim Crow "is the Negro's problem and he has got to pay for it." Bynum, *A. Philip Randolph and the Struggle for Civil Rights*, 127. While Randolph moved toward a race-first mentality beginning with the March on Washington Movement by 1940, his thinking on the matter was still evolving in the late 1920s—but he likely still valued working across lines of race to achieve shared class consciousness among Black and white workers.

71. BSCP membership dropped from 7,000 in the late 1920s to 771 in 1932. Erik S. Gellman, *Death Blow to Jim Crow: The National Negro Congress and the Rise of Militant Civil Rights* (Chapel Hill: University of North Carolina Press, 2012), 12–13.

72. FOR Minutes, 25 May 1929.

73. FOR Minutes, 23 May 1929.

74. FOR Minutes, "FOR Committee on Administration Personnel, Report 1," May 1929; FOR Minutes, 25 May 1929. Greene was a University of Chicago graduate and a leader in the New Americans Division of the Interchurch World Movement, a precursor to the National Council of Churches. "Interchurch World Movement: January 1919–April 1921," finding aid, Interchurch Center, accessed 30 December 2020, https://interchurch-center.org/wp-content/uploads/2015/09/Interchuurch-World-Movement-Guide.pdf.

75. FOR Minutes, 20 October 1927.

76. Collins and Kester were both working on race relations literature in March 1923. FOR Minutes, 22 March 1928; FOR Minutes, 2 November 1928.

77. FOR Minutes, April 1929.

78. FOR Minutes, 23 March 1929.

79. John Nevin Sayre, "Development of the Fellowship in the Next Ten Years," FOR Minutes, 1929.

80. While modern notions of race, particularly in the United States, are quite distinct from ancient notions of difference across lines of ethnicity, religion, and nation, Sayre sought to draw on the radical ideas of Christian community from the first century in his argument to FOR members in the United States in 1920. For an excellent accounting of race as a theological idea, see J. Kameron Carter, *Race: A Theological Account* (Oxford: Oxford University Press, 2008).

81. "Memorandum on Paul Jones Challenge to the FOR," FOR Minutes, May 1929.

82. Howard Kester, "Report from Interracial Conference in Memphis at LeMoyne Jr. College," 27–30 December 1929, John Nevin Sayre Papers (hereafter JNSP), Series A, Box 9, Folder John Nevin Sayre and Howard Kester Correspondence, SCPC.

83. Kester, "Report from Interracial Conference."

84. Kester.
85. Kester.
86. Kester.
87. Howard Kester, "March 1931–Interracial Work," Sayre and Kester Correspondence, JNSP.
88. Kester, "March 1931–Interracial Work."
89. Kester.
90. Robin D. G. Kelley provides crucial historical context for this violence:

By July 1931 the CFWU [Croppers and Farm Workers Union], now eight hundred strong, had won a few isolated victories in its battle for continuation of food advances. Most Tallapoosa landlords, however, just would not tolerate a surreptitious organization of black tenant farmers and agricultural workers. Camp Hill, Alabama, became the scene of the nation's first major confrontation with the local power structure. On July 15th, Taft Holmes organized a group of sharecroppers near Camp Hill and invited [CFWU organizer Mack] Coad, along with several other union members, to address the group in a vacant house that doubled as a church. In all, about 80 black men and women piled into the abandoned house to listen to Coad discuss the CFWU and the Scottsboro case. After a black informant notified Tallapoosa County Sheriff Kyle Young of the gathering, deputized vigilantes raided the meeting place, brutally beating men and women alike. The posse then regrouped at Tommy Gray's home and assaulted his entire family, including his wife who suffered a fractured skull, in an effort to obtain information about the CFWU. Only an agitated Gray, who had rushed into the house armed, saved them from possible fatal consequences. Union organizer Jasper Kennedy was arrested for possessing twenty copies of the *Southern Worker*, and Holmes was picked up by the police the following day, interrogated for several hours, and upon release fled to Chattanooga. Despite the violence, about 150 sharecroppers met with Coad the following evening in a vacant house southwest of Camp Hill. This time sentries were posted around the meeting place. When Sheriff Young arrived on the scene with Camp Hill Police Chief J. M. Wilson and Deputy A. J. Thompson, he found Ralph Gray standing guard about a quarter mile from the meeting. Although accounts differ as to the sequence of events, both Gray and the sheriff traded harsh words and, in the heat of argument, exchanged buckshot. Young, who received gunshot wounds to the stomach, was rushed to a hospital in nearby Alexander City while Gray lay on the side of the road, his legs riddled with bullets. Fellow union members carried Gray to his home but the group, including Mack Coad, barricaded themselves inside the house. The group held off a posse led by police chief J. M. Wilson long enough to allow most members to escape, but the wounded Ralph Gray opted to remain in his home until the end. The posse returned with reinforcements and found Gray lying in his bed and his family huddled in a corner. According to his brother, someone in the group "poked a pistol into brother Ralph's mouth and shot down his throat." The mob burned his home to the ground and dumped his body on the steps of the Dadeville Courthouse. The mangled and lifeless leader became an example for other black sharecroppers as groups of armed whites took turns shooting and kicking the bloody corpse of Ralph Gray. Over the next few days, between 34 and 55 black men were arrested near Camp Hill, nine of whom were under 18 years of age. Most of the defendants were charged with conspiracy to murder or with carrying a concealed weapon, but 5 union members, Dosie Miner, T. Patterson, William Gribb, John Finch, and Tommy Finch, were charged with assault to murder. Although police chief Wilson could not legally act out his wish to "kill every member of the 'red' there and throw them into this Creek," the Camp Hill Police Department stood idle as enraged white citizens waged genocidal attacks on the black community that left dozens wounded or dead and forced entire families to seek refuge in the woods. Union secretary Mack Coad, the vigilantes' prime target, fled all the way to Atlanta. But few Tallapoosa Communists were as lucky as Coad. Estelle Milner suffered a fractured vertebra at the hands of police after a local black Minister accused her of possessing ammunition.

Kelley explains that "behind the violence in Tallapoeaosa County loomed the Scottsboro case." Robin D. G. Kelley, *Hammer and Hoe: Alabama Communists during the Great Depression* (Chapel Hill: University of North Carolina Press, 1990), 40–42.

91. Howard Kester, "To Friend from Howard Kester," 15 August 1931, Sayre and Kester Correspondence, JNSP.

92. Kelley, *Hammer and Hoe*, 42.

93. Kelley, 42.

94. Kelley, 42.

95. Kelley, 42.

96. Howard Kester, "The Interracial Situation," Report to the FOR National Council, October 1931, JNSP.

97. Kester.

98. Kester.

99. Kester.

100. Howard Kester to John Nevin Sayre, 20 November 1931, JNSP; Kester, "Interracial Situation."

101. FOR Minutes, April 1931; FOR Minutes, 19 December 1931.

102. For a full accounting of the violence in Birmingham in August 1931, and the remarkable story of the attempted "legal lynching" of Willie Peterson, see Melanie S. Morrison, *Murder on Shades Mountain: The Legal Lynching of Willie Peterson and the Struggle for Justice in Jim Crow Birmingham* (Durham, NC: Duke University Press, 2018).

103. FOR Minutes, 19 December 1931.

104. FOR Minutes, 19 December 1931.

105. John Nevin Sayre, "Trip Memo Spring 1932," FOR Papers, Series E, Box 16, Folder Race Relations Misc. 1920–1930s, SCPC.

106. Sayre, "Trip Memo Spring 1932."

107. Sayre.

108. "Report of John Nevin Sayre, Oct. 1931–Oct. 1932," FOR Minutes, October 1932.

109. "Report of Wilder Emergency Relief Committee," 31 December 1932, Sayre and Kester Correspondence, JNSP; Helen Dahnke, "Their Leader Dead, Wilder's Striking Miners Say Their Cause 'Goes Marching On,'" *The Tennessean*, 7 May 1933, found in Sayre and Kester Correspondence, JNSP.

110. Howard Kester, "Trouble in the TN Coalfields, December 1932," Sayre and Kester Correspondence, JNSP.

111. Dahnke, "Their Leader Dead."

112. Howard Kester, "Annual Report of Southern Secretary, October 1933," Sayre and Kester Correspondence, JNSP.

113. Kester, "Annual Report of Southern Secretary, October 1933."

114. Kester.

115. Kester.

116. John Nevin Sayre to Howard Kester, 30 October 1933, Sayre and Kester Correspondence, JNSP.

117. Sayre to Kester, 30 October 1933.

118. John Nevin Sayre, "Written Statement in Conference of FOR Bulletin," November 1933, Sayre and Kester Correspondence, JNSP.

119. "The Newsletter," FOR, November 1933, p. 5, JNSP.

120. "Please Answer This Referendum Immediately," 22 November 1933, FOR Minutes, FOR Papers, SCPC, Reel 102.02.

121. "Please Answer This Referendum Immediately."

122. Howard Kester to John Nevin Sayre, 6 November 1933, Sayre and Kester Correspondence, JNSP.

123. Kester to Sayre, 6 November 1933.

124. Kester to Sayre, 6 November 1933; emphasis in original.

125. John Nevin Sayre to Howard Kester, 21 November 1933, Sayre and Kester Correspondence, JNSP.

126. Howard Kester to John Nevin Sayre, Telegram, 18 December 1933, Sayre and Kester Correspondence, JNSP.

127. Kester to Sayre, 18 December 1933.

128. Howard Kester to John Nevin Sayre, 4 January 1934, Sayre and Kester Correspondence, JNSP.

129. Kester to Sayre, 4 January 1934.

130. Alice Kester to John Nevin Sayre, 11 January 1934, Sayre and Kester Correspondence, JNSP.

131. A. Kester to Sayre, 11 January 1934.

132. Howard Kester to John Nevin Sayre, 16 January 1934, Sayre and Kester Correspondence, JNSP.

133. FOR Minutes, 24 June 1935.

134. Charles F. Howlett, "American Friends Service Committee and Peace Education," in *2008 Encyclopedia of Peace Education* (New York: Columbia University, 2008), https://www.tc.columbia.edu/epe/epe-entries/Howlett_american_friends.pdf.

135. Ray Newton to Claud Nelson, 28 September 1935, in *Quaker Brotherhood: Interracial Activism and the American Friends Service Committee, 1917–1950*, by Allan W. Austin (Urbana: University of Illinois Press, 2012), 98.

136. Austin, *Quaker Brotherhood*, 98.
137. Austin, 103.
138. Austin, 105.
139. FOR Minutes, 12 September 1939; FOR Minutes, 8 September 1940.
140. FOR Minutes, 11 February 1941.
141. J. Holmes Smith, "Report of Secretary of Committee on Non-violent Techniques, March 25 to November 25 1941," FOR Minutes, November 1941.
142. FOR Minutes, 7 September 1941.

Chapter 2

1. Howard W. Thurman, *With Head and Heart: The Autobiography of Howard Thurman* (New York: Harcourt Brace Jovanovich, 1979), 265–66.

2. Howard W. Thurman, "Relaxation and Race Conflict," 1929, in *The Papers of Howard Washington Thurman* [hereafter PHWT], vol. 1, *My People Need Me, June 1918–March 1936*, ed. Walter Earl Fluker (Columbia: University of South Carolina Press, 2009), 145.

3. Thurman first used the language of the religion of Jesus as a "technique of survival for an underprivileged minority" in his 1935 essay "Good News for the Under priveleged" cited below.

In Katie Cannon's pathbreaking text *Black Womanist Ethics*, Howard Thurman was a primary focus. Cannon writes, "The essence of Thurman's theological ethics is that the religion of Jesus is 'a technique of survival for the oppressed.' Each person's life must be defined, nurtured and transformed, wherein the self is actualized, affirming the inward authority which arouses greater meaning and potential with each mystical experience." Katie G. Cannon, *Black Womanist Ethics* (Eugene, OR: Wipf and Stock, 1988), 21. In this chapter, I hope to demystify the "mystical" moniker often attached to Thurman's ideas by exploring how his ethics were linked to a way of being in the world, and how this way of being became the foundation for a politics of collective nonviolent action in the Black freedom struggle.

4. Bulletin for 1937–1938 Academic Year, Howard University School of Religion Bulletins [hereafter HUSORB], Howard University School Records [hereafter HUSOR], Moorland Spingarn Research Center (MSRC), Howard University (HU).

5. Rayford W. Logan, *Howard University: The First Hundred Years, 1867–1967* (New York: New York University Press, 1969), 23.

6. Bulletin for 1928–1929 Academic Year, HUSORB, HUSOR. See also Logan, *Howard University: The First Hundred Years*, 4.

7. William Stuart Nelson, "School of Religion Annual Report Covering Period from 1931–1941," 30 June 1941, HUSOR. Attendees at the first prayer meeting outlined a plan for "a theological seminar, having in view the training of colored men for the ministry." In 1897, an "evening institute" was established to "aid preachers and workers" in teaching Sunday school classes, but this institute was discontinued in 1916. Such fits and starts were important preludes to the establishment of a formal seminary dedicated to preparing Black Americans for ministry in the years following the Civil War, a larger effort to define what Eric Foner has called "the

meaning of freedom" for Black Americans through the creation of public and private educational institutions. Eric Foner, "The Meaning of Freedom in the Age of Emancipation," *Journal of American History* 81, no. 2 (September 1994): 435–60.

8. In 1928, under Howard's first Black president, Mordecai Wyatt Johnson, the university's board of governors voted to authorize the graduate school administration to hire its own faculty, a significant boost to graduate education in religion that led to the arrival of some of the best Black religious intellectuals in the country. Nelson, "School of Religion Annual Report Covering Period from 1931–1941"; William Stuart Nelson, HUSORB, 1930–1931; William Stuart Nelson, HUSORB, 1932–1933; William Stuart Nelson, HUSORB, 1928–1929.

9. Nelson, HUSORB, 1930–1931.

10. Quoted in Richard I. McKinney and Mordecai W. Johnson, *Mordecai, the Man and His Message: The Story of Mordecai Wyatt Johnson* (Washington, DC: Howard University Press, 1997), 257. McKinney notes that Johnson was a "moral and spiritual engineer" (60).

11. As Zachery R. Williams notes, "About two years after his arrival as Howard's first black president, Mordecai Johnson gained annual appropriations for the university from the federal government, but these appropriations came at a very high price." Federal allocations for Howard came as a result of the Cramton Bill in 1928, but the price of these appropriations was often ensuring that the institutional commitments did not include actively supporting students in their demonstrations against Jim Crow, even if those demonstrations were nonviolent. As noted in chapter 3, Pauli Murray and a group of young women openly challenged Johnson on this in 1942 with support from Howard Thurman. Zachery R. Williams, *Howard University Public Intellectuals and the Dilemmas of Race, 1926–1970* (Columbia: University of Missouri Press, 2009), 16.

12. McKinney and Johnson, *Mordecai, the Man and His Message*, 258.

13. McKinney and Johnson, 258.

14. Nelson, "School of Religion Annual Report Covering Period from 1931–1941"; Nelson, HUSORB, 1932–1933. Nelson, HUSORB, 1934–1935 Benjamin E. Mays replaced D. Butler Pratt after seventeen years of service. The SOR officially ended the evening school, the correspondence courses, and ultimately the theological college itself to focus on graduate training.

15. William Stuart Nelson, "School of Religion Annual Report, July 1938–30 June 1939," HUSOR, MSRC, HU, p. 5. Gammon had sixty-seven students enrolled, but only thirty-four were college graduates. Notably, Oberlin had thirteen African Americans.

16. See Genna Rae McNeil and A. Leon Higginbotham Jr., *Groundwork: Charles Hamilton Houston and the Struggle for Civil Rights* (Philadelphia: University of Pennsylvania Press, 1984); Rawn James Jr., *Root and Branch: Charles Hamilton Houston, Thurgood Marshall, and the Struggle to End Segregation* (repr., New York: Bloomsbury Press, 2013).

17. James Nabrit, "From Prayer Meeting to University," *Faculty Reprints*, 1 September 1942, 32, https://dh.howard.edu/cgi/viewcontent.cgi?article=1150&context=reprints.

18. Nelson, "School of Religion Annual Report, July 1938–30 June 1939," 13.

19. See Robin D. G. Kelley, *Hammer and Hoe: Alabama Communists during the Great Depression* (Chapel Hill: University of North Carolina Press, 1990).

20. Mays, in Nelson, "School of Religion Annual Report, July 1938–30 June 1939," 16–17; emphasis in original.

21. Evelyn Higginbotham, *Righteous Discontent: The Women's Movement in the Black Baptist Church: 1880–1920* (Cambridge, MA: Harvard University Press, 1993), 227. While Higginbotham suggests that the politics of respectability ought not be discarded wholesale as an accommodation to white culture, noting instead the collective power that women generated within Black denominational structures—particularly over and against men—through practices of dress, decorum, and committee leadership. Higginbotham notes how these cultural practices proved insurgent to race, class, and sex norms. Similarly, while well-dressed nonviolent demonstrators with books can be described as practicing the politics of respectability and accommodating white cultural norms, this analysis elides the deeper vision animating their actions and obscures the deeper impact of their witness. These demonstrators, often from working-class families, were challenging the public dehumanization of Black people in Jim Crow America by asserting their freedom to be in public spaces—a far cry from accommodating white cultural norms.

22. Nelson noted growth from two full-time professors and eight part-time instructors in 1931. Nelson, "School of Religion Annual Report, July 1938–30 June 1939."

23. Nelson, HUSORB, 1937–1938, 1.

24. Nelson, HUSORB, 1937–1938, 2.

25. The growth in the library was due to a purchase of 39,000 volumes from Auburn Theological Seminary and Union Theological Seminary in New York City. "School of Religion NEWS," 1941, HUSOR, MSRC, HU. Of the 248 total Black students attending schools of religion across the United States in 1942, 106 were in white schools and 102 were in Black institutions. Of those attending Black schools, fifty-four, or more than half, attended Howard. William Stuart Nelson, "HUSOR Annual Report Covering 1941–1942," July 1942, MSRC, HU.

26. Howard Thurman to Mordecai Wyatt Johnson, 18 June 1918, PHWT, 1:2.

27. Mordecai Wyatt Johnson to Howard Thurman, 8 July 1918, PHWT, 1:4.

28. Imani Perry's book on the history of "Lift Every Voice and Sing" provides an excellent overview of the extent of the development of Black associational life in the first half of the twentieth century. See Imani Perry, *May We Forever Stand: A History of the Black National Anthem* (Chapel Hill: University of North Carolina Press, 2018).

29. Howard Thurman, "College and Color," April 1924, PHWT, 1:37.

30. Thurman was a contributor to William Stuart Nelson, ed., *The Christian Way in Race Relations* (Freeport, NY: Ayer, 1948).

31. Thurman, "College and Color," PHWT, 1:39.

32. Thurman, 1:40.

33. Thurman, 1:liii. Fluker also described Rochester as a seminary built around "modernistic liberalism."

34. Thurman, 1:liii.

35. Howard Thurman, "Let Ministers Be Christians," January 1925, PHWT, 1:46.

36. Howard Thurman, "The Perils of Immature Piety," May 1925, PHWT, 1:50.

37. Howard Thurman, "Can It Truly Be Said That the Existence of a Supreme Spirit Is a Scientific Hypothesis?" Fall 1925, PHWT, 1:60.

38. Howard Thurman, "The Basis of Sex Morality: An Inquiry into the Attitude toward Premarital Sexual Morality and Analysis of Its True Basis," April 1926, PHWT, 1:99.

39. William James, lecturing about pragmatism in 1907, stated, "Truth happens to an idea. . . . It *becomes* true, is *made* true by events. Its verity *is* in fact an event, a process: the process namely of its verifying self." Quoted in Louis Menand, *The Metaphysical Club: A Story of Ideas in America* (repr., New York: Farrar, Straus and Giroux, 2002), 353.

40. Howard Thurman to Mordecai Johnson, 23 September 1927, Handwritten, Mordecai Wyatt Johnson Papers, Box 178-11, Folder Correspondence with Howard Thurman, MSRC, HU.

41. Among Thurman's most prominent work in this era is a reinterpretation of the spirituals. Walter Fluker has written that Thurman emphasized the "relevance of the spirituals as religious documents," suggesting that in them it is possible to evidence "the primacy of religious experiences" as "the basis of hope and the tools for survival in an otherwise hopeless situation." See Fluker in PHWT, 1:127. See also Howard Thurman, *Deep River and the Negro Spiritual Speaks of Life and Death* (Richmond, IN: Friends United Press, 1975).

42. Howard Thurman, "The Message of the Spirituals," October 1928, PHWT, 1:132.

43. Thurman, "Let Ministers Be Christians," 1:44.

44. Howard Thurman, "The Task of the Negro Minister," October 1928, PHWT, 1:142.

45. Thurman, "Task of the Negro Minister," 1:142.

46. Thurman, "Relaxation and Race Conflict," PHWT, 1:146.

47. Thurman, 1:145.

48. Thurman, 1:112.

49. Thurman believed that pacifism "springs out of a sense of the unity, the basic interrelation and the vast sacredness of all life." It seems to acknowledge that all people are bound together at the level of the capacity for creativity, which means all are also promised the ability to grow into one's unique personality. Thurman, 1:112.

50. Thurman, 1:147.

51. Thurman stated also, "Perhaps this was in the mind of the spiritual geniuses of the race who felt that a man *ought* to love his neighbor as he *ought* to love himself." Thurman, 1:147.

52. Thurman, 1:149.

53. Thurman, 1:149.

54. D. Butler Pratt to Howard Thurman, 30 August 1932, PHWT, 1:168.

55. Pratt to Thurman, 1:168.

56. Howard Thurman to Winnifred Wygal, 24 March 1934, PHWT, 1:179.

57. Howard Thurman, "Good News for the Underprivileged," in *The Negro Caravan: The American Negro, His History, and Literature*, ed. Sterling A. Brown, Arthur P. Davis, and Ulysses Lee (New York: Arno Press, 1970), 687.

58. Thurman, "Good News for the Underprivileged," 688.

59. Thurman, 690.

60. Thurman, 691.

61. Thurman, 687.

62. Thurman, 689.

63. James Russell Brown, "An Examination of the Thesis That Christianity in Its Genesis Was a Technique of Survival for an Underprivileged Minority," master's thesis, 1935, HUSOR, MSRC, HU, 15; 9.

64. Brown, "Examination of the Thesis," 36.

65. Brown, 51, 54.

66. Brown, 57.

67. Brown, 57. Howard Thurman would use the phrase "psychology of Jesus" in his 1949 book *Jesus and the Disinherited*. Thurman was not simply inspiring his students. His students were also inspiring him, an important dialectic in Black religious education.

68. Brown, 58.

69. Brown, 59.

70. Brown, 60.

71. Brown, 60–61.

72. Brown, 61.

73. Brown, 64.

74. Brown, 64.

75. Lee C. Phillip, "A Critical Study of Two Minority Techniques in the Light of Christian Principles," master's thesis, 1939, HUSOR, MSRC, HU, iii.

76. Phillip, "Critical Study of Two Minority Techniques," iv.

77. Phillip, 4, 6.

78. Phillip, 6. The idea of Christian nonresistance occupied many writers seeking a nonviolent politics in the late nineteenth century and into the twentieth. For an explanation of Gandhi's response to this notion as well as an explanation for how nonviolence differed from nonresistance in the Black freedom struggle, see Anthony C. Siracusa, "Developing an American *Ahimsa*: James M. Lawson Jr.'s Paradigm of Protest," honors thesis, Rhodes College, Spring 2009, 42–45, http://dlynx.rhodes.edu:8080/jspui/bitstream/10267/7416/1/Siracusa_honors_2009.PDF.

79. Siracusa, "Developing an American *Ahimsa*," 12. Walter Wink discusses the insurgency of going the extra mile by explaining more carefully the context for the choice faced by the Jewish man in the story. See Walter Wink, *Naming the Powers: The Language of Power in the New Testament* (New York: Fortress Press, 1984); Walter Wink, *Unmasking the Powers: The Invisible Processes That Determine Human Existence* (New York: Fortress Press, 1986); Walter Wink, *Engaging the Powers: Discernment and Resistance in a World of Domination* (New York: Fortress Press, 1992); Walter Wink, *The Powers That Be: Theology for a New Millennium* (New York: Harmony Press, 1999), 98–111.

80. Siracusa, "Developing an American *Ahimsa*," 13.

81. Siracusa, 16.

82. Charles M. Campbell, "Educating Young People on the Philosophy and Technique of Nonviolence," master's thesis, 1941, HUSOR, MSRC, HU, preface.

83. Campbell, "Educating Young People," 22.

84. Campbell, 24.

85. Campbell, 38.

86. Campbell, 37. *Satyagraha* is the Sanskrit term that Gandhi famously used to describe his innovative conception of the force of nonviolence. *Satya* means "truth," and *agraha* implies seizing, clinging to, or clutching at. Gandhi intended the term to imply a complete dedication of one's life and way of being to the pursuit of truth, which included a commitment to do no violence to another person—an idea at the heart of the Sanskrit term *ahimsā*—as each individual has some element of truth to reveal. This is explained in detail in chapter 5.

87. James L. Farmer Jr., "The Relation between Religion and Racism with Special Reference to Christianity and the American Scene," master's thesis, 1941, HUSOR, MSRC, HU, ii.

88. Farmer, "Relation between Religion and Racism," 112.

89. Farmer, 114.

90. Farmer, 114.

91. Farmer, 114.

Chapter 3

1. Rosalind Rosenberg, *Jane Crow: The Life of Pauli Murray* (New York: Oxford University Press, 2017), 4.

2. Rosenberg, *Jane Crow*, 132.

3. Rosenberg, 137.

4. Rosenberg, 139.

5. Rosenberg, 120.

6. Kimberlé Crenshaw coined the phrase "intersectionality" in 1989—four years after Pauli Murray's death in 1985. See Kimberlé Crenshaw, "Demarginalizing the Intersection of Race and Sex: A Black Feminist Critique of Antidiscrimination Doctrine, Feminist Theory and Antiracist Politics," in *University of Chicago Legal Forum*, 1989, 139–67. Crenshaw showed that "a problematic consequence of the tendency to treat race and gender as mutually exclusive categories of experience and analysis" is that Black women have been "theoretically erased" in the "conceptualization, identification and remediation of race and sex discrimination by limiting inquiry to the experiences of otherwise privileged members of the group." The implications for this way of thinking about race and sex are "a distorted analysis of racism and sexism because the operative conceptions of race and sex become grounded in experiences that actually represent only a subset of a much more complex phenomenon" (139–40). This takes seriously the way race and sex informed Pauli Murray's vision of the world, and her vision for how to change it. The innovative vision of politics at the heart of nonviolent direct action was, in part, a

consequence of being locked out not just of first-class citizenship as a Black person, but the difficulty of advancing in the legal profession in part because of her identity as a woman in the 1940s.

7. The tension here with historically Black colleges and universities was apparent to Murray. "Again I want to emphasize that we radicals are not trying to destroy or limit the possibility of the ALL-NEGRO college. We want the opportunity and the right to attend white graduate schools if we desire. We are sure of equal education such as the South provides when we have this right—otherwise we must be in a constant state of struggle for small gain, wearing out our energies, building resentments, and wasting valuable time." Pauli Murray to Dr. James E. Shepard, 2 April 1940, Pauli Murray Papers (PMP), Radcliffe Institute for Advanced Study in the Schlesinger Library at Harvard University (hereafter RIASSLHU), Cambridge, Massachusetts.

8. Glenda Elizabeth Gilmore, *Defying Dixie: The Radical Roots of Civil Rights, 1919–1950* (New York: W. W. Norton, 2008), 317.

9. Gilmore, *Defying Dixie*, 319. The original source for this quote was the *Carolina Times*, 6 April 1940, PMP, Folder Petersburg Bus Incident 2. The full quote read as follows: "And so the yow-yow continued for more than a half hour, while the girls, using Mahatma Gandhi's technique with the British Lion, just sat—and sat." Murray had recently met Krishnalal Shirhadarni, whose book *War without Violence* later inspired activists in the Congress of Racial Equality (CORE).

10. Quoted in Sarah Azaransky, *The Dream Is Freedom: Pauli Murray and American Democratic Faith* (New York: Oxford University Press, 2011), 20.

11. Rosenberg, *Jane Crow*, 92.

12. Murray to Walter White, 29 March 1940, PMP, Folder Petersburg Bus Incident 1.

13. Murray to David L. Lendaman, 25 March 1940, PMP, Folder Petersburg Bus Incident 2.

14. Candace (Pan) Stone to Murray and Mac, 26 March 1940, PMP, Folder Petersburg Bus Incident 2.

15. Murray noted that India is a country with an oppressed majority, while the United States has an oppressed minority. She notes the tradition of nonviolence in religious traditions in India, noting that Black Americans had by and large been peaceful even amid severe violence and discrimination. "Notes Taken by P.M. on Non-violence," March 1940, PMP, Folder Petersburg Bus Incident 2.

16. "Notes Taken by P.M."

17. Murray to Jean and Pan, 2 April 1940, PMP, Folder Petersburg Bus Incident 2.

18. Pan to Murray, 6 April 1940, PMP, Folder Petersburg Bus Incident 3.

19. Pan to Murray, 6 April 1940.

20. Rosenberg writes of Murray's short stint in the Harlem Ashram, which she joined shortly after the bus incident: "Murray's residence at the ashram ended only after a few months. On January 4th, 1941, she was waiting with other residents for the arrival of A. J. Muste, a founding member of the FOR and for many years the head of the faculty at the Brookwood Labor College. Murray lit a cigarette as she waited. Haridas Muzumdar touched her on the shoulder and said, 'no smoking.'

Enraged, but mindful of her Satyagraha-inspired vow to control her temper and not show resentment, Murray retreated to the upstairs bedroom she shared with Mac. There she smoked while denying herself the chance to see Muste. As she explained her actions in her diary the next day, 'I agree with Haridas that we must have discipline, but it must be self inspired, not dictated from without.' She concluded by noting, 'if the ashram is to become a Convent or Monastery, then I have no place here.'" Rosenberg, *Jane Crow*, 101.

21. Murray to Jean and Pan, 9 April 1940, PMP, Folder Petersburg Bus Incident 3.

22. Murray to Jean and Pan, 9 April 1940. Murray expressed joy at "our realization that we were gaining sympathy from the white passengers through intelligent and restrained handling of our situation . . . our willingness to be arrested rather than submit to open discrimination . . . our refusal to respond to threats, discourteous treatment, or coercion . . . our duty to fight against any law which we felt was unjust . . . our identification with our negro fellow prisoners while in prison, and our attempt to carry on educational work among them."

23. Murray to Jean and Pan, 9 April 1940.

24. Murray to Jean and Pan, 9 April 1940.

25. Rosenberg, 95. A similar situation would play out in multiple cities more than a decade later, as notable challenges to the laws preventing segregation in interstate travel would not advance due to the perceived character of the person challenging the law. Among the most notable was Claudette Colvin from Montgomery, a fifteen-year-old who challenged segregation on a Montgomery bus nine months before Rosa Parks. While Colvin's case became part of the *Browder v. Gayle* (1956) case that overturned bus segregation laws in Alabama, when asked why she did not receive the attention that Parks later did, Colvin told National Public Radio, "The NAACP and all the other black organizations felt Parks would be a good icon because 'she was an adult. They didn't think teenagers would be reliable. . . . Her skin texture was the kind that people associate with the middle class. . . . She fit that profile.'" Margot Adler, "Before Rosa Parks, There Was Claudette Colvin," 15 March 2009, National Public Radio, https://www.npr.org/2009/03/15/101719889/before-rosa-parks-there-was-claudette-colvin.

26. "[To] challenge race taboos was one thing," Rosenberg has written of the men's decision. "[But] challenging cross-race sex taboos could get them all killed." Rosenberg, *Jane Crow*, 96. Glenda Gilmore has written that "Murray found in cross-dressing a respite from shouldering the cloak of middle-class female dignity that she had to wear as a black woman activist." Gilmore, *Defying Dixie*, 324.

27. Quoted in Azaransky, *Dream Is Freedom*, 22.

28. My amendment to the excellent work done by Rosenberg, Azaransky, and Gilmore on this question is to argue that the law itself was a big part of the problem. Not only was the law used to discipline and punish Black Americans in the early twentieth century, but the idiosyncrasies of the law were also used—as James M. Lawson Jr. later put it in 1960—as a gimmick to evade real and direct challenges to the legal and cultural bulwark of Jim Crow. In this case, Murray's case was not viable from the lawyer's perspective because she ultimately was not charged with violating segregation laws, even though she and Mac's defiance was

directed squarely at ways Jim Crow law and custom enabled whites to publicly degrade Black people.

29. Rosenberg, *Jane Crow*, 120.

30. Pauli Murray, "An American Negro Views the Indian Question," 4 September 1942, *The Call*, PMP, Howard NAACP Clippings Folder 1.

31. Murray, "American Negro Views the Indian Question." Murray was deeply inspired by the Mahatma and his campaign and sought to build peace at an international student assembly. In early September, 350 students from fifty countries assembled to talk about brokering a world peace amid a global war, and Murray was tasked alongside Dr. H. T. Chu from the University of Chicago "to work out an agreement between Indian and British delegations." *Journal and Guide*, 12 September 1942, PMP, Howard NAACP Clippings Folder 1.

32. Pauli Murray, *Song in a Weary Throat: An American Pilgrimage* (New York: HarperCollins, 1987), 201.

33. Murray, *Song in a Weary Throat*, 205.

34. Paula Giddings, *When and Where I Enter: The Impact of Black Women on Race and Sex in America* (repr., New York: Amistad Publishing, 2006), 278.

35. Morrow and her husband, Wallace Nelson, became active leaders in CORE and participated in sit-ins in the years that followed. Murray, *Song in a Weary Throat*, 209.

36. Pauli Murray, "A Blueprint for First Class Citizenship," PMP, Howard NAACP Clippings Folder 2.

37. "Confidential Report on Howard Chapter NAACP and Civil Rights Committee," 8 May 1944, PMP, Howard Civil Rights Committee 1944 Folder 1.

38. Murray, "Blueprint for First Class Citizenship." Rainse continued, "If the white people deny us service, let them pay for it. . . . Let's go downtown some lunch hour when they're crowded. They're open to the public. We'll take a seat on a lunch stool, and if they don't serve us, we'll just sit there and read our books. They lose trade while that seat is out of circulation. If enough people occupy seats, they'll lose so much trade they'll start thinking."

39. "To the Howard Student," 3 February 1943, PMP, Howard NAACP Clippings Folder 1.

40. Murray, "Blueprint for First Class Citizenship."

41. Juanita Morrow and James T. Wright, "Letter to Howard Campus," 16 March 1943, PMP, Howard NAACP Clippings Folder 1.

42. "Proposed Plan for Campus Campaign on Equal Rights Bill for the District of Columbia," 16 March 1943, PMP, Howard NAACP Clippings Folder 1.

43. "Howard Students Picket Jim Crow Restaurant," *Chicago Defender*, Washington Bureau, 24 April 1943, PMP, Howard NAACP Clippings Folder 1.

44. "Howard Students Picket."

45. "Howard Students Picket." Some Howard faculty were also on hand for this demonstration, including Dean Susie Lavell and Professors Caroline Ware and Leon Ransom.

46. In her biography of Baker, Barbara Ransby writes that during Baker and Murray's time together in Harlem in the 1930s, the two women became "fast friends,"

noting also that "the two women remained in touch off and on for over forty years." During the campaigns Murray helped to lead at Howard under the auspices of the NAACP during the Second World War, Baker was working as director of branches for the national staff of the NAACP. In a 1944 letter to Walter White and Roy Wilkins, Murray, hard at work seeking to transform Jim Crow conditions through organizing local students in an NAACP chapter in Washington, D.C., called "race relations" a "profession," adding that "its workers should be technically trained." "Who is more capable," she asked, "to lead off in the training process than the national staff?" Singling out Baker, Murray wrote, "I've seen Ella in action and they don't come finer." Barbara Ransby, *Ella Baker and the Black Freedom Movement: A Radical Democratic Vision* (Chapel Hill: University of North Carolina Press, 2003), 72, 140–41.

47. Rosenberg, *Jane Crow*, 127.

48. Rosenberg.

49. CORE experimented with nonviolent direct action as early as 1942 in Chicago. CORE in Chicago sent an interracial group to investigate the racial policies at Stoner's, a "white tablecloth restaurant in the heart of Chicago's Loop." CORE eventually investigated all of the restaurants in the sixteen-square-block downtown and found that only Stoner's practiced segregation. The group published "50 Loop Restaurants Which Do Not Discriminate" and continued attempts at negotiation with the owner. After these failed, CORE attempted a sit-in. Teams of two and three whites were seated quickly and without difficulty. But when an interracial group of six African Americans and two whites followed behind, Stoner kicked one of the white team members in the leg as they waited. He called the police three times as the interracial team waited, but upon finding no disturbance the police left. Before leaving the third time, the police warned Stoner that they would carry him to jail if he called again. Patrons throughout the restaurant perked up at the site of the interracial teams, and a passing hostess whispered to a participant, "Keep it up—we're all with you." "Suddenly," James Farmer wrote of the sit-in, the "deadlock was broken." An older woman not associated with the demonstration approached an African American woman in the interracial group of CORE demonstrators and asked her to have dinner. Other patrons followed suit, and soon only two demonstrators in the group were left waiting for service. A hostess seated the last two demonstrators, and the restaurant broke out into spontaneous applause as the final members of the CORE team were seated. "It was a fitting climax to a well-executed non-violent demonstration for racial justice," Farmer wrote. Anthony C. Siracusa, "Developing an American *Ahimsa*: James M. Lawson Jr.'s Paradigm of Protest," honors thesis, Rhodes College, 2009, 21–25.

50. Murray, *Song in a Weary Throat*, 222.

51. "What Took Place on 11th and Pennsylvania, April 22, 1944–April 23, 1944," PMP, Folder Howard Civil Rights Committee 1944. Two People's Drug Stores were also targeted by the Institute on Race Relations.

52. Murray, *Song in a Weary Throat*, 224. Notably, participation had grown from twelve demonstrators at the Little Palace Cafe to fifty-six at Thompson's, and at least fourteen were women—including Pauli Murray. "Were You There When We

All Took a Chair at Dear Old Thompson's?" 23 April 1944, Flier, PMP, Folder Howard Civil Rights Committee 1944. Thompson's had multiple locations in D.C., and it would take continued direct action and a Supreme Court decision to end segregation across all locations. https://historicsites.dcpreservation.org/items/show/971, accessed 1 January 2021.

53. Each student was asked to make a pledge: "to be prompt at all meetings; to fulfill any obligation or assignment which I undertake on behalf of the campaign, and to serve in whatever capacity I am best fitted—whether picketing, 'sitting in' restaurants, making posters and signs, handing out leaflets, or speaking." "The Civil Rights Committee, Howard Chapter NAACP, Washington, DC," 25 April 1944, PMP, Folder Howard Civil Rights Committee 1944.

54. "Howard University Students Demonstrate New Technique in Securing Equal Rights Noting Victory at Thompson's," 25 April 1944, Press Release, PMP, Folder Howard Civil Rights Committee 1944. Other slogans read, "We die together, why can't we eat together?"

55. "The Civil Rights Committee, Howard Chapter NAACP, Washington, DC."

56. "Howard University Students Demonstrate New Technique."

57. "Howard University Students Demonstrate New Technique."

58. "Howard University Students Demonstrate New Technique." The origins of the campaign were explained in more depth: "The Civil Rights Campaign grew out of an incident last February when three Howard University students were arrested and imprisoned for refusing to pay an up charge in a United cigar store, when they insisted upon being served. Stung into action, the Howard chapter, NAACP, organized the civil rights committee, made a survey of the laws in the District of Columbia, and unearthed a bill for equal rights, HR 1995, introduced by Congressman Rowan of Illinois and now buried in the district committee with about 15 signatures on a discharge petition. . . . The Howard students realizing the slow pace of remedial legislation decided to dramatize the need for an equal rights law in the District of Columbia by helping public opinion along a little."

59. Murray, *Song in a Weary Throat*, 203.

60. Horace Cayton, "New Technique: A Dramatic Program to Focus Attention on Negro Problems," 30 April 1944, *Pittsburgh Courier*, PMP, Folder Howard NAACP Clippings 2.

61. "A Thing or Two—One Elementary Step," *PM*, 29 April 1944, Folder Howard NAACP Clippings 2.

62. "We Ain't Ready," *Pittsburgh Courier*, 30 April 1944, Folder Howard NAACP Clippings 2.

63. "We Ain't Ready."

64. Murray and Powell to Johnson, 30 April 1944, PMP, Folder Howard Civil Rights Committee 1944.

65. "President Johnson's Letter to Professor Ransom re Statement of Policy on NAACP Civil Rights Activities," 2 May 1944, PMP, Folder Howard Civil Rights Committee 1944.

66. Howard University Civil Rights Committee to Professor Ransom, 2 May 1944, PMP, Folder Howard Civil Rights Committee 1944.

67. Murray to Eleanor Roosevelt, 4 May 1944, PMP, Folder Howard Civil Rights Committee 1944.
68. Murray to Eleanor Roosevelt, 4 May 1944.
69. Murray to Eleanor Roosevelt, 4 May 1944.
70. Murray to Eleanor Roosevelt, 4 May 1944.
71. Murray, *Song in a Weary Throat*, 228.
72. "Suggested Instructions to Be Issued on an 'Instruction Sheet' to Picketers, Sitters, and Other Demonstrators in Civil Rights Campaign," 24 May 1944, PMP, Folder Howard Civil Rights Committee.
73. Lawson's work is outlined in detail in chapter 5.
74. "Suggested Instructions to Be Issued on an 'Instruction Sheet.'"
75. "Suggested Instructions to Be Issued on an 'Instruction Sheet.'"
76. "Suggested Instructions to Be Issued on an 'Instruction Sheet.'"
77. "Suggested Instructions to Be Issued on an 'Instruction Sheet.'"
78. Murray, *Song in a Weary Throat*, 225.
79. Murray, *Song in a Weary Throat*, 229.
80. Murray, *Song in a Weary Throat*. Powell argued, "Non-violent resistance to gain civil rights did not begin with the bus boycott in Montgomery, Alabama in 1956. It began with bus incidents in 1940 and was perfected as a technique before 1945. The Negro movements for integration today [1963], like mass movements before it, had its dedicated *avant garde*." She notes that out of the anger Black Americans experienced came "the search for a new, dignified, and more direct way.... Perhaps the greatest gain from the war years is that they inspired the use of a tactic that would be consistent with militancy and peaceful protest." Murray, *Song in a Weary Throat*, 229.
81. "Howard Prexy Denies Disbanding NAACP," *Washington Tribune*, 13 May 1944, PMP, Folder Howard NAACP Clippings II.
82. "Student Pickets," Unnamed Clipping, PMP, Folder Howard NAACP Clippings II.
83. Pauli Murray, "An American Credo," *Common Ground*, Winter 1945, PMP, Folder Howard NAACP Clippings II.
84. Murray, "American Credo."
85. Murray, "American Credo."
86. Murray, "American Credo."
87. Murray, "American Credo."
88. Murray, "American Credo."
89. Murray, "American Credo."
90. Murray, "American Credo."
91. Murray, "American Credo."
92. "Both FOR and CORE seized on *Morgan* as an opportunity to take action. They devised a kind of traveling test of the decision that would be an opportunity to educate local communities about the case along the way. For two weeks in April 1947, an interracial team of 16 men, eight black and eight white, traveled on buses to Virginia, North Carolina, Tennessee, and Kentucky. The choice of route and riders was strategic and not without controversy. They went through the

Upper South to avoid what they anticipated to be more entrenched white racism that might be accompanied by deadly violence farther south. Women activists wanted to be a part of the rides. Pauli Murray; Juanita Morrow, who had also lived at the Harlem ashram; and Ella Baker, the great NAACP organizer, were all part of the planning team and wanted women to be among the protesters. Mail planners, who composed the majority, felt that having interracial teams of men and women would be too inflammatory (regardless, too, of the fact that the person whose name graced the high court decision was a woman)." Sarah Azaransky, *This Worldwide Struggle: Religion and the International Roots of the Civil Rights Movement* (Oxford: Oxford University Press, 2017), 115.

93. Rosenberg, *Jane Crow*, 95–96. As Azaransky writes, "Rustin's insights were nevertheless limited by his stubborn inability to see the significance of women's leadership—in Montgomery and elsewhere. As early as the planning for the Journey of Reconciliation, he had worked closely with brilliant and brave women, like Ella Baker, Pauli Murray, and Juanita Morrow. Someone with his organizing acumen would have seen and appreciated that women had organized the Montgomery boycott and women were crucial to its success. Surely his own experiences of multiple injustices, as a black gay person, could have fostered a solidarity with black women, who experienced the multiple oppressions that Pauli Murray had named Jane Crow. This blind spot of Rustin stayed with him through the decades. In the run-up to the 1963 March on Washington, Anna Arnold Edgerman, the only woman on the planning committee, argued forcefully for women's place on the podium, but he was unmoved. [Benjamin] Mays had proclaimed an egalitarian gospel; similarly, Rustin's own religious convictions required that he testify to equality. Like Mays, Rustin fell short of consistently living the faith he professed." Azaransky, *This Worldwide Struggle*, 199.

94. Azaransky, 139.

Chapter 4

1. John D'Emilio, *Lost Prophet: The Life and Times of Bayard Rustin* (Chicago: University of Chicago Press, 2003), 72.

2. D'Emilio, *Lost Prophet*, 76.

3. D'Emilio notes that COs were "turning the institutions upside down." *Lost Prophet*, 73.

4. D'Emilio, 81.

5. In 1939, *Time* magazine called Muste America's number one pacifist.

6. A. J. Muste to Bayard Rustin, 4 July 1945, Library of Congress [hereafter LOC], Washington, D.C.; Bayard Rustin Papers [hereafter BRP], Folder Correspondence 1945, Reel 40.

7. D'Emilio, *Lost Prophet*, 103–4.

8. D'Emilio, 107.

9. Muste to Rustin, 4 July 1945.

10. Rustin writes, "The failure of pacifist organizations in this country who have concerned themselves with denunciations of war and the causes of war has been to

develop a moral equivalent of war." Bayard Rustin, "The Green Revolution—'Forward to the Land' or Recentralism—A Way Out," Session number 5, 16 April 1944, BRP, Folder FOR, Reel 5. The phrase originally appeared in a William James speech at Stanford in 1906, which was later turned into a 1910 book.

11. Both Rustin and the FOR were explicit about the importance of building an interracial and interchurch movement. As Rustin wrote in 1943, "The formation of an inter-racial, inter-church organization" in communities across the United States "is of great importance not only because as a demonstrated united group your expressions of concern carry more weight but also because of the personal inspiration such an organization offers meeting individual parish problems." Bayard Rustin, "What Can Ministers Do to Forward the Cause of Inter-Racial Hebrew Christian Brotherhood?" October 1943, BRP, Folder Race Relations Institutes 1940s, Reel 5.

12. For more on this, see Sean Chabot, *Transnational Roots of the Civil Rights Movement: African American Explorations of the Gandhian Repertoire* (Lanham, MD: Lexington Books, 2012), 2.

13. For a discussion of how this process worked in a different context, see Larry W. Isaac, Daniel B. Cornfield, Dennis C. Dickerson, James M. Lawson, and Jonathan S. Coley, "'Movement Schools' and Dialogical Diffusion of Nonviolent Praxis: Nashville Workshops in the Southern Civil Rights Movement," in *Nonviolent Conflict and Civil Resistance*, ed. Sharon Erickson Nepstad and Lester R. Kurtz, Research in Social Movements, Conflicts, and Change 34 (Bingley, UK: Emerald Group, 2012), 155–84.

14. Sean Scalmer has written that these links between India and the United States were "a history not just of individuals and nations, but also of connections, campaigns, and international flows." Scalmer, *Gandhi in the West: The Mahatma and the Rise of Radical Protest* (Cambridge: Cambridge University Press, 2011), 5. For the role played by Black women in these international freedom spaces, see Keisha N. Blaine, *Set the World on Fire: Black Nationalist Women and the Global Struggle for Freedom* (Philadelphia: University of Pennsylvania Press, 2018). Nico Slate has called these connections between India and the United States part of the "larger history of racism and anti-racism, of empire and anti-imperialism, of civil rights and human rights." Slate, *Colored Cosmopolitan: The Shared Struggle for Freedom in the United States and India* (Cambridge, MA: Harvard University Press, 2012), 3.

15. Dennis C. Dickerson, "African American Religious Intellectuals and the Theological Foundations of the Civil Rights Movement, 1930–55," *Church History* 74, no. 2 (2005): 217–35; Leilah C. Danielson, "'In My Extremity I Turned to Gandhi': American Pacifists, Christianity, and Gandhian Nonviolence, 1915–1941," *Church History* 72, no. 2 (2003): 361–88; Leilah Danielson, *American Gandhi: A. J. Muste and the History of Radicalism in the Twentieth Century* (Philadelphia: University of Pennsylvania Press, 2014); Joseph Kip Kosek, *Acts of Conscience: Christian Nonviolence and Modern American Democracy* (New York: Columbia University Press, 2011); Chabot, *Transnational Roots of the Civil Rights Movement*; Scalmer, *Gandhi in the West*; Sudarshan Kapur, *Raising Up a Prophet: The African-American Encounter with Gandhi* (Boston: Beacon Press, 1992); Aldon D. Morris, *The Origins of the*

Civil Rights Movement: Black Communities Organizing for Change (New York: Free Press, 1986); Aldon D. Morris, "A Retrospective on the Civil Rights Movement: Political and Intellectual Landmarks," *Annual Review of Sociology* 25 (1999): 517-39.

16. Kapur, *Raising Up a Prophet*; Kosek, *Acts of Conscience*, 85-112; A. J. Muste, "The World Task of Pacifism," in *The Essays of A. J. Muste*, ed. Nat Hentoff (New York: Simon and Schuster, 1967), 215-34. Also see Quinton Hosford Dixie and Peter R. Eisenstadt, *Visions of a Better World: Howard Thurman's Pilgrimage to India and the Origins of African American Nonviolence* (Boston: Beacon Press, 2011); Gerald Horne, *The End of Empires: African Americans and India* (Philadelphia: Temple University Press, 2008), 98-124; Chabot, *Transnational Roots of the Civil Rights Movement*, 74.

17. "*How* different social movements affect one another," as David S. Meyer and Nancy Whittier put it, has been the subject of many studies. See Meyer and Whittier, "Social Movement Spillover," *Social Problems* 41, no. 2 (1994): 278. See also Larry Isaac and Lars Christiansen, "How the Civil Rights Movement Revitalized Labor Militancy," *American Sociological Review* 67, no. 5 (2002): 722-46; Larry Isaac, Steve McDonald, and Greg Lukasik, "Takin' It from the Streets: How the Sixties Mass Movement Revitalized Unionization," *American Journal of Sociology* 112, no. 1 (2006): 46-96. Also see Peter Stamatov, "Activist Religion, Empire, and the Emergence of Modern Long-Distance Advocacy Networks," *American Sociological Review* 75, no. 4 (2010): 618; Margaret E. Keck and Kathryn Sikkink, *Activists beyond Borders: Advocacy Networks in International Politics* (Ithaca, NY: Cornell University Press, 1998). Chabot takes up precisely this question by looking for the mechanisms by which ideas about nonviolence and nonviolent tactics were dispersed transnationally in the years before the Montgomery Bus Boycott. Chabot suggests that U.S. activists intent on "adopting Gandhian forms of discourse, organizing, and action on American soil" developed a "Gandhian Repertoire" of contentious politics through "trial and error" using noncooperation techniques. He argues that U.S. activists in the early 1940s engaged in "collective learning" about Gandhi's social movement techniques through experimentation with this "foreign repertoire" while on domestic soil. Chabot, *Transnational Roots of the Civil Rights Movement*, 4.

18. A Gandhian "frame alignment" sparked by the Second World War initiated concerted interracial collaboration between these otherwise distinct movements. Defined as the "linkage" or coupling of "interpretive orientations" among both individuals and social movement organizations, frame alignment is described by movement theorists as a process wherein the "interests, values, and beliefs" as well as the "activities, goals, and ideology" of distinct movement actors become aligned. David A. Snow, E. Burke Rochford Jr., Stephen K. Worden, and Robert D. Benford, "Frame Alignment Processes, Micromobilization, and Movement Participation," *American Sociological Review* 51, no. 4 (1986): 464.

19. Judith Brown, *Modern India: The Origins of an Asian Democracy* (New York: Oxford University Press, 1985), 311-12.

20. Arthur Hernan, *Gandhi and Churchill: The Epic Rivalry That Destroyed an Empire and Forged Our Age* (New York: Random House, 2008), 495; Bidyut Chakrabarty,

"Political Mobilization in the Localities: The 1942 Quit India Movement in Midnapur," *Modern Asian Studies* 26, no. 4 (1992): 791–814.

21. "Wake Up Negro America" flier, A. Philip Randolph Papers, LOC Manuscript Collections, Washington, D.C. [hereafter Randolph Papers], Box 26, Folder MOWM Press Releases 1942–1946.

22. A. Philip Randolph keynote address, MOWM Proceedings of Conference Held in Detroit, 26–27 September 1942, Series A-3, Box 15, Folder March on Washington, FOR, SCPC, 1–4.

23. The Quit India campaign revealed concentric space between Randolph's movement and the pacifist FOR. This moment of collaboration has either been incorrectly chronicled or, more commonly, dismissed. Despite the quality of her work on A. Philip Randolph, Cynthia Taylor incorrectly posits that A. J. Muste spoke at the MOWM's first national meeting in 1943. See Taylor, *A. Philip Randolph: The Religious Journey of an African American Labor Leader* (New York: New York University Press, 2006), 170. JoAnn Robinson says simply that the MOWM and FOR "used" one another to pursue their distinct goals. See JoAnn O. Robinson, *Abraham Went Out: The Biography of A. J. Muste* (Philadelphia: Temple University Press, 1981), 115. Joseph Kip Kosek cites meeting minutes from a FOR meeting to assert that Muste believed the MOWM was "a challenge to us." Kosek, *Acts of Conscience*, 184. Although Taylor at times gets the facts wrong, she does more than either Kosek or Robinson to explain the connections between FOR and the MOWM. Kosek argues that "race logic" prevented important collaboration between the two, and Robinson underplays the significance of their intermovement exchange in crafting and diffusing a new movement ideology. Neither of these approaches captures the importance of this intermovement collaboration between FOR and the MOWM during the Second World War.

24. "There is a mantra, a short one," Gandhi told the Indian National Congress at Gowalia Tank in Bombay before it voted to support the Quit India campaign of 1942. "You imprint it on your heart and let every breath of yours give an expression to it. The mantra is 'do or die.'" Mohandas Gandhi, "Do or Die" speech, 8 August 1942, http://nvdatabase.swarthmore.edu/content/indians-campaign-full-independence-quit-india-campaign-1942-1943. For examples of how some Christians actually interpreted such forceful action as following in the way of Jesus, see Warren Carter, *Matthew and Empire: Initial Explorations* (London: Bloomsbury, 2001).

25. Jill Wallis, *Valiant for Peace: History of the Fellowship of Reconciliation, 1914–89* (London: Fellowship of Reconciliation, 1991), 83. For Gandhi's contention that satyagraha is the opposite of pacifism, see M. K. Gandhi, *Nonviolent Resistance (Satyagraha)* (Mineola, NY: Dover Press, 2001), 6.

26. Paula Pfeffer calls Randolph an atheist multiple times throughout her 1996 text despite Randolph's intimate relationship with religious thought and the church throughout his life. Paula Pfeffer, *A. Philip Randolph, Pioneer of the Civil Rights Movement* (Baton Rouge: Louisiana State University Press, 1996), 7, 63, 84.

27. Taylor, *A. Philip Randolph*, 2. On the all-Black character of the BSCP, see Cornelius L. Bynum, *A. Philip Randolph and the Struggle for Civil Rights* (Urbana: University of Illinois Press, 2010). Bynum writes, "Randolph never considered the

organization of all-black unions as an end unto itself. Rather, he viewed the Brotherhood as one key step in the process of drawing black workers more deeply into the American labor movement" (105).

28. Taylor, *A. Philip Randolph*, 224.

29. Robinson, *Abraham Went Out*, 64. FOR was founded in England in August 1914. Muste cofounded the U.S. affiliate in November 1915. The distinction is an important one, as the organizations would reach different conclusions about pacifism and nonviolence over time—especially in regard to Gandhi. A. J. Muste, "Return to Pacifism," in *Essays of A. J. Muste*, 196. This idea was later adopted by James M. Lawson Jr., a Black Methodist minister who Martin Luther King later called the most knowledgeable and experienced nonviolent organizer in the United States. Lawson's first inspiration to pursue a life of nonviolent resistance came from hearing Muste speak at his alma mater, Baldwin Wallace College, in the late 1940s (detailed in chapter 5). See Leilah Danielson's excellent biography of Muste, *American Gandhi: A. J. Muste and the History of Radicalism in the Twentieth Century* (Philadelphia: University of Pennsylvania Press, 2014).

30. A. J. Muste, "Sit-Downs and Lie-Downs," in *Essays of A. J. Muste*, 206.

31. Lewis Perry, *Civil Disobedience: An American Tradition* (New Haven, CT: Yale University Press, 2013), 175.

32. Bynum, *A. Philip Randolph and the Struggle for Civil Rights*, 170–71.

33. Muste, "Sit-Downs and Lie-Downs," 206.

34. A. J. Muste, Memo, 14 March 1941, FOR Papers, Section II, Series A, Sub-Series A-1, Box 3, Folder Nonviolent Direct Action Program, SCPC.

35. A. J. Muste to James Farmer, 3 January 1942, FOR Papers, Section II, Series A-3, Box 2, Folder A. J. Muste Correspondence with James Farmer, SCPC.

36. All quotes from James Farmer, "Memorandum to A. J. Muste on Brotherhood Mobilization," 8 January 1942, Series C, Box 3, Folder Misc. Material, FOR, SCPC. Farmer's Brotherhood Mobilization coalesced into the interracial Congress of Racial Equality (CORE), which scholars have referenced extensively for decades—but only recently have we seen in-depth local studies of CORE. Meier and Rudwick argue that CORE "articulated the philosophy and applied the tactics of nonviolent direct action for nearly two decades before the 'civil rights revolution' burst upon the national scene in 1960." August Meier and Elliot Rudwick, *CORE: A Study in the Civil Rights Movement, 1942–1968* (New York: Oxford University Press, 1973), 3. Chabot also deals extensively with CORE in *Transnational Roots of the Civil Rights Movement*. Later works detailing local CORE chapters on the East and West Coasts offer a promising look into the development of this grassroots organization in places outside the South. See Brian Purnell, *Fighting Jim Crow in the County of Kings: The Congress of Racial Equality in Brooklyn* (Lexington: University of Kentucky Press, 2015); Joan Singler, Jean Durning, Bettylou Valentine, and Maid Adams, *Seattle in Black and White: The Congress of Racial Equality and the Fight for Equal Opportunity* (Seattle: University of Washington Press, 2011).

37. "Calling All Negroes to Attend 'We Are Americans, Too,' Conference," n.d., Box 26, Folder Press Releases 1942–1946, MOWM, Randolph Papers, LOC. At the MOWM's national policy conference in Detroit in September 1942, participants

discussed how nonviolent civil disobedience might be treated: "Where no civil rights legislation is in force, disciplined and trained leaders, students and young people should use a carefully planned non-violent technique of refusal to accept such discriminations; such groups must be prepared in advance to face the consequences of civil proceedings; test cases should be developed and handled by existing legal agencies; refusals should be organized and continuous until the pattern is broken down, or public action is taken to eliminate such discriminations." Strategy committee participants included Pauli Murray, Theodore Brown, J. L. McLemore, and J. Conyers. See "Techniques for Breaking Down Discrimination in Restaurants, Hotels, Busses, Movies, etc.," in "MOWM Proceedings of Conference Held in Detroit," 26–27 September 1942, Series A-3, Box 15, Folder March on Washington, FOR, SCPC, 35.

38. "March on Washington May Conference Will Pioneer Program of Civil Disobedience and Non-Cooperation," press release, 30 December 1942, Box 26, MOWM, press release folder 1942–1946, Randolph Papers, LOC.

39. A. J. Muste to A. Philip Randolph, 11 January 1943, FOR Papers, Series A-3, Box 15, Folder March on Washington, SCPC.

40. A. Philip Randolph to A. J. Muste, 26 January 1943, FOR Papers, Series A-3, Box 15, Folder March on Washington, SCPC.

41. A. Philip Randolph to A. J. Muste, 30 April 1943, FOR Papers, Series A-3, Box 15, Folder March on Washington, SCPC.

42. A. J. Muste to A. Philip Randolph, 21 May 1943, FOR Papers, Series A-3, Box 15, Folder March on Washington, SCPC. E. Stanley Jones worked with Gandhi throughout the 1920s and penned *Christ of the Indian Road* in 1925.

43. Bayard Rustin to A. J. Muste, 22 February 1943, FOR Papers, Section II, Series A-3, Box 4, Muste Correspondence, Rustin folder, SCPC. This letter is quoted also in JoAnn Robinson, *Abraham Went Out*, 112. Robinson tracks the relationship between Randolph and Muste and, more broadly, the links between FOR, CORE, and the MOWM throughout the 1940s. But Robinson concludes her discussion of the relationships between each movement succinctly, claiming "in one sense or another each side (FOR and MOWM) probably did incline to 'use' the other, but the integrity of both leaders kept that inclination in check" (116). Robinson diminishes the importance of this cooperation between the MOWM and FOR by focusing on personalities. The cooperation between each movement was integral to developing a nonviolent direct-action praxis that superseded the discrete aims and ideologies of either movement. In particular, Rustin labored for both organizations throughout 1943 and developed a pamphlet outlining nonviolent action that was distributed throughout the MOWM network. See minutes of NVDA committee, 25 January 1943, FOR Papers, Section II, Series A-1, Box 3, Non-Violent Direct Action Folder, FOR.

44. Chabot offers little empirical evidence to explain what was transmitted between pacifists and African American civic organizations in the nonviolent institutes these groups hosted together that were the most significant sites of collective learning in the early 1940s. Chabot, *Transnational Roots of the Civil Rights Movement*, 78. For a relevant theoretical framework that considers the idea of collective

learning, see Colin Barker and John Krinsky, "Movement Strategizing as Developmental Learning: Perspectives from Cultural-Historical Activity Theory," in *Culture, Social Movements, and Protest,* ed. Hank Johnston (Burlington, VT: Ashgate Publishing, 2009), 212, 225.

45. "Mapping a Broad National Program in the Interest of Abolishing Jim Crow," 1 July 1943, Randolph Papers, Box 24, Folder MOWM Conferences, LOC.

46. "Town Hall Meeting Tonight," 2 July 1943, Box 24, Folder MOWM Conferences, Randolph Papers, LOC; "Flier for Independence Day Service," Box 24, Folder MOWM Conferences, Randolph Papers, LOC; B. M. Philips, "Chicago Convention Votes for a New March on Capital: Randolph Says," *Baltimore Afro-American,* 10 July 1943, 1.

47. Bayard Rustin, "Race Relations Department of the FOR Plan, 1943–1944," n.d., BRP, Folder FOR, Reel 1, LOC.

48. Among those Rustin hoped to have write for a nonviolence bulletin were Walter White, Rabbi Cronbach, Howard Thurman, George Schuyler, "Phil" Randolph, Algernon Black, Cary McWilliams, Dr. Riddich, Pearl Buck, Frances Gunther, Haridas Muzumdar, Otto Kleinberg, Ruth Benedict, Charles Wesley, and Hideo Hasimoto. Maurice Dawkins would serve as associate editor. Rustin, "Race Relations Department of the FOR Plan."

49. Bayard Rustin, "FOR Draft Report—Commission on Inter-racial and Minorities," BRP, Folder FOR, Reel 1.

50. "Institute on Race Relations and Non-Violent Solutions, April 16–18, 1943, Detroit Michigan," program, BRP, Folder Race Relations Institute/Workshops, Reel 5.

51. "Conference on Creative Non-violence as an Aid to Racial Understanding, Avalon Boulevard Christian Church, Los Angeles, California, April 30–May 2, 1943," program, BRP, Folder Race Relations Institute/Workshops, Reel 5, LOC.

52. Henry J. Richardson Jr., "Speech Delivered before the Indianapolis Institute on Race Relations and Non-Violent Solutions at the Senate Avenue Research Branch of the YMCA," 12 June 1943, BRP, Folder Race Relations Institute/Workshops, Reel 5, LOC.

53. "Report from Dayton Race Relations Institutes," 14–15 June 1943, BRP, Folder Race Relations Institute/Workshops, Reel 5, LOC.

54. "Dayton Inter Racial Institute," program, BRP, Folder Race Relations Institute/Workshops, Reel 5, LOC.

55. "Columbus Institute on Race Relations and Non-Violent Solutions at the Second Baptist Church," program, 16 June 1943, BRP, Folder Race Relations Institute/Workshops, Reel 5, LOC.

56. "Columbus Institute on Race Relations."

57. See Tom Sugrue, *The Origins of the Urban Crisis: Race and Inequality in Postwar Detroit* (Princeton, NJ: Princeton University Press, 2005), 29. See also Heather Ann Thompson, *Whose Detroit? Politics, Labor, and Race in a Modern American City* (Ithaca, NY: Cornell University Press, 2004), 16.

58. Bayard Rustin, "A Statement on the Race Relations Crisis in June of 1943," BRP, Folder FOR, Reel 1, LOC.

59. Bayard Rustin, "FOR Draft Report—Commission on Inter-racial Work and Minorities," BRP, Folder FOR, Reel 1, LOC. The report contains a mention of the so-called Zoot Suit Riots, which means it was likely written in May or June 1943.

60. Bayard Rustin to A. J. Muste, 18 October 1943, FOR Papers, Section II, Series D, Box 51, Folder 2, SCPC; "Mixed Groups Test Capital's Jim Crow," *Baltimore Afro-American*, 14 August 1943, 13.

61. "Institute for Race Relations," March 1943, FOR Papers, Section II, Series D, Box 51, Folder Rustin 2, SCPC.

62. W. Astor Kirk, "Institute on Race Relations Progress Note," 11 September 1943, BRP, Folder Fellowship of Reconciliation, Reel 1, LOC.

63. "Non-Violent Direct Action Group Girds to Break D.C. Restaurant Ban," *New York Amsterdam News*, 9 October 1943, 12.

64. Bayard Rustin, "Race Relations Department of the FOR Plan for 1943–1944," n.d., BRP, Folder Race Relations Institutes/Workshops, Reel 5, LOC. Rustin and FOR also hoped that local chapters would form partnerships with the NAACP, the ACLU, the Urban League, the War Resisters League, and the Women's Defense Leagues. Among the cities mentioned as targets by Rustin and FOR were Kansas City, Pittsburgh, Toledo, St. Louis, Baltimore, Chicago, Dayton, Indianapolis, Cleveland, Detroit, Richmond, Philadelphia, and Syracuse.

65. Isaac et al., "'Movement Schools' and Dialogical Diffusion of Nonviolent Praxis," 158.

66. "To Bayard, AJ, and John from Jean," 11 August 1943, BRP, Folder Race Relations Institute/Workshops, Reel 5, LOC.

67. "Workshops on Race and Nonviolence, Lecture and Discussion, Sunday Evening, 17 October (1943), the March on Washington Movement and the Detroit and Harlem Riots," BRP, Folder Race Relations Institutes 1940s, Reel 5, LOC.

68. Randolph had direct experience with the threat of takeover by white communists, as they had attempted to steer the direction of the National Negro Congress (NNC), which Randolph had cofounded in the mid-1930s. For an analysis of Randolph's public denouncement of communists as president of the NNC, see Erik S. Gellman, *Death Blow to Jim Crow: The National Negro Congress and the Rise of Militant Civil Rights* (Chapel Hill: University of North Carolina Press, 2014), 151–53.

69. "Workshops on Race and Nonviolence, Lecture and Discussion, Sunday Evening, 17 October (1943)."

70. Bayard Rustin, "Workshops on Race and Nonviolence, Discussion—14 October," 1943, BRP, Folder Race Relations Institutes 1940s, Reel 5, LOC. The list of targeted businesses and institutions comes from "Workshops on Race and Nonviolence, Discussion—31 October," BRP, Folder Race Relations Institutes 1940s, Reel 5, LOC.

71. Peg Deuel to Bayard Rustin, 9 February 1944, BRP, Folder Race Relations Institute/Workshops, Reel 5, LOC.

72. Bayard Rustin, "Workshops on Race and Nonviolence, Project No. 1. An Interracial Primer for Negroes," BRP, Folder Race Relations Institutes 1940s, Reel 5, LOC.

73. Bayard Rustin, "Workshops on Race and Nonviolence, Panel Discussion, Saturday Evening October 30," 1943, BRP, Folder Race Relations Institutes 1940s, Reel 5, LOC.

74. Bayard Rustin, "Workshops on Race and Nonviolence, Sheet No. 6: Lesson Plan on Faith, Discipline, Action," BRP, Folder Race Relations Institutes 1940s, Reel 5, LOC.

75. Bayard Rustin, "Workshops on Race and Nonviolence, Sheet No. 1: Lesson Plan on Nonviolent Action," BRP, Folder Race Relations Institutes 1940s, Reel 5. Interestingly, Rustin suggested using the "why" method in the South—by which he meant questioning whites who asked African Americans to remove themselves to segregated seating areas on street cars. "One reason why racial prejudice has flourished in the South," he wrote, "has been the docile acceptance by Negroes of segregation in principle. Another reason is the consequent conditioning of white people since childhood to be unaware of segregation as an issue." The why method, Rustin suggested, challenges whites to think about their participation in a system they have not considered carefully.

76. Rustin, "Workshops on Race and Nonviolence, Sheet No. 1: Lesson Plan on Nonviolent Action."

77. Bayard Rustin, "Workshops on Race and Nonviolence, Sheet No. 5: The American Racial Scene Today," BRP, Folder Race Relations Institutes 1940s, Reel 5, LOC.

78. Bayard Rustin, "Workshops on Race and Nonviolence, Suggestions to Ministers," n.d., BRP, Folder Race Relations Institutes 1940s, Reel 5, LOC.

79. Brown, Jean McKay, Berger, and Bayard Rustin, "Workshops on Race and Nonviolence, Workshop Report on Action in Specific Instances of Discrimination," BRP, Folder Race Relations Institutes 1940s, Reel 5, LOC.

80. Bayard Rustin to Doris Grotewohl, 5 May 1944, BRP, Folder FOR, Reel 1, LOC.

81. Bayard Rustin, "Basic Principles," n.d., BRP, Folder FOR, Reel 1, LOC.

82. Bayard Rustin, "Forward from Pacifism: Our Need to Shift Our Emphasis from Pacifism to a Program of Positive Social Goals, Part I, Session #3," 2 April 1944, BRP, Folder FOR, Reel 1, LOC.

83. Bayard Rustin, "Sunday Seminar, 16 April 1944, 'The Green Revolution—"Forward to the Land" or Recentralism—A Way Out,' Session Number 5," BRP, Folder FOR, Reel 1, LOC.

84. Excerpts from Eleanor Clark to Doris Grotewohl, 3 May 1944, BRP, Folder FOR, Reel 1, LOC. John D'Emilio also covers this episode in *Lost Prophet*, 84–85. *The Power of Nonviolence* was published in 1934 and became a staple of nonviolent trainings in the decades that followed. Joseph Kipp Clark and Lewis Perry, among others, have written about the book's importance to nonviolence and civil disobedience movements. See Richard Bartlett Gregg, *The Power of Non-Violence* (Philadelphia: J. B. Lippincott, 1934); Joseph Kipp Kosek, *Acts of Conscience: Christian Nonviolence and American Democracy* (New York: Columbia University Press, 2009); Lewis Perry, *Civil Disobedience: An American Tradition* (New Haven, CT: Yale University Press, 2013).

85. Eleanor Clark to Doris Grotewohl, 3 May 1944.

86. William Greiner to Peton Price, quoted by Bayard Rustin, "Sunday Seminar, 16 April 1944."

87. William Greiner to Peton Price, quoted by Bayard Rustin, "Sunday Seminar, 16 April 1944."

88. William Greiner to Peton Price, quoted by Bayard Rustin, "Sunday Seminar, 16 April 1944."

89. D'Emilio, *Lost Prophet*, 108.

90. D'Emilio writes, "Rustin appeared confident, assured, and free of guilt. . . . His homosexuality was an integral part of him, openly accepted by the heterosexuals in his life" (109). This is a remarkable disposition for a gay man in 1940s America.

91. A. J. Muste to Rustin, 18 June 1945, BRP, LOC.

92. D'Emilio, *Lost Prophet*, 70.

93. D'Emilio, 114–15.

94. Unless otherwise noted, the information in this paragraph is taken from two letters: Bayard Rustin to Davis Platt, 5 April 1945 and 20 April 1945, quoted in D'Emilio, *Lost Prophet*, 110.

95. "Kansas City Race Institute, 14–16 April 1945," program, BRP, Folder Race Relations Institute/Workshops, Reel 5, LOC. For information on the Toledo institute, see George Houser to Shizu Proctor, 24 January 1946, BRP, Folder Race Relations Institute/Workshops, Reel 5, LOC. A race relations institute in Cleveland with no recorded date included more than 350 participants. See "Statistics on Cleveland Race Relations Institute," BRP, Folder Race Relations Institute/Workshops, Reel 5, LOC.

96. "Race Relations Institute Emphasizing Democratic and Non-violent Solutions of Present Day Race Problems," program, n.d., BRP, Folder Race Relations Institute/Workshops, Reel 5, LOC; "The Interracial Workshop, Washington, DC," July 1947, BRP, Folder Race Relations Institute/Workshops, Reel 5, LOC.

97. "List of Interracial Workshop Participants," n.d., BRP, Folder Race Relations Institute/Workshops, Reel 5, LOC.

98. Bayard Rustin, "The Interracial Workshop, Observations," BRP, Folder Race Relations Institute/Workshops, Reel 5, LOC.

99. "Front Cover of Program Announcements—New York (or Boston, St. Louis, Detroit) Institute on Race Relations and Non-Violent Solutions," BRP, Folder Race Relations Institute/Workshops, Reel 5, LOC.

100. James M. Lawson interview with Joan Beifuss, Memphis Sanitation Strike Special Collection, University of Memphis Ned McWhiter Library, Folder 130, p. 3.

101. Lawson interview with Beifuss, 1–2.

102. A host of scholars have noted the rapid and widespread rise of American religiosity in the postwar era. See, among others, Paul Harvey and Philip Goff, eds., *The Columbia Documentary History of Religion in America since 1945* (New York: Columbia University Press, 2005); Darren Dochuk, *From Bible Belt to Sunbelt: Plain-Folk Religion, Grassroots Politics, and the Rise of Evangelical Conservatism* (New York: W. W. Norton, 2011); James David Hudnut-Beumler, *Looking for God in the Suburbs: The Religion of the American Dream and Its Critics, 1945–1965* (New Brunswick, NJ: Rutgers University Press, 1994).

103. David Chappell, *A Stone of Hope: Prophetic Religion and the Death of Jim Crow* (Chapel Hill: University of North Carolina Press, 2004).

Chapter 5

1. David Halberstam, *The Children* (New York: Random House, 1998), 136–37.

2. Wesley Hogan, *Many Minds, One Heart: SNCC's Dream for a New America* (Chapel Hill: University of North Carolina Press, 2007), 38.

3. Halberstam, *Children*, 136–37.

4. Sociologists and historians have collaborated recently to produce outstanding insights into the Nashville movement. See Larry W. Isaac, Daniel B. Cornfield, Dennis C. Dickerson, James M. Lawson, and Jonathan S. Coley, "'Movement Schools' and Dialogical Diffusion of Nonviolent Praxis: Nashville Workshops in the Southern Civil Rights Movement," in *Nonviolent Conflict and Civil Resistance*, ed. Sharon Erickson Nepstad, Lester R. Kurtz (Bingley, UK: Emerald Group, 2012), 155–84; Larry W. Isaac, Jonathan S. Coley, Daniel B. Cornfield, and Dennis C. Dickerson "Preparation Pathways and Movement Participation: Insurgent Schooling and Nonviolent Direct Action in the Nashville Civil Rights Movement," *Mobilization: An International Quarterly* 21, no. 2 (June 2016): 155–76; Daniel B. Cornfield, Jonathan S. Coley, Larry W. Isaac, and Dennis C. Dickerson, "Occupational Activism and Racial Desegregation at Work: Activist Careers after the Nonviolent Nashville Civil Rights Movement," in *Race, Identity, and Work*, ed. Ethel L. Mickey and Adia Harvey Wingfield (Bingley, UK: Emerald Group, 2018), 217–48; Larry W. Isaac, Jonathan S. Coley, Daniel B. Cornfield, Dennis C. Dickerson, "Pathways to Modes of Movement Participation: Micromobilization in the Nashville Civil Rights Movement," *Social Forces*, December 2019, 1–28.

5. The late 1950s were not dissimilar to the 1930s, a moment Harvard Sitkoff described as "a time of planting, not harvesting" for Black Americans. Harvard Sitkoff, *A New Deal for Blacks: The Emergence of Civil Rights as a National Issue* (New York: Oxford University Press, 1978), ix. The long process of attempting to develop a moral form of nonviolent political action among Black intellectuals is perhaps best evidenced the essays in W. S. Nelson, ed., *The Christian Way in Race Relations* (Freeport, NY: Ayer, 1948).

6. Wesley Hogan notes Lawson's particular role in linking ideas and action. See Hogan, *Many Minds, One Heart*, 9.

7. Lawson appears frequently throughout the historical and sociological literature, but little work has been done on his intellectual contributions to nonviolence. Eminent sociologist and historian of the civil rights movement Aldon Morris described Lawson as "an expert tactician of nonviolent protest." See Morris, *The Origins of the Civil Rights Movement: Black Communities Organizing for Change* (New York: Free Press, 1986), 204. Many scholars cite the importance of Lawson's nonviolent workshops in Nashville in late 1959 and 1960, but there is less explanation about the theoretical work Lawson did in arranging the curricula for these workshops. For good work on the Nashville movement and Lawson's workshops, see Benjamin Houston, *The Nashville Way: Racial Etiquette and the Struggle for Social Justice in a Southern City* (Athens: University of Georgia Press, 2012), 83. For Lawson's workshops as a model of how ideas are diffused, see Isaac et al., "'Movement Schools' and Dialogical Diffusion of Nonviolent Praxis," and Isaac et al., "Preparation Pathways

and Movement Participation." Hogan provides a brief treatment of how Lawson's ideas impacted a cadre of Nashville students in *Many Minds, One Heart*, 13–45. For an older work on the Nashville movement and Lawson's workshops, see Halberstam, *Children*, 4–10, 40, 50–90. For work on how the Nashville students carried lessons from Lawson's workshop to the wider southern movement after 1960, and for a brief treatment of the workshops, see Raymond Arsenault, *Freedom Riders: 1961 and the Struggle for Racial Justice* (New York: Oxford University Press, 2006), especially pp. 53–55. See also John Lewis and Michael D'Orso, *Walking with the Wind: A Memoir of the Movement* (New York: Simon & Schuster, 1998), 70–190. Taylor Branch also follows the Nashville students in his history of America in the King years and describes Lawson as the "mentor of the Nashville movement." Branch, *Pillar of Fire: America in the King Years, 1963–65* (New York: Simon & Schuster, 1998), 122. For detailed information about King's relationship to the Nashville movement in 1960, see Branch, *Parting the Waters: America in the King Years, 1954–63* (New York: Simon & Schuster, 1988), especially pp. 260–97 and 391–95. For a brief but important overview of Lawson and his relationship to Gandhism, see Harvard Sitkoff, *The Struggle for Black Equality, 1954–1992* (New York: Hill and Wang, 1993), 67–84. David Chappell calls Lawson "a veteran of nonviolent warfare" in Chappell's work on Black religion and the challenge to Jim Crow in, *A Stone of Hope: Prophetic Religion and the Death of Jim Crow* (Chapel Hill: University of North Carolina Press, 2004), 68. Lawson is also mentioned regularly in David J. Garrow's *Bearing the Cross*, but little attention is given to the ideas Lawson synthesized and diffused. See Garrow, *Bearing the Cross: Martin Luther King Jr. and the Southern Christian Leadership Conference*, collector's ed. (Norwalk, CT: Easton Press, 1989).

8. Report to the FOR National Council and the Racial Industrial Work, 30 May 1947, Series E, Folder FOR Race Relations, FOR Projects and Co-sponsorship, Institutes, Workshops, etc. 1944–1959.

9. Bulletin, Interracial Workshops, July 1948, Washington, D.C. and Southern California, Folder FOR Race Relations, FOR Projects and Co-sponsorship, Institutes, Workshops, etc. 1944–1959.

10. Summer Interracial Workshop Bulletin, 15 July 1949, Folder FOR Race Relations, FOR Projects and Co-sponsorship, Institutes, Workshops, etc. 1944–1959.

11. Summer Interracial Workshop Bulletin, 15 July 1949.

12. Glenn Smiley, "The FOR and Race Relations," 1959, Series E, Folder FOR Race Relations, FOR Projects and Co-sponsorship, Institutes, Workshops, etc. 1944–1959.

13. As the historian Joel Williamson has written, "Between 1889 and 1946 . . . almost 4,000 black men, women, and children had been mobbed to their deaths." Joel Williamson, *The Crucible of Race: Black/White Relations in the American South since Emancipation* (New York: Oxford University Press, 1984), 120. For a collection of primary sources dealing with lynching, see Ralph Ginzburg, *100 Years of Lynchings* (Baltimore: Black Classic Press, 2013). See also Amy Louise Wood, *Spectacle and Lynching: Witnessing Racial Violence in America, 1890–1940* (Chapel Hill: University of North Carolina Press, 2011); James Allen, ed., *Without Sanctuary:*

Lynching Photography in America (Santa Fe, NM: Twin Palms Publishing, 2000). For work on how criminality and Blackness were linked, often through accusations of rape leveled against Black men, see Khalil Gibran Muhammad, *The Condemnation of Blackness* (Cambridge, MA: Harvard University Press, 2010). See also Philip Dray, *At the Hands of Persons Unknown: The Lynching of Black America* (repr., New York: Modern Library, 2007).

14. Mark M. Smith, *How Race Is Made: Slavery, Segregation, and the Senses* (Chapel Hill: University of North Carolina Press, 2006), 60; Andrew Zimmerman, *Alabama in Africa: Booker T. Washington, the German Empire, and the Globalization of the New South* (Princeton, NJ: Princeton University Press, 2010), 40.

15. Amy Wood focuses on the lynching of men, suggesting that 3,200 Black men were killed between 1880 and 1940. Wood, *Spectacle and Lynching*, 3. The Equal Justice Initiative has put the total number of lynchings between the end of Reconstruction and the end of the Second World War at 4,400. Equal Justice Initiative, *Lynching in America: Confronting the Legacy of Racial Terror*, 3rd ed., 2017, https://lynchinginamerica.eji.org/report.

16. Charles M. Payne, *I've Got the Light of Freedom: The Organizing Tradition and the Mississippi Freedom Struggle* (Berkeley: University of California Press, 1995), 15. Beverly Guy Shefftal describes lynching as "public ritual" in Wilma Pearl Mankiller, *The Reader's Companion to U.S. Women's History* (Boston: Houghton Mifflin, 1998), 351.

17. The Dyer Anti-Lynching Bill failed in 1922 after years of work by the NAACP to pass such a bill. More than a decade later, in 1935, southern lawmakers again prevailed and defeated the Costigan-Wagner Bill, which would have ended lynching through a federal law. President Franklin Delano Roosevelt did not support the bill. In 2020, the Emmett Till Antilynching Act was passed by the House of Representatives in a 410-4 vote and has the backing of ninety-nine senators. But at the time of this writing, the bill is being held up by Rand Paul of Kentucky. Nicholas Fandos, "Frustration and Fury as Rand Paul Holds Up Anti-Lynching Bill in Senate," *New York Times*, 5 June 2020.

18. Reverdy C. Ransom, "Gandhi: Indian Messiah and Saint," in *A.M.E. Church Review* 38 (October 1921): 87. See also Dennis C. Dickerson, "African American Religious Intellectuals and the Theological Foundations of the Civil Rights Movement, 1930-55," *Church History* 74, no. 2 (June 2005): 221; Kapur, *Raising Up a Prophet*, 26, 28, 48-49; and Leilah Danielson, "'In My Extremity I Turned to Gandhi': American Pacifists, Christianity, and Gandhian Nonviolence, 1915-1941," *Church History* 72, no. 2 (June 2003): 361-88.

19. Ransom, "Gandhi: Indian Messiah and Saint," 88.

20. For detailed analysis of the role of Howard faculty and administrators in advancing Gandhism and discerning a moral methodology for challenging Jim Crow, see Dickerson, "African American Religious Intellectuals." See also Randal Maurice Jelks, *Benjamin Elijah Mays: Schoolmaster of the Movement* (Chapel Hill: University of North Carolina Press, 2012). For Mays's autobiography, see Benjamin E. Mays, *Born to Rebel: An Autobiography* (Athens: University of Georgia Press, 2003). For a biography on Johnson, see Richard I. McKinney and Mordecai W. Johnson,

Mordecai, the Man and His Message: The Story of Mordecai Wyatt Johnson (Washington, DC: Howard University Press, 1997). For the most thorough work to date on this cohort of Black religious intellectuals, see Clarence Taylor, *Black Religious Intellectuals: The Fight for Equality from Jim Crow to the 21st Century* (New York: Routledge, 2002). For additional literature on Houston and the role of Howard Law School in ending legal segregation, see Gordon Andrews, *Undoing Plessy: Charles Hamilton Houston, Race, Labor, and the Law, 1895–1950* (Newcastle, UK: Cambridge Scholars Publishing, 2014). For an older work on Houston, see Genna Rae McNeil and A. Leon Higginbotham Jr., *Groundwork: Charles Hamilton Houston and the Struggle for Civil Rights* (Philadelphia: University of Pennsylvania Press, 1984). For more information about Thurgood Marshall's tutelage under Houston at Howard Law School, see Rawn James Jr., *Root and Branch: Charles Hamilton Houston, Thurgood Marshall, and the Struggle to End Segregation* (repr., New York: Bloomsbury Press, 2013). For a critical history of Houston, Marshall, and the NAACP, see Risa Lauren Goluboff, *The Lost Promise of Civil Rights* (Cambridge, MA: Harvard University Press, 2007). See also chapter 2 of this book.

21. Kapur, *Raising Up a Prophet*, 72–101. See also "The Negro Pilgrimage to India," in *Visions of a Better World: Howard Thurman's Pilgrimage to India and the Origins of African American Nonviolence*, by Quinton Hosford Dixie and Peter R. Eisenstadt (Boston: Beacon Press, 2011). For more on Thurman's encounter with Gandhi as well as the trips by Johnson and Mays, see Gerald Horne, *The End of Empires: African Americans and India* (Philadelphia: Temple University Press, 2008), 88–119. See also Anthony C. Siracusa, "Developing an American *Ahimsa*: James M. Lawson Jr.'s Paradigm of Protest," honors thesis, Rhodes College, 2009, 45–48.

22. Howard Thurman, *Jesus and the Disinherited* (Boston: Beacon Press, 1996), 113–14.

23. Thurman, *Jesus and the Disinherited*, 15.

24. Thurman believed American Christianity "lacked much that was fundamental to the genius of the faith itself." Howard Thurman, *With Head and Heart: The Autobiography of Howard Thurman* (New York: Harcourt Brace Jovanovich, 1979), 104.

25. Thurman, *Jesus and the Disinherited*, 35.

26. Thurman, 35.

27. Thurman, 86–88.

28. It's also critical to acknowledge that violent insurrection as an imminently anticipated and easily quelled response was countered by a host of authors who argued that a nonviolent response would destabilize their attacker to quickly reconsider his or her method of intimidation and control. These tactical expressions were popularly presented as "moral jiu-jitsu" in Richard Bartlett Gregg, *The Power of Non-Violence* (Philadelphia: J. B. Lippincott, 1934).

29. For an extensive discussion of the ways in which prominent Black intellectuals and writers discussed Gandhi in Jesus-like terms, see Kapur, *Raising Up a Prophet*, 35–45, 98–102, 140.

30. Gandhi, *Nonviolent Resistance*, 6, 375. See Leo Tolstoy, *The Kingdom of God Is within You: Christianity Not as a Mystical Teaching but as a New Concept of Life* (Rockville, MD: Wildside Press, 2006), 17.

31. Gandhi, *Nonviolent Resistance*, 375.

32. Gandhi, 3.

33. A cohort of contemporaries celebrated Lawson's work on nonviolence. Martin Luther King called Lawson "the leading theorist of nonviolence in the world." See "Reverend James M. Lawson Jr.," Martin Luther King Jr. Research and Education Institute, Stanford University, https://kinginstitute.stanford.edu/reverend-james-m-lawson-jr. John Lewis said that Lawson's trainings in Nashville "turned my world around." "Jim Lawson knew—though we had no idea when we began—that we were being trained for a war unlike any this nation had seen up to this time, a nonviolent struggle that would force this nation to face its conscience." Lewis and D'Orso, *Walking with the Wind*, 70, 78. Diane Nash was skeptical of nonviolence when she first attended Lawson's workshops but concluded, "In the process of using it . . . I finally became convinced." Lisa Mullins, *Diane Nash: The Fire of the Civil Rights Movement* (Miami: Barnhadt and Ashe, 2007), 18. Marion Barry said, "Jim Lawson was the foremost proponent of the philosophical construct around nonviolence." Henry Hampton, Steve Fayer, and Sarah Flynn, eds., *Voices of Freedom: An Oral History of the Civil Rights Movement from the 1950s through the 1980s* (New York: Bantam Books, 1991), 63. Julian Bond described Lawson's vision as "a militant nonviolence, an aggressive nonviolence." Hampton et al., *Voices of Freedom*, 63. Tom Kahn, a close assistant to Bayard Rustin and co-organizer of the 1963 March on Washington, told Lawson he was "most impressed and appreciative" of his role in the sit-in movement of 1960. Tom Kahn to James Lawson, 29 June 1960, James M. Lawson Manuscript Collection (hereafter JLMC), Box 39, Folder Incoming and Outgoing Correspondence, Jane and Alexander Heard Library (hereafter JAHL), Vanderbilt University (VU).

34. After visiting her home in Dover, Delaware, Pauline Morris told Lawson she believed "non-violence is the best practice" for the difficult process of advancing integration. Pauline Morris to James Lawson, 20 May 1958, JLMC, Box 36, Folder Incoming Correspondence, JAHL.

35. Lawson consistently maintained the importance of religion to nonviolence. He wrote Tom Kahn, "Your point about the religious character of the struggle is highly complex and, to be treated justly, would require considerable discussion." Tom Kahn to James Lawson, 21 July 1960, JLMC, Box 39, Folder Incoming and Outgoing Correspondence, JAHL. The final section of this chapter details the religious ideas running throughout Lawson's conception of nonviolence. See also Isaac et al., "'Movement Schools' and Dialogical Diffusion of Nonviolent Praxis."

36. Vincent Harding and Rosemarie Freeney Harding, eds. "James M. Lawson Jr.: The Seamless Cloth of Faith and Struggle," in *The Veterans of Hope Pamphlet Series* vol. 1, no. 2 (Denver: Center for the Study of Religion and Democratic Renewal at Iliff School of Theology, 2000), 9.

37. *Time* magazine called Muste the "number one U.S. pacifist" in 1939.

38. The debate about Christian "nonresistance" as a biblical imperative is covered throughout this book. Gandhi maintained that such "passive resistance" is in fact, no resistance at all. For Gandhi's contention that satyagraha is the opposite of pacifism, see Gandhi, *Nonviolent Resistance*, 6. The broader debate on passive and

active resistance stems from differing interpretations of Jesus' Sermon on the Mount in Matthew 5–7. The British FOR, for example, interpreted Jesus' admonition to "resist not evil" as a counsel to passively accept violence against oneself. Other writers and activists, perhaps first among them the Russian writer Leo Tolstoy, believed Jesus counseled followers to "resist not evil in the way of evil." Tolstoy was among the first to argue that the use of nonviolent force in resisting evil was a Christian idea. Tolstoy described "passive" interpretations of Jesus' teachings in the face of evil as "a perversion" of Christian doctrine, arguing instead that nonresistance should be interpreted "in the exact sense of our Saviour's teaching—that is, not repaying evil for evil. We ought to oppose evil by every righteous means in our power, but not by evil." Tolstoy, *Kingdom of God Is within You*, 18. Tolstoy's ideas deeply impacted Gandhi. In part 2 of his autobiography, *My Experiments with Truth*, Gandhi wrote, "Tolstoy's *The Kingdom of God is Within You* overwhelmed me. It left an abiding impression on me. Before the independent thinking, profound morality, and the truthfulness of this book, [most other books] pale into insignificance." See chapter 15, "Religious Ferment." For the full text of Gandhi's *My Experiments with Truth* (1925), see http://www.columbia.edu/itc/mealac/pritchett/00litlinks/gandhi/#part2. For a fuller discussion of this debate, see Siracusa, "Developing an American *Ahimsa*," 42–45.

39. By 1932, Muste had become a self-described Trotskyist who embraced a "qualified defense of labor violence" before returning to an unqualified position of Christian pacifism by 1936. JoAnn O. Robinson, *Abraham Went Out: The Biography of A. J. Muste* (Philadelphia: Temple University Press, 1981), 64. See also A. J. Muste, *Nonviolence in an Aggressive World* (New York: Harper, 1940).

40. For more on Rustin and Farmer, see Joseph Kip Kosek, *Acts of Conscience: Christian Nonviolence and Modern American Democracy* (New York: Columbia University Press, 2011), 146–91. For the best work on Rustin, see John D'Emilio, *Lost Prophet: The Life and Times of Bayard Rustin* (New York: Free Press, 2003). See also Jervis Anderson, *Bayard Rustin: Troubles I've Seen* (Berkeley: University of California Press, 1998). For excellent primary sources from Rustin himself, see Bayard Rustin, *Time on Two Crosses: The Collected Writings of Bayard Rustin*, ed. Devon W. Carbado and Donald Weise (San Francisco: Cleis Press, 2003). For more on Farmer's experience founding CORE, see James Farmer, *Lay Bare the Heart: An Autobiography of the Civil Rights Movement* (New York: Arbor House, 1985), 101–17.

41. James M. Lawson Jr. interview with Joan Turner Beifuss, 10 September 1968, Sanitation Strike Collection, University of Memphis Library, Folder 29, p. 20. FOR was at the forefront of nonviolent theory and practice with regard to race in America during the 1940s.

42. Lawson interview with Beifuss, 10 September 1968, Folder 130, p. 7.

43. Lawson interview with Beifuss, 10 September 1968, Folder 129, p. 19.

44. A. J. Muste to James M. Lawson Jr., 17 November 1950, JLMC, Box 36, no folder, JAHL.

45. Lawson interview with Beifuss, 10 September 1968, Folder 130, pp. 19–24. For an extended explanation of Lawson's time in jail, see Siracusa, "Developing an American *Ahimsa*," 24–31.

46. A. J. Muste to "Friends in India," 5 November 1952, JLMC, Box 36, no folder, JAHL.

47. Harding and Harding, eds. "James M. Lawson Jr.: The Seamless Cloth of Faith and Struggle," 11.

48. Lawson interview with Harding, 10.

49. James M. Lawson Jr., "Raleigh Institute of Religion: Lecture on Non-Violent Solutions of South and Its Effects Abroad," 30 January 1961, JLMC, Box 21, Folder Speeches on NV Movement (Race), JAHL.

50. James M. Lawson Jr., "The Case for Christian Nonviolence/Backdraft—Chapter 1," n.d., JLMC, Box 45, Folder Correspondence Undated, JAHL.

51. For a discussion of Rustin's and Smiley's role in convincing King to remain nonviolent, see Christopher Strain, *Pure Fire: Self-Defense as Activism in the Civil Rights Era* (Athens: University of Georgia Press, 2005), 40.

52. Lawson, "Case for Christian Nonviolence/Backdraft—Chapter 1." Lawson wrote, "For at least two decades Randolph has urged and sponsored mass nonviolent action for the Negro. . . . Rustin remains the Negro-American with the depth of experience and breadth of imagination in various situations of conflict and racial discrimination." Lawson continued: "Gandhi insisted that nonviolence has to be practiced daily and in the intricate situations to be confirmed and to be understood. Rustin did exactly that. As he travelled about the country, he met segregation both north and south with love-force, often opening a restaurant or converting a would be opponent on the spot."

53. Lawson. Lawson says outright, "Nonviolence is revolutionary."

54. James M. Lawson Jr., "Non-violence: A Relevant Power for Constructive Social Change, Fisk Race Institute, 1958," JLMC, Box 38, Folder NV Workshops 1958, JAHL. Lawson wrote, "One can discover [nonviolence] explicitly in the doctrine of ahimsa (hinduism), non-retaliation (buddhism), doctrine of the cross (Christianity). The spiritual giants of all ages concur in this concept."

55. James M. Lawson Jr. "The Measure of a Movement," Gandhi Memorial Lecture at Howard University, 10 April 1961, JLMC, Box 21, Folder—Speeches on NV Movement (Race), JAHL. Lawson notes also that Gandhi admitted it was his reading of the New Testament that "confirmed the idea of moral resistance." In drawing together the Black Christian heritage, ideas common to major religions, and the politics of Gandhian nonviolence, Lawson reconceived of nonviolence as religion in itself; Lawson notes he gave up violence well before he knew of Gandhi—in the seventh grade. In Gandhi, Lawson saw a "clarification" of much of what Jesus taught. See Lawson, "Case for Christian Nonviolence/Backdraft—Chapter 1."

56. *Wu-wei*, the idea of "not forcing," is likely the idea Lawson emphasized from the Daodejing. The practice of wu-wei is supposed to explain the path of harmony with the Dao, or ziran. Sufism included a set of inner laws, *fiqh*, intended to govern one's own behavior as well as outer laws, *qanun*, which referred to social concerns such as marriage and criminal law. In addition to *ahimsā*, the notion of truth (the Sanskrit word *satya*), or no illusion in word or thought, was drawn from Pantanjail and the Baghavad Gita. The idea of universal love, or *jiān ài*, is likely the idea from Mohism that Lawson emphasized. *Jiān ài* was the idea Mozi used to capture his

belief that Confucius overemphasized loving people within clans and family structures. Early Sufis, like Christian monks and Hindu mystics, professed the subjugation of selfish desire in order to know God.

57. James M. Lawson Jr., "What Is Nonviolence?" n.d., JLMC, Box 45, Folder Backdraft Chapter II—Chapter III, JAHL.

58. M. K. Gandhi in Jeffery D. Long, *Jainism: An Introduction* (London: I. B. Tauris, 2009), 166.

59. Jeffery Long calls this "the Jainist system of relativity." Long, *Jainism*, 164.

60. Arvind Sharma, *Gandhi: A Spiritual Biography* (New Haven, CT: Yale University Press, 2013), 58.

61. Sharma, *Gandhi*.

62. The document from FOR spelled it out this way: "The goal is God; the second thing is that He can be directly known in this life and in this body; the third thing is that spiritual practices are imperative if one is to know God." "The Basis and Power of Love, Preliminary Reading for Feb 1959 Boston FOR Discussion Group," JLMC, Box 36, Folder FOR I, JAHL.

63. James M. Lawson Jr., "Chapter II Clarifying Violence and Nonviolence," JLMC, Box 45, JAHL.

64. James M. Lawson Jr., "(SCLC) Annual Meeting," August 1961, JLMC, Box 39, Folder 1961, JAHL.

65. James M. Lawson Jr., handwritten notes, JLMC, Box 38, Folder NV Workshops 1958, Folder JAHL.

66. Lawson, "(SCLC) Annual Meeting," August 1961.

67. Lawson, "Measure of a Movement."

68. Lawson described his work as FOR's southern secretary as "a unique task in the South today . . . [because] only the FOR has the broad Christian tradition which can appeal to the church leaders of the South." Lawson estimated that between 75 and 90 percent of Black leaders were clergy or lay Christians who saw the struggle as part of their "Christian witness." James M. Lawson Jr. to Dr. George Brown, 15 April 1958, JLMC, Box 36, Folder 1958 Correspondence Incoming and Outgoing, JAHL. Lawson was not the first FOR staff member to work in the South. Howard Kester, a FOR staffer and former Vanderbilt Divinity student in the late 1920s, had organized sharecroppers in communities across the South—but he not only struggled to preach nonviolence in the 1930s but faced the constant threat of personal violence against himself. For more on Howard Kester, see chapter 1 as well as Howard Kester, *Revolt among the Sharecroppers* (Knoxville: University of Tennessee Press, 1997). The University of North Carolina also has extensive oral histories with Kester. See http://docsouth.unc.edu/sohp/B-0007-1/menu.html. Lawson did not tap the "radical roots" common to the 1930s popular front for organizing because the anticommunist efforts of the late 1940s and 1950s had effectively eroded many of those relationships, though people radicalized by their experiences were often essential to the southern civil rights movement. Glenda Elizabeth Gilmore cites the local newspaper in Chapel Hill, North Carolina, which wrote in 1935, "We can use a few more radicals whose roots are set deeply into native soil." Gilmore,

Defying Dixie: The Radical Roots of Civil Rights, 1919–1950 (New York: W. W. Norton, 2008), 204. Gilmore's book does excellent work on the role on the communist alliance with labor and Black Americans in the South during the 1930s, but the largely failed efforts of both communists and organized labor to advance racial equality made new approaches all the more significant by the late 1950s—a time when, arguably, anticommunist crackdowns were at their height. For more on the failure of organized labor to advance civil rights in the South, see Barbara S. Griffith, *The Crisis of American Labor: Operation Dixie and the Defeat of the CIO* (Philadelphia: Temple University Press, 1988). On smaller victories by the Congress of Industrial Organizations (CIO) in Memphis, see Michael K. Honey, *Southern Labor and Black Civil Rights: Organizing Memphis Workers* (Urbana: University of Illinois Press, 1993). Robin Kelley has done excellent work on communist organizing in the 1930s, particularly in response to the Scottsboro trials, where the NAACP faltered. See Robin D. G. Kelley, *Hammer and Hoe: Alabama Communists during the Great Depression* (Chapel Hill: University of North Carolina Press, 1990), 23–43.

69. A host of broader national shifts help us account for the ascent of this unique form of politics in the postwar South. Sociologist Aldon Morris has suggested that the NAACP's blossoming in the immediate postwar years contributed greatly to the development of widespread Black protest beginning in 1960; indeed, following Ruby Hurley's appointment as Southeast Region director of the NAACP in 1951, the total number of NAACP chapters across the former Confederacy rose to more than 500. See "Ruby Hurley, Southeast Region Director," in *NAACP: A Century in the Fight for Freedom—The Civil Rights Era*, Library of Congress, http://www.loc.gov/exhibits/naacp/the-civil-rights-era.html#obj14. But the rise of the NAACP should be understood alongside the near complete banishment of Black Americans from electoral politics in the South. The more than four million Black Americans who left the South for the North and West during the Great Migration often sought to join the Republican Party, but their arrival served only to hasten the pursuit of a "lily white" strategy in "the party of Lincoln." Slowly ostracized from their base of formal political power in the Republican Party, Black Americans began joining FDR's Democratic Party in the late 1930s and early 1940s. But the cumulative effect of these party realignments for Black Americans in the South was a doubling down on Black exclusion by a group of Southern Democrats waging the "Dixiecrat Revolution" in 1948. Bruce J. Schulman suggests, however, that a new breed of "whiggish" southern businessmen would emerge as a more moderate and stable force in the Southern Democratic party. Schulman, *From Cotton Belt to Sunbelt: Federal Policy, Economic Development, and the Transformation of the South, 1938–1980* (Durham, NC: Duke University Press, 1994), 133. Regardless, with the exception of Memphis, Black voting was almost nonexistent in the former Confederacy before the Voting Rights Act of 1965. As Hasan Kwame Jefferies points out about Lowndes County, Alabama, for example, more than 5,000 voting age Black Americans lived in the county at the beginning of 1965, and not one was on the voting roles. Jefferies, *Bloody Lowndes: Civil Rights and Black Power in Alabama's Black Belt* (New York: New York University Press, 2009), 1. By the time the 1956 "Southern Manifesto" was issued by southern lawmakers engaged in "massive resistance" to

integration, Blacks were almost completely disenfranchised from formal electoral politics in the South. The city of Memphis was an exception to this rigid political exclusion. G. Wayne Dowdy has written about the massive voter registrations among Black Memphians in the lead-up to the 1959 election, which Black Americans called a "great crusade for freedom." See Dowdy, *Crusades for Freedom: Memphis and the Political Transformation of the American South* (Jackson: University Press of Mississippi, 2010).

70. James M. Lawson Jr., "Address at Penn State University," 30 March 1960, JLMC, Box 45, Folder Students vs Segregation, JAHL, 3. Lawson went on to say, "What we in the movement in Nashville understand is that we are committed to this building of a climate in which democratic law will have some real relevance. We see ourselves trying to persuade people, to change the attitudes of people, in such a fashion that the Supreme Court decisions can really be relevant." Lawson was publicly critical of the law not only as a limited venue for achieving Black freedom but also in criticizing the law as a "gimmick" used to shut down legitimate civil rights demonstrations. His public criticism of the law was a consequential element in the decision to expel him from Vanderbilt Divinity School. https://whospeaks.library.vanderbilt.edu/sites/default/files/James%20Lawson%20daysofthunder.pdf, accessed 4 January 2020. See also A. W. Martin, "The Lawson Affair, the Sit-Ins, and Beyond," *Tennessee Historical Quarterly* 75, no. 2 (Summer 2016): 142–65.

71. Lawson, "Address at Penn State University," 2.

72. Lawson, "Measure of a Movement." Lawson also wrote that "Negro leadership has not been amenable to an approach which would not only change the laws and customs but transform the power structures which made and sustains those laws and customs." Lawson, "Case for Christian Nonviolence/Backdraft—Chapter 1."

73. James M. Lawson Jr., handwritten note, n.d., JLMC, Box 38, Folder NV Workshops 1958, JAHL.

74. Lawson, "Chapter II Clarifying Violence, and Nonviolence." Lawson wrote, "There is a powerful and significant reception to the idea of non-violence. When I spoke on campuses in Texas in 1953, I did not find this openness to the ideals of pacifism at all. I suggest that recent months (Montgomery, Orangeburg) has paved the way for responsible Negro leaders to see the unlimited possibilities in what we of the Fellowship [of Reconciliation] have been preached [sic] for 43 years." Lawson to Brown, 15 April 1958. Lawson also remarked, "I strongly believe that the FOR has an opportunity to make the ministry of reconciliation felt as never before in its history." James M. Lawson Jr. to Dr. George Brown, 23 June 1958, JLMC, Box 36, Folder Outgoing Correspondence, JAHL. He also told Brown of his intent to remain in the South for a "number of years": "While there are dangers involved in the work, there is also realization that right now I belong there." Lawson to Brown, 15 April 1958. A host of movements in nonwhite countries also shifted discourse on race and resistance in the United States. Gandhi's rise in international politics, despite his never being elected to office, was already a strong source of inspiration for Black Americans by the late 1950s. The high politics of Gandhi's col-

league Jawaharlal Nehru and the collection of nonaligned nations at the Bandung Conference of 1955 signaled to the Soviet Union and the United States that nonwhite peoples across the globe would not simply be folded into their geopolitical calculations. The South African Defiance Campaign of 1948, the armed Mau Mau uprising of the mid-1950s, and Kwame Nkrumah's successful push for Ghanaian independence in 1960 proved to be only the beginning of independence movements in Africa. By 1962, twenty-five new nations emerged in formerly colonized territories and effectively shifted global discourses on race, freedom, and resistance in the United States. James Hunter Meriwether, *Proudly We Can Be Africans: Black Americans and Africa, 1935-1961* (Chapel Hill: University of North Carolina Press, 2002).

75. "Minutes of National Council of the FOR, 21-23 April 1960," JLMC, Box 39, Folder 1961 Clippings/King, JAHL.

76. Lawson was also sought for a number of tasks across the country in places to which he did not travel. Lawson was asked by the Ohio United Campus Christian Fellowship to write an article on world problems and student challenges. David Shaw, pastor of St. Luke's in Odessa, Texas, requested "The Montgomery Story" and "Walk to Freedom" comic books for his congregation. David Shaw to James M. Lawson Jr., 2 April 1959, JLMC, Box 36, Folder Incoming Correspondence, JAHL. Lawson also turned down a Danforth Foundation request to be at a conference with 325 college students in August 1959.

77. James M. Lawson Jr., "Memphis Report," JLMC, Box 38, Folder NV Workshops 1958, JAHL.

78. Lawson, "Memphis Report."

79. Glenn Smiley to James M. Lawson Jr., 19 May 1958, JLMC, Box 36, Folder Incoming Correspondence, JAHL.

80. James M. Lawson Jr. to Glenn Smiley, 2 July 1958, JLMC, Box 36, Folder Outgoing Correspondence, JAHL.

81. James M. Lawson Jr. to Dr. Major Jones, Chattanooga, 10 March 1960, JLMC, Box 36, Folder Outgoing Correspondence, JAHL.

82. While Howard Kester led interracial meetings in the South in the 1930s, nonviolence as a political philosophy and nonviolent direct action as a strategic tactic that could lead to mass mobilization remained a distant possibility.

83. James M. Lawson Jr. to Rev. S. M. Riley Jr., 5 July 1958, JLMC, Box 36, Folder Outgoing Correspondence, JAHL. Lawson also told Riley that much could happen if "ministers could be jarred out of their fear and see the possibility for creative preaching and action."

84. Hogan, *Many Minds, One Heart*, 9.

85. James M. Lawson Jr., "Theology and Social Change" handwritten notes, JLMC, box 45, Folder Notes for chapter three, JAHL, 5.

86. Lawson, "Theology and Social Change" handwritten notes, 5. On humans as social beings in a historical process, see also James M. Lawson Jr., "Approach to Seminary," JLMC, Box 45, Folder Notes for Chapter Three.

87. James M. Lawson Jr., "The Theological Basis of Nonviolence," JLMC, Box 45, Folder Chapter 3, JAHL.

88. James M. Lawson Jr., "A Christian Theology of Nonviolence," handwritten notes, JLMC, Box 45, Folder Notes for Chapter Three Theology and Social Change, JAHL.

89. James M. Lawson Jr., "Cruciality of the Cross," handwritten notes, Box 45, Folder Notes for Chapter Three Theology and Social Change, 5.

90. Lawson, "Cruciality of the Cross," 5.

91. James M. Lawson Jr., "SNCC Conference," handwritten speech, Fall 1960, JLMC, Box 21, Folder Speeches on NV Movement (race), JAHL.

92. "Jesus was nailed to a cross," Lawson wrote, "six bullets were pumped into Gandhi." James M. Lawson Jr., "Non-violence: A Relevant Power for Constructive Social Change," 1958, JLMC, Box 38, Folder NV Workshops 1958, JAHL. Lawson argued that these men had become world historical figures precisely because they chose suffering and sacrifice. Lawson also intoned sardonically, "Perhaps your crucifixion will come out alright as well." James M. Lawson Jr., Handwritten Notes, JLMC, Box 45, Folder Notes for Chapter Three, JAHL.

93. Mullins, *Diane Nash*, 18.

94. James M. Lawson Jr., "Chapter III—What Is Nonviolence," Box 45, Folder CH. III, JAHL.

95. Lawson, "Non-violence: A Relevant Power for Constructive Social Change," 1958. "With the exception of a distinctive segment represented by Mary McLeod Bethune, the Negro has not been non-violent, but rather acquiescent. We, in part, suffer from decades of perpetrating violence against ourselves."

96. James M. Lawson Jr., interview by Anthony C. Siracusa, July 2007.

97. James M. Lawson Jr., "The Womb of Revolution," August 1961, JLMC, Box 39, Folder 1961 (SCLC) Annual Meeting, JAHL.

98. James M. Lawson Jr., "Thoughts on Nonviolence," n.d., JLMC, Box 45, Folder Chapter IV, JAHL. Lawson goes further: "Nonviolent action must not be taken as a political or social means apart from the fundamental approach to life which makes it an outgrowth of faith." It is only over time, a time that likely outstrips political cycles, where nonviolence might be assessed. "The nonviolent action which does not achieve the immediate objectives may actually have the greater meaning to a life of a community than the easy success of an action," Lawson wrote.

99. Bimal Krishna Matilal, *The Central Philosophy of Jainism (Anekånta-Våada)* (Ahmedabad, India: L. D. Institute of Indology, 1981), 61.

100. Long, *Jainism*, 76.

101. Long, 76.

102. Quoted in Long, *Jainism*, 166.

103. James Russell Brown, "An Examination of the Thesis That Christianity in Its Genesis Was a Technique of Survival for an Underprivileged Minority," master's thesis, 1935, Howard University School of Religion Records, Moorland Spingarn Special Collections, Howard University, 60.

104. Lawson, "Cruciality of the Cross."

105. James M. Lawson Jr., "Raleigh Institute of Religion Lecture on Non-Violent Solutions of South and Its Effects Abroad." Lawson was militant, perhaps to a fault,

in emphasizing the importance of accepting violence and suffering by remaining in jail. Lawson argued that nonviolence "does not debate" whether to go to jail and stay there. "Jail going and staying symbolizes the cross," he told his students. It "represents [the] cheerful suffering" at the "heart" of nonviolence. Suffering was at the heart of the politics of revolutionary nonviolence, and Lawson held that "accepting jail sentences tests the fiber of love," which he called "the root law and sustaining spirit of *insistent resistance*. Cut out jail-occupation and you of necessity cut out suffering—cut out suffering and you no longer have [nonviolence]." James M. Lawson Jr., handwritten notes from SNCC Conference, Fall 1960, JLMC, Box 21, Folder Speeches on NV Movement (Race), JAHL.

106. Lawson argued for four categories of force: physical, spiritual/moral, psychological, and sociopolitical. Lawson, "Clarifying Violence and Nonviolence."

107. "Through Negroes nonviolence arrived in America to confound Negroes, challenge the life of a nation, and demand a hearing in a world of violence." Lawson, "Case for Christian Nonviolence/Backdraft—Chapter 1."

108. Lawson, "Womb of Revolution." Lawson believed that self-control, as counseled by Gandhi, "includes this element of meditation and other forms of training." He cites "simple living, recognition of the unity of all life and disinterested service. The vows were: truth, nonviolence, chastity, fearlessness, control of the palate, non-possession, non-stealing, bread-labor, equality of religions, anti untouchability and self-rule. By these daily observances was truth-force to be developed." Quoted in "Basis and Power of Love, Preliminary Reading for Feb 1959 Boston FOR Discussion Group."

109. Lawson, "Womb of Revolution."

110. James M. Lawson Jr., "Handwritten Notes for SNCC Conference Fall 1960." Lawson quotes Philippians 1:12–14 in the speech: " Now I want you to know, brothers and sisters, that what has happened to me has actually served to advance the gospel. As a result, it has become clear throughout the whole palace guard and to everyone else that I am in chains for Christ. And because of my chains, most of the brothers and sisters have become confident in the Lord and dare all the more to proclaim the gospel without fear."

111. James M. Lawson Jr., "NV Workshop Materials," JLMC, Box 38, Folder NV Workshops 1958, JAHL.

112. Robin D. G. Kelley used the phrase "freedom dreams" to describe the variegated strains of the Black radical imagination across the 20th century. Robin D. G. Kelley, *Freedom Dreams: The Black Radical Imagination* (Boston: Beacon Press, 2002)

113. Lawson, "Womb of Revolution."

114. Leon F. Litwack, *Trouble in Mind: Black Southerners in the Age of Jim Crow* (New York: Knopf, 1998), 373.

115. Lawson, "Womb of Revolution."

116. Todd Gitlin, *The Sixties: Years of Hope, Days of Rage* (New York: Bantam Books, 1987).

Epilogue

1. James M. Lawson, "Eulogy of John R. Lewis," 30 July 2020, https://www.youtube.com/watch?v=YOxpSPT5PnI.

2. "Agnostic nonviolent technicians" was coined by a participant in Oxford in 1964 to describe these volunteers. See Lewis Perry, *Civil Disobedience: An American Tradition* (New Haven, CT: Yale University Press, 2013), 244n88.

3. Ellen Barnes, "Journal of Ellen Barnes Experiences at Western College during the Mississippi Freedom Project," June 1964, Freedom Summer Text and Photo Archive, Miami University Digital Library, http://digital.lib.miamioh.edu/cdm/ref/collection/fstxt/id/1146, 18.

4. Barnes, "Journal of Ellen Barnes," 20.

5. Barnes, 22.

6. Barnes, 24.

7. Barnes, 24.

8. Karen Grigsby Bates, "Stokely Carmichael: A Philosopher behind the Black Power Movement," National Public Radio, 10 March 2014.

9. Barnes, "Journal of Ellen Barnes," 24.

10. James M. Lawson Jr., "Student Nonviolent Coordinating Committee Statement of Purpose," in *Black Protest*, ed. Joanne Grant (New York: Random House, 1968), 273. See also Clayborne Carson, *In Struggle: SNCC and the Black Awakening of the 1960s* (Cambridge, MA: Harvard University Press, 1995), 23-24.

11. Charles Tilly has used the notion of "repertoires" to capture the idea that collective nonviolent political action can take many forms, all of which combined form a "repertoire of contentious politics." Those include strikes, boycotts, sit-downs, work stoppages, and many other direct-action tactics. See Charles Tilly, *The Politics of Collective Nonviolence* (Cambridge: Cambridge University Press, 2003).

12. James M. Lawson Jr., interview with Anthony C. Siracusa, 23 July 2007.

13. For an excellent treatment of the Meredith March against Fear, see Aram Goudsouzian, *Down to the Crossroads: Civil Rights, Black Power, and the Meredith March against Fear* (New York: Farrar, Straus and Giroux, 2014).

14. Peniel E. Joseph, *Stokely: A Life* (New York: Basic Books, 2014), 114.

15. Martin Luther King Jr., *All Labor Has Dignity*, ed. Michael K. Honey (Boston: Beacon Press, 2011), 170-71.

16. James M. Lawson Jr., interview by David Yellin and Joan Turner Beifuss, 24 September 1969, Box 22, Folder 139, p. 18, University of Memphis.

17. Lawson, interview by Yellin and Beifuss, Folder 134, p. 22, and Folder 137, p. 32.

18. Sarah Azaransky, *The Dream Is Freedom: Pauli Murray and the Democratic American Faith* (New York: Oxford University Press, 2011), 96.

19. Cannon wrote, "Black women are the most vulnerable and the most exploited members of the American society. The structure of the capitalist political economy in which Black people are commodities combined with patriarchal contempt for women has caused the Black woman to experience oppression that knows no ethical or physical bounds." Cannon sought to show "how Black women

live out a moral wisdom in their real-lived context that does not appeal to the fixed rules or absolute principles of the white-oriented, male structured society. Black women's analysis and appraisal of what is right and wrong and good or bad develops out of the various coping mechanisms related to the conditions of their own cultural circumstances. In the face of this, Black women have justly regarded survival against the tyrannical systems of triple oppression as a true sphere of moral life." Cannon may have agreed that gender-nonconforming Black people, like Murray, may be even more vulnerable than Black women. Katie G. Cannon, *Black Womanist Ethics* (Eugene, OR: Wipf and Stock, 1988), 4.

20. Rosalind Rosenberg, *Jane Crow: The Life of Pauli Murray* (New York: Oxford University Press, 2017), 359.

21. Azaransky, *Dream Is Freedom*, 100.

22. Martin Marty, *Martin Luther: A Life* (New York: Penguin Books, 2004), 68.

23. Rosenberg, *Jane Crow*, 374.

Bibliography

Primary Source Manuscript Collections

Cambridge, Massachusetts
    Radcliffe Institute for Advanced Study in the Schlesinger Library
        at Harvard University
        Pauli Murray Papers
Memphis, Tennessee
    Special Collections in the Ned McWhirter Library
        Memphis Search for Meaning Committee Sanitation Strike Collection
Nashville, Tennessee
    Jean and Alexander Heard Library at Vanderbilt University
        James M. Lawson Jr. Manuscript Collection
Swarthmore, Pennsylvania
    Swarthmore College Peace Collection
        Fellowship of Reconciliation Papers
        John Nevin Sayre Papers
Washington, D.C.
    Library of Congress Manuscript Collections
        A. Philip Randolph Papers
        Bayard Rustin Papers
    Moorland Spingarn Special Collections at Howard University
        Mordecai Wyatt Johnson Papers

Secondary Sources

Allen, James, ed. *Without Sanctuary: Lynching Photography in America*. Santa Fe, NM: Twin Palms, 2000.

Anderson, Carol. *Bourgeois Radicals: The NAACP and the Struggle for Colonial Liberation, 1941–1960*. Cambridge: Cambridge University Press, 2014.

——. *Eyes off the Prize: The United Nations and the African American Struggle for Human Rights, 1944–1955*. New York: Cambridge University Press, 2003.

Anderson, Jervis. *A. Philip Randolph: A Biographical Portrait*. New York: Harcourt Brace Jovanovich, 1974.

——. *Bayard Rustin: Troubles I've Seen*. Berkeley: University of California Press, 1998.

Andrews, Gordon. *Undoing Plessy: Charles Hamilton Houston, Race, Labor, and the Law, 1895–1950*. Newcastle. UK: Cambridge Scholars Publishing, 2014.

Arsenault, Raymond. *Freedom Riders: 1961 and the Struggle for Racial Justice*. New York: Oxford University Press, 2006.

Austin, Allan W. *Quaker Brotherhood: Interracial Activism and the American Friends Service Committee, 1917–1950*. Urbana: University of Illinois Press, 2012.

Azaransky, Sarah. *The Dream Is Freedom: Pauli Murray and American Democratic Faith*. New York: Oxford University Press, 2011.

——. *This Worldwide Struggle: Religion and the International Roots of the Civil Rights Movement*. Oxford: Oxford University Press, 2017.

Barker, Colin, and John Krinsky. "Movement Strategizing as Developmental Learning: Perspectives from Cultural-Historical Activity Theory." In *Culture, Social Movements, and Protest*, edited by Hank Johnston. Burlington, VT: Ashgate Publishing, 2009.

Bederman, Gail. *Manliness and Civilization: A Cultural History of Gender and Race in the United States, 1880–1917*. Women in Culture and Society ed. Chicago: University of Chicago Press, 1996.

Blackmon, Douglas A. *Slavery by Another Name: The Re-Enslavement of Black Americans from the Civil War to World War II*. New York: Anchor Books, 2008.

Blackwell, Joyce. *No Peace without Freedom: Race and the Women's International League for Peace and Freedom, 1915–1975*. Carbondale: Southern Illinois University Press, 1991.

Blaine, Keisha N. *Set the World on Fire: Black Nationalist Women and the Global Struggle for Freedom*. Philadelphia: University of Pennsylvania Press, 2018.

Branch, Taylor. *At Canaan's Edge: America in the King Years, 1965–68*. New York: Simon & Schuster, 2007.

——. *Parting the Waters: America in the King Years, 1954–63*. New York: Simon & Schuster, 1988.

——. *Pillar of Fire: America in the King Years, 1963–65*. New York: Simon & Schuster, 1999.

Brown, Judith. *Modern India: The Origins of an Asian Democracy*. New York: Oxford University Press, 1985.

Brown, Sterling A., Arthur P. Davis, and Ulysses Lee. *The Negro Caravan: Writings by American Negros*. New York: Arno Press, 1970.

Butler, Anthea D. *Women in the Church of God in Christ*. Chapel Hill: University of North Carolina Press, 2006.

Bynum, Cornelius L. *A. Philip Randolph and the Struggle for Civil Rights*. Urbana: University of Illinois Press, 2010.

Camp, Stephanie. *Closer to Freedom: Enslaved Women and Everyday Resistance in the Plantation South*. Chapel Hill: University of North Carolina Press, 2004.

Cannon, Katie. *Black Womanist Ethics*. Eugene, OR: Wipf and Stock, 1988.

Carmichael, Stokely, Ekwueme Michael Thelwell, and John Edgar Wideman. *Ready for Revolution: The Life and Struggles of Stokely Carmichael*. Reprint, New York: Scribner, 2005.

Carson, Clayborne. *In Struggle: SNCC and the Black Awakening of the 1960s*. Cambridge, MA: Harvard University Press, 1995.

Carter, J. Kameron. *Race: A Theological Account*. Oxford: Oxford University Press, 2008.

Carter, Warren. *Matthew and Empire: Initial Explorations*. London: Bloomsbury, 2001.

Chabot, Sean. *Transnational Roots of the Civil Rights Movement: African American Explorations of the Gandhian Repertoire*. Lanham, MD: Lexington Books, 2012.

Chakrabarty, Bidyut. "Political Mobilization in the Localities: The 1942 Quit India Movement in Midnapur." *Modern Asian Studies* 26, no. 4 (1992): 791–814.

Chappell, David. *A Stone of Hope: Prophetic Religion and the Death of Jim Crow*. Chapel Hill: University of North Carolina Press, 2004.

Clark, Septima. *Ready from Within: A First Person Narrative*. Trenton, NJ: Africa World Press, 1990.

Cobb, Charles E. *This Nonviolent Stuff'll Get You Killed: How Guns Made the Civil Rights Movement Possible*. Boston: Basic Books, 2014.

Cone, James. *A Black Theology of Liberation*. Maryknoll, NY: Orbis Books, 1986.

———. *Martin and Malcolm and America: A Dream or a Nightmare?* 20th anniversary ed. New York: Orbis Books, 2012.

Cooper, Brittney C. *Beyond Respectability: The Intellectual Thought of Race Women*. Urbana: University of Illinois Press, 2017.

Cornfield, Daniel B., Jonathan S. Coley, Larry W. Isaac, and Dennis C. Dickerson. "Occupational Activism and Racial Desegregation at Work: Activist Careers after the Nonviolent Nashville Civil Rights Movement." In *Race, Identity, and Work*, edited by Ethel L. Mickey and Adia Harvey Wingfield, 217–48. Research in the Sociology of Work 32. Bingley, UK: Emerald Group, 2018.

Cornish, Dudley Taylor. *The Sable Arm: Black Troops in the Union Army, 1861–1865*. Reprint, Lawrence: University Press of Kansas, 1987.

Cott, Nancy F. *The Grounding of Modern Feminism*. New Haven, CT: Yale University, Press, 1987.

Crenshaw, Kimberlé. "Demarginalizing the Intersection of Race and Sex: A Black Feminist Critique of Antidiscrimination Doctrine, Feminist Theory and Antiracist Politics." *University of Chicago Legal Forum* 1989, no. 1 (1989): 139–67.

Crowley, Ashon T. *Blackpentecostal Breath: The Aesthetics of Possibility*. New York: Fordham University Press, 2017.

Dailey, Jane Elizabeth, Glenda Elizabeth Gilmore, and Bryant Simon. *Jumpin' Jim Crow: Southern Politics from Civil War to Civil Rights*. Princeton, NJ: Princeton University Press, 2000.

Danielson, Leilah C. *American Gandhi: A. J. Muste and the History of Radicalism in the Twentieth Century*. Philadelphia: University of Pennsylvania Press, 2014.

———. "'In My Extremity I Turned to Gandhi': American Pacifists, Christianity, and Gandhian Nonviolence, 1915–1941." *Church History* 72, no. 2 (2003): 361–88.

Danielson, Leilah, Marian Mollin, and Doug Rossinow, eds. *The Religious Left in America: Doorkeepers of a Radical Faith*. Palgrave Studies in the History of Social Movements. New York: Palgrave Macmillan, 2018.

Dellinger, David T. *Revolutionary Non-Violence*. Indianapolis: Bobbs-Merrill, 1970.

D'Emilio, John. *Lost Prophet: The Life and Times of Bayard Rustin*. 2nd ed. New York: Free Press, 2004.

Dickerson, Dennis C. "African American Religious Intellectuals and the Theological Foundations of the Civil Rights Movement, 1930–55." *Church History* 74, no. 2 (2005): 217–35.

———. "Gandhi's India and Beyond: Black Women's Religious and Secular Internationalism, 1935–1952." *Journal of African American History* 104, no. 1 (2019): 59–83.

Dixie, Quinton Hosford, and Peter R. Eisenstadt. *Visions of a Better World: Howard Thurman's Pilgrimage to India and the Origins of African American Nonviolence*. Boston: Beacon Press, 2011.

Dochuk, Darren. *From Bible Belt to Sunbelt: Plain-Folk Religion, Grassroots Politics, and the Rise of Evangelical Conservatism*. New York: W. W. Norton, 2011.

Douglass, Frederick. "An Appeal to Congress for Impartial Suffrage." In *Foundations of American Political Thought*, edited by Constance Polin and Raymond Polin, 420–40. New York: Peter Lang, 2006.

Dowdy, Wayne. *Crusades for Freedom: Memphis and the Political Transformation of the American South*. Jackson: University Press of Mississippi, 2010.

Drake, St. Clair, Horace R. Cayton, and Mary Pattillo. *Black Metropolis: A Study of Negro Life in a Northern City*. Enlarged ed. Chicago: University of Chicago Press, 2015.

Dray, Philip. *At the Hands of Persons Unknown: The Lynching of Black America*. Reprint, New York: Modern Library, 2007.

Dubofsky, Melvyn. *We Shall Be All: A History of the Industrial Workers of the World*. 2nd ed. Urbana: University of Illinois Press, 1988.

Du Bois, W. E. B. *The Negro Church Report of a Social Study Made under the Direction of Atlanta University: Together with the Proceedings of the Eighth Conference for the Study of the Negro Problems*. Atlanta: Atlanta University Press, 1903.

Duziak, Mary L. *Cold War Civil Rights: Race and the Image of American Democracy*. Princeton, NJ: Princeton University Press, 2000.

Egerton, John. *Speak Now against the Day: The Generation before the Civil Rights Movement in the South*. New York: Knopf, 1994.

Equal Justice Initiative. *Lynching in America: Confronting the Legacy of Racial Terror*. 3rd ed. 2017. https://lynchinginamerica.eji.org/report.

Evans, Sara M. *Personal Politics: The Roots of Women's Liberation in the Civil Rights Movement and the New Left*. New York: Vintage Books, 1980.

Ewing, Adam. *The Age of Garvey: How a Jamaican Activist Created a Mass Movement and Changed Global Black Politics*. America in the World. Princeton, NJ: Princeton University Press, 2014.

Fairclough, Adam. *To Redeem the Soul of America: The Southern Christian Leadership Conference and Martin Luther King, Jr.* Athens: University of Georgia Press, 1987.

Farmer, James. *Lay Bare the Heart: An Autobiography of the Civil Rights Movement*. New York: Arbor House, 1985.

Foner, Eric. "The Meaning of Freedom in the Age of Emancipation." *Journal of American History* 81, no. 2 (September 1994): 435–60.

———. *Nothing but Freedom: Emancipation and Its Legacy.* Walter Lynwood Fleming Lectures in Southern History. Baton Rouge: Louisiana State University Press, 2007.

Frazier, E. Franklin. *The Free Negro Family: A Study of Family Origins before the Civil War.* Nashville: Fisk University Press, 1932.

———. *The Negro Church in America.* New York: Schocken Books, 1964.

———. "The Negro Family in Bahia, Brazil." *American Sociological Review* 7, no. 4 (1942): 465–78.

Gaines, Kevin Kelly. *American Africans in Ghana: Black Expatriates and the Civil Rights Era.* Chapel Hill: University of North Carolina Press, 2006.

Gandhi, M. K. *Nonviolent Resistance (Satyagraha).* Mineola, NY: Dover Press, 2001.

Garrow, David. *Bearing the Cross: Martin Luther King Jr. and the Southern Christian Leadership Conference.* Collector's ed. Norwalk, CT: Easton Press, 1989.

———. *We Shall Overcome: The Civil Rights Movement in the United States in the 1950s and 1960s.* Brooklyn: Carlson Publishing, 1989.

Gellman, Erik S. *Death Blow to Jim Crow: The National Negro Congress and the Rise of Militant Civil Rights.* John Hope Franklin Series in African American History and Culture. Chapel Hill: University of North Carolina Press, 2014.

Genovese, Eugene D. *Roll, Jordan, Roll: The World the Slaves Made.* New York: Pantheon Books, 1974.

Gerstle, Gary. *American Crucible: Race and Nation in the Twentieth Century.* Princeton, NJ: Princeton University Press, 2001.

———. "Theodore Roosevelt and the Divided Character of American Nationalism." *Journal of American History* 86, no. 3 (1999): 1280–1307.

Giddings, Paula J. *Ida: A Sword among Lions.* New York: Amistad, 2008.

———. *When and Where I Enter: The Impact of Black Women on Race and Sex in America.* 2nd ed. New York: Amistad Publishing, 2006.

Gilbert, Alan. *Black Patriots and Loyalists: Fighting for Emancipation in the War for Independence.* Reprint, Chicago: University of Chicago Press, 2013.

Gilmore, Glenda Elizabeth. *Defying Dixie: The Radical Roots of Civil Rights, 1919–1950.* New York: W. W. Norton, 2008.

———. *Gender and Jim Crow: Women and the Politics of White Supremacy in North Carolina, 1896–1920.* Chapel Hill: University of North Carolina Press, 1996.

———. *Who Were the Progressives? Readings.* Boston: Bedford/St. Martin's, 2002.

Gilroy, Paul. *The Black Atlantic: Modernity and Double Consciousness.* Cambridge, MA: Harvard University Press, 1993.

Ginzburg, Ralph. *100 Years of Lynchings.* Baltimore: Black Classic Press, 2013.

Gitlin, Todd. *The Sixties: Years of Hope, Days of Rage.* New York: Bantam Books, 1987.

Goluboff, Risa Lauren. *The Lost Promise of Civil Rights.* Cambridge, MA: Harvard University Press, 2007.

Goudsouzian, Aram. *Down to the Crossroads: Civil Rights, Black Power, and the Meredith March against Fear.* New York: Farrar, Straus and Giroux, 2014.

Grant, Colin. *Negro with a Hat: The Rise and Fall of Marcus Garvey.* New York: Oxford University Press, 2010.

Gregg, Richard Bartlett. *The Power of Non-Violence.* Philadelphia: J. B. Lippincott, 1934.

Griffith, Barbara S. *The Crisis of American Labor: Operation Dixie and the Defeat of the CIO.* Philadelphia: Temple University Press, 1988.

Halberstam, David. *The Children.* New York: Random House, 1998.

Hall, Jacquelyn Dowd. "The Long Civil Rights Movement and the Political Uses of the Past." *Journal of American History* 91, no. 4 (2005): 1233–63.

Hampton, Henry, Steve Fayer, and Sarah Flynn, eds. *Voices of Freedom: An Oral History of the Civil Rights Movement from the 1950s through the 1980s.* New York: Bantam Books, 1991.

Harding, Vincent, and Rosemarie Freeney Harding, eds. "James M. Lawson Jr.: The Seamless Cloth of Faith and Struggle," in *The Veterans of Hope Pamphlet Series*, vol. 1, no. 2. Denver: Center for the Study of Religion and Democratic Renewal at Iliff School of Theology, 2000.

Harvey, Paul. *Freedom's Coming: Religious Culture and the Shaping of the South from the Civil War through the Civil Rights Era.* Chapel Hill: University of North Carolina Press, 2005.

Harvey, Paul, and Philip Goff, eds. *The Columbia Documentary History of Religion in America since 1945.* New York: Columbia University Press, 2005.

Haynes, Robert V. *A Night of Violence: The Houston Riot of 1917.* Baton Rouge: Louisiana State University Press, 1976.

Haynes, Stephen R. *The Last Segregated Hour: The Memphis Kneel-Ins and the Campaign for Southern Church Desegregation.* New York: Oxford University Press, 2013.

———. *Noah's Curse: The Biblical Justification of American Slavery.* Oxford: Oxford University Press, 2007.

Hernan, Arthur. *Gandhi and Churchill: The Epic Rivalry That Destroyed an Empire and Forged Our Age.* New York: Random House, 2008.

Herskovits, Melville J. "The Negro in Bahia, Brazil: A Problem in Method." *American Sociological Review* 8, no. 4 (1943): 394–404.

Higginbotham, Evelyn. *Righteous Discontent: The Women's Movement in the Black Baptist Church: 1880–1920.* Cambridge, MA: Harvard University Press, 1993.

Hill, Lance. *The Deacons for Defense: Armed Resistance and the Civil Rights Movement.* Chapel Hill: University of North Carolina Press, 2006.

Hobsbawm, Eric. *The Invention of Tradition.* Cambridge: Cambridge University Press, 1983.

Hodgkin, Henry. "Quakers and Peace." In *Publications: Texts for Students of International Law.* London: Sweet Publishing, 1921.

Hogan, Wesley C. *Many Minds, One Heart: SNCC's Dream for a New America.* Chapel Hill: University of North Carolina Press, 2007.

Holsaert, Faith S., et al. *Hands on the Freedom Plow: Personal Accounts by Women in SNCC*. Urbana: University of Illinois Press, 2010.

Honey, Michael K. *Going Down Jericho Road: The Memphis Strike, Martin Luther King's Last Campaign*. New York: W. W. Norton, 2007.

———. *Southern Labor and Black Civil Rights: Organizing Memphis Workers*. Urbana: University of Illinois Press, 1993.

Horne, Gerald. *The End of Empires: African Americans and India*. Philadelphia: Temple University Press, 2008.

Houston, Benjamin. *The Nashville Way: Racial Etiquette and the Struggle for Social Justice in a Southern City*. Athens: University of Georgia Press, 2012.

Howlett, Charles F. "American Friends Service Committee and Peace Education." In *2008 Encyclopedia of Peace Education*. New York: Columbia University, 2008. https://www.tc.columbia.edu/epe/epe-entries/Howlett_american_friends.pdf.

Hudnut-Beumler, James David. *Looking for God in the Suburbs: The Religion of the American Dream and Its Critics, 1945–1965*. New Brunswick, NJ: Rutgers University Press, 1994.

Hunter, Tera W. *To 'Joy My Freedom: Southern Black Women's Lives and Labors after the Civil War*. Cambridge, MA: Harvard University Press, 1997.

Hunter Meriwether, James. *Proudly We Can Be Africans: Black Americans and Africa, 1935–1961*. Chapel Hill: University of North Carolina Press, 2002.

Isaac, Larry, and Lars Christiansen. "How the Civil Rights Movement Revitalized Labor Militancy." *American Sociological Review* 67, no. 5 (2002): 722–46.

Isaac, Larry W., Jonathan S. Coley, Daniel B. Cornfield, and Dennis C. Dickerson. "Pathways to Modes of Movement Participation: Micromobilization in the Nashville Civil Rights Movement." *Social Forces*, December 2019, 1–28.

———. "Preparation Pathways and Movement Participation: Insurgent Schooling and Nonviolent Direct Action in the Nashville Civil Rights Movement." *Mobilization: An International Quarterly* 21, no. 2 (June 2016): 155–76.

Isaac, Larry W., Daniel B. Cornfield, Dennis C. Dickerson, James M. Lawson, and Jonathan S. Coley. "'Movement Schools' and Dialogical Diffusion of Nonviolent Praxis: Nashville Workshops in the Southern Civil Rights Movement." In *Nonviolent Conflict and Civil Resistance*, edited by Sharon Erickson Nepstad and Lester R. Kurtz, 155–184. Research in Social Movements, Conflicts, and Change 34. Bingley, UK: Emerald Group, 2012.

Isaac, Larry, Steve McDonald, and Greg Lukasik. "Takin' It from the Streets: How the Sixties Mass Movement Revitalized Unionization." *American Journal of Sociology* 112, no. 1 (2006): 46–96.

James, Rawn, Jr. *Root and Branch: Charles Hamilton Houston, Thurgood Marshall, and the Struggle to End Segregation*. Reprint, New York: Bloomsbury Press, 2013.

Jefferies, Hasan Kwame. *Bloody Lowndes: Civil Rights and Black Power in Alabama's Black Belt*. New York: New York University Press, 2009.

Jelks, Randal Maurice. *Benjamin Elijah Mays: Schoolmaster of the Movement*. Chapel Hill: University of North Carolina Press, 2012.

Johnson, Nicholas. *Negroes and the Gun: The Black Tradition of Arms*. Amherst, NY: Prometheus Books, 2014.

Johnson, Walter. "On Agency." *Journal of Social History* 37, no. 1, special issue (Autumn 2003): 113–24.
Jones, William Powell. *The March on Washington: Jobs, Freedom, and the Forgotten History of Civil Rights*. New York: W. W. Norton, 2013.
Joseph, Peniel. *Stokely: A Life*. New York: Basic Books, 2014.
Kapur, Sudarshan. *Raising Up a Prophet: The African-American Encounter with Gandhi*. Boston: Beacon Press, 1992.
Keck, Margaret E., and Kathryn Sikkink. *Activists beyond Borders: Advocacy Networks in International Politics*. Ithaca, NY: Cornell University Press, 1998.
Kelley, Robin D. G. *Freedom Dreams: The Black Radical Imagination*. Boston: Beacon Press, 2002.
———. *Hammer and Hoe: Alabama Communists during the Great Depression*. Chapel Hill: University of North Carolina Press, 1990.
Kersten, Andrew Edmund. *A. Philip Randolph: A Life in the Vanguard*. Lanham, MD: Rowman & Littlefield, 2007.
Kester, Howard. *Revolt among the Sharecroppers*. Knoxville: University of Tennessee Press, 1997.
King, Martin Luther, Jr. *All Labor Has Dignity*. Edited by Michael K. Honey. Boston: Beacon Press, 2011.
———. "Suffering and Faith." *Christian Century*, 27 April 1960.
———. *A Testament of Hope: The Essential Writings and Speeches of Martin Luther King Jr.* Edited by James M. Washington. Reprint, San Francisco: HarperOne, 2003.
Korstad, Robert R. *Civil Rights Unionism: Tobacco Workers and the Struggle for Democracy in the Mid-Twentieth-Century South*. Chapel Hill: University of North Carolina Press, 2003.
Kosek, Joseph Kip. *Acts of Conscience: Christian Nonviolence and Modern American Democracy*. New York: Columbia University Press, 2011.
Kruse, Kevin Michael, and Stephen G. N. Tuck, eds. *Fog of War: The Second World War and the Civil Rights Movement*. New York: Oxford University Press, 2012.
Lake, Marilyn, and Henry Reynolds. *Drawing the Global Colour Line: White Men's Countries and the International Challenge of Racial Equality*. Critical Perspectives on Empire Series. Cambridge: Cambridge University Press, 2008.
Lartey, James. "Diane Nash: 'Non-violent Protest Was the Most Important Invention of the 20th Century.'" *The Guardian*, 6 April 2017.
Lauterbach, Preston. *Beale Street Dynasty: Sex, Song, and the Struggle for the Soul of Memphis*. New York: W. W. Norton, 2015.
Lawson, James M. Jr., "Student Nonviolent Coordinating Committee Statement of Purpose," in *Black Protest*, ed. Joanne Grant (New York: Random House, 1968), 273.
Leiker, James N. *Racial Borders: Black Soldiers along the Rio Grande*. College Station: Texas A&M University Press, 2002.
Levine, Ellen S. *Freedom's Children: Young Civil Rights Activists Tell Their Own Stories*. New York: Puffin Books, 2000.
Lewis, David L. *King: A Biography*. 3rd ed. Urbana: University of Illinois Press, 2012.
———. *W. E. B. Du Bois: Biography of a Race, 1868–1919*. New York: Henry Holt, 1993.

———. *W. E. B. Du Bois: The Fight for Equality and the American Century, 1919–1963.* New York: Henry Holt, 2000.
Lewis, John, and Michael D'Orso. *Walking with the Wind: A Memoir of the Movement.* New York: Simon & Schuster, 1998.
Lincoln, C. Eric. *The Black Church in the African-American Experience.* Durham, NC: Duke University Press, 1990.
———. *The Negro Church since Frazier.* New York: Schocken Books, 1974.
Litwack, Leon F. *Trouble in Mind: Black Southerners in the Age of Jim Crow.* New York: Knopf, 1998.
Locke, Alain, ed. *The New Negro.* Reprint, New York: Touchstone Press, 1997.
Logan, Rayford W. *The Betrayal of the Negro: From Rutherford B. Hayes to Woodrow Wilson.* New York: Da Capo Press, 1997.
———. *Howard University: The First Hundred Years, 1867–1967.* New York: New York University Press, 1969.
Long, Jeffery D. *Jainism: An Introduction.* I. B. Tauris Introductions to Religion. London: I. B. Tauris, 2009.
Lucander, David. *Winning the War for Democracy: The March on Washington Movement, 1941–1946.* Urbana: University of Illinois Press, 2015.
Maffly-Kipp, Laurie F. *Setting Down the Sacred Past: African-American Race Histories.* Cambridge, MA: Harvard University Press, 2010.
Manela, Erez. *The Wilsonian Moment: Self-Determination and the International Origins of Anticolonial Nationalism.* Oxford: Oxford University Press, 2009.
Mankiller, Wilma Pearl, et al., eds. *The Reader's Companion to U.S. Women's History.* Boston: Houghton Mifflin, 1998.
Martin, A. W. "The Lawson Affair, the Sit-Ins, and Beyond." *Tennessee Historical Quarterly* 75, no. 2 (Summer 2016): 142–65.
Marty, Martin. *Martin Luther: A Life.* New York: Penguin Books, 2004.
Matilal, Bimal Krishna. *The Central Philosophy of Jainism Anekånta-Våada.* Ahmedabad, India: L. D. Institute of Indology, 1981.
Mays, Benjamin E. *Born to Rebel: An Autobiography.* Athens: University of Georgia Press, 2003.
Mays, Benjamin E., and Joseph William Nicholson. *The Negro's Church.* New York: Institute of Social and Religious Research, 1933.
McAdam, Doug. *Political Process and the Development of Black Insurgency, 1930–1970.* 2nd ed. Chicago: University of Chicago Press, 1999.
McKinney, Charles W., Jr. *Greater Freedom: The Evolution of the Civil Rights Struggle in Wilson, North Carolina.* Lanham, MD: University Press of America, 2010.
McKinney, Richard I., and Mordecai W. Johnson. *Mordecai, the Man and His Message: The Story of Mordecai Wyatt Johnson.* Washington, DC: Howard University Press, 1997.
McLean, Nancy K. *Behind the Mask of Chivalry: The Making of the Second Ku Klux Klan.* Oxford: Oxford University Press, 1995.
McNeil, Genna Rae. "Before Brown: Reflections on Historical Context and Vision." *American University Law Review* 52, no. 6 (2003): 1431–60.

McNeil, Genna Rae, and A. Leon Higginbotham Jr. *Groundwork: Charles Hamilton Houston and the Struggle for Civil Rights*. Philadelphia: University of Pennsylvania Press, 1984.

McPherson, James M. *The Negro's Civil War: How American Blacks Felt and Acted during the War for the Union*. New York: Vintage Books, 2003.

McWhirter, Cameron. *Red Summer: The Summer of 1919 and the Awakening of Black America*. Boston: St. Martin's Press, 2012.

Meier, August. *Negro Thought in America, 1880–1915: Racial Ideologies in the Age of Booker T. Washington*. Ann Arbor: University of Michigan Press, 1963.

Meier, August, and Elliot Rudwick. *Along the Color Line: Explorations in the Black Experience*. 1st paperback ed. Urbana: University of Illinois Press, 2002.

———. *Black Detroit and the Rise of the UAW*. New York: Oxford University Press, 1981.

———. *CORE: A Study in the Civil Rights Movement, 1942–1968*. New York: Oxford University Press, 1973.

Mellen Charron, Katherine. *Freedom's Teacher: The Life of Septima Clark*. Chapel Hill: University of North Carolina Press, 2012.

Menand, Louis. *The Metaphysical Club: A Story of Ideas in America*. Reprint, New York: Farrar, Straus and Giroux, 2002.

Meriwether, James Hunter. *Proudly We Can Be Africans: Black Americans and Africa, 1935–1961*. Chapel Hill: University of North Carolina Press, 2002.

Meyer, David S., and Nancy Whittier. "Social Movement Spillover." *Social Problems* 41, no. 2 (1994): 277–98.

Morris, Aldon D. *The Origins of the Civil Rights Movement: Black Communities Organizing for Change*. New York: Free Press, 1986.

———. "A Retrospective on the Civil Rights Movement: Political and Intellectual Landmarks." *Annual Review of Sociology* 25 (1999): 517–39.

Morrison, Melanie S. *Murder on Shades Mountain: The Legal Lynching of Willie Peterson and the Struggle for Justice in Jim Crow Birmingham*. Durham, NC: Duke University Press, 2018.

Muhammad, Khalil Gibran. *The Condemnation of Blackness*. Cambridge, MA: Harvard University Press, 2010.

Mullins, Lisa. *Diane Nash: The Fire of the Civil Rights Movement*. Miami: Barnhadt and Ashe, 2007.

Murray, Pauli. *Song in a Weary Throat: An American Pilgrimage*. New York: HarperCollins, 1987.

Muste, A. J. *Non-violence in an Aggressive World*. New York: Harpers Publishing, 1940.

———. "Return to Pacifism." In *The Essays of A. J. Muste*, edited by Nat Hentoff, 195–202. New York: Simon & Schuster, 1967.

———. "Sit-Downs and Lie-Downs." In *The Essays of A. J. Muste*, edited by Nat Hentoff, 203–6. New York: Simon & Schuster, 1967.

———. "The World Task of Pacifism." In *The Essays of A. J. Muste*, edited by Nat Hentoff, 215–33. New York: Simon & Schuster, 1967.

Nabrit, James. "From Prayer Meeting to University." *Faculty Reprints*. 1 September 1942, 29–34. https://dh.howard.edu/cgi/viewcontent.cgi?article =1150&context=reprints.

Nelson, Williams S., ed. *The Christian Way in Race Relations*. Freeport, NY: Ayer, 1948.

Newman, Richard S. *Freedom's Prophet: Bishop Richard Allen, the AME Church, and the Black Founding Fathers*. New York: New York University Press, 2009.

Patterson, Orlando. *Slavery and Social Death: A Comparative Study*. Cambridge, MA: Harvard University Press, 1982.

Payne, Charles M. *I've Got the Light of Freedom: The Organizing Tradition and the Mississippi Freedom Struggle*. Berkeley: University of California Press, 1995.

Perry, Imani. *May We Forever Stand: A History of the Black National Anthem*. John Hope Franklin Series in African American History and Culture. Chapel Hill: University of North Carolina Press, 2018.

Perry, Lewis. *Civil Disobedience: An American Tradition*. New Haven, CT: Yale University Press, 2013.

Pfeffer, Paula F. *A. Philip Randolph, Pioneer of the Civil Rights Movement*. Baton Rouge: Louisiana State University Press, 1990.

Purnell, Brian. *Fighting Jim Crow in the County of Kings: The Congress of Racial Equality in Brooklyn*. Civil Rights and the Struggle for Black Equality in the Twentieth Century. Lexington: University of Kentucky Press, 2015.

Raboteau, Albert J. *Slave Religion: The "Invisible Institution" in the Antebellum South*. Updated ed. Oxford: Oxford University Press, 2004.

Ransby, Barbara. *Ella Baker and the Black Freedom Movement: A Radical Democratic Vision*. Chapel Hill: University of North Carolina Press, 2003.

Ransom, Reverdy C. "Gandhi: Indian Messiah and Saint," in *A.M.E. Church Review* 38 (October 1921): 87.

Robinson, Daniel N. *An Intellectual History of Psychology*. 3rd ed. Madison: University of Wisconsin Press, 1995.

Robinson, JoAnn O. *Abraham Went Out: The Biography of A. J. Muste*. Philadelphia: Temple University Press, 1981.

Rodgers, Daniel T. *Age of Fracture*. Cambridge, MA: Belknap Press of Harvard University Press, 2011.

Rosenberg, Rosalind. *Jane Crow: The Life of Pauli Murray*. New York: Oxford University Press, 2017.

Rosenfeld, Seth. *Subversives: The FBI's War on Student Radicals and Reagan's Rise to Power*. New York: Picador, 2013.

Rossinow, Douglass. *The Politics of Authenticity: Liberalism, Christianity, and the New Left in America*. New York: Columbia University Press, 1998.

Rudwick, Elliott. *Race Riot at East St. Louis: July 2, 1917*. Urbana: University of Illinois Press, 1982.

Rupp, Leila J. *Worlds of Women: The Making of an International Women's Movement*. Princeton, NJ: Princeton University Press, 1997.

Rustin, Bayard. *Time on Two Crosses: The Collected Writings of Bayard Rustin.* Edited by Devon W. Carbado and Donald Weise. San Francisco: Cleis Press, 2003.

Sanford, Otis L. *From Boss Crump to King Willie: How Race Changed Memphis Politics.* Knoxville: University of Tennessee Press, 2017.

Scalmer, Sean. *Gandhi in the West: The Mahatma and the Rise of Radical Protest.* Cambridge: Cambridge University Press, 2011.

Schulman, Bruce J. *From Cotton Belt to Sunbelt: Federal Policy, Economic Development, and the Transformation of the South, 1938–1980.* Durham, NC: Duke University Press, 1994.

Self, Robert O. *American Babylon: Race and the Struggle for Postwar Oakland.* Princeton, NJ: Princeton University Press, 2003.

Sharma, Arvind. *Gandhi: A Spiritual Biography.* New Haven, CT: Yale University Press, 2013.

Singler, Joan, Jean Durning, Bettylou Valentine, and Maid Adams. *Seattle in Black and White: The Congress of Racial Equality and the Fight for Equal Opportunity.* Seattle: University of Washington Press, 2011.

Siracusa, Anthony C. "Developing an American *Ahimsa*: James M. Lawson Jr.'s Paradigm of Protest." Honors thesis, Rhodes College, 2009.

———. "Nonviolence, Black Power, and the Surveillance State in Memphis' War on Poverty." In *An Unseen Light: Black Freedom Struggles in Memphis, Tennessee,* edited by Aram Goudsouzian and Charles McKinney, 279–305. Lexington: University of Kentucky Press, 2018.

Sitkoff, Harvard. *A New Deal for Blacks: The Emergence of Civil Rights as a National Issue.* New York: Oxford University Press, 1978.

———. *The Struggle for Black Equality, 1954–1992.* New York: Hill and Wang, 1993.

Slate, Nico. *Colored Cosmopolitanism: The Shared Struggle for Freedom in the United States and India.* Cambridge, MA: Harvard University Press, 2012.

———. "From Colored Cosmopolitanism to Human Rights: A Historical Overview of the Transnational Black Freedom Struggle." *Journal of Civil and Human Rights* 1, no. 1 (2015): 3–24.

Smallwood, Stephanie. *Saltwater Slavery: A Middle Passage from Africa to American Diaspora.* Cambridge, MA: Harvard University Press, 2008.

Smith, Mark M. *How Race Is Made: Slavery, Segregation, and the Senses.* Chapel Hill: University of North Carolina Press, 2006.

Snow, David, E. Burke Rochford Jr., Stephen K. Worden, and Robert D. Benford. "Frame Alignment Processes, Micromobilization, and Movement Participation." *American Sociological Review* 51, no. 4 (1986): 464–81.

Stamatov, Peter. "Activist Religion, Empire, and the Emergence of Modern Long-Distance Advocacy Networks." *American Sociological Review* 75, no. 4 (2010): 607–28.

Strain, Christopher. *Pure Fire: Self-Defense as Activism in the Civil Rights Era.* Athens: University of Georgia Press, 2005.

Sugrue, Thomas J. *The Origins of the Urban Crisis: Race and Inequality in Postwar Detroit.* 1st Princeton Classic ed. Princeton, NJ: Princeton University Press, 2005.

———. *Sweet Land of Liberty: The Forgotten Struggle for Civil Rights in the North.* New York: Random House, 2008.

Taylor, Clarence. *Black Religious Intellectuals: The Fight for Equality from Jim Crow to the 21st Century.* New York: Routledge, 2002.

Taylor, Cynthia. *A. Philip Randolph: The Religious Journey of an African American Labor Leader.* New York: New York University Press, 2006.

Thompson, Edward Palmer. *The Essential E. P. Thompson.* New York: New Press, 2001.

Thompson, Heather Ann. *Whose Detroit? Politics, Labor, and Race in a Modern American City.* Ithaca, NY: Cornell University Press, 2004.

Thornton, John. *Africa and Africans in the Making of the Atlantic World, 1400–1800.* Cambridge: Cambridge University Press, 1998.

Thurman, Howard W. *Deep River and the Negro Spiritual Speaks of Life and Death.* Richmond, IN: Friends United Press, 1975.

———. *The Papers of Howard Washington Thurman.* Vol. 1, *My People Need Me, June 1918–March 1936*, edited by Walter Earl Fluker. Columbia: University of South Carolina Press, 2009.

———. *The Papers of Howard Washington Thurman.* Vol. 2, *Christian, Who Calls Me Christian? April 1936–August 1943*, edited by Walter Earl Fluker. Columbia: University of South Carolina Press, 2012.

———. *The Papers of Howard Washington Thurman.* Vol. 3, *The Bold Adventure, September 1943–May 1949*, edited by Walter Earl Fluker. Columbia: University of South Carolina Press, 2015.

———. *The Papers of Howard Washington Thurman.* Vol. 4, *The Soundless Passion of a Single Mind, June 1949–December 1962*, edited by Walter Earl Fluker. Columbia: University of South Carolina Press, 2017.

———. *The Papers of Howard Washington Thurman.* Vol. 5, *The Wider Ministry, January 1963–April 1981*, edited by Walter Earl Fluker. Columbia: University of South Carolina Press, 2019.

———. *With Head and Heart: The Autobiography of Howard Thurman.* New York: Harcourt Brace Jovanovich, 1979.

Tilly, Charles. *The Politics of Collective Nonviolence.* Cambridge: Cambridge University Press, 2003.

———. *Regimes and Repertoires.* Chicago: University of Chicago Press, 2006.

Tilly, Charles, and Sidney Tarrow. *Contentious Politics.* 2nd ed. Oxford: Oxford University Press, 2015.

Tolstoy, Leo. *The Kingdom of God Is within You: Christianity Not as a Mystical Teaching but as a New Concept of Life.* Rockville, MD: Wildside Press, 2006.

Tuttle, William M. *Race Riot: Chicago in the Red Summer of 1919.* Urbana: University of Illinois Press, 1996.

Tyrell, Ian. *Reforming the World: The Creation of America's Moral Empire.* Princeton, NJ: Princeton University Press, 2013.

———. *Woman's World/Woman's Empire: The Woman's Christian Temperance Union in International Perspective, 1880–1930.* Chapel Hill: University of North Carolina Press, 1991.

Tyson, Timothy B. *Radio Free Dixie: Robert F. Williams and the Roots of Black Power.* Chapel Hill: University of North Carolina Press, 1999.

Umoja, Akinyele Omowale. *We Will Shoot Back: Armed Resistance in the Mississippi Freedom Movement.* New York: New York University Press, 2013.

Von Eschen, Penny M. *Race against Empire: Black Americans and Anticolonialism, 1937–1957.* Ithaca, NY: Cornell University Press, 1997.

———. *Satchmo Blows Up the World: Jazz Ambassadors Play the Cold War.* Cambridge, MA: Harvard University Press, 2004.

Wallis, Jill. *Valiant for Peace: History of the Fellowship of Reconciliation, 1914–89.* London: Fellowship of Reconciliation, 1991.

Wendt, Simon. *The Spirit and the Shotgun: Armed Resistance and the Struggle for Civil Rights.* Gainesville: University Press of Florida, 2007.

Whitaker, Robert. *On the Laps of Gods: The Red Summer of 1919 and the Struggle for Justice That Remade a Nation.* New York: Crown, 2008.

White, Calvin. *The Rise to Respectability: Race, Religion, and the Church of God in Christ.* Fayetteville: University of Arkansas Press, 2012.

Wiebe, Robert H. *The Search for Order, 1877–1920.* New York: Hill and Wang, 1967.

Wilkerson, Isabel. *The Warmth of Other Suns: The Epic Story of America's Great Migration.* Reprint, New York: Vintage, 2011.

Williams, Rhonda Y. *The Politics of Public Housing: Black Women's Struggle against Urban Inequality.* Oxford: Oxford University Press, 2004.

Williams, Zachery R. *Howard University Public Intellectuals and the Dilemmas of Race, 1926–1970.* Columbia: University of Missouri Press, 2009.

Williamson, Joel. *The Crucible of Race: Black/White Relations in the American South since Emancipation.* New York: Oxford University Press, 1984.

Wilson, Joseph T. *The Black Phalanx: African American Soldiers in the War of Independence, the War of 1812, and the Civil War.* New York: Da Capo Press, 1994.

Wood, Amy Louise. *Spectacle and Lynching: Witnessing Racial Violence in America, 1890–1940.* Chapel Hill: University of North Carolina Press, 2011.

Woodson, Carter Godwin. *The History of the Negro Church.* Washington, DC: Associated Publishers, 1921.

Zimmerman, Andrew. *Alabama in Africa: Booker T. Washington, the German Empire, and the Globalization of the New South.* America in the World. Princeton, NJ: Princeton University Press, 2010.

Index

Notes: Page numbers in *italics* refer to illustrative matter.

AFL. *See* American Federation of Labor (AFL)
African Americans: armed self-defense and, 10, 18, 22–23, 37–46, 178, 196n22, 199n26; Black Lives Matter movement on, 6, 173; Christianity and enslavement of, 1–2, 32, 185n3, 187n4; constitutional freedoms of, 187n6; dehumanization of, 1–2, 5, 7, 23–24, 88–89, 144, 185n3; freedom to be of (*See* politics of being); Gandhian nonviolence and, overview, 10, 148, 179, 225n17, 242n74; Great Migration of, 22, 33, 203n19, 241n69; lynchings of (*See* lynchings); political disenfranchisement of, 49, 145, 147, 158, 160, 175, 198n23, 241n69; religious education of (*See* religious education); segregation of, 7–8, 23–24, 187n6; spirituals of, 1, 185n1; university enrollment statistics of, 212n15; violence against (*See* white violence); war and, 21, 48, 187n6. See also *names of specific persons;* nonviolence, as ethic; nonviolent direct actions
African Methodist Episcopal (AME) Church, 21, 117, 123, 148
"aggressive pacifism," Kester on, 38–40. *See also* pacifism
"agnostic nonviolent technicians," as phrase, 246n2
ahiṃsā, 150, 155–56, 165, 166, 216n86, 239n56. *See also* nonviolence, as ethic
Akron Rubber Plant, 118

Allen, Richard, 117, 121, 185n3, 189n7
All-India Congress Committee, 115
"All Ohio Collegiate Workshop in Minority Problems" (1948), 136
Aluminum Ore Company, 23
American Association of Theological Schools, 53
"American Christianity," 74–76, 149, 236n24. *See also* Christianity
American Civil Liberties Union (ACLU), 47, 204n33
American Civil War, 21, 187n3, 187n6. *See also* war
American Federation of Labor (AFL), 29, 30, 152, 206n57. *See also* union organizing
American Friends Service Committee (AFSC), 40, 46, 204n33. *See also* Quakerism
"The American Racial Scene Today" (Rustin), 131
American Revolutionary War, 21. *See also* war
American Steel Company, 23
American Thread Company, 29
Andrews, C. F., 32
anekāntavāda, 165
aparigraha, 165, 166
armed self-defense. *See* self-defense, armed
asceticism, 69, 87, 114, 150, 162, 179, 190n13. *See also* nonviolence, as ethic
Ashby, Clyde, 126
Ashland Federal Penitentiary, Kentucky, 111, 131

Attucks, Crispus, 21
Austin, Allan, 46
Austin, Lewis E., 86

Baghavad Gita, 239n56. *See also* Hinduism
Baker, Ella Jo: on Citizenship Schools, 189n9; gender discrimination against, 110; Murray and, 219n46; NAACP work of, 93, 103, 170, 219n46; SNCC and, 190n10; women-led actions and, 189n9, 222nn92–93
barbershop protests (1948), 137
Barnes, Ellen, 173–76
Barry, Marion, 237n33
Beaver, Gilbert A., 19
being. *See* politics of being
Berea, Kentucky, 136–37
Berkeley Free Speech movement, 177
Berry, Marion, 172
Bethune, Mary McLeod, 244n95
Bevel, Jim, 172, 196n22
biblical citations. *See* Christianity
Birmingham, Alabama, 35, 40, 151, 188n7
Birmingham Age Herald (publication), 37
Black cultural life and experience. *See* African Americans
Black Lives Matter movement, 6, 173
Blackmon, Douglas A., 2
Black Power movement, 178
Black religious education. *See* religious education
Black women-led direct actions, 11, 91, 93–94, 103, 172, 188n7, 191n14, 195n21, 222nn92–93. *See also* African Americans; Murray, Pauli; nonviolent direct actions
Blanche Greene, Amy, 32
blind men and the elephant parable, 165
Bond, Julian, 237n33
Boos, Margaret, 136
Bowles, Luanna J., 33–34, 35
Bradshaw, Michael, 123
Brandeis, Louis, 57

British India. *See* Indian civil disobedience movement
Brotherhood of Sleeping Car Porters (BSCP), 31, 117, 122, 206n57, 207n71, 226n27. *See also* union organizing
Browder v. Gayle, 157, 188n7, 218n25
Brown, James Russell, 68–71, 130, 149, 165
Brown, Judith, 116
Brown, Morris, 185n3
Brown v. Board of Education, 11, 81, 157
BSCP. *See* Brotherhood of Sleeping Car Porters (BSCP)
buses, nonviolent direct actions and desegregation of: by Colvin, 188n7, 218n25; Freedom Rides, 4; Montgomery Bus Boycott, 153–54, 157, 190n10; Morgan's case on, 88, 222n92; by Murray, 83–85, 87, 106, 222n80; by NAACP, 88, 89; by Parks, 189n7, 218n25
Bush, George W., 171
Butler, Angeline, 3–4, 172, 173, 178
Bynum, Cornelius, 204n25, 206n57, 206n69, 207n70, 226n27

Camp, Stephanie, 188n7, 192n18
Campbell, Charles M., 73–74
"Can Guns Settle Strikes" (FOR pamphlet), 46
Cannon, Katie G., 181, 182, 211n3, 246n19
Carmichael, Stokely, 12, 175–77, 179–80, 190n13
Carolina Times (publication), 84
Carter, Jimmy, 171
caste system, 54, 75, 90, 108, 143. *See also* segregation
Chafe, William, 168
Cheek, Cord, 45
Chicago, Illinois, 86, 93, 220n49
Chicago Defender (publication), 92, 104, 114
"Children's Crusade" (1963), 188n7
Christianity: "American Christianity," 74–76, 149, 236n24; Black enslave-

264 Index

ment and, 1–2, 32, 185n3, 187n4; Gospel of Matthew, 28, 150, 237n38; of King, 193n19; Philippians 1:12–14, 245n110; response to war and, 19, 21; Thurman application of, 56–60, 65–66, 148–49. *See also* Jesus Christ (political archetype); Jesus of Nazareth (historical person); Quakerism; religious education
Church of God in Christ, 158, 180
Citizenship Schools, 189n9
Civil Rights Act (1866), 187n6, 192n15
Civil Rights Act (1871), 192n15
Civil Rights Act (1875), 187n6, 192n15
Civil Rights Act (1964), 173
civil rights cases: *Browder v. Gayle,* 157, 188n7, 218n25; *Brown v. Board of Education,* 11, 81, 157; *Plessy v. Ferguson,* 81, 97, 187n6; Scottsboro case, 37, 38, 298n90, 240n68; *Shelley v. Kramer,* 157; *Smith v. Allwright,* 157
Civil War. *See* American Civil War
Clark, Bronson, 132
Clayton, Horace, 98–99
Clinton, Bill, 171
Coad, Mack, 208n90
Cobb, Charles, 196n22
Coke Company strike (1932), 41–42
Collins, George L., 29–30, 32, 34, 206n61
colonialism, 49, 187n6, 242n74
Colvin, Claudette, 188n7, 218n25
Comant, James B., 81
communism, 37–39, 76
Communist Party (US), 53
Cone, James, 181
Congress of Industrial Organizations (CIO), 29, 122
Congress of Racial Equality (CORE), 76, 127, 145, 216n9; nonviolent direct actions by, 86, 93, 220n49, 227n36
Connor, Eugene "Bull," 188n7
conscientious objectors (COs), 111–13, 131–32, 153. *See also* nonviolent direct actions; war

conscription laws, 7–8, 111, 153, 182
CORE. *See* Congress of Racial Equality (CORE)
Costigan-Wagner Bill (proposed), 235n17
cotton mill strike (1925), 29
courage, 2, 3, 60, 72, 106–7, 130, 143. *See also* creative action and expression; nonviolence, as ethic; politics of being
Cramton Bill (1928), 212n11
creative action and expression, 3; FOR on, 25; Brown on, 70; Howard student group on, 101, 107; King on, 190n13; Lawson on, 143, 163, 164, 174; Mordecai Johnson on, 56; Quakers on inner light and, 4, 46, 49, 55; religion and, 185n3; sanitation workers strike on, 181; Thurman on, 49–50, 61, 64, 66, 67, 143, 149, 150, 173, 177. *See also* courage; nonviolence, as ethic; politics of being
Crenshaw, Kimberlé, 83, 216n6
"A Critical Study of Two Minority Techniques in the Light of Christian Principles" (Phillip), 71
Croppers and Farm Workers Union (CFWU), 208n90
Cross, George, 59
Cummings, Elijah E., 171

Daley, Helen S., 19
Davis, Jerome, 28, 29
dehumanization, Black, 1–2, 5, 7, 23–24, 88–89, 144, 185n3. *See also* African Americans; politics of being; slavery; white supremacy
D'Emilio, John, 112, 134, 135, 199n26
Democratic Party, 241n69
Detroit, Michigan, 124, 128, 136, 204n26
Deuel, Peg, 130
dharna, 150, 190n13
Douglass, Frederick, 21
draft resistance, 111–13, 131–32, 153. *See also* nonviolent direct actions; war

Index 265

Du Bois, W. E. B., 21, 22, 51, 57, 128
Dyer Anti-Lynching Bill (proposed), 235n17

East St. Louis massacre (1917), 23, 204n27
Edgerman, Anna Arnold, 223n93
Edmund Pettus Bridge march (1965), 171
"Educating Young People on the Philosophy and Technique of Nonviolence" (Campbell), 73
Elaine, Arkansas, massacre (1919), 23
Emerson, Alfred, 123
Emmett Till Antilynching Act (proposed), 235n17
ethics of nonviolence. *See* nonviolence, as ethic
Evans, Edward W., 19, 24, 26, 47
"An Examination of the Thesis That Christianity in Its Genesis Was a Technique of Survival for an Underprivileged Minority" (Thurman), 68
Executive Order 8802 (1941), 116

Fair Employment Practice Committee, 116
false revolutions, 8
Farmer, James L., Jr., 18, 47, 74–76, 119, 121
Federal Council of Churches, 24, 204n32, 206n63
Fellowship of Reconciliation (FOR), 9; on armed self-defense, 37–46; black leadership of, 47; establishment of, 17–26, 117, 152, 205n46; Farmer's work at, 119; on interracialism, 38–40, 46–47, 224n11; Kester's work with, 18, 33–46; Lawson's work for, 138, 145, 152, 154, 158–60, 240n68; MOWM and, 113, 137, 228n43; Muste's work at, 27, 47, 120, 121; pacifist methodology of, 28–31, 118–19; philosophical nonviolence of, 26–28, 199n26, 237n38; race relations institutes, 12, 121–27, 124, 135–38, 145–47; religious forums of, 25–26, 211n7; Rustin and, 112, 113; Sayre's work with, 32–33; Thurman's work with, 12, 18, 28–29, 33, 48. *See also* Lawson, James M., Jr.; Muste, Abraham Johannes "A. J."; pacifism; Quakerism
Fentress Coal strike (1932), 41–42
Fifteenth Amendment (US Constitution), 187n6, 192n15
Fisher, Bernice, 127
Fisk University, 3, 33, 50
FOR. *See* Fellowship of Reconciliation (FOR)
Fourteenth Amendment (US Constitution), 187n6, 192n15
freedom dreams, as phrase, 245n112
Freedom Rides, 4. *See also* buses, nonviolent direct actions and desegregation of
Freedom Schools, 189n9
freedom to be. *See* politics of being
The Free Speech (publication), 22

Gandhi, Mohandas Karamchand: Campbell on, 74; historical overview of Black activism and, 10, 114–15, 148, 179, 225n17, 242n74; Kester on, 44; Lawson on, 3, 152, 154, 166, 167, 168, 244n92, 245n108; Murray on, 76, 84, 85, 102; on pacifism *vs.* nonviolence, 129, 237n38; Powell on, 107; Quit India campaign by, 85, 90, 98, 114–17; Ransom on, 148; religious traditions of, 8, 143, 150, 155–56; *satyagraha* and, 74, 84–86, 117, 119, 172, 216n86, 217n20; Sayre on, 43; on truth, 74, 165, 237n38, 245n108
Garfinkel, Herbert, 84
Garvey, Marcus, 22, 128, 203n21
gender identity, 82, 84, 88, 89–90
Ghana, 242n74
Giddings, Paula, 3
Gilmore, Glenda, 170
Gilroy, Paul, 191n14
Gitlin, Todd, 170

Gladden, Washington, 20
"Good News for the Underprivileged" (Thurman), 65–66, 149
Gort, Solomon, 141–42, 166
Gospel of Matthew, 28, 150, 237n38
Graham, Barney, 41
Grant, Jackie, 181
Gray, Ralph, 208n90
Great Migration, 22, 33, 203n19, 241n69
Great War. *See* World War I
Gregg, Richard, 132
Grotewahl, Doris, 134

Harding, Vincent, 153
Harlem, New York, 26, 47, 203n21
Hastie, William, 88
Hayden, Tom, 177
Hayes, Janetta, 172
Haywood, William "Big Bill," 30
Hebrew enslavement, 1–2, 7, 185n3. *See also* Judaism
Higginbotham, Evelyn, 54, 213n21
Hinduism, 8, 150, 239n56
Hodgkin, Henry, 19
Holmes, John Haynes, 47
Hose, Sam, 22
Houser, George, 145, 146, 151, 154
Houston, Charles Hamilton, 53, 81
Howard University, 5; Johnson's response to student activism at, 107–8; leadership of, 22–23; Murray's work at, 11, 90–93; NAACP student group, 83, 94–108, 221n58; FOR race relations institutes at, 125–26; School of Law, 81, 89–90; School of Religion (SOR), 49, 50–56, 67–71, 148, 212n8, 212n14; Thurman's work at, 10, 52, 64, 148
Howell, Clarence V., 25–26, 205n43
Hughes, Langston, 101

Indian civil disobedience movement, 85, 90, 98, 114–17, 216n15, 226nn23–24, 242n74. *See also* Gandhi, Mohandas Karamchand

Industrial Workers of the World (IWW), 30
"inner light," as concept, 4, 46, 49, 55. *See also* creative action and expression; politics of being; Quakerism
"Institute on Race Relations and Non-Violent Solutions" (1943), 123
interracialism: FOR's work and, 9, 33–46, 137–38, 224n11; Randolph on, 203n21, 207n70; WWII and, 225n18
intersectionality, 30, 82–83, 216n6. *See also* Murray, Pauli; Rustin, Bayard
interstate travel. *See* buses, nonviolent direct actions and desegregation of
Irwin, Sydney, 136

"Jacob's Ladder" (spiritual), 1
Jainism, 8, 143, 155, 165–66
James, William, 58, 61, 205n46, 214n39
Jesus and the Disinherited (Thurman), 149–50, 163–64, 215n67
Jesus Christ (political archetype), 9, 19–20, 42, 49, 75, 110, 117, 150. *See also* Christianity
Jesus of Nazareth (historical person): Gandhi on, 150–51; historical framework of, 7, 68–69; Lawson's teachings on, 3, 161–62, 180, 244n92; Murray on, 182–83; Rustin on, 130; Thurman on, 49–50, 62, 65–66, 149–50. *See also* Christianity
jiān ài, 239n56
John Dewey Educational Society, 85
Johnson, Andrew, 50, 187n6
Johnson, James Weldon, 24
Johnson, Link, 88
Johnson, Lyndon, 104, 107–8
Johnson, Mordecai Wyatt: on nonviolent direct actions, 11, 99–100; personal philosophy of, 22–23, 51–52; role at Howard University, 61, 212n8, 212nn10–11; Thurman and, 56–57, 61–62, 64, 148
Johnson, Nicholas, 10

Index 267

Jones, Absalom, 182
Jones, E. Stanley, 120
Jones, Paul, 31–32
Jones, Rufus, 19, 33, 58
Josif, Emily, 136
Judaism, 7, 68–69, 70, 75. *See also* Hebrew enslavement

Kahn, Tom, 237n33, 237n35
Kavjka, Frank, 136
Kelley, Robin D. G, 37, 208n90, 245n112
Kester, Alice, 45–46
Kester, Howard, 18, 32, 33–46, 36, 103
King, Martin Luther, Jr.: assassination of, 13; criticisms of, 176, 190n10, 190n13, 199n26; Lawson and, 168, 180; nonviolent direct actions led by, 153; philosophical nonviolence and, 199n26; on suffering, 190n13; work in Memphis, xi
Kirk, W. Astor, 125–26
Knight, Paulina, 172
Ku Klux Klan, 28, 43

labor strikes, 29–30, 117–18; of 1919, 152; of 1925, 29; of 1932, 41–42; of 1968, xi, 180. *See also* nonviolent direct actions; union organizing
Lafayette, Bernard, 141–42, 172
Lawrence Textile Strike (1919), 152
Lawson, James M., Jr., 162; as 1964 protest speaker, 173–76; on categories of force, 245n106; on creative action and expression, 143, 163, 164, 174; early life of, 151–52; on false revolutions, 8; on Gandhi, 3, 152, 154, 166, 167, 168, 244n92, 245n108; Howard University student activism and, 105; influence of, 237nn33–34; inspiration of, 3, 143, 180, 239n52; interference tactics of, 142; on Jesus, 3, 161–62, 180, 244n92; King and, xi, 199n26, 237n33; Lewis and, 171–72, 237n33; Muste and, 144, 152–53; nonviolent direct actions led by, 137, 168–70;

philosophical nonviolence of, 12, 144–51, 154–58, 161–69, 196n22, 244n98, 244n105; as SCLC speaker, 168, 169; FOR work by, 138, 145, 152, 154, 158–60, 240n68. *See also* Fellowship of Reconciliation (FOR)
Lawson, James M., Sr., 151
Lawson, Philane May Cover, 152
LeMoyne College, 33–35, 138, 158
Lerner, Max, 101
"Lesson Plan on Faith, Discipline, Action" (Rustin), 130
"Lesson Plan on Nonviolent Action" (Rustin), 129–30
Lewis, John, 171, 172–73, 178, 179, 180, 196n22, 237n33
Little Palace Café sit-in (1943), 93, 94, 101, 108
Litwack, Leon, 170
Locke, Alain, 191n14
Long, Jeffrey, 155
Lorde, Audre, 1
Lorraine Hotel, Memphis, 13
Luther, Martin, 183
lynchings, 2, 147, 187n6; FOR on, 17; during 1919 Red Summer, 23, 57, 148; of Cord Cheek, 45; Du Bois on, 22; of Emmett Till, 157, 163; Evans on, 24–25; proposed laws against, 235n17; Randolph on, 206n69; statistics on, 234n13, 235n15. *See also* African Americans; white violence

marches, protest, 87, 116, 128, 130, 141–42, 171, 179. *See also* nonviolent direct actions
March on Washington Movement (MOWM): FOR and, 113, 137, 228n43; philosophical nonviolence of, 227n37; race relations institutes and, 11–12, 121–27; Randolph on nonviolent direct action of, 76. *See also* Randolph, A. Philip
Marshall, Thurgood, 11, 81, 88
Marx, Karl, 75

268 Index

Mason, Charles H., 158
mass mobilization. *See* nonviolent direct actions
master-slave ethic, 2, 187n4. *See also* slavery
Matilal, Bimal Krishna, 165
Matthew, J. B., 43
Mays, Benjamin, 35, 52–55, 148, 212n14
McKinney, Charles, 195n21, 212n10
Memphis, Tennessee, xi, 13, 151, 158, 180, 181
Meredith March against Fear (1966), 179
"Message to Men and Women of Goodwill" (Hodgkin), 19
The Messenger (publication), 21, 23, 30
Methodist Episcopal Church, 25, 26
military draft resistance, 111–12, 131–32, 153. *See also* nonviolent direct actions; war
Mississippi Freedom Summer (1964), 173–76
Mohism, 155, 239n56
Montgomery Bus Boycott (1955), 153–54, 157, 190n10. *See also* Parks, Rosa
Moore, Douglass, 168
Moore, Eleanor Perry, 128
Morehouse College, 9, 28, 35, 48, 50, 51, 55
Morgan, Irene, 88
Morris, Aldon, 193n19, 198n25, 233n7, 241n69
Morris, Pauline, 237n34
Morrow, Juanita, 91, 93, 110, 222nn92–93
Moses, Bob, 175–76, 196n22
MOWM. *See* March on Washington Movement (MOWM)
Murray, Pauli, 13, 95, 183; Baker and, 219n46; correspondence with Eleanor Roosevelt, 81, 100, 101, 104; on discrimination against women, 53, 81, 110; education of, 81, 89, 90, 217n7; in Harlem ashram, 87, 217n20, 222n92; on India's history *vs.* Black Americans, 216n15; nonviolent direct actions led by, 11, 76–77, 82–86, 87, 90–93, 106, 212n11, 216n9, 222n80; personal identity of, 82, 84, 88, 89–90, 108–9, 181–84, 202n30, 216n6, 218n26; philosophical nonviolence of, 87–89, 99, 100–104, 108–10; Thurman's inspiration of, 3
Musgrave, Marian, 93
Muste, Abraham Johannes "A. J.": King and, 199n26; Lawson and, 144, 152–53; on pacifism, 117–18; philosophical nonviolence of, 119, 125; Rustin and, 112, 113, 134–35, 136; FOR work by, 27, 47, 120, 121. *See also* Fellowship of Reconciliation (FOR)
Muste, A. J., 29–30
Myrdal, Gunnar, 102

NAACP (National Association for the Advancement of Colored People), 5; Baker's work at, 93, 103, 170, 219n46; establishment of, 17, 22, 128; Howard University student group of, 83, 94–108, 221n58; Lawson and, 154–55; Niagara Movement and, 24; protests organized by, 23, 88, 89; Randolph as convention speaker of, 118; role in 1920s and 1930s, 53
Nash, Diane: influence of, 172; "Jail, No Bail!" campaign by, 3; philosophical nonviolence of, 4, 196n22, 237n33; politics of being and, 163, 173, 178
Nashville, Tennessee: desegregation of, 4; student movement in, 105, 141–42, 151, 160, 162, 168, 171–72, 196n22
National Civil Rights Museum, 5
National Negro Congress (NNC), 230n68
National Sharecroppers Awareness Week, 103
Nehru, Jawaharlal, 90, 242n74
Nelson, Claud, 46

Nelson, Juanita, 222nn92-93
Nelson, William Stuart, 55, 129, 148
Newton, Ray, 46
New World (publication), 25
New York Amsterdam News (publication), 126
New York Times (publication), 171
Niagara Movement, 22, 24
Niebuhr, Reinhold, 152, 206n54
noncooperation, as tactic, 17. *See also* nonviolent direct actions; pacifism
nonviolence, as ethic, 193n19; armed self-defense and, 196n22; Brown on, 70-71; Campbell on, 73-74; Carmichael on, 175, 176, 177; Clayton on, 98-99; *vs.* direct actions, 10, 12, 193n19; Gandhi on, 10, 129, 150-51, 237n38; historical overview of, 2-6, 10, 184; Howard University student group on, 105-7; Lawson on, 12, 144-51, 154-58, 161-69, 244n98, 244n105; Murray on, 87-89, 99, 100-104, 108-10; Muste on, 119, 125; Phillip on, 71-73; politics of being and, 4-9; Rustin on, 113-14, 129-30; *satyagraha*, 74, 84-86, 117, 119, 172, 216n86, 217-18n20; Thurman on, 9-10, 48-50, 62-67, 117, 129. *See also* courage; creative action and expression; politics of being
nonviolence, as term, 10, 188n7
nonviolent direct actions, 193n19; by FOR, 18, 116, 118-19; by Allen, 117, 121, 185n3, 188-89n7; barbershop protests, 137; by Black women during enslavement and segregation, 188n7; Bowles on, 34; "Children's Crusade," 188n7; by Colvin, 188n7, 218n25; by CORE, 86, 220n49, 227n36; by Howard University student group, 94-101, 108, 125, 126, 220n52; in India, 85, 90, 98, 114-17, 216n15, 226nn23-24; by Lawson, 137, 142, 168-69; led by Black women, 11, 91, 93-95, 103, 172, 188n7, 191n14, 195n21; by Lewis, 171; military draft resistance, 111-13, 131-32, 153; Mississippi Freedom Summer, 173-76; Montgomery Bus Boycott, 153-54, 157, 190n10; by Murray, 11, 76-77, 82-89, 90-93, 212n11, 216n9; in Nashville, 105, 141-42, 151, 160, 168, 196n22; by Parks, 188n7, 218n25; protest marches, 87, 116, 128, 130, 141-42, 171, 179; by Randolph, 76, 116, 120-21; by Rustin, 11-12, 107, 111, 121-31; sanitation workers strike, xi, 180; sit-ins, 86, 93, 94-98, 141-44, 167-68; against slavery, 188n7, 192n18; as tactic *vs.* ethic, 10, 12, 193n19. *See also* labor strikes; *names of specific leaders;* race relations institutes (FOR); segregation; self-defense, armed
"nonviolent institutes." *See* race relations institutes (FOR)
NVDA. *See* nonviolent direct actions

Obama, Barack, 171
Oberlin School of Theology, 153, 212n15
Opportunity Magazine (publication), 84
Owen, Chandler, 21, 23, 29

pacifism: FOR's work and, 38-47; Lawson on, 167; Muste on, 117-18; *vs.* nonviolence, 12, 113, 129, 237n38; Rustin on, 113, 129, 132-33, 223n10; Thurman on, 9-10, 48-49, 63-64, 85, 129, 214n49; white movement on, 9, 85-86, 111, 128. *See also* conscientious objectors (COs); Fellowship of Reconciliation (FOR); nonviolence, as ethic; Quakerism
Palmer, Benjamin J., 185n3
"Pan" (Candace Stone), 85-87, 103
Parks, Rosa, 188n7, 218n25. *See also* Montgomery Bus Boycott (1955)
paternalism, 85-86, 128. *See also* white pacifist movement

Payne, Charles, 147, 173
Philippians 1:12–14, 245n110
Phillip, Lee C., 68, 71–73
philosophical nonviolence. *See* nonviolence, as ethic
"Pilgrimage to Nonviolence" (King), 199n26
Pittsburgh Courier (publication), 76, 84, 92–93, 98, 99, 114
Platt, Davis, 134–35
Plessy v. Ferguson, 81, 97, 187n6
political disenfranchisement, 49, 145, 147, 158, 160, 175, 198n23, 241n69. *See also* African Americans; white supremacy
politics of being, 4–9, 12, 104–5, 114, 129, 161–64, 173. *See also* courage; creative action and expression; "inner light," as concept; nonviolence, as ethic
Pope, H. W., 35
Pope, Ned, 40, 41
Poston, Ted, 84
Powell, Ruth, 93, 99, 107
Power of Nonviolence (Gregg), 132
Pratt, D. Butler, 64–65, 212n14
Price, Hollis, 158
protest, as term, 6

Quakerism, 17; on freedom, 114; on "inner light," 4, 46, 49, 55. *See also* American Friends Service Committee (AFSC); Christianity; Fellowship of Reconciliation (FOR); pacifism; Rustin, Bayard
The Quest for the Historical Jesus (Schweitzer), 58
Quit India campaign. *See* Indian civil disobedience movement

Raboteau, Albert J., 185n3, 187n4
"Race Relations Institute Emphasizing Democratic and Non-violent Solutions of Present Day Race Problems" (1947), 136

race relations institutes (FOR), 12, 121–27, *124*, 135–38, 145–47. *See also* nonviolent direct actions
Randolph, A. Philip: on armed self-defense, 204n25; on citizenship, 101; interest in Gandhi's work and mass mobilization, 115, 116; on interracialism, 29, 203n21, 207n70; NNC and, 230n68; nonviolent direct actions led by, 76, 87, 116, 120–21; response to white violence, 21, 23, 206n69. *See also* March on Washington Movement (MOWM)
Ransom, Reverdy C., 148
Rauschenbusch, Walter, 20, 57
Reconstruction Acts (1867), 50
Red Summer (1919), 23, 57, 148, 204n25
"The Relation between Religion and Racism with Special Reference to the American Scene" (Farmer), 74
religion. *See* Christianity; Hinduism; Jainism; Judaism; Mohism; Quakerism; Sufism
religious education, 211n7; American Association of Theological Schools, 53; Howard SOR, 49, 50–56, 67–71, 148, 212n8, 212n14; Oberlin School of Theology, 153, 212n15; Rochester Theological Seminary, 59, 213n33; Union Theological Seminary, 71. *See also names of specific leaders*
religious forums (FOR), 25–26, 211n7. *See also* race relations institutes (FOR)
repentance, 70, 158
repertoires, as term, 246n11
Republican Party, 241n69
Richardson, Henry, 123
Roberts, Helen, 172
Rochester Theological Seminary, 59, 213n33
Rock Hill campaign (1960), 3
Roosevelt, Eleanor, 81, 100, 101, 104
Roosevelt, Franklin Delano, 87, 116, 235n17

Rosenberg, Rosalind, 182, 218nn25–26
Rustin, Bayard, *124*; draft resistance by, 111–13, 131–32; female leaders and, 110, 136, 223n93; King and, 199n26; nonviolent direct actions led by, 11–12, 107; on pacifism, 113, 129, 132–33, 223n10; philosophical nonviolence of, 113–14, 129–30; race relations institutes by, 12, 121–27, *124*, 135–37, 138, 145, 146; sexuality of, 112–13, 133–35, 178, 223n93, 232n90; Thurman's inspiration of, 3; FOR work by, 18, 47, 154

sanitation workers strike (1968), xi, 180
Sarnes, Raymond, 93
Sartre, John Paul, 152
satya, 155, 216n86, 239n56. See also *satyagraha*; truth
satyagraha, 74, 84–86, 117, 119, 172, 216n86, 217n20. See also nonviolence, as ethic
Savio, Mario, 177
Sayre, John Nevin, 32–33, 37, 42–46, 207n80. See also Fellowship of Reconciliation (FOR)
Schweitzer, Albert, 20, 58
Scottsboro trial, 37, 38, 208n90, 240n68
segregation, 7–8, 23–24, 116, 187n6, 231n75. See also African Americans; caste system; dehumanization, Black; slavery; white supremacy
Seitter, Lynn, 136
self-control, Lawson on, 245n108
self-defense, armed, 10, 18, 22–23, 37–46, 178, 196n22, 199n26. See also nonviolent direct actions
self-estimate, 64–65, 67
self-reliance, 189nn9–10
Selma, Alabama, 151, 171
sexuality: of Murray, 90, 113, 181; of Rustin, 112–13, 133–35, 178, 223n93, 232n90

sharecroppers, organization of, 37, 208n90
Shaw University, 50, 55
Shelley v. Kramer, 157
"Should the Civil Rights Cases and *Plessy v. Ferguson* Be Overturned?" (Murray), 81
sit-ins, 86, 93, 94–98, 141–44, 167–68. See also nonviolent direct actions
slavery: domination and, 192n18; nonviolent direct actions against, 188n7, 192n18; religion and, 1–2, 7, 32, 185n3, 187n4. See also African Americans; dehumanization, Black; segregation; white violence
Smiley, Glenn, 147, 154, 158, 199n26
Smith, Kelly Miller, 172
Smith, Ruby Doris, 3
Smith v. Allwright, 157
SNCC. See Student Nonviolent Coordinating Committee (SNCC)
Social Gospel, 20, 57
SOR. See under Howard University
South Africa, 242n74
Southern Christian Leadership Conference (SCLC), 32, 151, 168–69, 188n7
Southern Tenant Farmers Union (STFU), 37
Spanish-American War, 21
Spelman College, 1, 2, 3, 7
spirituals (songs), 1, 185n1. See also Christianity
"Statement on Christianity and the Negro Problem" (Johnson and Wood), 24
Stone, Candace "Pan," 85–87, 103
Student Challenge (publication), 58, 59
Student Christian Movement, 19
Student Nonviolent Coordinating Committee (SNCC), 103, 190n10, 193n19, 196n22
Students for a Democratic Society (SDS), 177

suffering, 161, 179, 190n13, 244n105
Sufism, 155, 239n56
Swomley, John, 118, 123, 125

Tallapoosa County, Alabama, incidents (1931), 37–38, 208n90
Taylor, Clarence, 10
Taylor, Cynthia, 117
Terrell, Joanne, 181
textile strike (1925), 29
Thirteenth Amendment (US Constitution), 187n6, 192n15
Thompson's restaurant sit-in (1944), 94–96, 97, 101, 108, 125, 126, 220n52
Thurman, Howard, 60; chapel talks by, 1–2, 7; on creative action and expression, 49–50, 61, 64, 66, 67, 143, 149, 150, 173, 177; FOR's methods and work of, 12, 18, 28–29, 33, 47; "Good News for the Underprivileged," 65–66, 149; *Jesus and the Disinherited*, 149–50, 163–64, 215n67; Mordecai Johnson and, 56–57, 61–62, 64; Murray and, 103; on pacifism, 9–10, 48–49, 63–64, 85, 129, 214n49; philosophical nonviolence of, 9–10, 48–50, 62–67, 117, 129; religious development of, 57–61, 211n3, 214n41; role at Howard School of Religion, 10, 52, 64, 148
Thurman, Sue Bailey, 148
Till, Emmett, 157, 163
Tolstoy, Leo, 152, 237n38
truth: in Baghavad Gita, 239n56; blind men and the elephant parable on, 165; Gandhi on, 74, 155, 156, 165, 237n38, 245n108; James on, 205n46, 214n39; Lawson on, 164; *satya*, 155, 216n86, 239n56; Sayre on, 43; Thurman on, 61, 63, 65, 130
Turner, Nat, 185n3

union organizing: of AFL, 29, 30, 152, 206n57; of BSCP, 31, 117, 122, 206n57, 226n27; of CFWU, 208n90; of CIO, 29, 122; by Kester, 37, 41; by Randolph, 21, 29, 117, 125, 206n57; of STFU, 37. *See also* labor strikes; nonviolent direct actions
Union Theological Seminary, 71
United Mine Workers (UMW), 122
universal love, 239n56
Universal Negro Improvement Association (UNIA), 128

Vanderbilt Divinity School, 31, 154, 168, 240n68, 242n70
Vesey, Denmark, 185n3
violence: armed self-defense against, 10, 18, 22–23, 39, 42, 45, 178, 199n26; against oneself, 163, 244n95; slave rebellions, 185n3. *See also* lynchings; *names of specific conflicts*; white violence
Vivian, C. T., 171, 172
Voting Rights Act (1965), 192n15, 241n69

war: African Americans and, 21, 48, 187n6; FOR's stand against, 19, 21; military draft resistance against, 111–13, 131–32, 153; Rustin on, 111. *See also names of specific conflicts*; pacifism
Washington, Booker T., 51, 57
Washington Tribune (publication), 107, 108
Wells, Ida B., 22, 57
Wendt, Simon, 196n22
Western College for Women protest (1964), 173–76
White, Andrew, 172
White, Walter, 84
white pacifist movement, 9, 38–49, 85–86, 111, 128. *See also* pacifism
white supremacy, 6, 63–64, 144, 187n6, 195n20. *See also* African Americans; segregation; white violence

white violence: in Birmingham, 40, 188n7; of colonialism, 49; in Detroit, 124, 128, 136; in East St. Louis, 23, 204n27; FOR's interpretations of, 17; against Nashville student protestors, 141–42; as political method of control, 8; politics of being against, 4–6, 187n5; prevalence of, 147; (1919) Red Summer, 23, 57, 148, 204n25; statistics on, 234n13, 235n15; in Tallapoosa, Alabama, 37, 38, 44, 208n90. *See also* African Americans; lynchings; *names of specific incidents;* slavery

Wiebe, Robert, 57
Wilder Coal Strike (1932), 41–42
Wilkerson, Dolores, 172
Wilkerson, Isabel, 203n19
Wilkins, Roy, 168
Williams, Rhonda, 195n21
women-led nonviolence. *See* Black women-led direct actions
Women's International League for Peace and Freedom, 19
Wood, L. Hollingsworth, 24, 204n33
Workers Defense League (WDL), 88, 103
workplace desegregation, 116
World Alliance of Churches for Promoting International Friendship, 19
The World Tomorrow (publication), 32
World War I, 17, 19, 21. *See also* war
World War II, 82, 90, 130, 225n18. *See also* military draft resistance; war
Wright, Richard, 21–22
wu-wei, 239n56

YMCA (Young Men's Christian Association), 19, 31, 35, 40, 122, 145
YWCA (Young Women's Christian Association), 31

Zellner, Bob, 175
Zimmerman, Andrew, 147

www.ingramcontent.com/pod-product-compliance
Lightning Source LLC
Chambersburg PA
CBHW031801220426
43662CB00007B/486